T0136401

Machine Learning and Probabilistic Graphical Models for Decision Support Systems

Editor

Kim Phuc Tran

Univ. Lille, ENSAIT, ULR 2461 - GEMTEX - Génie et Matériaux Textiles
F-59000 Lille, France

CRC Press
Taylor & Francis Group
Boca Raton   London   New York

CRC Press is an imprint of the
Taylor & Francis Group, an **informa** business
A SCIENCE PUBLISHERS BOOK

First edition published 2022
by CRC Press
6000 Broken Sound Parkway NW, Suite 300, Boca Raton, FL 33487-2742

and by CRC Press
4 Park Square, Milton Park, Abingdon, Oxon, OX14 4RN

© 2022 Taylor & Francis Group, LLC

CRC Press is an imprint of Taylor & Francis Group, LLC

Library of Congress Cataloging-in-Publication Data (applied for)

ISBN: 978-1-032-03948-0 (hbk)
ISBN: 978-1-032-03950-3 (pbk)
ISBN: 978-1-003-18988-6 (ebk)

DOI: 10.1201/9781003189886

Typeset in Times New Roman
by Radiant Productions

Preface

The last decades have witnessed the rapid growth of advanced technologies and their application that is leading to the fourth industrial revolution. The recent development of information and communication technologies has engendered to add intelligence into the industrial process to drive continuous improvement, knowledge transfer, and data driven-based decision-making. The Internet of Things (IoT) is one of the main technologies used to enable enabling industrial organizations to rapidly automate and digitize traditional business processes. A huge volume of data collected can feed real-time analytic solutions provided by Artificial Intelligence (AI), Big Data Analytics, and Decision Support Systems (DSS), which can lead to optimal industrial operations. Based on modern technologies of the IoT, the process of collecting, transforming, and storing data from all stages of the industrial process becomes easier and more efficient, promoting the era of Big Data. AI algorithms provide powerful tools for exploiting the wealth of data generated in the IoT. By extracting useful information and features from Big Data, the AI algorithms allow complex tasks such as monitoring, and optimizing the production process to be performed smartly and efficiently. To combine human knowledge with these above results, DSS is integrated to help managers to make better decisions in their work.

In the era of Big Data, DSS has become vital for organizations. Machine Learning, a subfield of AI, is a useful technology to process and analyze Big Data are a useful methodology for DSS with a combination of data dictated and human-driven analytics. DSS applications can be used in a vast array of diverse fields, such as making operational decisions, medical diagnosis, and predictive maintenance. There is a lot of research in the literature regarding the development and application of DSS. In this book, the chapters are proposed in such a way as to explore every important aspect of Machine Learning and Probabilistic Graphical Models for Decision Support Systems. This book presents recent advancements in research, new methods and techniques, and applications of DSS with Machine Learning and Probabilistic Graphical Models, which are very powerful techniques to extract knowledge from Big Data effectively and interpret decisions. The book undertakes to stimulate scientific exchange, ideas, and experiences in the field of DSS applications. Researchers and practitioners alike will benefit from this book to enhance the understanding of machine learning, Probabilistic Graphical Models, and, especially, their use in DSS in the context of decision making with uncertainty. The real-world case studies in various fields with guidance and recommendations for the practical applications of these studies are introduced in each chapter. Current researches, trends, future directions, opportunities, etc. will be discussed, making it friendly for beginners and young researchers.

20 November 2021   **Kim Phuc Tran**

Univ. Lille, ENSAIT, ULR 2461 - GEMTEX - Génie et Matériaux Textiles
F-59000 Lille, France.
kim-phuc.tran@ensait.fr

Contents

Acronyms

5G	5 Generation	DSSS	Direct-Sequence Spread Spectrum
AD	Anomaly Detection		
AE	Autoencoder	DT	Decision Tree
AHC	Agglomerative Hierarchical Clustering	ECG	Electrocardiograph
		ED	Economic Design
AI	Artificial Intelligence	EKNS	Enhanced Kernel Null Space
ANN	Artificial Neural Network	ELBO	Evidence Lower Bound
ARL	Average Run Length	EM	ElectroMagnetic
ARP	Address Resolution Protocol	EML	Edge-Machine-Learning
ASC	Agriculture Supply Chain	ERP	Enterprise Resource Planning
AUC	Area Under the ROC Curve	ESD	Economic Statistical Design
BC	Blockchain	EWMA	Exponentially Moving Average
BN	Bayesian Network	FL	Federated Learning
BO	Bayesian Optimization	FN	False Negative
BS	BackSpace	FP	False Positive
BT	Blockchain Technique	FPR	False Positive Rate
CE	Cross Entropy	GA	Genetic Algorithm
CL	Centralized Learning	GAN	Generative Adversarial Networks
CLSC	Closed-Loop Supply Chain	HTM	Hierarchical Temporal Memory
CNN	Convolutional Neural Network	IC	In-control
CoDa	Compositional Data	ICS	Industrial Control System
CPD	Conditional Probability Distribution	IDS	Intrusion Detection System
		IF	Isolation Forest
CPS	Cyber-Physical System	IIoT	Industrial Internet of Thing
CS	Computer Science	IoT	Internet of Thing
DBN	Deep Belief Network	IPS	Intrusion Prevention System
DDoS	Distributed DoS	IT	Information Technology
DDS	Decision Support System	KDE	Kernel Density Estimation
DL	Deep Learning	KL	Kullback-Leibler
DNN	Deep Neural Network	KNN	K-Nearest Neighbors
DOE	Design of Experiment	KPCA	Kernel Principle Component Analysis
DoS	Denial of Service		
DR	Detection Rate	KQE	Kernel Quantile Estimator
DSS	Decision Support System	LCL	Lower Control Limit

LOCF	Last Observation Carried Forward	RL	Reinforcement Learning
LoS	Line of Sight	RMSE	Root Mean Squared Error
LR	Linear Regression	RNN	Recurrent Neural Network
LSTM	Long-Short Term Memory	ROC	Receiver Operating Characteristic
M2M	Machine-to-Machine	RSME	Root Mean Square Error
MAD	Mean Absolute Deviation	RSSI	Received Signal Strength Indicator
MAPE	Mean Absolute Percentage Error		
MAR	Missing at Random	RUL	Remaining Useful Lifetime
MCAR	Missing Completely at Random	SCA	Side Channel Attack
ML	Machine Learning	SCADA	Supervisory Control and Data Acquisition
MLP	Multi Layer Perceptron		
MNAR	Missing not at Random	SCM	Supply Chain Management
MQTT	Message Queuing Telemetry Transport	SDN	Software Defined Network
		SM	Smart Manufacturing
MRF	Markov Random Field	SN charts	Shewhart charts using the Sign Statistics
MSE	Mean Square Error		
MU-MIMO	Multi User-Multiple-Input Multiple-Output	SPC	Statistical Process Control
		SPM	Statistical Process Monitoring
NN	Neural Network	SR charts	Shewhart charts using the Wilcoxon Signed-rank Statistics
NR	New Radio		
OC	Out-of-control	SSH	Secure Shell
OCSVM	One Class Support Vector Machine	SVc	Support Vector classification
		SVDD	Support Vector Data Description
OFDM	Orthogonal Frequency Division Multiplexing	SVM	Support Vector Machine
		TDA	Topological Data Analysis
OoS	Out of Sight	TETRA	TErrestrial Trunked RAdio
PCA	Principal Component Analysis	UCL	Upper Control Limit
PdM	Predictive Maintenance	URL	Uniform Resource Locator
PDR	Packet Delivery Ratio	VAE	Variational Autoencoder
PGM	Probabilistic Graphical Models	VR	Virtual Reality
PLM	Product Lifecycle Management	Wi-Fi	Wireless Fidelity
QoS	Quality of Service	WSN	Wireless Sensor Network
RBF NN	Radial Basis Function Neural Network	XAI	Explainable Artificial Intelligence
RF	Random Forest	XGBoos	eXtreme Gradient Boosting
RFID	Radio Frequency IDentification		

Chapter 1

Introduction to Machine Learning and Probabilistic Graphical Models for Decision Support Systems

Kim Phuc Tran

1 Scope of the Research Domain

We are now witnessing the rapid development and powerful application of advanced technologies, leading to the 4th industrial revolution or Industry 4.0[1]. Digitization is changing every aspect of society and industry. Sensors with integrated Internet of Things (IoT) technology are being used more and more widely in the digital transformation process of businesses. The wide use of cyber-physical systems and the IoT lead to the era of Big Data. The massiveness, complexity, and heterogeneity of data streams require advanced computing technologies which are now performed efficiently thanks to the availability of Artificial Intelligence (AI) and Cloud Computing[2].

Industry 4.0 can provide automatic solutions to different sectors such as manufacturing, healthcare, automation, supply chain management. However, there are many challenges in Industry 4.0 such as shorter product life cycles, the need for resources to design, manufacture, and quality control that decision-making processes in companies are becoming extremely complex and require more and more knowledge[3]. In this context, decision-making based on the data gathered from the process of data-driven decision-making is essential. Data-driven decision-making is a technology that brings a lot of benefits to the decision-making process of enterprises. As an essential tool, Decision Support System (DSS) is designed to assist companies to support the decision-making process and making more effective decisions. A DSS is an information system that analyses data from organizations and presents it so that managers can make decisions more easily[4].

In the era of Big Data, DSS has become vital for organizations. DSS applications can be used in a vast array of diverse fields, such as making operational decisions, medical diagnosis, and predictive maintenance. In industry 4.0, the emergence of increasingly complex Big Data brings more challenges to the current DSS technology. As a powerful solution, in this case, Machine learning is a useful technology for decision support systems to solve complex decision

---

Univ. Lille, ENSAIT, ULR 2461 - GEMTEX - Génie et Matériaux Textiles, F-59000 Lille, France.
Email: kim-phuc.tran@ensait.fr

problems[5]. In addition, in the context of decision-making under uncertainty, Probabilistic Graphical Modeling (PGM) is a rich framework that provides a powerful formal framework to model complex data[6]. PGM is widely used throughout machine learning and in many real-time applications in various fields of engineering. These are the primary reasons for using PGMs. PGMs are acknowledged as a powerful framework for complex domains. Bringing together graph theory and probability theory, PGMs can be used to represent relations compactly and permit efficient inference in the presence of uncertainty[7]. This book is devoted to the development of a decision support system based on machine learning and PGMs with applications in many fields such as manufacturing, healthcare, supply chain management, predictive maintenance, cybersecurity, etc.

2 Structure of the Book

This is the first book that presents recent advancements of research, new methods, and techniques with applications in DSS using Machine Learning and PGMs which are very powerful techniques to extract knowledge from Big Data effectively and interpret decisions. It explores Bayesian Network[6], Long Short-Term Memory (LSTM) networks[1], Reinforcement Learning[8;5], Anomaly Detection[9], Intrusion Detection[10], etc. The book contains 12 chapters.

In the Introductory chapter "Introduction to Machine Learning and Probabilistic Graphical Models for Decision Support Systems", the book editor Kim Phuc Tran elaborates on the peculiarities of Decision Support Systems using Machine Learning and Probabilistic Graphical Models. He determines recent research streams and summarizes the structure and contributions of the book.

Ali Raza, Kim Phuc Tran, Ludovic Koehl, and Shujun Li investigate in their chapter, "Decision Support Systems for Healthcare based on Probabilistic Graphical Models: a survey and perspective", a survey and perspective about the development of Probabilistic Graphical Models based Decision Support Systems for Healthcare. This chapter fills the gap in the literature by identifying and analyzing research on the application of DSSs for Healthcare. The authors review and discuss open research issues that are important for this research stream.

Quoc-Thong Nguyen, Tung Nhi Tran, Cédric Heuchenne, and Kim Phuc Tran develop in their chapter, "Decision Support Systems for Anomaly Detection with the Applications in Smart Manufacturing: a survey and perspective", a survey of the key techniques that enable SM, including IIoT, Big Data, DSS and AI with several important perspectives for the decentralised techniques in Smart Manufacturing.

Ayeley Tchangani develop in his chapter, 'Decision Support System for Complex Systems Risk Assessment with Bayesian Networks, an overview of how to use different Bayesian technology tools to model and analyze risk management problems.

Huu Du Nguyen and Kim Phuc Tran develop in their chapter, "Decision Support System using LSTM with Bayesian optimization for Predictive Maintenance: Remaining Useful Life Prediction" an ML based method to build a DSS using the LSTM with a Bayesian optimization algorithm for predicting Remaining Useful Life Prediction.

Zaohao Lu, Zhenglei He, Kim Phuc Tran, Sebastien Thomassey, Xianyi Zeng, and Mengna Hong develop in their chapter, "Decision Support Systems for Textile Manufacturing Process with Machine Learning" a decision support system combining the Artificial Neural Network model, Analytic Hierarchy Process and Q-learning for supporting the decision-making of textile manufacturing process.

Truong Thu Huong, Nguyen Minh Dan, Le Anh Quang, Nguyen Xuan Hoang, Le Thanh Cong, Kieu Ha Phung, and Kim Phuc Tran develop in their chapter, "Anomaly Detection enables Cybersecurity with Machine Learning techniques" an overview of Cybersecurity issues for Industrial systems, IoT-based Industrial systems, and the cyberattack detection issues for Industrial Control Systems.

Thi Thuy Van Nguyen, Cédric Heuchenne and Kim Phuc Tran develop in their chapter, "Machine learning for compositional data analysis in Support of the Decision Making Process" a review of several researches related to applying ML to compositional data, including principal component analysis, clustering, classification, and regression. They introduced a transformation method based on Dirichlet density estimation to transform CoDa into real data and apply this transformed data in anomaly detection using Support Vector Data Description.

Alejandro Marcos Alvarez, Cédric Heuchenne, Phuong Hanh Tran and Alireza Faraz develop in their chapter, "Decision support system with Genetic Algorithm for economic statistical design of Nonparametric control chart" an economic statistical design (ESD) for two nonparametric control charts based on the sign and the Wilcoxon signed-rank tests. Genetic Algorithm based DSS is used to find the optimal parameters of the designed charts.

Jonathan Villain, Virginie Deniau and Christophe Gransart develop in their chapter, "Jamming Detection in Electromagnetic communication with Machine Learning: a survey and perspective" an overview on the threat of the jamming on the use of wireless communication and they shown the interest of ML to help to counter this threat.

Yanni Xu and Xiaofen Ji develop in their chapter, "Intellectual Support with Machine Learning for Decision-making in Garment Manufacturing Industry: A Review" insights and relevant references for both researchers and practitioners on the machine learning-based decision support for smart manufacturing in garment industry 4.0.

Thi Hien Nguyen, Huu Du Nguyen, Kim Duc Tran, Dinh Duy Kha Nguyen, and Kim Phuc Tran develops in their chapter, "Enabling Smart Supply Chain Management with Artificial Intelligence" a comprehensive overview of the applications of the AI Technique in Supply Chain Management.

3   Conclusion

The book undertakes to stimulate scientific exchanges, ideas, and experiences in the field of DSS applications. Researchers, postgraduate students, and practitioners alike will benefit from this book to enhance the understanding of Machine Learning, Probabilistic Graphical Models, and their use in DSS in practice, and especially in the context of decision making with uncertainty. The real-world case studies in various fields with guidance and recommendations for the practical applications of these studies are introduced in each chapter.

References

[1] H.D. Nguyen, K.P. Tran, S. Thomassey and M. Hamad. Forecasting and anomaly detection approaches using LSTM and LSTM Autoencoder techniques with the applications in supply chain management. *International Journal of Information Management*, 57: 102282, 2021.

[2] K.P. Tran. Artificial intelligence for smart manufacturing: Methods and applications. *Sensors*, 21(16): 5584, 2021.

[3] K.P. Tran, S. Thomassey, X. Zeng, C. Yi, Z. He and J. Xu. Modeling of textile manufacturing processes using intelligent techniques: A review. *The International Journal of Advanced Manufacturing Technology*, pp. 1–29, 2021.

[4] C.W. Holsapple, R.H. Bonczek and A.B. Whinston. *Foundations of Decision Support Systems*. Academic Press, 2014.

[5] J. Xu, S. Thomassey, X. Zeng, C. Yi, Z. He and K.P. Tran. Multi-objective optimization of the textile manufacturing process using deep-q-network based multi-agent reinforcement learning. *Journal of Manufacturing Systems*, 2021.

[6] K. Topuz and D. Delen. A probabilistic bayesian inference model to investigate injury severity in automobile crashes. *Decision Support Systems*, p. 113557, 2021.

[7] D. Koller and N. Friedman. *Probabilistic Graphical Models: Principles and Techniques*. MIT Press, 2009.

[8] J. Xu, S. Thomassey, X. Zeng, C. Yi, Z. He and K.P. Tran. A deep reinforcement learning based multi-criteria decision support system for optimizing textile chemical process. *Computers in Industry*, 125: 103373, 2021.

[9] T.H. Nguyen, K.D. Tran, P.H. Tran, A. Ahmadi Nadi and K.P. Tran. *Application of Machine Learning in Statistical Process Control Charts: A Survey and Perspective*, pp. 7–42. Springer International Publishing, Cham, 2022.

[10] M.L. Dao, D.L. Tran, M.D. Nguyen, A.Q. Le, D.T. Bui, K.P. Tran, T.H. Truong and P.B. Ta. Detecting cyberattacks using anomaly detection in industrial control systems: A federated learning approach. *Computers in Industry*, 132: 103509, 2021.

Chapter 2

Decision Support Systems for Healthcare based on Probabilistic Graphical Models: A Survey and Perspective

Ali Raza,[1,2] Kim Phuc Tran,[1,*] Ludovic Koehl[1] and Shujun Li[2]

1 Introduction

Probabilistic graphical modeling (PGM) deals with the branch of machine learning which studies the use of probability distributions to describe a given event to make useful predictions about it. PGM is widely used throughout machine learning and in many real-world applications. Such techniques can be used to address problems in fields such as medicine, language processing, and computer vision. This combination of theory and powerful applications makes PGMs one of the most interesting topics in the modern era of artificial intelligence (AI). One major advantage of probabilistic models is that they provide an idea about the uncertainty associated with predictions. Such ideas related to uncertainty and confidence are of extreme utility when it comes to sensitive and critical machine learning applications, such as clinical healthcare. To understand probabilistic models at the abstract level, let us consider a classification problem with N classes. If the model is probabilistic it will provide a probability for each of the N classes for a given input, i.e., the model which provides a probability distribution over the N classes. Usually, we consider the class with the highest probability as the output class. Typical examples of probabilistic models in machine learning are logistic regression, hidden Markov models and Bayesian classifiers, and neural networks with the softmax function (we will discuss in detail in later sections). Note that logistic regression based on the sigmoid function can be considered as an exception, as it provides the probability in relation to one class only.

Another way to understand the difference between probabilistic and non-probabilistic models is their respective objective functions. For example, in linear regression, the objective function is based on the squared, where the objective is to minimize the Mean Squared Error (MSE) or Root Mean Squared Error (RMSE), the later is defined by Eq. 1.

$$\text{RMSE} = \sqrt{\frac{1}{n}\sum_{i=1}^{n}(y-y')^2}, (y_i - y_i')^2 \tag{1}$$

---

[1] Univ. Lille, ENSAIT, ULR 2461 - GEMTEX - Génie et Matériaux Textiles, F-59000 Lille, France.

[2] School of Computing & Institute of Cyber Security for Society (iCSS), University of Kent, UK.

* Corresponding author: kim-phuc.tran@ensait.fr

Here, n is the total number of data samples, y_i is the true label, and y_i' is the predicted label. The intuition behind this is to calculate the RSME by predicting a given data point based on the difference between the actual value and the predicted value. As the objective function here is not based on probabilities, but on the absolute difference between the actual value and the predicted value they can be considered as non-probabilistic models. Typical examples of non-probabilistic models are Support Vectors Machines (SVMs) and @Shujun: sigmoid predicts the probability of occurrence of a binary outcome. It is a special case of linear regression as it predicts the probabilities of outcome using log function. We use the activation function (sigmoid) to convert the outcome into categorical value. In regards to probabilistic models, such as neural networks with softmax output function, the objective function is usually cross-entropy (binary cross-entropy in case of a binary classifier), given by Eq. 2. Here, $p(y_i)$ and y_i is the predicted label and true label of data sample i respectively. The intuition behind cross-entropy is; if the probabilistic model predicts the true class of a data point with high confidence, the loss will be less.

$$\text{CS} = -\frac{1}{n}\sum_{i=1}^{n}\left(\log\left(p(y_i)\right)\right) \tag{2}$$

As we notice that cross-entropy is based on probabilities, such models can be regarded as probabilistic models. Therefore, to differentiate between probabilistic and non-probabilistic models, one of the easiest ways is to analyze the loss function of the model.

1.1 Probabilistic Modeling

To understand probabilistic modeling, the simplest way would be to define a real-world model in the form of the mathematical equation.

$$y = \boldsymbol{\alpha x}, \tag{3}$$

where y is the dependent variable which we want to predict, and x is the independent variable, upon which y is dependent, paramaterized by $\boldsymbol{\alpha}$. For example, y may be the price of a car, and $\boldsymbol{x}$ are features that affect price, e.g., color, the number of seats, the engine size, etc. We assume that y is a linear function of $\boldsymbol{x}$. However, real-world events are very complicated to model because they involve a certain amount of uncertainty. Therefore, we model such events in the form of probability distributions, represented as $p(\boldsymbol{x}, y)$. The probabilistic aspect of modeling has significant importance, because we cannot perfectly predict the future as the world is often stochastic. Moreover, we need to assess the confidence of our predictions. It is often the case that predicting a single value is not enough, we need the system to output its beliefs about what is going on in the event. To overcome this, we can write the probability model as a product of conditional probabilities.

$$P(y, x_1, x_2, \ldots, x_n) = p(y)\prod_{i=1}^{n} p(x_i|y) \tag{4}$$

A small number of parameters (e.g., weights in case of machine learning) can be used to describe each factor $p(x_i|y)$.

1.2 Applications of PGMs

PGMs have a number of diverse real-world applications. Typical examples of such applications include image generation, inpainting, denoising, language translation, speech recognition, and diagnosis in clinical healthcare and medicine. In this subsection, we provide an overview of applications in healthcare and medicine.

PGMs can assist clinical practitioners in diagnosing diseases and prognoses. For example, in[1] Bayesian networks (which we will discuss later) based model has been developed for diagnosing pneumonia. Their model was able to distinguish patients with pneumonia from patients with other diseases with high sensitivity (0.95) and specificity (0.965), and was used for many years in the clinical practice. Figure 1 outlines the network proposed in[1].

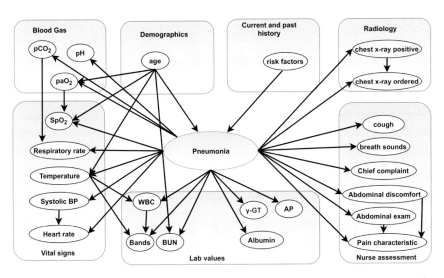

Figure 1: Structure of Bayesian network. Reprinted from Aronsky and Haug[1].

Regarding the application of PGMs in healthcare, probabilistic methods lie primarily in the realm of AI. The AI community first encountered these methods in the search of building computerized systems designed to perform complex tasks, such as medical diagnosis, at an expert level. Researchers in this domain quickly realized the need for methods that allow the integration of evidence and information to provide support for decision making under certain uncertainty. Furthermore, academia has recognized that Decision Support Systems (DSS) have the utmost important role in computer-based information systems and play a crucial role in supporting managers in their semi-structured or unstructured decision-making activities. Using a predefined set of rules, DSS extracts knowledge from complex data and presents it in an appropriate way. For instance, Gorry and Scott Morton[2] claimed that information systems should exist only to support decisions. Thereafter, there has been an exponentially growing amount of research in the area of DSS. Medical diagnosis is one of the most important research subjects in medical informatics. Hence, a lot of research is being carried out in the application of DSS in healthcare. By adopting proper DSS, healthcare can be made easily accessible to remote and large populations. Furthermore, physicians can have easy access to medical records, medical test results, medical images, and information about medication remotely anytime[3]. Moreover, healthcare requires responsibility in managing a large amount of healthcare-related information. It can be done by proper modeling of information that field experts can continuously build a strong policy of welfare. The main goal of DSS is to provide experts with information when it is needed. Such systems provide knowledge, models, and data processing tools to help the experts in making efficient and better decisions in many situations. The goal of such systems is to resolve several problems in healthcare to help patients and their families, and the clinical practitioners manage their healthcare by providing better access to these services[4].

A lot of research has been carried in the application of DSS in healthcare. Feinleib[5] suggest that data mining methods are promising in the application of DSS in healthcare. A prototype of a system for self-management in healthcare to assist patients with diabetes and to track their blood glucose levels has been developed in[6]. Goldberg et al.[7] used web-based DSS for departments related to emergency to assess the performance features source of the recommendations generated by experts. The results show that a remote clinical decision support system decreases time-to-trial in the decision support to clinical interventions.

In regards to the importance of DSS in healthcare, this chapter reviews some of the research work on healthcare DSS based on Probabilistic Graphical Models (PGMs)[8] and machine learning. The rest of the chapter is organized as follows: Section 2 discusses decision support systems in Healthcare. Section 3 presents a review about the application of artificial intelligence in healthcare. Section 4 discusses healthcare DSSs based on PGMs. Section 5 provides perspectives for Healthcare DSSs based on PGMs. Section 6 provides case studies of DSS in healthcare. Section 7 concludes the chapter.

2 Decision Support Systems in Healthcare

DSS in healthcare are intended to assist physicians and other health practitioners in decision-making tasks. It can be also defined as a computerized algorithm that uses data from a number of patients to generate case-specific or encounter-specific advice[9]. Decision support systems in healthcare have been studied and explored extensively in the healthcare industry. These systems links observations with health knowledge to determine health options by health practitioners for improved healthcare. The main idea of healthcare DSS is a set of rules derived from medical professionals applied to dynamic knowledge. Data mining is well suited to give decision support for healthcare. There are several probabilistic classification techniques available that can be used for healthcare decision support systems. Various techniques are being used for differential diagnoses. Health decision support systems provide a number of soft computing techniques to derive useful information from data repositories, human knowledge, and literature to support decision-making across operational and clinical healthcare processes.

DSSs are an important part of modern healthcare organizations. They help felicitate patients, practitioners, and healthcare stakeholders by providing patient-centered information and expert health knowledge[10]. To improve the efficiency and quality of healthcare, healthcare decision-making uses the knowledge obtained from the smart decisions systems. For example, automated DSSs for ECG is available in primary health care units and hospitals to fulfill the increasing healthcare requirements of prognosis in the domain of heart diseases. A lot of studies have used healthcare DSSs to promote individualized cardiovascular prevention[11;12;13]. DSSs provide timely information at the point of care to inform patient care decisions. The use cases of decision support systems can be summarized as follow;

1. Clinical Management: DSS can alert healthcare practitioners to reach out to patients who have not followed management schedules, or are due for a follow-up, and help identify patients eligible for research based on specific criteria[14].

2. Diagnosis Support: DSSs for healthcare diagnosis, known as diagnostic decision support systems (DDSs) have traditionally provided computerized support, whereby they might be provided an input (data/user selections), and then the output of possible diagnoses[15;16;17].

Moreover, the healthcare industry generates a large amount of data. Consequently, DSSs are used extensively to capture and transfer information. Therefore, in this section, we will briefly overview various classification techniques for healthcare decision support systems. In other words, this section summarizes some of the historical and state of the art decision support systems in healthcare, and analyzes the success factors needed for widespread deployment, and postulates the future trends of the field in the context of a new decision management paradigm.

2.1 Probabilistic Graphical Models

PGMs were developed in the early 1980s by researchers working in mathematics, AI, and economy with the purpose of solving complex problems which were proven not to be solvable by methods existing so far. PGMs are a rich framework for encoding probability distributions over complex domains: joint (multivariate) distributions over large numbers of random variables that interact with each other. These representations exist in the intersection of statistics and computer science, depending on concepts from probability theory, graph algorithms, machine learning, and more. They are the basis for the state-of-the-art methods in a number of applications, such as healthcare, image processing, speech, and natural language processing, etc. They are also the building blocks in the formulation of many machine learning problems. PGMs allow dealing with problems that were not solvable with traditional probabilistic methods or other artificial intelligence techniques.

Depending on whether the graph is directed or undirected, we can classify graphical models into Bayesian networks (BN) and Markov networks (MN), respectively, as shown in Figure 2.

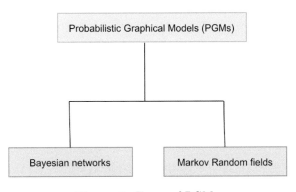

Figure 2: Types of PGMs.

Both types contain the properties of conditional probabilities and independence. However, they can encode the different sets of independence and the conditional probabilities of the distribution. Each type is discussed as follows.

2.2 Bayesian Networks: Directed Graphical Models

BN is a knowledge-based graphical representation[18;19] that depicts a set of variables and their probabilistic relationships among diseases and the corresponding symptoms. In other words, BN represent probability distributions that can be calculated by-product of the local conditional probability distribution. To understand, let us use the notation $I(p)$ to denote the set of all independencies for a joint distribution p. If $p(x|y) = p(x)p(y)$, we say $x \perp y \in I(p)$. The Bayesian network can describe many independencies in $I(p)$; such independencies can be retrieved from the directed graphs. For example, a Bayes net G with three nodes A, B and C could have essentially three different possible structures with different independence assumptions, as shown in Figure 3.

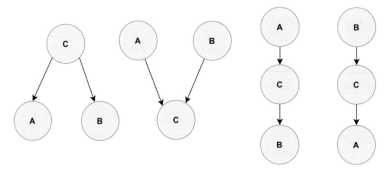

Figure 3: Bayesian networks over three variables, encoding different types of dependencies.

These structures describe the independencies in a three-variable BN. We can extend it to general networks by recursively applying them over any larger graph. This leads to a notion called d-separation (where d stands for directed).

BN are used to find the probability of possible diseases to occur, given their symptoms. These networks take advantage of their property to require the knowledge and conclusions of domain experts in the form of probabilities. However, it is not viable for large complex systems given multiple symptoms. To understand the BN, let us consider a canonical example of a researchers network. The setting of the graph, as shown in Figure 4, consists of four variables which are given as follows.

1. *Difficulty:* Takes values 0 and 1 for minimum and maximum difficulty, respectively.

2. *Intelligence:* Takes values 0 and 1 for not intelligent and intelligent, respectively.

3. *Research output:* Takes values 1, 2 and 3 for good, average and bad research, respectively.

4. *Research articles:* shows the number of research articles published.

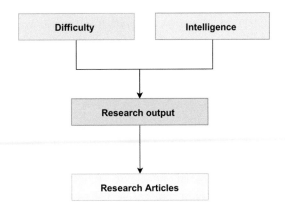

Figure 4: Bayesian networks: Directed graphical models.

The edges in the graph show the dependencies in the graph. The *Research Output* of a researcher depends on the *Difficulty* of the research area and the *Intelligence* of the researcher. The *Research output*, in turn, determines the number of publications. Note that the direction of arrows shows the cause-effect relationships. *Difficulty* affects the *Research Output* score, but the *Research Output* does not influence the *Difficulty*. Finally, let us look at the tables associated with each of the nodes. Formally, these are called conditional probability distributions (CPDs), as shown in Figure 5. The CPDs for *Difficulty* and *Intelligence* are easy to compute, because these variables are independent. The tables basically encode the probabilities of these variables, taking values from 0 to 1. You might have noticed, the values in each of the rows must sum to 1.

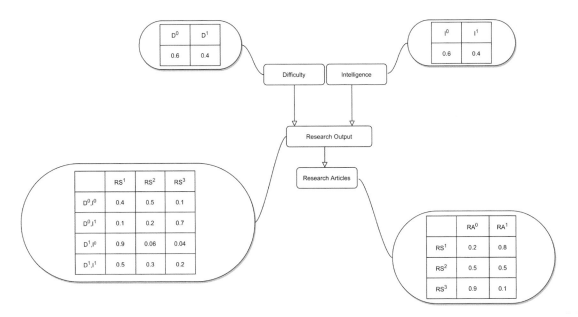

Figure 5: Bayesian network with conditional probability distributions (CPDs).

Next, let us look at the CPD for *Research Output*. Each row corresponds to the values that its parent (*Difficulty* and *Intelligence*) can take, and each column corresponds to the values that *Research Output* can take. Each cell has the conditional probability $p(RsearchOutput = RS|Intelligence = I, Difficulty = D)$, that is, given that the value of *Intelligence* and *Difficulty* , what is the probability of the value of *Research Output* being RS. For example, as $P(ResearchOutput = RS^1|Difficulty = D^1, Intelligence = I^1)$ is 0.5, that is, if the intelligence of the researcher and the difficulty of the research area is high, then the probability of the research output to be good is 0.5. The CPD for Research Articles is easy to understand with the above knowledge. Because it has one parent, the conditional probabilities will be of the form $P(ResearchArticles = RA^1|ResearchOutput = RS^1)$, that is, what is the probability of Research Articles being RA, given that the value of Research Output is RS. Each row now corresponds to a pair of values of Research Output. Again, the row values add up to 1. An essential requirement for BN is that the graph must be a directed acyclic graph (DAG).

Thanathornwong[20] designed a clinical decision support system to help general practitioners assess the need for orthodontic treatment in patients with permanent dentition. Particularly, a BN is used as the underlying model for assessing the need for orthodontic treatment. Around one thousand permanent dentition patient's datasets chosen from a hospital record system were prepared in which one data element represented one participant with information for all variables and their stated need for orthodontic treatment. The proposed system in this work provided promising results; it showed a high classification accuracy for classifying groups into needing and not needing orthodontic treatment.

2.3 Markov Random Fields

Although BN can compactly represent interesting probability distributions some distributions may have independent assumptions that cannot be well represented by the structure of a BN. To address such challenges there exists another technique for compactly representing and visualizing a probability distribution that is based on the language of undirected graphs called Markov random fields (MRF)[21;22]. Let us take a motivating example to understand the MRF. Suppose that we are modeling voting preferences among persons W, X, Y, and Z. Let us say that (W,X), (X,Y), (Y,Z), and (Z,W), are relatives. Moreover, suppose that relatives have similar voting preferences. These relationships can be naturally depicted by undirected graphs, as shown in Figure 6.

A MRF is a probability distribution p over variables defined by an undirected graph G in which nodes represent variables x_i $i = 1, \ldots, N$. The probability p is given by.

$$p(x_1, ..., x_N) = \frac{1}{Z} \prod_{c \in C} \beta_c(X_c)$$

Where C denotes the set of cliques of G, and each factor β_c is a non-negative function over cliques. The partition function

$$Z = \sum_{x_1,...,X_N} \prod_{c \in C} \beta_c(X_c),$$

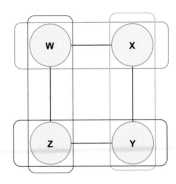

Figure 6: Undirected graphical representation of a joint probability of voting preferences over four individuals. Colors illustrates the pairwise preference present in the model.

is a normalizing constant which sums the distribution to one. Hence, given a graph G, there might be factors in the probability distribution whose scope is any clique in G, it can be a single node, an edge, etc. It is important to note that there is no need to specify a factor for each clique. In the example above, a factor is defined over each edge (which is a clique of two nodes). Nevertheless, cliques over single nodes have been specified.

In regards to the application of BN and MRF Rajinikanth et al.[23] present a Firefly Algorithm and Shannon Entropy (FA+SE) based multi-threshold to increase the pneumonia lesion and implements MRF segmentation to identify the lesions with better accuracy.[24] developed a system based on BN which uses Bayesian reasoning to compute posterior probabilities of possible diagnoses depending on the given symptoms. This system was developed for diagnosis in Internal Medicine and now covers about 1500 diagnoses in this domain, based on thousands of findings. Barnett et al.[25] proposed a system called DXplain which uses a modified form of the BN. It generates a list of ranked diagnoses associated with the given symptoms. It finds its use particularly for healthcare practitioners who lack computer expertise. It is also used as a reference with a searchable database of diseases and clinical manifestations. SimulConsult[26], utilizes BN to input data in a scalable fashion and compute probabilities, accomplishing it by focusing specialty by specialty. It uses a statistical pattern-matching method which consists of the onset and offset of the findings in each disease. Table 1 presents a summary of a few past developments and applications of BN and MRF in the healthcare sector.

Table 1: Applications of MRF and BN in healthcare.

Scheme	Method	Use Case
27	MRF	Vertebral Tumor Prediction
28	MRF	Tumor segmentation and gene-expression based classification
29	MRF	Segmented MRI-based partial volume correction in PET
30	MRF	Unsupervised 4D myocardium segmentation
31	MRF	EMR-based medical knowledge representation and inference
32	BN	Identifying Risk Factors of Depression in Middle-Aged Persons
33	BN	Electrocardiogram (ECG) or Heart rate monitoring
34	BN	Human activity recognition (HAR)

2.4 Deep Neural Networks

Deep Neural Networks (DNN)[35;36] are non-knowledge-based decision support systems which are adaptive in nature. They learn from existing knowledge and experiences (data). A typical workflow of neural networks in healthcare is shown in Figure 7.

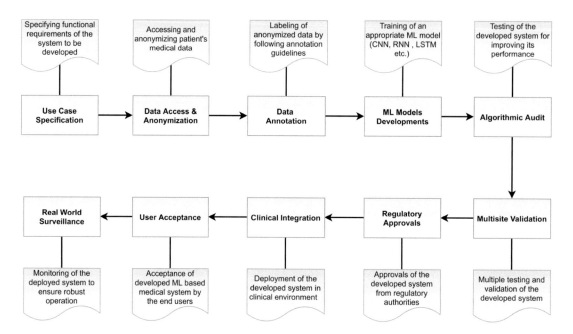

Figure 7: The illustration of major phases for development of DNN based healthcare systems. Figure adopted from[37].

The architecture of DNN mainly consists of three layers: Input, Output, and Hidden layer(s). These networks are made of nodes called neurons. Weights and biases are the connection between nodes of different layers, which are used to propagate the input between the nodes. DNN are able to work with incomplete data which gives educated guesses about missing data and gets improved with adaptive system learning. A method for training an unsupervised fashion is autoencoders[38]. An autoencoder learns features of a dataset, typically of lower dimensions. Autoencoder is a type of DNN that learns to reconstruct its input in the output. It has an internal representation layer that describes a code used to represent the input, and it is made up of an encoder that translates the input into the latent space, and a decoder that maps the latent space to reconstructed input. A lot of improvement has been made so far in the architecture and algorithm of DNN to make them learn without any supervised pretraining. Such as, the use of RELU activation $f(z) = max(z, 0)$, which learns more efficiently in a multi-layer model.

A typical DNN is depicted in Figure 8. In this DNN the convolutional layer along with the max-pooling layers are used for feature extraction and the dense layer is used for classification. The output dense layer often uses a sigmoid function in the case of binary classification and a softmax function in the case of multiclass classification. DNN have been used in several applications, such as image classification, computer vision, activity recognition, and deep reinforcement learning. For example, Kharat and Dudul [39] proposed a healthcare decision support system based on Jordan/Elman neural network for the diagnosis of epilepsy. The proposed system obtained comparatively a high overall training accuracy 99.83% and testing accuracy of 99.92%. A decision support system based on a DNN for the classification of heart-related diseases into 5 categories of heart disease with 97.5% accuracy by using multilayer perceptron with backpropagation training algorithm is proposed in [40]. Janghel et al. [41] proposed a decision support system using an artificial neural network to classify the fetal delivery method into normal or surgical. They primarily used three different algorithms to train the neural network: radial basis function, back propagation algorithm, and learning vector quantization network with an accuracy 99%, 93.75%, and 87.5% respectively. Researchers have proposed a large number of methods to apply DSS in healthcare. For example, [42] explains the role played by the DSS. Luque Gallego [43] describes the medical decision-support system for the mediastinal staging of non-small cell lung cancer, which is also known as called Mediastinet. Table 2 presents summary of selected works in the applications of DNN for healthcare.

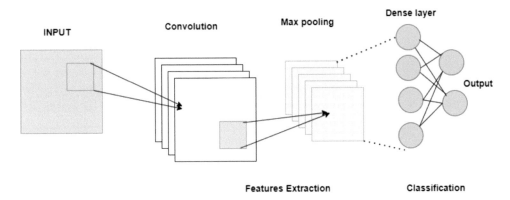

Figure 8: A typical deep Neural Network (DNN) architecture.

Table 2: Applications of DNN in healthcare.

Scheme	Method	Use Case
44	MLP	Diagnosing diabetes
45	RNN	Clinical intervention prediction and understanding
46	NN	Emotion recognition for healthcare surveillance
47	CNN	ECG biometric recognition
48	RNN	ECG signal denoising
49	DNN	ECG-based cardiac arrest pulse detection
50	CNN	ECG classification
51	CNN	ECG arrhythmias detection

2.5 Neural Networks with Probabilistic Graphical Models

There are certain limitations and challenges for neural networks NN.

1. Explanations: DNN are often complex and difficult to explain the reasons behind their predictions and decisions. Explanations about the model's decision making important for some applications such as medical prognosis and diagnosis[52].

2. Uncertainty measure: DNN cannot provide a quantification of the uncertainty of their decisions and outputs.

3. Robustness: similar to the first point, it is hard to know about the aspect of input DNN are using to take decisions.

PGM can help to solve these shortcomings, thereafter there is an opportunity to use these approaches to take advantage of their complementary strengths. For example, PGM provides a practical way to represent dependence relationships between variables and spatial relations[53;54]. DNN outperforms other approaches in classification. Thus to integrate PGM and DNN is by representing the structure of a complex problem through PGM, followed by the use of DNNs as classifiers for different elements of the underlying problem. The DNN, trained on labeled data, provide an initial estimation; then these initial estimates can be combined and improved through belief propagation in the graphical model. This approach can be used for efficient training of the model, as each one only considers a particular dataset. Spatial analysis problems are hybrid systems in which the above-mentioned systems can be useful. For instance, human activity estimation, in which body parts have a certain spatial structure; this structure provides constraints that can be used by a graphical model. The spatial constraints between the distinct elements in the model can be represented in terms of a Markov network, showing the constraints as the local joint probabilities of neighboring elements. These elements are detected and classified using a DNN. Another type of such problem is temporal modeling. In temporal modeling, the outputs change and evolve over the time usually depending on the previous state, for example, time-series. Markov chain and hidden Markov are often used to represent such problems. In the hybrid system, DNN can be used to classify the state-based observation, and the Markov model can be used for encoding the temporal relations. The application of such systems is human activity recognition and speech recognition. A toy example of such hybrid systems has been shown in Figure 9. Variational Autoencoders (VAE) are another such example. Due to the increasing popularity of VAEs in anomaly detection, they have been used in various fields, such as, Healthcare[55], cybersecurity[56] and various other applications being discovered with time. One of the important use of VAE in healthcare is anomaly detection. The idea is to train the VAE using normal data and note down the corresponding reconstruction error. When the VAE is subjected to anomaly data the reconstruction error is usually high. Hence, data with reconstruction error more than that of the normal data is considered anomalous. In order to give more in-depth details owing to the growing utility of VAEs in anomaly detection, we will discuss a case study about VAE in healthcare anomaly detection in Section 6.2. Researchers have proposed such hybrid architectures for human activity recognition. For example, in[57] an architecture for the recognition of the human posture in video sequences was developed. The proposed model consists of a convolutional neural network-based detector and a hidden markov

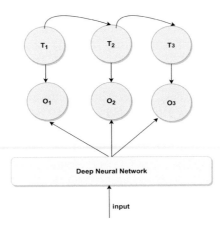

Figure 9: A hybrid DNN classifier and a hidden Markov model architecture.

model (CoHMM). The integration of both models allows learning spatial and temporal dependencies. The detector recognizes the different joints based on a convolutional neural network (CNN), and uses the spatial correlations between neighboring regions through a conditional random field (CRF)[58]. Whereas, the CoHMMs computes the best possible movement sequence among interacting processes.

More interesting research that combines deep neural networks and graphical models include: conditional random fields as recurrent neural networks have been summarized in[59].

3 Artificial Intelligence in Healthcare Applications

In the last decade, Artificial intelligence (AI) has revolutionized the healthcare system[60;61]. AI is bringing a paradigm shift to healthcare, powered by the increasing availability of healthcare data and rapid progress of analytic techniques. AI can be applied to various types of healthcare data (structured and unstructured) to help practitioners diagnose the underlying health issue in the early stages with more accuracy and efficiency. In this section, we review selected current AI applications in healthcare and also discuss their future applications. The usefulness and the advantages of AI have been extensively discussed in[62;63;64]. AI constructs data analysis algorithms to extract features from data. AI algorithm's inputs include patient 'traits' and sometimes medical outcomes of interest. A patient's traits commonly include baseline data, such as age, gender, disease history, Xray-images, ECG. This may also include disease-specific data, gene expressions, physical examination results, clinical symptoms, medication. Depending on the outcomes and the input data, machine learning (ML) (a subclass of AI, which has been extensively used in healthcare) can be classified into two major categories: unsupervised learning and supervised learning. Unsupervised learning (UL) is a type of algorithm that learns patterns from untagged data. In unsupervised learning, through mimicry, the machine is forced to build a compact internal representation of the underlying traits of data. In supervised learning (SL) the data is tagged or labeled by a human, e.g., as "car" or "fish", etc. Unsupervised learning is well known for feature extraction, while supervised learning is suitable for predictive modeling by building some relationships between the input and the outcome of interest. Recently, a hybrid of unsupervised learning and supervised learning, known as semisupervised learning has been proposed which is suitable for scenarios where the outcome is missing for certain subjects. Clustering and principal component analysis (PCA) are two famous and extensively used unsupervised learning techniques. Clustering groups data points with similar features together into clusters, without using the labeled outcome information. Clustering algorithms predict the cluster labels as output for the given input data point by maximizing and minimizing the similarity of the data within and between the clusters. Most popular clustering algorithms include k-means, hierarchical, and Gaussian mixture clustering. On the other hand, PCA plays a key role in the dimension reduction of complex data. Especially, when the recorded data is multi-dimensional. For example, the number of genes in a genome-wide association study. PCA works by projecting data into a few principal component (PC) directions, without losing too much information about the underlying data. It is sometimes recommended to use PCA for multi-dimensional data and then use clustering for better, and efficient clustering of data.

In regards to supervised learning, it considers the subject's outcomes together with their features, and goes through a certain training process to determine the best outputs associated with the inputs that are closest to the mean outcomes. Usually, the output formulations vary and are dependent on the underlying method and problem being solved. For example, the outcome can be the probability of getting a particular clinical event, the expected value of a disease level, or the expected survival duration.

The application of AI especially in healthcare is well studied in literature[65]. For example, the internet of medical things (IoMT) integrates healthcare devices, sensors and machine learning algorithms to provide new applications in healthcare[66]. Machines based on AI can add support in healthcare by providing continuous automatic monitoring and alerting the healthcare provider or clinical practitioners through an alert system. Moreover, these devices can also help in decision-making through DSS. One of the major advantages of this transformation is the transition of tasks from a manual, hectic and time-consuming methodology to smart, automatic, and time-efficient systems in healthcare. Additionally, these systems help clinical practitioners to attend to patients in emergency cases by providing timely information. DNN has always outperformed in healthcare by providing hybrid architectures and blended concepts like CNN, to enable new healthcare solutions. Due to the variety of healthcare data including clinical data, HAR data, it is difficult for humans to infer the data for decision making. Accordingly, ML has been used in healthcare for better understanding of data and for better decision-making process[67]. For example, Azimi et al.[68] proposed a CNN-based classifier architecture for a health case study on an ECG classification. Tahmassebi et al.[69] proposed ML-based algorithms for early prediction of pathological complete response (PCR) to neoadjuvant chemotherapy and survival outcome of breast cancer patients using multiparametric magnetic resonance imaging (mpMRI) data and eight different ML-based classifiers. In this regard, decision-making is incorporated at the edge thereby sending notifications to the user in the case of disease detection. This gives timely information for decision-making at the initial stage of the healthcare monitoring and improving the healthcare system.

In conclusion, we believe that AI has an important role to play in healthcare in the future. In the form of machine learning, it plays a primary role in the development of precision medicine, and healthcare solutions. Although early efforts at providing prognosis, diagnosis, and treatment recommendations are challenging, it can be seen that AI will ultimately cope with these challenges as well. Given the fast research advances in AI for imaging analysis, it can be seen that most radiology and pathology images will be examined at some point by machines using AI. As for now, automatic speech and text recognition systems are already employed for tasks like patient communication and for clinical notes, and usage of such systems is continuously increasing.

One of the greatest challenges to AI application in healthcare is to ensure their adoption in daily clinical practice. For adoption to take place, AI systems must be approved by regulators, and standardized to the extent that similar products work in a similar way. Such challenges will be overcome ultimately, but they will take time for the technologies themselves to be practical enough. As a result, we see limited use of AI in clinical practice for the coming decade, but with the rapidly improving research can make use of such systems in real life soon. For more interesting works about the application of artificial intelligence in DSS, we recommend to read [70;71].

4   Healthcare Decision Support Systems based on Probabilistic Graphical Models

DSS [72;73;74] have been widely used in the field of healthcare for assisting physicians and other healthcare professionals with decision-making tasks, for example, for analyzing patient data [75;76;77;78]. DSS are mainly based on two mainstream approaches: knowledge-based and non-knowledge based. The knowledge-based DSS consists of two principal components: the knowledge database and the inference engine. The knowledge database contains the rules and associations of compiled data which often take the form of if–then rules, whereas the inference engine combines the rules from the knowledge database with the real patients' data in order to generate new knowledge and to propose a set of suitable actions. Different methodologies have been proposed for designing healthcare knowledge databases and inference engines, such as the ontological representation of information [79]. The nonknowledge-based DSS have no direct clinical knowledge about a particular healthcare process, however, they learn clinical rules from past experiences and by finding patterns in clinical data. For example, various machine learning algorithms such as decision trees represent methodologies for learning healthcare and clinical knowledge. Both of these approaches could be used in conjunction with Ambient Intelligence (AmI) technologies. Indeed, the sensitive, adaptive, and unobtrusive nature of AmI is particularly suitable for designing decision support systems capable of supporting medical staff in critical decisions. In particular, AmI technology enables the design of the third generation of telecare systems. The first generation was the panic-alarms gadgets, often worn as pendants or around the wrist to allow a person to summon help in the case of a fall or other kinds of health emergencies. The second generation of telecare systems uses sensors to automatically detect situations where assistance or medical decisions are needed. Finally, the third generation represents AmI-based systems that move away from the simple reactive approach and adopt a proactive strategy capable of anticipating emergency situations. As a result, DSS could be used with multimodal sensing and wearable computing technologies for constantly monitoring all important signs of a patient and for analyzing such data in order to take real-time decisions and opportunely support people. Finally, DSS are jointly used with the AmI paradigm for enhancing communications among health personnel such as doctors and nurses. For example,[80] introduced a DSS based on context-aware knowledge modeling aimed at facilitating the communication and improving the capability to take decisions among clinical practitioners located in different locations.

5 Perspectives for Healthcare Decision Support Systems based on Probabilistic Graphical Models

Probabilistic models such as deep neural networks have become popular in medical applications, especially as healthcare support for computerized-aided diagnosis and prognosis. Although, such probabilistic models provide promising results and attract attention in healthcare research, real-world implementation of such models would not be that easy. Firstly, there are no clear regulations. Current regulations lack standards to measure the safety and efficacy of probabilistic models. In order to overcome such issues, the United-States food and drug administration provided guidance for assessing probabilistic models systems[81]. It classifies probabilistic models to be general wellness products, which are loosely regulated as long as the models are intended for general wellness and have low risk to the users. They also provide guidance for adaptive design in healthcare trials. Secondly, since healthcare data is highly sensitive, exchanging it among geographically distributed parties governs privacy and security challenges. Moreover, the data should be protected under general data protection regulations. Techniques like encryption, differential privacy, and federated learning can be applied to provide security and privacy to the data. However, such techniques come with a trade-off between privacy, security, and efficiency. Another hurdle in the implementation of probabilistic systems in healthcare is data ownership and incentives. Currently, there are no clearly defined regulations for the ownership of data. Moreover, most of the current healthcare environment does not provide incentives to the data owners for sharing data on the system. Nevertheless, research is underway to stimulate data sharing. The research is oriented toward changing the health service payment systems. Many payers, such as insurance companies, have shifted from rewarding the physicians by shifting the treatment volume to the treatment outcome. Additionally, the payers are also reimbursed for a medication or a treatment procedure by considering its efficiency. Under such an environment, all the parties in the healthcare system, the clinical physicians, pharmaceutical companies, and patients, have more incentives to compile and exchange information.

Other than the regulations, the key challenges and perspectives for the implementation of probabilistic systems in healthcare include those intrinsic to the science of ML, logistical difficulties in implementation, and consideration of the barriers to adoption as well as of the necessary socio-cultural or pathway changes. Robust peer-reviewed clinical evaluation as part of randomized controlled trials should be developed as a standard for evidence generation, but in practice, it may not always be appropriate or feasible. Performance evaluations should focus to capture real clinical applicability and be interpretable and understandable to the intended users. Research for regulation to access the innovation with the potential for harm, alongside thoughtful post-market surveillance is needed to ensure that patients are not exposed to dangerous health and finical risks. Methodologies should be developed to enable and make direct comparisons of probabilistic models, including the use of independent, local, and baseline test datasets. Research and development of probabilistic algorithms must be vigilant to potential dangers, including dataset shift, accidental fitting of confounders, unintended bias, the issues of generalization to new datasets, and the unintended bad consequences of new algorithms on health outcomes.

In summary, the key future perspectives about the implementation of probabilistic models in healthcare are as follow.

1. The data should be regulated properly by clear regulatory policies. The proper mechanism should be developed to ensure the security and privacy of data under general data protection regulations. For example, techniques like federated learning[82] can address such issues, but issues in federated learning like data heterogeneity, privacy leakages needed to be addressed[83;84].

2. Proper metrics should be developed to measure the risk and unintended harm to users by probabilistic models for healthcare and clinical practice.

3. Proper interpretable guidance and mechanisms should be developed to understand the results of probabilistic models for healthcare and clinical practice. For example, explainable artificial intelligence can be used to interpret the result of deep neural networks[51].

4. Proper incentive mechanisms should be developed to reward the data owners[85].

6   Case Studies

Discriminative and generative models are widely used machine learning models for ECG classification in healthcare. For example, logistic regression, support vector machines, are popular discriminative models and VAE and autoencoder are examples of generative models. In this section, we provide a case study to explore the discriminative model's graphical structure as PGM, using logistic regression as an example for ECG classification. We also provide a case study to explore the generative model's graphical structure as PGM, using VAEs as an example for ECG anomaly detection.

6.1   Logistic Regression for ECG Classification

Suppose that we are solving a classification problem to decide if an ECG signal is benign or not. We have a joint model over labels $Y = y$, and features $X = x_1, ... x_n$. The joint distribution of the model is represented as $p(Y, X) = P(y, x_1, ... x_n)$. Our aim is to estimate the probability of benign ECG signal: $P(Y = 1|X)$. To get the conditional probability $P(Y|X)$, discriminative models assume the functional form for $P(Y|X)$ and estimate parameters of $P(Y|X)$ directly from training data.

In Figure 10, the circles represent variable(s) and the arrow indicates what probabilities can be inferred. In our example, X is the ECG signal and Y is the unknown class of the ECG signal. We see that the arrow is pointing from X to Y, indicating that we can infer $P(Y|X)$ directly from the given X.

Figure 10: Directed graphical model.

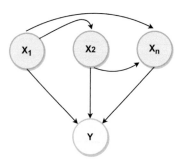

Figure 11: Graphical representation of input and output relationship.

Figure 11 represents the probability distribution of the model when feature X is expanded. We can see that each feature x_i depends on all the previous features. This will have no effect as the model simply treats X as given facts and it estimates $P(Y|X)$. As mentioned earlier that the model estimates the probability from the training data:

$$P(Y|X) = p(y|x_1 \dots x_n) \tag{5}$$

In logistic regression, we parameterize the probability as

$$P(Y = 1|X; \beta) = \frac{1}{1 + \exp(\beta_0 + \sum_{i=1}^{n} \beta_i x_i)} \tag{6}$$

Here, maximum likelihood estimation is used to estimate the parameters, followed by classification into benign and not benign ECG.

6.2 Variational Autoencoder for ECG Anomaly Detection

In this section, we will present VAEs as a case study. VAE are a type of generative deep learning method which learns latent representations. Figure 12 shows a typical structure of a VAE. VAE have also been used to draw images.

VAE consist of two main parts: encoder and decoder, where the encoder part models $E(Z|X)$, Z is the latent representation, and X is the data. $E(Z|X)$ is the function that maps the data to the latent variables. The decoder function $D(X|Z)$ learns to generate

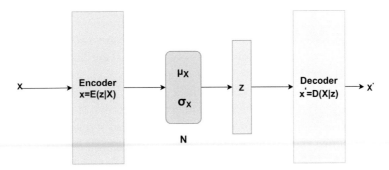

Figure 12: The structure of the variational autoencoder.

new data using the latent variables. It should be noted that in VAE, unlike the autoencoders, the distribution of Z is forced to be close to normal distribution as possible. With VAE parametric distribution can be achieved. Hence, during the run time, we can construct new samples from the normal distribution and feed them to the encoder function to generate samples, as depicted in Figure 14. The main difference between traditional autoencoder and VAE is that the former has no continuous latent space, while the latter has continuous latent space (a sample is mapped to a probability distribution with a certain mean and variance). Figure 13 depicts a comparison between the mapping of input data to latent space by an autoencoder and a VAE.

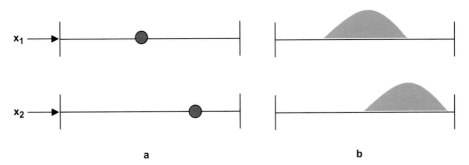

Figure 13: (a) mapping of an input to latent space by autoencoder, (b) mapping of an input to latent space by VAE.

The main objective of this case study is to use the VAE to learn the latent representations of the data. We will use the VAE to map the data to latent representation. Thereafter, we will visualize features to see the model has generalized enough to learn the data clustering or to differentiate the data as normal or not normal. Note that we do not use labels because VAE are unsupervised machine learning approaches. To show the applicability, we will use the ECG healthcare dataset for anomaly detection and visualize the features that the model has learned. The reason for using VAE is to get rid of labeling the data, as labeling data can be a hectic task. In this case study, we trained a convolutional VAE for ECG anomaly detection. We trained the VAE on normal (a particular distribution) ECG signals so that, when not normal (different distribution) ECG signals are fed into the VAE, the reconstruction loss is expected to be higher than a certain threshold. The threshold is usually the reconstruction error of VAE for normal data. If for certain data, the reconstruction error crosses the threshold, we see that data point as not normal. In other words, via the reconstruction loss, we can keep track if an ECG signal belongs to a particular distribution or not. The VAE has optimized over 2 losses, the Kullback–Leibler (kl)-loss and reconstruction loss (the difference between the input ECG and the reconstructed ECG). The kl-loss is the difference between the distribution of the latent space and a standard Gaussian with mean zero and standard deviation one. In other words, kl-loss is used the minimize the distance between the distribution between distinct classes yet keep them separable. The kl loss between two distributions A and B can be calculated as the negative sum of probability of each event in A, multiplied by the log probability of B over the probability of the event in A, as given by Eq. 7.

$$KL(A||B) = -\sum_{x \in X} A(x) \log(\frac{B(x)}{A(x)}) \tag{7}$$

Where, $||$ is divergence. This is to compress the distribution of the latent space to the standard distribution. This helps the decoder to map from every area of the latent space when decoding the input ECG signal. Figure 14 shows a graphical representation of the VAE for new sample generation.

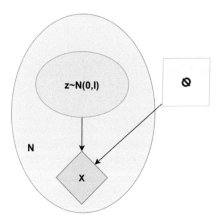

Figure 14: VAE as a graphical model and its use to generate new samples.

We used the public baseline ECG dataset[86] to train and test our VAE for anomaly detection. Figure 15 shows a scatter plot of the latent space generated by the encoder for the test dataset, after training for 50 epochs, with stochastic gradient descent optimization. The color of each point reflects its associated reconstruction error. In other words, it shows the marking of each data point that has crossed the error threshold as an anomaly in dark violet color, and the normal data point as yellow. We can clearly see one large cluster of points that seem quite on the normal side (yellow dots), with a dark-colored cluster with a relatively high error term on the sides. It should be noted that this VAE was just a toy example without any hyper-parameter tuning. The performance can be enhanced by optimizing the hyper-parameters and adjusting the layer structure of the VAE.

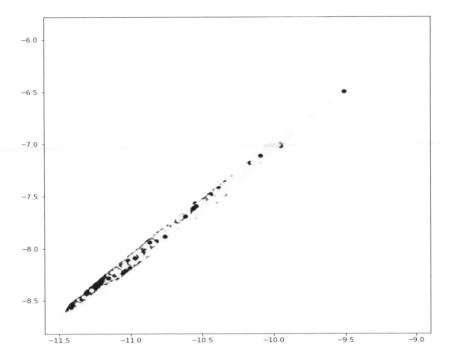

Figure 15: Anomaly detection using VAE.

VAE are widely used for a variety of machine learning tasks. This case study was an example to show VAE's application. The applicability of VAE can be enhanced by using XAI. While reconstructing a sample in anomaly detection methods such as class activation maps can be utilized to tap the neurons which fire for a given input and by applying max-polling over the activation maps we can generate a spatial saliency map which shows the regions of input signal that contribute more tho the output signal. For a reconstruction which is marked as an anomaly, the regions with high vales of gradient mapping will be the contributor. Hence, the region which cause the anomalous behaviour can be trace out. The example shown in Figure 16

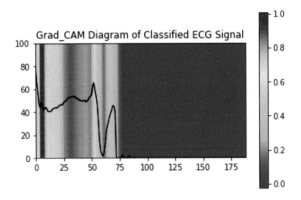

Figure 16: Explanation of the regions responsible for a particular class.

was introduced in[51] to trace back the regions which are responsible for predicting a particular class. The regions in red are responsible for classification of the ECG signal in to the output class (color weighted scale shows contribution of each region). Similar approaches can be adopted in anomaly detection to trace and explain the regions which cause the anomalous behaviour.

7   Conclusions

In this chapter, we discussed different DSS based on probabilistic graphical methods and machine learning. DSS were proven to be a useful tool. They help in the reduction of prescription errors, and help in prognosis, with a higher capacity than the previously used methods. DSS has been shown to help healthcare practitioners and providers and in a variety of decisions making and diagnosis tasks, and as of now, they actively and efficiently support in providing quality healthcare service. Moreover, they were proved to be useful in the standardization of protocols, adjustments with a target, and warning systems. We noticed that both DSS based on classical PGM and DSSs based on advanced machine learning methods are extensively used in healthcare. However, PGM has fallen out a little due to the ubiquity of probabilistic methods like neural networks. Nevertheless, we believe they still have the potential to be relevant in the future, because of their explanatory and intuitive nature. They can be used for modeling casual relationships and can be useful in learning the representation of abstract or high-level concepts. As we saw in the chapter that combining neural networks with graphical models could be very useful in the domain of machine learning, especially in healthcare DSS.

Meanwhile, we must take extra measures and precautions and careful analysis when creating, implementing, and maintaining DSS. In this regard complete solutions will be required in practice, especially as DSS continue to evolve in complexity through advances in AI, interoperability, explanations, and new sources of data.

References

[1] D. Aronsky and P.J. Haug. Diagnosing community-acquired pneumonia with a Bayesian network. In: *Proceedings of the AMIA Symposium, American Medical Informatics Association*, p. 632, 1998.

[2] G.A. Gorry and M.S. Scott Morton. A framework for management information systems, 1971.

[3] J. Horsky, J. Aarts, L. Verheul, D.L. Seger, H. van der Sijs and D.W. Bates. Clinical reasoning in the context of active decision support during medication prescribing. *International Journal of Medical Informatics*, 97: 1–11, 2017.

[4] M.W.L. Moreira, J.J.P.C. Rodrigues, V. Korotaev, J. Al-Muhtadi and N. Kumar. A comprehensive review on smart decision support systems for health care. *IEEE Systems Journal*, 13: 3536–3545, 2019.

[5] D. Feinleib. *Big Data Bootcamp: What Managers Need to know to Profit from the Big Data Revolution*. A Press, 2014.

[6] A. Sunyaev and D. Chornyi. Supporting chronic disease care quality: Design and implementation of a health service and its integration with electronic health records. *Journal of Data and Information Quality (JDIQ)*, 3: 1–21, 2012.

[7] Howard S. Goldberg, Marilyn D. Paterno, Robert W. Grundmeier, Beatriz H. Rochaab, Jeffrey M. Hoffman, Eric Tham, Marguerite Swietlik, Molly H. Schaeffer, Deepika Pabbathi, Sara J. Deakyne, Nathan Kuppermann and Peter S. Dayan. Use of a remote clinical decision support service for a multicenter trial to implement prediction rules for children with minor blunt head trauma. *International Journal of Medical Informatics*, 87: 101–110, 2016.

[8] D. Koller and N. Friedman. *Probabilistic Graphical Models: Principles and Techniques.* MIT Press, 2009.

[9] J. Wyatt and J. Liu. Basic concepts in medical informatics. *Journal of Epidemiology & Community Health*, 56: 808–812, 2002.

[10] S.B. Clauser, E.H. Wagner, E.J.A. Bowles, L. Tuzzio and S.M. Greene. Improving modern cancer care through information technology. *American Journal of Preventive Medicine*, 40: S198–S207, 2011.

[11] Jason Chiang, John Furler, Douglas Boyle, Malcolm Clark and Jo-Anne Manski-Nankervis. Electronic clinical decision support tool for the evaluation of cardiovascular risk in general practice: A pilot study. *Australian Family Physician*, 46: 764, 2017.

[12] P.A. Williams, R.D. Furberg, J.E. Bagwell and K.A. LaBresh. Usability testing and adaptation of the pediatric cardiovascular risk reduction clinical decision support tool. *JMIR Human Factors*, 3: e17, 2016.

[13] A.A. Montgomery, T. Fahey, T.J. Peters, C. MacIntosh and D.J. Sharp. Evaluation of computer based clinical decision support system and risk chart for management of hypertension in primary care: Randomised controlled trial. *Bmj*, 320: 686–690, 2000.

[14] R.T. Sutton, D. Pincock, D.C. Baumgart, D.C. Sadowski, R.N. Fedorak and K.I. Kroeker. An overview of clinical decision support systems: Benefits, risks, and strategies for success. *NPJ Digital Medicine*, 3: 1–10, 2020.

[15] E.S. Berner and T.J. La Lande. Overview of clinical decision support systems. In: *Clinical Decision Support Systems*, Springer, pp. 3–22, 2007.

[16] S. Belciug and F. Gorunescu. *Intelligent Decision Support Systems—A Journey to Smarter Healthcare*, Springer, 2020.

[17] C. Schaarup, L.B. Pape-Haugaard and O.K. Hejlesen. Models used in clinical decision support systems supporting healthcare professionals treating chronic wounds: Systematic literature review. *JMIR Diabetes*, 3: e8316, 2018.

[18] J. Pearl. Bayesian networks, 2011.

[19] D. Heckerman. A tutorial on learning with Bayesian networks. *Innovations in Bayesian Networks*, 33–82, 2008.

[20] B. Thanathornwong. Bayesian-based decision support system for assessing the needs for orthodontic treatment. *Healthcare Informatics Research*, 24: 22, 2018.

[21] G.R. Cross and A.K. Jain. Markov random field texture models. *IEEE Transactions on Pattern Analysis and Machine Intelligence*, 25–39, 1983.

[22] C. Wang, N. Komodakis and N. Paragios. Markov random field modeling, inference & learning in computer vision & image understanding: A survey. *Computer Vision and Image Understanding*, 117: 1610–1627, 2013.

[23] V. Rajinikanth, S. Kadry, K.P. Thanaraj, K. Kamalanand and S. Seo. Firefly-algorithm supported scheme to detect covid-19 lesion in lung ct scan images using shannon entropy and markov-random-field. *arXiv preprint arXiv:2004.09239*, 2020.

[24] Depeursinge Adrien, Vargas Alejandro, Gaillard Frédéric, Platon Alexandra, Geissbuhler Antoine, Poletti Pierre-Alexandre and Müller Henning. Case-based lung image categorization and retrieval for interstitial lung diseases: Clinical workflows. *International Journal of Computer Assisted Radiology and Surgery*, 7(1): 97–110, 2012.

[25] G.O. Barnett, J.J. Cimino, J.A. Hupp and E.P. Hoffer. DXplain: An evolving diagnostic decision-support system. *Jama*, 258: 67–74, 1987.

[26] SimulConsult Inc. A simultaneous consult on your patient's diagnosis, 2022.

[27] A. Alsiddiky, W. Awwad, K. Bakarman, H. Fouad and N.M. Mahmoud. Magnetic resonance imaging evaluation of vertebral tumor prediction using hierarchical hidden markov random field model on internet of medical things (iomt) platform. *Measurement*, 159: 107772, 2020.

[28] A.B. Ashraf, S.C. Gavenonis, D. Daye, C. Mies, M.A. Rosen and D. Kontos. A multichannel markov random field framework for tumor segmentation with an application to classification of gene expression-based breast cancer recurrence risk. *IEEE Transactions on Medical Imaging*, 32: 637–648, 2012.

[29] A. Bousse, S. Pedemonte, B.A. Thomas, K. Erlandsson, S. Ourselin, S. Arridge and B.F. Hutton. Markov random field and gaussian mixture for segmented mri-based partial volume correction in pet. *Physics in Medicine & Biology*, 57: 6681, 2012.

[30] L. Cordero-Grande, G. Vegas-Sánchez-Ferrero, P. Casaseca-de-la Higuera, J.A. San-Román-Calvar, A. Revilla-Orodea, M. Martín-Fernández and C. Alberola-López. Unsupervised 4d myocardium segmentation with a markov random field based deformable model. *Medical Image Analysis*, 15: 283–301, 2011.

[31] C. Zhao, J. Jiang, Y. Guan, X. Guo and B. He. Emr-based medical knowledge representation and inference via markov random fields and distributed representation learning. *Artificial Intelligence in Medicine*, 87: 49–59, 2018.

[32] F.J. Costello, C. Kim, C.M. Kang and K.C. Lee. Identifying high-risk factors of depression in middle-aged persons with a novel sons and spouses bayesian network model 8: 562, 2020.

[33] P. Gupta, B. Bhowmick and A. Pal. Mombat: Heart rate monitoring from face video using pulse modeling and bayesian tracking. *Computers in Biology and Medicine*, 121: 103813, 2020.

[34] Z. Zhou, H. Yu and H. Shi. Human activity recognition based on improved bayesian convolution network to analyze health care data using wearable IOT device. *IEEE Access*, 8: 86411–86418, 2020.

[35] O.I. Abiodun, A. Jantan, A.E. Omolara, K.V. Dada, N.A. Mohamed and H. Arshad. State-of-the-art in artificial neural network applications: A survey, *Heliyon*, 4: e00938, 2018.

[36] W. Liu, Z. Wang, X. Liu, N. Zeng, Y. Liu and F.E. Alsaadi. A survey of deep neural network architectures and their applications. *Neurocomputing*, 234: 11–26, 2017.

[37] A. Qayyum, J. Qadir, M. Bilal and A. Al-Fuqaha. Secure and robust machine learning for healthcare: A survey. *IEEE Reviews in Biomedical Engineering*, 14: 156–180, 2021.

[38] I. Goodfellow, Y. Bengio, A. Courville and Y. Bengio. *Deep Learning*, volume 1. MIT Press Cambridge, 2016.

[39] P. Kharat and S. Dudul. Clinical decision support system based on jordan/elman neural networks. In: *2011 IEEE Recent Advances in Intelligent Computational Systems.* IEEE, pp. 255–259, 2011.

[40] M. Gudadhe, K. Wankhade and S. Dongre. Decision support system for heart disease based on support vector machine and artificial neural network. In: *2010 International Conference on Computer and Communication Technology (ICCCT).* IEEE, pp. 741–745.

[41] R. Janghel, A. Shukla, R. Tiwari and P. Tiwari. Clinical decision support system for fetal delivery using artificial neural network. In: *2009 International Conference on New Trends in Information and Service Science.* IEEE, pp. 1070–1075, 2009.

[42] K. Rajalakshmi, S.C. Mohan and S.D. Babu. Decision support system in healthcare industry. *International Journal of Computer Applications*, 26: 42–44, 2011.

[43] M. Luque Gallego. Probabilistic graphical models for decision making in medicine, 2009.

[44] O. Karan, C. Bayraktar, H. Gümüşkaya and B. Karlık. Diagnosing diabetes using neural networks on small mobile devices. *Expert Systems with Applications*, 39: 54–60, 2012.

[45] H. Suresh, N. Hunt, A. Johnson, L.A. Celi, P. Szolovits and M. Ghassemi. Clinical intervention prediction and understanding with deep neural networks, 322–337, 2017.

[46] M. Dhuheir, A. Albaseer, E. Baccour, A. Erbad, M. Abdallah and M. Hamdi. Emotion recognition for healthcare surveillance systems using neural networks: A survey. In: *2021 International Wireless Communications and Mobile Computing (IWCMC).* IEEE, pp. 681–687, 2021.

[47] R.D. Labati, E. Muñoz, V. Piuri, R. Sassi and F. Scotti. Deep-ecg: Convolutional neural networks for ecg biometric recognition. *Pattern Recognition Letters*, 126: 78–85, 2019.

[48] K. Antczak. Deep recurrent neural networks for ecg signal denoising. *arXiv preprint arXiv:1807.11551*, 2018.

[49] A. Elola, E. Aramendi, U. Irusta, A. Picón, E. Alonso, P. Owens and A. Idris. Deep neural networks for ecg-based pulse detection during out-of-hospital cardiac arrest. *Entropy*, 21: 305, 2019.

[50] Y. Wu, F. Yang, Y. Liu, X. Zha and S. Yuan. A comparison of 1-d and 2-d deep convolutional neural networks in ecg classification. *arXiv preprint arXiv:1810.07088*, 2018.

[51] A. Raza, K.P. Tran, L. Koehl and S. Li. Designing ecg monitoring healthcare system with federated transfer learning and explainable AI. *arXiv preprint arXiv:2105.12497*, 2021.

[52] F.K. Došilović, M. Brčić and N. Hlupić. Explainable artificial intelligence: A survey. In: *2018 41st International Convention on Information and Communication Technology, Electronics and Microelectronics (MIPRO)*, IEEE, pp. 0210–0215, 2018.

[53] M.J. Johnson, D. Duvenaud, A.B. Wiltschko, S.R. Datta and R.P. Adams. Structured vaes: Composing probabilistic graphical models and variational autoencoders. *arXiv preprint arXiv:1603.06277 2 (2016)*, 2016.

[54] F. Le, M. Srivatsa, K.K. Reddy and K. Roy. Using graphical models as explanations in deep neural networks, 283–289, 2019.

[55] T. Fernando, H. Gammulle, S. Denman, S. Sridharan and C. Fookes. Deep learning for medical anomaly detection—A survey. *arXiv preprint arXiv:2012.02364*, 2020.

[56] Truong Thu Huong, Ta Phuong Bac, Dao Minh Long, Tran Duc Luong, Nguyen Minh Dan, Le Anh Quang, Le Thanh Cong, Bui Doan Thang and Kim Phuc Tran. Detecting cyberattacks using anomaly detection in industrial control systems: A federated learning approach. *Computers in Industry*, 132: 103509, 2021.

[57] R.B. Zebadúa. Human body pose tracking based on spatio-temporal joints dependency learning, 2018.

[58] X. Chu, W. Yang, W. Ouyang, C. Ma, A.L. Yuille and X. Wang. Multi-context attention for human pose estimation. In: *Proceedings of the IEEE Conference on Computer Vision and Pattern Recognition*, pp. 1831–1840, 2017.

[59] S. Zheng, S. Jayasumana, B. Romera-Paredes, V. Vineet, Z. Su, D. Du, C. Huang and P.H. Torr. Conditional random fields as recurrent neural networks. In: *Proceedings of the IEEE International Conference on Computer Vision*, pp. 1529–1537, 2017.

[60] A. Panesar. *Machine Learning and AI for Healthcare*. Springer, 2019.

[61] R. Shah and A. Chircu. Iot and AI in healthcare: A systematic literature review. *Issues in Information Systems*, 19, 2018.

[62] S.E. Dilsizian and E.L. Siegel. Artificial intelligence in medicine and cardiac imaging: Harnessing big data and advanced computing to provide personalized medical diagnosis and treatment. *Current Cardiology Reports*, 16: 441, 2014.

[63] V.L. Patel, E.H. Shortliffe, M. Stefanelli, P. Szolovits, M.R. Berthold, R. Bellazzi and A. Abu-Hanna. The coming of age of artificial intelligence in medicine. *Artificial Intelligence in Medicine*, 46: 5–17, 2009.

[64] S. Jha and E.J. Topol. Adapting to artificial intelligence: Radiologists and pathologists as information specialists. *Jama*, 316: 2353–2354, 2016.

[65] A. Qayyum, J. Qadir, M. Bilal and A. Al-Fuqaha. Secure and robust machine learning for healthcare: A survey. *arXiv preprint arXiv:2001.08103*, 2020.

[66] S. Durga, R. Nag and E. Daniel Survey on machine learning and deep learning algorithms used in internet of things (iot) healthcare. In: *2019 3rd International Conference on Computing Methodologies and Communication (ICCMC)*, pp. 1018–1022, 2019.

[67] K.R. Bisaso, G.T. Anguzu, S.A. Karungi, A. Kiragga and B. Castelnuovo. A survey of machine learning applications in hiv clinical research and care. *Computers in Biology and Medicine*, 91: 366–371, 2017.

[68] I. Azimi, J. Takalo-Mattila, A. Anzanpour, A.M. Rahmani, J.-P. Soininen and P. Liljeberg. Empowering healthcare iot systems with hierarchical edge-based deep learning. In: *Proceedings of the 2018 IEEE/ACM International Conference on Connected Health: Applications, Systems and Engineering Technologies*, pp. 63–68, 2018.

[69] Amirhessam Tahmassebi, Georg J. Wengert, Thomas H. Helbich, Zsuzsanna Bago-Horvath, Sousan Alaei, Rupert Bartsch, Peter Dubsky, Pascal Baltzer, Paola Clauser, Panagiotis Kapetas, Elizabeth A. Morris, Anke Meyer-Baese and Katja Pinker. Impact of machine learning with multiparametric magnetic resonance imaging of the breast for early prediction of response to neoadjuvant chemotherapy and survival outcomes in breast cancer patients. *Investigative Radiology*, 54: 110, 2019.

[70] S. Montani and M. Striani. Artificial intelligence in clinical decision support: A focused literature survey. *Yearbook of Medical Informatics*, 28: 120–127, 2019.

[71] M. Fernandes, S.M. Vieira, F. Leite, C. Palos, S. Finkelstein and J.M. Sousa. Clinical decision support systems for triage in the emergency department using intelligent systems: A review. *Artificial Intelligence in Medicine*, 102: 101762, 2020.

[72] E. Turban. Implementing decision support systems: A survey. In: *1996 IEEE International Conference on Systems, Man and Cybernetics*. Information Intelligence and Systems (Cat. No. 96CH35929), volume 4, IEEE, pp. 2540–2545, 1996.

[73] S.B. Eom, S.M. Lee, E. Kim and C. Somarajan. A survey of decision support system applications (1988–1994). *Journal of the Operational Research Society*, 49: 109–120, 1998.

[74] S. Eom and E. Kim. A survey of decision support system applications (1995–2001). *Journal of the Operational Research Society*, 57: 1264–1278, 2006.

[75] M. Omichi, Y. Maki, T. Ohta, Y. Sekita and S. Fujisaku. A decision support system for regional health care planning in a metropolitan area. *Japan-hospitals: The Journal of the Japan Hospital Association*, 3: 19–23, 1984.

[76] G. Acampora, D.J. Cook, P. Rashidi and A.V. Vasilakos. A survey on ambient intelligence in healthcare. *Proceedings of the IEEE*, 101: 2470–2494, 2013.

[77] R. Snyder-Halpern. Assessing health care setting readiness for point of care computerized clinical decision support system innovations. *Outcomes Management for Nursing Practice*, 3: 118–127, 1999.

[78] Mohammad Raza Perwez, Naveed Ahmad, Muhammad Sajid Javaid and Muhammad Ehsan ul Haq. A critical analysis on efficacy of clinical decision support systems in health care

domain. In: *Advanced Materials Research*, volume 383, Trans. Tech. Publ., pp. 4043–4050, 2012.

[79] M.C. Kaptein, P. Markopoulos, B. De Ruyter and E. Aarts. Persuasion in ambient intelligence. *Journal of Ambient Intelligence and Humanized Computing*, 1: 43–56, 2010.

[80] O. Anya, H. Tawfik, S. Amin, A. Nagar and K. Shaalan. Context-aware knowledge modelling for decision support in e-health. In: *The 2010 International Joint Conference on Neural Networks (IJCNN)*, pp. 1–7, 2010.

[81] J. Graham. Artificial intelligence, machine learning, and the fda, 2016.

[82] M. Aledhari, R. Razzak, R.M. Parizi and F. Saeed. Federated learning: A survey on enabling technologies, protocols, and applications. *IEEE Access*, 8: 140699–140725, 2020.

[83] J.H. Yoo, H. Jeong, J. Lee and T.-M. Chung. Federated learning: Issues in medical application, 2021.

[84] N. Papernot, P. McDaniel, A. Sinha and M. Wellman. Towards the science of security and privacy in machine learning. *arXiv preprint arXiv:1611.03814*, 2016.

[85] Y. Zhan, J. Zhang, Z. Hong, L. Wu, P. Li and S. Guo. A survey of incentive mechanism design for federated learning. *IEEE Transactions on Emerging Topics in Computing*, 2021.

[86] G.B. Moody and R.G. Mark. The impact of the mit-bih arrhythmia database. *IEEE Engineering in Medicine and Biology Magazine*, 20: 45–50, 2001.

Chapter 3

Decision Support Systems for Anomaly Detection with the Applications in Smart Manufacturing: A Survey and Perspective

Quoc-Thông Nguyen,[1,2,#] Tung Nhi Tran,[1,#] Cédric Heuchenne[3,*] and
Kim Phuc Tran[2]

1 Introduction

With the growth of the volume of data collected in manufacturing, Big Data offers a tremendous opportunity in the transformation of today's manufacturing paradigm to smart manufacturing (SM) and helps the scientists and engineers have Artificial Intelligence (AI)-driven Industrial Internet of Things (IIoT) solutions working in real-time and being more accurate and efficient[1]. The development of AI algorithms and Big Data analytic helps to transfer a human experience to technological developments, providing ways for IIoT solutions to maximize value creation across asset and operations life-cycles while improving profitability. Machine Learning (ML) and Deep Learning (DL) are AI subsets that are used to assess produced data and provide useful information about the manufacturing industry[2]. Therefore, ML and DL play important roles in the development of SM with various applications especially anomaly detection in[3], machine fault diagnosis[4], intrusion detection[5], production monitoring[6]. Furthermore, to react and adapt to the constantly changing industrial environment, manufacturers nowadays need a support system that allows them analyze information to come up with reasonable decisions. Decision support systems (DSS) in this scenario integrate human talents with computer capabilities to offer effective data administration, reporting, analytics, modeling, and planning. By integrating these advanced technologies in manufacturing, the factories enable it to optimize the performance, quality, control, and transparency of the manufacturing process. While there is a large amount of research related to these technologies in the context of SM, there are still challenges in applying them in a practical setting[7;8;9].

---

[1] International Research Institute for Artificial Intelligence and Data Science, Dong A University, Danang, Vietnam.

[2] Univ. Lille, ENSAIT, ULR 2461 - GEMTEX - Génie et Matériaux Textiles, F-59000 Lille, France.

[3] HEC Management School, University of Liège, Liège, Belgium.

* Corresponding author: C.Heuchenne@uliege.be

# These authors contributed equally

The first problem is that, to have a flexible and scalable IIoT platform, the central computing of all data collected in manufacturing is the way for growth and innovation. Thus, cloud computing is important to empower the workloads and applications, reduce costs, and increase release velocity, and agility. With the recent advancements in cloud computing, enterprises can have large storage and enough computing capacity to process collected data from IIoT devices. Traditionally, IIoT is only used for data collection and offloads computationally intensive tasks to cloud servers. Yet, offloading computationally intensive tasks to a cloud centre may result in a delay, due to the time needed to transmit, process, and receive a large amount of data. This is a serious drawback in a smart factory that must perform massive analysis in real-time. To overcome this limitation, the concept of edge computing can be used in a smart factory[10]. Edge computing is the technology that makes it possible to quickly perform the necessary computational task in the network edge, i.e., between data producers and the cloud centre. The workload that is concentrated in the central cloud can be reduced. Moreover, in some situations, traditional ML approaches require combining data at one location which not only prevents systems from dealing with vastly distributed data and training models on the edge nodes but also presses communication systems in factories. In that case, Federated Learning (FL) approach can represent a good solution. In[11], the authors mentioned that operating an FL system can decrease the amount of bandwidth used in transferring data between the edge and the cloud by 35%. Integrating FL with other learning frameworks is a potential method that can solve existing problems in SM. Therefore, this chapter is the first to show a survey on ML and DL techniques used for anomaly detection in some aspects of SM. Then, difficulties and challenges in applying them in a real context are discussed. Finally, our perspectives for solving these problems are recommended.

The chapter is organised as follows: In Section 2, we briefly describe the concept of DSS. The IIoT-based background and techniques for anomaly detection in SM are presented in Section 3. Some difficulties and challenges also mentioned in Section 4. In Section 5, we propose an alternative approach for the decentralised system. The case studies are given in Section 6. Section 7 provides some concluding remarks.

2 Decision Support Systems for Smart Manufacturing

In SM, the future factory will be more conscious and intelligent to independently perform complex tasks, i.e., "smart factory"[12]. It leads to increased demand in making precise decisions as soon as possible. In addition, with the wide use of electronic sensing devices, wireless sensor networks and other advanced technologies in the IIoT, there would be a tremendous amount of information that needs to be processed to come up with rational decisions. Thus, decision makers will encounter complex situations in the decision-making. This process becomes more challenging due to insufficient and complex data, it is difficult to do it in the traditional way. The formulation process is due to failed and weak decisions. Thanks to the development of technology such as cloud computing, the Internet of Things (IoT), and Big Data which are key elements in digital transformation, decision support and decision support system (DSS) turn into accessible and reliable. However, it seems difficult to have an exact definition of it. In[13] and[14], DSS is mentioned as human and management systems that depend on management science and adapt technologies tools through simulation and information technology. In some recent researches, a DSS includes all of the people who are in the organisation and the hardware, software, models and data[15]. According to[16], DSS is described as an interactive computer-based system or subsystem designed to help decision-makers use communication technology, data, documents, knowledge, and/or models to identify and solve problems, complete tasks in the decision-making process, and make decisions. DSS are divided into five categories depending on their major sources of information[17]:

1. **Communication-Driven DSS** is a type that uses communication technologies and networks to facilitate the communication and collaboration of decision-relevant. It emphasizes communication, collaboration, and shared decision-making support using technology. The most fundamental level of functionality is a simple bulletin or threaded e-mail. Communications-driven DSS allows two or more individuals to interact, share and coordinate their activities.

2. **Data-Driven DSS** emphasize access to and manipulation of a time series of internal company data and in some systems real-time and external data. Business intelligence systems for operational or strategic use are most often data-driven.

3. **Document-Driven DSS** integrate a variety of storage and processing technologies to provide complete document retrieval and analysis. A search engine is a powerful decision-aiding tool associated with a document-driven DSS.

4. **Model-Driven DSS** emphasize access to and manipulation of a quantitative model (e.g., an algebraic, financial, optimization, or simulation model). Model-driven DSS use data and parameters provided by decision makers to aid them in analyzing a situation, but they are not usually data-intensive.

5. **Knowledge-Driven DSS** suggest or recommend actions to managers. These DSS are person–computer systems with specialized problem-solving expertise. A knowledge-driven DSS uses AI and statistical technologies. Knowledge storage and processing technologies are the dominant component in the architecture of these systems.

As mentioned above, DSS plays an important role in SM. Promoting effective strategies to support decision-making can not only be through a comprehensive understanding of the dynamics involved, but also the possibility of enriching these processes with the valuable information collected at different levels. The last point represents a key aspect of effective decision-making, especially when we consider decentralization. In addition, it is necessary to analyze the amount of information collected to avoid the overloading of decision variables and the increasing complexity of the decision-making process. Another problem is how to integrate different tasks (that is, decisions at different levels) that need to be made so that the existing system works more efficiently. There are 2 common methods to overcome this challenge: centralized or decentralized.

1. In the centralized decision-making process, a single, decision center is acquainted with all the system information. The central node is responsible for system planning and has the ability to manage the operations performed by all nodes on the network. The central node makes decisions with the aim to optimize the objectives of the entire network[18].

2. In the decentralized decision-making models each individual independent network entity makes its own decisions in order to optimize its own objectives. In this process, there is more than one decision-maker so the collaboration of these nodes is an essential component. They need to be connected and to exchange their information as well as decisions. Moreover, depending on the degree of collaboration, the nodes' decisions are impacted by the other ones in the network[19].

In this chapter, we will focus on the Anomaly Detection approaches used as DSS in SM that we will discuss in the next section.

3 Anomaly Detection in Smart Manufacturing

With the emerged industry in the last decade under the name SM, the maintenance, protection, and cybersecurity systems have been evolved to face the novel challenges and conditions. In the chapter, we will focus on 4 most important axes of anomaly detection in SM: Smart Predictive Maintenance, Integrated Wearable Technology, Production Monitoring, and Real-time Cybersecurity.

3.1 Smart Predictive Maintenance

Equipment maintenance is a vital factor in SM and directly affects the service life of the equipment and its production efficiency. By using IIoT and wireless sensors devices to monitor equipment status, advanced and pervasive Predictive Maintenance (PdM) applications can be developed, thus reducing maintenance costs, and avoiding dangerous situations. PdM is generally indicated based on the assessment of the health status of key components, regardless of the maintenance status, and its fundamental purpose is to make predictability achievable. That is, the incipient problems that may evolve into catastrophic failures can be predicted accurately, and effective measures can be applied to avoid these failures on the basis of the prediction results. This approach can minimise maintenance costs and also extend the useful life of the equipment. With the rise of AI, data-driven methods for fault diagnosis and remaining useful life prediction have been popular issues in PdM system research. The process of data-driven PdM can be divided into four stages: (1) operational assessment; (2) data acquisition; (3) feature engineering, and (4) modelling.

Currently, with the massively available data used to solve numerous problems, ML has been widely used in computer science and other fields, e.g., the PdM of industrial equipment, such as Linear Regression (LR), Support Vector Machine (SVM), Decision Tree (DT), Random Forest (RF). Although high-performance algorithms are continually developed, generally, employing efficiently and straightforward methods were only first considered by[20;21]. An LR model can be provided to industry experts with interpretability and that its predictive performance outperformed in terms of predicting whether mechanical equipment or components run correctly[22]. The SVM model is used to tackle the tasks for binary classification. Specifically, the SVM model and its extension can be utilised to solve multi-class tasks since the diversity of fault types and the ability of mapping low dimension features to hyperplanes[23]. A Digital Twin model can decompose a complex decision-making process into a collection of more straightforward decisions by recursively partitioning the co-variate space into sub-spaces, thus providing a solution that is prone to interpretation. Furthermore, RF is an ensemble learning algorithm composed of multiple DT classifiers, and the category of its output is determined jointly by these individual trees[24]. The RF is provided with many significant advantages. For instance, it can handle high dimensional data without feature selection; trees are independent of each other during the training process, and the implementation is relatively simple; besides, the training speed is usually fast, and at the same time the generalisation ability is strong enough. Moreover, there have some DL models that are used in PdM, such as Artificial Neural Network (ANN), Deep Neural Network (DNN), and Auto-Encoder (AE). ANN is designed to address nonlinear problems. It is a massively parallel computing system consisting of an extremely large number of simple processors with many interconnections. It learns underlying rules from the given collection of representative examples[25]. It is especially suitable for systems with a large scale, a complex structure, and unclear information. DNNs can self-adaptively extract fault features to effectively represent crucial information and realise intelligent diagnosis; they can also improve identification accuracy and are extremely effective in reducing defects in manual design features. And an AE model belongs to the type of unsupervised learning methods that only require unlabelled measurement data. In terms of model performance, these algorithms are applicable to most industrial applications.

3.2   Integrated Wearable Technology

Besides, in SM, data can be not only used for predicting the states of machines but also utilized to help workers in factories. The development of IoT devices encourages wearable technology that provides employees with real-time access to useful information. Thus, IoT-enabled wearable boost safety in the smart factory is essential to prevent hazards, benefit for industrial work safety and augment their performance in challenging environments[26]. Health monitoring and management for manufacturing workers in adverse conditions is not only their safety but also cost efficiency[27]. The wearable technologies can be categorized based on their functional properties and capabilities[28]:

1. Smartwatch: displays information, payment, fitness/activity tracking, communication, navigation.

2. Smart eyewear: visualisation, language interpretation, communication, task coordination.

3. Fitness tracker: physiological wellness, navigation, fitness/activity tracking, heart rate monitor.

4. Smart clothing: heart rate, daily activities, temperature, body position tracking, heating or cooling the body, automatic payment.

5. Wearable camera: captures real-time first-person photos and videos, live streaming, fitness/activity tracking.

6. Wearable medical device: cardiovascular diseases, physiological disorders, chronic diseases, diabetes, surgery, neuroscience, dermatology, rehabilitation.

The sensor-based data-driven on the clothes has been used for monitoring in sport, healthcare, the fashion industry[29;30;31;32;33;34]. The proposed embedded wearable system shown at a mining site using sensor-equipped safety vest, Smart Eyewear, sensor-equipped helmet, the smartwatch has shown that by introducing wearable device technology to mining sites, the safety of mining operations can be enhanced[28]. The example of solutions using smartwatches to improve workplace safety is also described in[35]. Specifically, the beacons are attached to the personal equipment, these beacons are connected to a smartwatch via Bluetooth. The goal of the system is to ensure that the right personal protective equipment required for a specific task is worn. A wearable system for monitoring health care workers and patients to comply with the hygiene in facilities[36]. The application of sensors in the undergarment for monitoring physiological extreme in firefighting in referred to in Deutsch[37]. The information from the sensors is analyzed to monitor worker fatigue[38]. Particularly, the sensor-based changes relate to the change in gait parameters of participants, which subjects to fatigue ratings. With the advent of voice-first technology, wearable will start incorporating voice technology into their designs, eventually developing into hands-free devices. Wearable tech will remove the friction that exists with handheld devices and enable a more seamless workflow, translating to greater productivity among workers. Workers can also use wearable technology to improve existing processes and functions within industrial and commercial settings. On the production line, for example, staff members could use wearable devices to stay focused on the tasks, obtain additional information, or deliver remote orders. Wearable technology can speed up operations, in warehouse and order fulfilment settings as well. Wearable technology will make workplaces virtually accident-proof by reversing the faulty human judgment, especially in construction workplace. For example, when a worker is wearing a smart vest and a driver on a forklift is coming around the corner and does not realise another worker is standing there, the smart vest he is wearing will beep an alarm and inform him about your presence around the corner. Another example on designing alerting vests to protect construction workers on roadside construction sites is presented in[39]. In 2018, a published study proposes a prototype integrating textile electrodes, motion sensors, and real-time data processing through a mobile application for automatic risk assessment of physical workload[40]. The ML techniques are applied in Human Activity Recognition for physical workload tracking[29;41]. The sensors are placed on clothes to alert the nurses when they are in the wrong posture at work[42]. Another example, a sensor is worn by workers that can relay temperature automatically to the cloud when the worker touches an electronic component to make sure it has been welded at the correct temperature. This will allow the company's management to monitor product quality in real-time. In the manufacturing sector, it is mandatory to maintain proper security protocols and authenticate third parties or each worker before they access any property. Therefore, wearable technology can restrict, allow, and location-track any sort of worker movement. There are huge potentials for wearable technology to improve and upgrade the things we operate. The human effort, in combination with AI-powered wearable devices, can help boost productivity, safety, and efficiency in the manufacturing industry. In recent years, the development of Intelligent Connected E-Textiles to benefit IoT Wearables and Garments has drawn much attention[43].

In order to collect the worker's health status data, we can use the "intelligent garment" instead of wearable sensors. In the intelligent garment, body sensors are integrated with a textile garment, which shall take various factors into consideration, such as sensor type, strategic location for sensor placement, the layout of flexible electricity cable, weak signal acquisition equipment, low-power wireless communications, and user comfortableness. The pulse sensor, body temperature sensor, electrocardiography sensor, myocardial sensor, blood oxygen sensor, electroencephalographic sensor, and batteries are all connected with flexible wires. In order to facilitate the washing of intelligent garments, the non-waterproof components can be removed by taking off the buttons from the clothing. Users can remove these components before washing and then reinstall them to the garment by snap on the buttons back. When we have the whole system connected, not only the health condition of everyone is monitored in real-time, but also any potential issue can be alerted beforehand. For example, the system can detect an early seizure and send alerts to nearby machines in order to stop their work, and to medical staff in order to help as soon as possible the patient. Of course, the information is stored and used for the training model at the local server. This contributes to the privacy and security of cybersecurity, which will be discussed further in Section 4.

3.3 Production Monitoring

Another important task in a smart factory is production monitoring because it enables the enterprise to detect timely abnormalities in the production line and then reduce waste. In industry, there are two commonly used techniques for anomaly detection: statistical process monitoring techniques and ML. The traditional methods in statistical process monitoring such as Shewhart chart and EWMA (Exponentially Weighted Moving Average) chart[44] have been widely used. The approaches using statistical analysis usually assume a normal distribution for the data. Without the assumption of normality, ML algorithms, such as SVM, emerge to be suitable approaches[6;45;46;47]. Thus, ML algorithms are effective analytic tools that can be integrating to statistical process control. A survey on the application of ML in statistical process control charts is presented in[48]. The study of using classification algorithms (e.g., linear discriminant analysis, k-nearest neighbours, logistic regression) in[49;50] has shown to outperform Hotelling's T2 control charts in monitoring a multivariate process. The use of IIoT technologies for the large production lines operating continuously creates real-time data. A Scalable On-line Anomaly Detection System is implemented to detect process anomalies via real-time processing[51;52;53]. The anomalies of the real-time event streams and derived subsequence patterns were scored using the Smith-Waterman algorithm. This system can analyze large amounts of process execution data in autonomous and adaptive manufacturing processes. Later, in[54], a hybrid off-line/on-line monitoring scheme is developed to advance the capability of quality control system for high density dataset. The recent application of ML algorithms (RF, SVM, Naive Bayes) in predicting manufacturing performance shown some advantages over the classical quality management technique[55], especially when the dataset is becoming large. In[56], authors adopt Reinforcement Learning to Statistical Process Control (SPC) in monitoring the quality of products. An ensemble ML model also offers a promising result in Steel Quality Control[57]. This paper compares the performance of 11 models: linear models (linear, ridge, LASSO, elastic net), SVM, Kernel Ridge Regression, KNN, RF, gradient boosting techniques. Recently, Wei Chen[58] proposed a reference architecture and construction path for smart factories. Particularly, the IIoTs solution for manufacturing workshops, integrated key technologies such as WSN and RFI, is described. This architecture takes advantage of the wireless sensors to real-time monitor manufacturing production line data. Online anomaly detection integrated ML that benefits the emergence of IoT is developed for many particular cases in manufacturing[58;59;60;61]. In addition, data in the smart factory are nowadays collected with a high frequency, high dimension and large variety which cannot be treated straightforwardly. Therefore, advanced models for real-time Big Data monitoring are required. Recently, the approach for anomaly detection with the idea of IoT has been exploited by[62]. A method using AE in anomaly detection was studied in[63]. In that paper, this AE is applied to reconstruct the data, and they use reconstruction error to identify an anomaly if the test data is inconsistent with the trained model. Comparing to kernel PCA, the property and the effectiveness of AEs are clarified. Recently, the Topological Data Analysis (TDA) is recognized as an efficient method to extract insights from high-dimensional, incomplete and noisy data. By identifying the shape, the structure of shapes or low-dimensional features of data, TDA simplifies the difficulty of processing the complicated structure and huge data. The application of TDA in manufacturing was first introduced in Sakurada and Yairi[64]. In[65], TDA is used to describe the time-series DL for analyzing time series data and anomaly-detection. Besides that, the data is becoming more and more related to functional data. The studies on monitoring functional data have drawn a lot of attention[66;67;68]. Anomaly detection methods for functional data based on functional principal component analysis[69], wavelet functional principal component analysis[67] are developed.

3.4 Real-time Cybersecurity

However, the exponential rise of IIoT brings with it not only enormous benefits, but also major obstacles in terms of developing and deploying industrial systems that are connected to cyber-security issues. In reality, the control systems in many factories, especially smart factories, are no longer isolated systems, but rather are linked to the Internet. As a result, if hackers were to take control of the network and steal the secrets, the repercussions would be catastrophic. The IIoT-based manufacturing systems are now one of the top industries targeted by a variety of attacks. Many real reported attacks against SM systems have been provided in[70]. The issue of protecting IIoT systems from cyber-attacks is becoming increasingly vital and critical in their development. Moreover, since threats become gradually complicated, many present cybersecurity solutions have grown outdated.

There are several threats present within IIoT-based SM systems such as a denial of service (DoS), spoofing, traffic sniffing, data manipulation of sensitive information, code injections, and unauthorised access. There are many vulnerable points in the system and, depending on the attack's objectives, the threat actors can have different methods which stresses the importance of cybersecurity. An access attack is an act of gaining unauthorized access to a network, a system, application software, or other resources without permission. In the context of manufacturing, attackers could gain unauthorised access to sensitive systems (e.g., product data management systems) and data. A DoS attack is often implemented by a hacker as a means of denying a service that is normally available to a user or organization. In the context of manufacturing, attackers could disrupt Cloud computing services for data-intensive applications. Data manipulation is a fraudulent cyber activity wherein attackers alter, tweak, or modify the valuable digital documents and critical data instead of straight away stealing the data to damage the organization and make of the misery. In the context of manufacturing, attackers could change part dimensions in data files or manufacturing process parameters. Changing those data might cause physical damage to the machinery, low quality products, and harm or death to the operator. Among the security control methods in cybersecurity, Intrusion detection involves the monitoring of system activities, auditing of system vulnerabilities, statistical analysis of activity patterns, and abnormal activity analysis. AI will offer better solutions for IIoT cybersecurity that aim to identify threats even if it requires a short learning phase to establish which events are potential attacks. For instance, an attack detection method using ANN and SVM[71] is capable of detecting anomalies and known intrusions. A hybrid attack detection method by combining ANNs and DT algorithms[72] can detect DoS and Probing attacks more effectively than detecting unauthorised access from a remote machine and authorised access to local superuser attacks. ML and algorithms for regression, classification, and clustering are powerful tools to detect and identify different classes of network attacks.

4 Difficulties and Challenges of Anomaly Detection Applications in Smart Manufacturing

Anomaly analysis in highly heterogeneous and dynamic environments (such as smart factories) requires complex mechanisms. Research done so far shows that ML-based technologies work very well in these types of scenarios. However, putting it into practical environments without decreasing its efficiency is not simple.

Firstly, in the aspect of revealing the essential reasons, the existing algorithms not only lack interpretability but also lack the ability to explain specific phenomena. This problem of traditional AI models is also known as "black box" concept. Generally, designers cannot figure out the reason when an AI arrived at a specific decision. This drawback becomes more serious in many applications such as healthcare, finance where rational decisions are important to ensure the reliability of the system. In the manufacturing context, if supervisors can understand the reasons for AI predictions, it is easier to identify problems and take appropriate actions. Obviously, it is necessary to build frameworks to help manufacturers understand AI output and build trust and confidence when applying AI models into production activity.

Secondly, most of the current commercial initiatives related to wearable and smart clothing do not use a blockchain or any other Distributed Ledger Technology to receive, validate, store and share the collected data with the objective of avoiding untrusted sources. It means that they cannot be considered IoT-enabled. Roughly speaking, an intelligent garment can be simply understood as the normal garments equipped with connected sensors to capture the internal or/and surrounding information without interfering with the users' activities. As we have mentioned in some examples above, the integrated devices not only capture information but also be able to interact with the surrounding environment to improve safety and productivity. Moreover, privacy and trustworthy data must be guaranteed. The existing products are developed based on each application and are not yet practical in mass production due to their complexity and economic profit. Therefore, it is desirable to develop the intelligent garments to improve safety at the workplace and to monitor the health status of workers, especially those with health problems. The edge computing framework for the intelligent garment can also be constructed.

Thirdly, the application of advanced ML on functional data still needs to be discovered. Although the current studies have eliminated a lot of assumptions about the distribution of data when designing control charts with ML techniques, there are still independent data assumptions that do not exist in the data environment collected from IIoT sensors. In general, there is still very little research on this promising approach and further researches need to be carried out to discover its numerous applications to the smart factory.

Fourthly, in cybersecurity, several traditional existing cybersecurity solutions have become obsolete. There are two issues that should be addressed:

- The joint problem of multi-source data mining and data security in the IIoT. On one hand, gathering multi-source IIoT data together is helpful for mining more effective knowledge, especially in the same industrial alliance. On the other hand, data security should be protected in order to prevent the disclosure of information.

- A comprehensive framework using ontology and knowledge reasoning to address the afore-mentioned issue.

Lastly, the growing variety and number of IIoT data collection devices have driven the trend towards Big Data. The expansion of data is already exponential, which is mainly accelerated by expanding data gathering and other cloud services[73]. When the large scale SM is applied in practice, it might very soon lead to a situation in which we can hardly handle the huge volume of collected data[74]. These datasets are too large specifically to be stored on a single machine and so must be distributed. Thus, centralized system gradually shows its disadvantages in storing and processing a huge amount of data. A decentralized system, where much smaller data is analyzed on the edge nodes, provide promising opportunities to overcome these limitations. Along with building this type of system, the development and adoption of advanced AI algorithms and IIoT architecture have to be taken seriously to reach a wide scale SM.

5 Perspectives for Anomaly Detection in Smart Manufacturing

As mentioned in the previous section, there are a lot of difficulties when applying the anomaly detection approach in SM. Most of them are how to collect, process and store a huge amount of complex data efficiently. Therefore, this section discusses some research perspectives to the above real needs by addressing these concrete challenges:

1. Online monitoring of daily processes in a factory, using cutting-edge ICT sensing solutions meeting exclusively the following constraints: wireless connected, cost-affordable and privacy respectful,

2. IIoT platform implementation for data security, processing and storage while being interpretable,

3. Targeting interpretable AI techniques where data have to meet high level of privacy, security and confidentiality constraints, and

4. Decentralised structure communication system where the processing intelligence is performed near to the data sources.

Although traditional ML and DL techniques have been researched and developed, there are some limits to apply in the large scale. Fortunately, recent advancements in ML show great promises for dealing with these challenges. The state-of-art techniques such as FL, Edge Computing, Probabilistic Graphical Models (PGMs), hybrid models are able to construct an effective, adaptable, and reliable system based Anomaly Detection in SM.

As well known, processing and storing complex data require a huge amount of variables. Generally, it is impossible to manipulate so many parameters from all angles. In terms of computation, it is expensive to store and process such many parameters. In practice, to learn such a density from the data, it would require access to many samples to have a proper assessment of the joint distribution that underlies it[75]. PGMs, in particular its branches such as Bayesian Network, Markov Network, has numerous ML applications due to their flexibility and interpretation. Bayesian Network can be used for anomaly detection and data correction in mixed tabular data[76], while the gradient descent version of Hidden Markov Network is able to monitor computer user actions and detect abnormal behaviors[77]. Another type of PGMs, Variational Autoencoder (VAE), is also developed in recent years. A deep support vector data description based on VAE (Deep SVDD-VAE) is introduced in[78] for anomaly detection in the image dataset. Even when not combining with the other algorithms, VAE is also a potent method in anomaly detection, which is presented in Section 6.

In terms of the big data analytic solutions, the collected data will be pre-processed, then fed to the AI algorithm. DL, as an emerging branch of ML, will be applied and compared with conventional ML techniques. For the cooperation of distributed smart factories and scalability of the whole system, new FL approaches with DL for event detection and maintenance prediction with privacy security in the smart factory will be developed. Particularly, FL approaches allow improving and sharing models without sharing the original private dataset. The encrypted model is sent to the individual local servers, which decrypt within a secure enclave in hardware and then train the local data by the DL algorithm. Only the model updates are shared with the central model aggregator (aggregation server). This provides protection to both the model and the data. The raw data never leaves the factories, which not only prevents large data transfers on the network but also removes privacy concern in edge computing. There are many solutions that can integrate real-time approaches for many important problems in SM, such as PdM, production monitoring, cybersecurity, and the applications of wearable technology by adapting the edge computing concept and developing the novel FL algorithms. One way to address these problems is by employing FL. FL is one of the modern ML approaches that empower edge computing by applying the technique of model iteration instead of fetching data from the device

FL enables devices/servers to collaboratively learn a shared prediction or detection model while keeping all the training data on devices/servers. The proposed approach is composed of three key components:

1. FL models that are trained using data stored at multiple different production sites of a factory or multiple different smart factories without sharing data on servers,

2. one or more computing devices that serve as the "edge" servers locally, and

3. the IIoT integrated sensors in the production sites/factories that can communicate with these edge device(s).

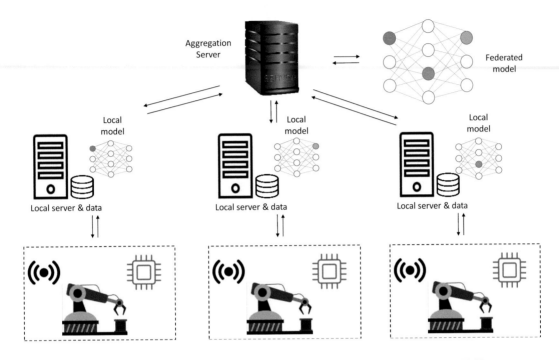

Figure 1: Federated learning architecture in smart factories enabled by IIoT.

It does this by first training separate models at each "edge" servers locally with the local data available and then sending those models to the cloud service to be combined into a master model. When the "edge" servers acquire more data, they can download the latest master model from the server, update it with the new data, and send it back to the server. Throughout the process, raw data are never exchanged—only the models, which cannot be reverse-engineered to reveal that data. The edge servers will be equipped with some ML models to allow local factory responses to the requisite and intervene in real-time, but will also be able to infer when requests, as well as processed (e.g., anonymised) data should be sent to the remote cloud server for getting additional support from the more advanced DL models there. By doing so, we will have an Edge-Machine-Learning-based (EML-based) smart system (for PdM or production monitoring for example) to provide a personalised resource service (provided by the local edge servers) for factories (or different production sites of the same factory), to save the storage space at the remote cloud server, and to improve privacy and security protection of factories' data. Considering the constrained resources of edge devices, we will propose an efficient way of training the local ML models and the request inference module for handling high-density IIoT data streams.

Although data-driven methods have achieved excellent performance in PdM applications, there is still a large potential for improvement and optimization, especially for practical applications. A comprehensive framework of the PdM should be developed, i.e., the framework will include the following layers: a physical layer, perception layer, signal analysis layer, performance prediction layer, and decision-making layer. Then, we will develop new FL (a hybrid CNN-LSTM model) based PdM system for Remaining Useful Life[79] prediction that can learn predictive models through peer-to-peer collaboration without raw data exchanges to accurately predict local equipment status. The structure of this approach consists of the following steps: (1) delivering the master predictive model to the edge device(s), (2) consuming input, making a prediction and storing the differences as the training data, (3) using this training data to improve the local predictive models at different edge devices, (4) sending these re-trained local models from multiple edge devices to a central server, (5) re-distributing and aggregating weights from all the different local models to create one master model, (6) repeating steps 1–5. Step 6 is needed to enable the process of continuous learning. These approaches will bring benefits about data security and privacy for the system since the training happens on the local device and only trained models are shared, real-time prediction since the prediction happens on the local device, offline (i.e., without an Internet connection) prediction made possible since the models are present on the local device.

In production monitoring, to reduce human intervention and maintain a high level of accuracy in the process, the advanced techniques need to eliminate most of the assumptions of traditional SPC and focus on complex data types (multivariate time series data, image data, and Big Data with complex structures). The FL approaches will be based on advanced DL algorithms such as long short-term memory (LSTM)[80], convolution neural network[81], Hierarchical Temporal Memory (HTM)[4] combined with anomaly detection methods[82;5], kernel density estimation (KDE)[83], e.g., AEs, for real-time multivariate time series data and image data monitoring.

In cybersecurity, FL approach also shows its potential in dealing with complicated problems. Besides, ML and DL algorithms for regression, classification, and clustering are powerful tools to detect and identify different classes of network attacks. We can develop new FL algorithms without the necessity to centralise the training data based on nested one-class SVMs or SVDD[84], LSTM networks[85], hybrid VAE - LSTM model[11] and HTM to solve cybersecurity problem in SM. Collecting multi-source IIoT data from similar SM can offer a promising opportunity to mine valuable knowledge, especially the SM belonging to the same vertical industrial alliance. In the recent review of Digital Twin technologies in manufacturing systems and processes[86], a Digital Twin-driven approach potentially plays a significant role in SM in the context of SM. In general concept, a Digital Twin is seen as the simulation of the physical system. More than a simulation, a twin system can behave according to near real-time data coming from the actual physical counterpart. Under the current circumstances, the ability of Digital Twin is only promoted to optimise the industrial process when important issues in manufacturing are solved by applying ML and IIoT technology. Moreover, digital twins are based in the cloud and the massive amounts of data being collected and utilised are drawn from numerous endpoints that leads to the face of new security threats. Although this technology has it owns challenges, the benefits are much bigger. Digital Twin is still far from reaching its full potential therefore obtaining the entire view of Digital Twin, including its characteristics, benefits, implementation and its challenges, is essential in order to unlock the true power of this technology[87]. In the context of SM, Digital Twins can be applied in diagnostics, monitoring the system/production line. With the rapid communication between devices, real-time system maintenance with high efficiency can be developed.

6 Case Studies

We present two applications of AI-based DSS in SM, in which the Anomaly Detection approach is considered to solve the specific problems in Production Monitoring and PdM. The source code is available here: https://github.com/tungnhitran/Anomaly-Detection-in-Smart-Manufacturing.

6.1 Anomaly Detection in Production Monitoring

For the first case, we illustrate a scenario for real-time production monitoring to detect anomaly in production line using the combination of Convolutional Neural Network (CNN) and Isolation Forest (IF) methods. A similar hybrid approach based on LSTM-AE and IF is introduced in[88]. In our example, the pre-trained CNN can be used as the feature extractor. In particular, we use the pre-trained AlexNet CNN algorithm to extract the feature vectors at the 'fc7' layer.

As described in[89], the pre-trained CNN AlexNet is trained on 1.2 million images and can classify images into 1000 object categories. It consists of 8 weight layers including 5 convolutional layers and 3 fully-connected layers, and three max-pooling layers are used following the first, second and fifth convolutional layers. The first convolutional layer has 96 filters of size 11×11 with a stride of 4 pixels and padding with 2 pixels. The stride and padding of other convolutional layers are set as 1 pixel. The second convolutional layer has 256 filters of size 5×5. The third, fourth and fifth convolutional layers have 384, 384 and 256 filters with size of 3×3 respectively.

In the CNN, after extracting features from input data, the classifier like SoftMax regression, see[90], is applied to classify the input. However, in this method, it is necessary to label all possible classes for the object of interest. This requirement might be difficult to meet in many practical manufacturing processes, since in these processes the practitioners cannot predetermine what kind of failures could be possible. Instead, the manufacturing data are mainly collected under normal operation condition. Therefore, we suggest to use one-class algorithm to classify the abnormal product from the normal one based on the features extracted from the CNN, particularly, the IF is applied in this example.

By using IF, the real-time monitoring problem is transferred to a one-class classification problem. In particular, the method is implemented as follows. Suppose that we have a dataset of images of normal samples to train the model. At the first step, we use the CNN to extract features of these training images, particularly, the feature vectors at the 'fc7' layer are extracted by the pre-trained AlexNet CNN. In the second step, the extracted features are then used to train the IF model to detect anomalies. In one-class classification approach, normal data are used to build isolation trees (iTrees). The iTree, which is defined as a decision tree, is built by recursively splitting the sub-sample points/instances over a split value of a randomly selected attribute, with the instances whose corresponding attribute value is smaller than the split value going left and the others going right. Then, each sample in testing data is transferred through these iTrees to test whether it is normal or defective. According to[91], the IF method is based on the idea that anomalies are made up of a small number of distinct observations, therefore if the iTrees are fitted on all training observations, anomalies should be found closer to the root of the tree than the normal ones.

Considering an example for the detection of defected nuts with their captured images*. In this example, a dataset containing 100 images of normal nuts is considered as the one-class training set. Since the data are not enough to train the model, we use a transfer learning method, which is the method of storing knowledge gained while solving one problem and applying it to a different but related problem. As mentioned, the pre-trained AlexNet CNN is used to extract the feature vectors at the 'fc7' layer.

The feature vectors extracted using the Alexnet method will be trained with IF. In[92], the kernel method with a one-class SVM and a pre-trained AlexNet CNN was developed for Image anomaly detection for production line. In the real-time monitoring, one of advantage of the IF is achieving low linear time-complexity and reducing memory requirement. Moreover, after the process was running for a long time, we can collect the dataset of the images of defected nuts. The updated dataset can be used to retrain the feature vectors for the interested system, the new feature vectors are then updated to the dataset to estimate the parameters for the IF classification. Figure 2 presents the scheme of the detection system.

In this specific example, 100 images of normal nuts are trained with IF for anomaly detection model. The testing data consists of 96 images of normal nuts and 48 images of defective ones which are generated from 4 images by rotating and adding Gaussian noise. The performance of our model is presented in Table 1. The metrics used in evaluating the performance are:

- Accuracy $= \frac{TP+TN}{TP+FP+TN+FN}$
- Recall $= \frac{TP}{TP+FN}$
- Precision $= \frac{TP}{TP+FP}$
- F-score $= 2 \times \frac{Precision \times Recall}{Precision+Recall}$

where TP (True Positive) is the number of anomalies correctly diagnosed, TN (True Negative) stands for the number of normal events correctly diagnosed as normal, FP (False Positive) is the number of normal events incorrectly diagnosed as anomalies, and FN (False Negative) stands for the number of anomalies undetected. By their definition, Precision is used to evaluate how accurate the result is, and Recall is used to evaluate how complete the result is. Also, F-score is used to seek a balance between Precision and Recall.

As can be seen from the table, most of anomalies are detected when the Precision is 92%. This result can be improved with a larger dataset and real-time data-driven parameter tuning. Practically, this example shows a possible method to integrate machine learning with the machine vision system to implement the real-time intelligent monitoring of production line, as discussed in detail by[93].

Table 1: Performance metrics of CNN-IF one-class classification.

Method	Recall	Precision	Accuracy	F-score
CNN + IF	0.9583	0.92	0.9583	0.9388

*https://github.com/mathworks/Deep-Learning-Image-anomaly-detection-for-production-line/releases/tag/1.0.1.

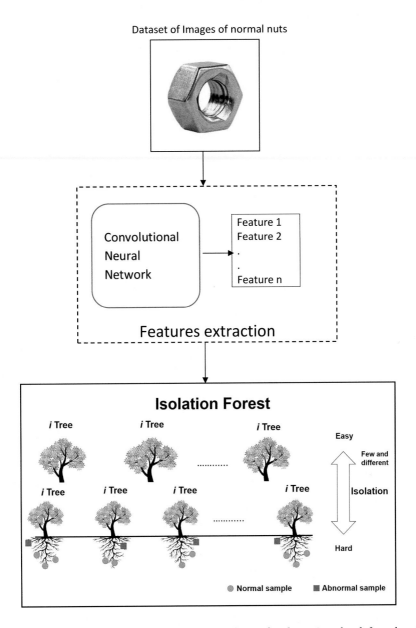

Figure 2: Procedure of real-time monitoring scheme for detecting the defected nut.

6.2 Anomaly Detection in Predictive Maintenance

In the second case, we present a situation for anomaly detection using VAEs method in PdM. This example shows a demonstration of collecting the physical health aspects of a specific machine and analyzing these information by ML algorithms for early fault detection, health assessment and prediction of this machine. It results in an optimal schedule to avoid the damage of unseasonable maintenance.

In the recent years, with others deep generative models such as Generative Adversarial Networks (GANs), VAEs has attracted increasing attention due to its potential in solving complex problems. First introduced in[94] as a stochastic variational inference and learning algorithm, VAEs are appealing because they are built on top of standard function approximators (neural networks)[95]. A VAE is a graphical model that combines variational inference and DL[96]. From generative modeling to semi-supervised learning and representation learning, the VAE framework has a wide range of applications[97]. There are a lot of researches showed that VAE is an effective method for dealing with complicated data, including handwritten digits, CIFAR images, faces[94], house numbers[98], segmentation[99]. Basically, VAE has an AE's architecture which composed of encoder, decoder and latent space. The difference is that VAE provides a probabilistic manner for describing an observation in latent space. Thus, instead of building an encoder that maps input into a single value in latent space, VAE's encoder aims to describe a probability distribution for each latent attribute. The mathematical basis of VAE is briefly presented through steps of training model:

1. To begin, let us define a probabilistic graphical model to describe our data. We denote our data by $\mathbf{x}$ which is mapped into a normal distribution $\mathbf{N}(\mu, \sigma)$ by the encoder $q_\phi(z|x)$.

2. A latent representation $\mathbf{z}$ is sampled from the prior distribution.

3. The decoder $p_\theta(x|z)$ maps a latent space sample to reconstruct the input data.

4. The loss function of VAE is composed of the reconstruction loss and Kullback-Leibler (KL) divergence.
$$L(\theta, \phi) = \mathbb{E}_{q_\phi(z|x)}[\log(p_\theta(x|z))] - KL(q_\phi(z|x)||q_\phi(z))$$

Particularly, for anomaly detection task, an anomaly score can be calculated using the VAE reconstruction error[100;101;64;102]. In An and Cho[96], authors utilized a reconstruction likelihood rather than a reconstruction error because they considered that it was a more objective anomaly metric. However, their technique required several VAE runs, which is computationally costly, that's why we utilize the usual reconstruction error approach.

In this example, we use bearing data provided by Case Western Reserve University (CWRU) Bearing Data Center[†]. The CWRU bearing dataset has been broadly utilized for examining fault diagnosis techniques[103;104], data-driven methods deploying ML[105;106] and DL algorithms[107;108;109]. The data is collected from a bearing testing platform consisting of a 2 hp[‡] motor, a torque transducer/encoder, a dynamometer and control electronic. The test bearing support motor shaft. Vibration signal was collected using accelerometers attached to the drive end (close to the bearing) and the fan end (remote from the bearing). Data was collected from 0 to 3 hp motor load for normal condition and 5 types of bearing fault, including ball fault, inner race fault, and outer fault (at 3 different locations). In spite of large information presented in this dataset, in this example, we use the 12 kHz sampled vibration signals when the motor load is 0 hp. The data is divided into two parts: the normal condition data consisting of 80496 samples, used for training, and the remaining 366117 samples are testing data. Testing data

---

[†]http://csegroups.case.edu/bearingdatacenter/home.
[‡]hp: horse power.

includes 122571 samples of ball fault, 122281 samples of outer fault at orthogonal position and 121265 samples of inner fault.

The anomaly detection result is illustrated in Figure 3, in which, the observations and the anomaly score are presented on x-axis and y-axis respectively. The red line represents for the anomaly threshold, which involves the calculation of maximum value from reconstruction error of training data. As illustrated, the threshold separated normal data and anomalies into two different groups.

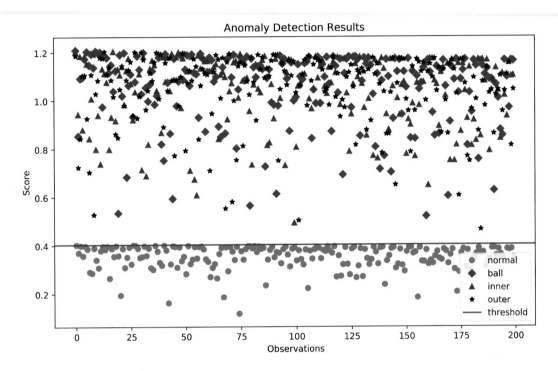

Figure 3: VAE for detecting anomalies of bearing faults.

The performance of our model is presented in Table 2. As observed, the VAE model brings result with an Accuracy of 97.23%, most of anomalies are detected. Although a few false positives can be observed, the verification of these few samples can be done manually to reduce waste.

Table 2: Performance metrics of VAE model.

Method	Recall	Precision	Accuracy	F-score
VAE	0.9782	0.9813	0.9723	0.9797

7 Concluding Remarks

In this chapter, we have presented a survey on enabling IIoT, AI, and DSS in Anomaly Detection in SM. We have discussed some perspectives for the potential frameworks of these components in large scale SM. The deployment of IIoT makes the collecting and processing of data at all stages in smart factories more convenient and precise. AI algorithms provide powerful tools to extract useful information from data and solve various problems in PdM, Wearable Technology, Production Monitoring, and Cybersecurity, the important factors of SM in anomaly detection. Then, the results can be combined with human knowledge by DSS to manage, organize, analyze massive amount of data and help manufacturers make reasonable decisions. However, when expanding the scale of SM, traditional model has its own disadvantages, therefore, FL and Edge computing can be promising methods to construct distributed systems where data is collected, processed and stored at the edge nodes, so that the stress of communication systems and central server is reduced. Finally, we presented two case studies in anomaly detection in production monitoring and PdM. Particularly, in the first case, we demonstrated an example of real-time detecting defected nuts in production line by combining CNN and IF techniques. In the second case, we showed how to deploy a VAE model to detect bearing faults based on vibration signals. Although there are a huge amount of studies contributing to the development of SM, further researches are needed to enable intelligent factories and realize Industry 4.0 vision.

References

[1] H. Nguyen, K. Tran, S. Thomassey and M. Hamad. Forecasting and anomaly detection approaches using lstm and lstm autoencoder techniques with the applications in supply chain management. *International Journal of Information Management*, 57: 102282, 2021.

[2] K.P. Tran. Artificial intelligence for smart manufacturing: Methods and applications, 2021.

[3] T. Kotsiopoulos, P. Sarigiannidis, D. Ioannidis and D. Tzovaras. Machine learning and deep learning in smart manufacturing: The smart grid paradigm. *Computer Science Review*, 40: 100341, 2021.

[4] L. Jing, M. Zhao, P. Li and X. Xu. A convolutional neural network based feature learning and fault diagnosis method for the condition monitoring of gearbox. *Measurement*, 111: 1–10, 2017.

[5] Q.T. Nguyen, K.P. Tran, P. Castagliola, T.T.H.M.K. Nguyen and S. Lardjane. Nested one-class support vector machines for network intrusion detection. In: *2018 IEEE Seventh International Conference on Communications and Electronics (ICCE)*, pp. 7–12, 2018.

[6] Q. Nguyen, H. Nguyen, K.P. Tran, P. Castagliola and E. Frénod. Real-time production monitoring approach for smart manufacturing with artificial intelligence techniques, 2019.

[7] K.T.S.T.X.Z.C.Y.Z. He and J. Xu. Modeling of textile manufacturing processes using intelligent techniques: A review. *The International Journal of Advanced Manufacturing Technology*, 1–29, 2021.

[8] J.X.S.T.X.Z.C.Y.Z. He and K.P. Tran. A deep reinforcement learning based multicriteria decision support system for optimizing textile chemical process. *Computers in Industry*, 125: 103373, 2021.

[9] J.X.S.T.X.Z.C.Y.Z. He and K.P. Tran. Multi-objective optimization of the textile manufacturing process using deep-q-network based multi-agent reinforcement learning. *Journal of Manufacturing Systems*, 2021.

[10] W. Yu, F. Liang, X. He, W.G. Hatcher, C. Lu, J. Lin and X. Yang. A survey on the edge computing for the internet of things. *IEEE Access*, 6: 6900–6919, 2018.

[11] T.H. Truong, T.P. Bac, D.M. Long, T.D. Luong, N.M. Dan, B.D. Thang and K.P. Tran. Detecting cyberattacks using anomaly detection in industrial control systems: A federated learning approach. *Computers in Industry*, 132: 103509, 2021.

[12] H.D. Nguyen, K.P. Tran, X. Zeng, L. Koehl and P. Castagliola. Industrial internet of things, big data, and artificial intelligence in the smart factory: A survey and perspective, 2019.

[13] D.T. Zhu and H. Zhang. Study on expressway meta-synthesis management decision support system. In: *2009 Chinese Control and Decision Conference, IEEE*, pp. 4951–4956, 2009.

[14] G.M. Marakas. *Decision Support Systems in the 21st Century*. Prentice Hall; US Ed edition, 2003.

[15] J. Angalakuditi and R. Kurnool. Decision support system (dss) for capacity planning: A case study. *International Journal of Advance Research in Computer Science and Management Studies*, 1: 24–30, 2013.

[16] D.J. Power. *Decision Support Systems: Concepts and Resources for Managers*. Greenwood Publishing Group, 2002.

[17] D. Power and C. Heavin. *Decision Support, Analytics, and Business Intelligence, Information Systems Collection*. Business Expert Press, 2017.

[18] I.-H. Hong, J.C. Ammons and M.J. Realff. Centralized versus decentralized decision-making for recycled material flows. *Environmental Science & Technology*, 42: 1172–1177, 2008.

[19] C. Schneeweiss. Distributed decision making in supply chain management. *International Journal of Production Economics*, 84: 71–83, 2003.

[20] D.N. Vu, N.N. Dao, Y. Jang, W. Na, Y.B. Kwon, H. Kang, J.J. Jung and S. Cho. Joint energy and latency optimization for upstream iot offloading services in fog radio access networks. *Transactions on Emerging Telecommunications Technologies*, 30: e3497, 2019.

[21] J.J. Jung, D. Camacho and C. Badica. Intelligent distributed processing methods for big data. *Journal of Universal Computer Science*, 2015.

[22] J. Phillips, E. Cripps, J.W. Lau and M.R. Hodkiewicz. Classifying machinery condition using oil samples and binary logistic regression. *Mechanical Systems and Signal Processing*, 60-61: 316–325, 2015.

[23] S. Zgarni and A. Braham. Classification of bearing fault detection using multiclass svm: A comparative study. In: *2018 15th International Multi-Conference on Systems, Signals Devices (SSD)*, pp. 888–892, 2018.

[24] S. Safavian and D. Landgrebe. A survey of decision tree classifier methodology. *IEEE Transactions on Systems, Man, and Cybernetics*, 21: 660–674, 1991.

[25] A. Jain, J. Mao and K. Mohiuddin. Artificial neural networks: A tutorial. *Computer*, 29: 31–44, 1996.

[26] E. Svertoka, S. Saafi, A. Rusu-Casandra, R. Burget, I. Marghescu, J. Hosek and A. Ometov. Wearables for industrial work safety: A survey. *Sensors*, 21, 2021.

[27] T.H. Truong, P.B. Ta, Q.T. Nguyen, H. Du Nguyen and K.P. Tran. A data-driven approach for network intrusion detection and monitoring based on kernel null space. In: *International Conference on Industrial Networks and Intelligent Systems*, Springer, pp. 130–140, 2019.

[28] X. Xu, M. Zhong, J. Wan, M. Yi and T. Gao. Health monitoring and management for manufacturing workers in adverse working conditions. *Journal of Medical Systems*, 40: 222, 2016.

[29] M. Mardonova and Y. Choi. Review of wearable device technology and its applications to the mining industry. *Energies*, 11: 547, 2018.

[30] H.D. Nguyen, K.P. Tran, X. Zeng, L. Koehl and G. Tartare. An improved ensemble machine learning algorithm for wearable sensor data based human activity recognition. *Reliability and Statistical Computing: Modeling, Methods and Applications*, 207–228, 2020.

[31] K. Liu, X. Zeng, P. Bruniaux, X. Tao, X. Yao, V. Li and J. Wang. 3d interactive garment pattern-making technology. *Computer-Aided Design*, 104: 113–124, 2018.

[32] K. Liu, X. Zeng, J. Wang, X. Tao, J. Xu, X. Jiang, J. Ren, E. Kamalha, T.K. Agrawal and P. Bruniaux. Parametric design of garment flat based on body dimension. *International Journal of Industrial Ergonomics*, 65: 46–59, 2018.

[33] Y. Hong, X. Cao, Y. Chen, Z. Pan, Y. Chen and X. Zeng. A conceptual wearable monitoring system for physiological indices and clothing microclimate measurement. *International Journal of Clothing Science and Technology*, 31: 318–325, 2019.

[34] X. Zhao, X. Zeng, L. Koehl, G. Tartare and J. De Jonckheere. A wearable system for in-home and long-term assessment of fetal movement. *IRBM*, 2019.

[35] E. Bertaux, S. Derler, R.M. Rossi, X. Zeng, L. Koehl and V. Ventenat. Textile, physiological, and sensorial parameters in sock comfort. *Textile Research Journal*, 80: 1803–1810, 2010.

[36] M. Kritzler, M. Bäckman, A. Tenfält and F. Michahelles. Wearable technology as a solution for workplace safety. In: *Proceedings of the 14th International Conference on Mobile and Ubiquitous Multimedia, MUM '15, Association for Computing Machinery, New York, NY, USA*, pp. 213–217, 2015.

[37] R. Deutsch. Systems and methods for monitoring health care workers and patients. US Patent 7,893,842, 2011.

[38] F. Salim, D. Prohasky, A. Belbasis, S. Houshyar and F.K. Fuss. Design and evaluation of smart wearable undergarment for monitoring physiological extremes in firefighting. In: *Proceedings of the 2014 ACM International Symposium on Wearable Computers: Adjunct Program*, pp. 249–254, 2014.

[39] A. Baghdadi, L.A. Cavuoto, A. Jones-Farmer, S.E. Rigdon, E.T. Esfahani and F.M. Megahed. Monitoring worker fatigue using wearable devices: A case study to detect changes in gait parameters. *Journal of Quality Technology*, 0: 1–25, 2019.

[40] K. Hines, W. Lages, N. Somasundaram and T. Martin. Protecting workers with smart e-vest. In: *Adjunct Proceedings of the 2015 ACM International Joint Conference on Pervasive and Ubiquitous Computing and Proceedings of the 2015 ACM International Symposium on Wearable Computers*, pp. 101–104, 2015.

[41] L. Yang, K. Lu, J.A. Diaz-Olivares, F. Seoane, K. Lindecrantz, M. Forsman, F. Abtahi and J.A.E. Eklund. Towards smart work clothing for automatic risk assessment of physical workload. *IEEE Access*, 6: 40059–40072, 2018.

[42] J. Manjarres, P. Narvaez, K. Gasser, W. Percybrooks and M. Pardo. Physical workload tracking using human activity recognition with wearable devices. *Sensors*, 20: 39, 2020.

[43] R. Bootsman, P. Markopoulos, Q. Qi, Q. Wang and A.A. Timmermans. Wearable technology for posture monitoring at the workplace. *International Journal of Human-Computer Studies*, 132: 99–111, 2019.

[44] D.C. Montgomery. *Introduction to Statistical Quality Control*. John Wiley & Sons, 2020.

[45] S. He, W. Jiang and H. Deng. A distance-based control chart for monitoring multivariate processes using support vector machines. *Annals of Operations Research*, 263: 191–207, 2018.

[46] T. Sukchotrat, S.B. Kim and F. Tsung. One-class classification-based control charts for multivariate process monitoring. *IIE Transactions*, 42: 107–120, 2009.

[47] R. Sun and F. Tsung. A kernel-distance-based multivariate control chart using support vector methods. *International Journal of Production Research*, 41: 2975–2989, 2003.

[48] P.H. Tran, A. Ahmadi Nadi, T.H. Nguyen, K.D. Tran and K.P. Tran. *Application of Machine Learning in Statistical Process Control Charts: A Survey and Perspective*. Springer International Publishing, Cham, pp. 7–42, 2022.

[49] A. Faraz, K. Chalaki, E.M. Saniga and C. Heuchenne. The robust economic statistical design of the hotelling's t2 chart. *Communications in Statistics—Theory and Methods*, 45: 6989–7001, 2016.

[50] T. Sukchotrat, S.B. Kim, K.L. Tsui and V.C.P. Chen. Integration of classification algorithms and control chart techniques for monitoring multivariate processes. *Journal of Statistical Computation and Simulation*, 81: 1897–1911, 2011.

[51] S. Choi, S. Youm and Y.S. Kang. Development of scalable on-line anomaly detection system for autonomous and adaptive manufacturing processes. *Applied Sciences*, 9: 4502, 2019.

[52] G. Celano and P. Castagliola. On-line monitoring of extreme values of geometric profiles in finite horizon processes. *Quality and Reliability Engineering International*, 36: 1313–1332, 2020.

[53] D.T. Nguyen and J.J. Jung. Real-time event detection on social data stream. *Mobile Networks and Applications*, 20: 475–486, 2015.

[54] R. Dastoorian and L.J. Wells. A hybrid off-line/on-line quality control approach for real-time monitoring of high-density datasets. *Journal of Intelligent Manufacturing*, 2021.

[55] S.C. Khoza and J. Grobler. Comparing machine learning and statistical process control for predicting manufacturing performance. In: *EPIA Conference on Artificial Intelligence*, Springer, pp. 108–119, 2019.

[56] Z.J. Viharos and R. Jakab. Reinforcement learning for statistical process control in manufacturing. *Measurement*, 182: 109616, 2021.

[57] F. Li, J. Wu, F. Dong, J. Lin, G. Sun, H. Chen and J. Shen. Ensemble machine learning systems for the estimation of steel quality control. In: *2018 IEEE International Conference on Big Data (Big Data), IEEE*, pp. 2245–2252, 2018.

[58] W. Chen. Intelligent manufacturing production line data monitoring system for industrial internet of things. *Computer Communications*, 151: 31–41, 2020.

[59] K.H.N. Bui and J.J. Jung. Aco-based dynamic decision making for connected vehicles in iot system. *IEEE Transactions on Industrial Informatics*, 15: 5648–5655, 2019.

[60] G. Loganathan, J. Samarabandu and X. Wang. Sequence to sequence pattern learning algorithm for real-time anomaly detection in network traffic. In: *2018 IEEE Canadian Conference on Electrical & Computer Engineering (CCECE), IEEE*, pp. 1–4, 2018.

[61] J. Liu, J. Guo, P. Orlik, M. Shibata, D. Nakahara, S. Mii and M. Takáč. Anomaly detection in manufacturing systems using structured neural networks. In: *2018 13th World Congress on Intelligent Control and Automation (WCICA), IEEE*, pp. 175–180, 2018.

[62] G.A. Susto, M. Terzi and A. Beghi. Anomaly detection approaches for semiconductor manufacturing. *Procedia Manufacturing*, 11: 2018–2024, 2017.

[63] A. Marchioni, M. Mangia, F. Pareschi, R. Rovatti and G. Setti. Subspace energy monitoring for anomaly detection @sensor or @edge. *IEEE Internet of Things Journal*, 1–1, 2020.

[64] M. Sakurada and T. Yairi. Anomaly detection using autoencoders with nonlinear dimensionality reduction. In: *Proceedings of the MLSDA 2014 2nd Workshop on Machine Learning for Sensory Data Analysis, MLSDA'14, Association for Computing Machinery, New York, NY, USA*, pp. 4–11, 2014.

[65] W. Guo and A.G. Banerjee. Identification of key features using topological data analysis for accurate prediction of manufacturing system outputs. *Journal of Manufacturing Systems*, 43: 225–234, 2017.

[66] Y. Umeda, J. Kaneko and H. Kikuchi. Topological data analysis and its application to timeseries data analysis. *FUJITSU Sci. Tech. J.*, 55: 7, 2019.

[67] B.M. Colosimo and M. Pacella. A comparison study of control charts for statistical monitoring of functional data. *International Journal of Production Research*, 48: 1575–1601, 2010.

[68] J. Liu, J. Chen and D. Wang. Wavelet functional principal component analysis for batch process monitoring. *Chemometrics and Intelligent Laboratory Systems*, 196: 103897, 2020.

[69] M. Flores, S. Naya, R. Fernández-Casal, S. Zaragoza, P. Raña and J. Tarrío-Saavedra. Constructing a control chart using functional data. *Mathematics*, 8: 58, 2020.

[70] S. Kapoor. Multi-agent reinforcement learning: A report on challenges and approaches. *arXiv:1807.09427 [cs, stat]*, 2018.

[71] S. Luo. Dynamic scheduling for flexible job shop with new job insertions by deep reinforcement learning. *Applied Soft Computing*, 91: 106208, 2020.

[72] N. Tuptuk and S. Hailes. Security of smart manufacturing systems. *Journal of Manufacturing Systems*, 47: 93–106, 2018.

[73] R. Yang and J. Xu. Computing at massive scale: Scalability and dependability challenges. In: *2016 IEEE Symposium on Service-Oriented System Engineering (SOSE), IEEE*, pp. 386–397.

[74] D.W. McKee, S.J. Clement, J. Almutairi and J. Xu. Massive-scale automation in cyberphysical systems: Vision amp; challenges. In: *2017 IEEE 13th International Symposium on Autonomous Decentralized System (ISADS)*, pp. 5–11, 2017.

[75] R. Laby. Détection et localisation d'anomalies dans des données hétérogènes en utilisant des modèles graphiques non orientés mixtes. Theses, Télécom ParisTech, 2017.

[76] E. Dufraisse, P. Leray, R. Nedellec and T. Benkhelif. Interactive anomaly detection in mixed tabular data using bayesian networks. In: *International Conference on Probabilistic Graphical Models, PMLR*, 2020.

[77] A. Saaudi, Y. Tong and C. Farkas. Probabilistic graphical model on detecting insiders: Modeling with sgd-hmm. In: *ICISSP*, pp. 461–470, 2019.

[78] Y. Zhou, X. Liang, W. Zhang, L. Zhang and X. Song. Vae-based deep svdd for anomaly detection. *Neurocomputing*, 453: 131–140, 2021.

[79] X. Li, Q. Ding and J.Q. Sun. Remaining useful life estimation in prognostics using deep convolution neural networks. *Reliability Engineering & System Safety*, 172: 1–11, 2018.

[80] G. Yu, C. Zou and Z. Wang. Outlier detection in functional observations with applications to profile monitoring. *Technometrics*, 54: 308–318, 2012.

[81] K.P. Tran, H.D. Nguyen and S. Thomassey. Anomaly detection using long short term memory networks and its applications in supply chain management. *IFAC-PapersOnLine*, 52: 2408–2412, 2019.

[82] J. Wu, W. Zeng and F. Yan. Hierarchical temporal memory method for time-series-based anomaly detection. *Neurocomputing*, 273: 535–546, 2018.

[83] V.V. Trinh, K.P. Tran and T.T. Huong. Data driven hyperparameter optimization of one-class support vector machines for anomaly detection in wireless sensor networks. In: *2017 International Conference on Advanced Technologies for Communications (ATC)*, pp. 6–10. 2017.

[84] R. Sadeghi and J. Hamidzadeh. Automatic support vector data description. *Soft Computing*, 22: 147–158, 2018.

[85] R. Meyes, H. Tercan, S. Roggendorf, T. Thiele, C. Büscher, M. Obdenbusch, C. Brecher, S. Jeschke and T. Meisen. Motion planning for industrial robots using reinforcement learning. *Procedia CIRP*, 63: 107–112, 2017.

[86] Y. Lu, C. Liu, K.I.-K. Wang, H. Huang and X. Xu. Digital twin-driven smart manufacturing: Connotation, reference model, applications and research issues. *Robotics and Computer-Integrated Manufacturing*, 61: 101837, 2020.

[87] M. Singh, E. Fuenmayor, E. Hinchy, Y. Qiao, N. Murray and D. Devine. Digital twin: Origin to future. *Applied System Innovation*, 4: 36, 2021.

[88] P.H. Tran, C. Heuchenne and S. Thomassey. An anomaly detection approach based on the combination of lstm autoencoder and isolation forest for multivariate time series data. *Developments of Artificial Intelligence Technologies in Computation and Robotics*, 2020.

[89] A. Krizhevsky, I. Sutskever and G.E. Hinton. Imagenet classification with deep convolutional neural networks. In: *Advances in Neural Information Processing Systems*, pp. 1097–1105, 2012.

[90] D. Heckerman and C. Meek. Models and selection criteria for regression and classification. In: *Proceedings of the Thirteenth Conference on Uncertainty in Artificial Intelligence.* Morgan Kaufmann Publishers Inc., pp. 223–228, 1997.

[91] F.T. Liu, K.M. Ting and Z.H. Zhou. Isolation forest. In: *2008 Eighth IEEE International Conference on Data Mining*, pp. 413–422, 2008.

[92] T. Fukumoto. Deep learning: Image anomaly detection for production line, 2021.

[93] S.F. Désage, G. Pitard, M. Pillet, H. Favrelière, F. Frelin, S. Samper, G. Le Goic, L. Gwinner and P. Jochum. Visual quality inspection and fine anomalies: Methods and application. In: *International Precision Assembly Seminar*, Springer, pp. 94–106, 2014.

[94] D.P. Kingma and M. Welling. Auto-encoding variational bayes. *arXiv preprint arXiv:1312.6114*, 2013.

[95] C. Doersch. Tutorial on variational autoencoders. *arXiv preprint arXiv:1606.05908*, 2016.

[96] J. An and S. Cho. Variational autoencoder based anomaly detection using reconstruction probability. *Special Lecture on IE*, 2: 1–18, 2015.

[97] D.P. Kingma and M. Welling. An introduction to variational autoencoders. *Foundations and Trends® in Machine Learning*, 12: 307–392, 2019.

[98] D.P. Kingma, S. Mohamed, D.J. Rezende and M. Welling. Semi-supervised learning with deep generative models. In: *Advances in Neural Information Processing Systems*, pp. 3581–3589, 2014.

[99] K. Sohn, H. Lee and X. Yan. Learning structured output representation using deep conditional generative models. *Advances in Neural Information Processing Systems*, 28: 3483–3491, 2015.

[100] R.Q. Chen, G.H. Shi, W.L. Zhao and C.H. Liang. A joint model for it operation series prediction and anomaly detection. *Neurocomputing*, 448: 130–139, 2021.

[101] E. Marchi, F. Vesperini, F. Eyben, S. Squartini and B. Schuller. A novel approach for automatic acoustic novelty detection using a denoising autoencoder with bidirectional lstm neural networks. In: *2015 IEEE International Conference on Acoustics, Speech and Signal Processing (ICASSP)*, pp. 1996–2000, 2015.

[102] A. Borghesi, A. Bartolini, M. Lombardi, M. Milano and L. Benini. Anomaly detection using autoencoders in high performance computing systems. *Proceedings of the AAAI Conference on Artificial Intelligence*, 33: 9428–9433, 2019.

[103] X. Lou and K.A. Loparo. Bearing fault diagnosis based on wavelet transform and fuzzy inference. *Mechanical Systems and Signal Processing*, 18: 1077–1095, 2004.

[104] W.A. Smith and R.B. Randall. Rolling element bearing diagnostics using the case western reserve university data: A benchmark study. *Mechanical Systems and Signal Processing*, 64: 100–131, 2015.

[105] M. Yuwono, Y. Qin, J. Zhou, Y. Guo, B.G. Celler and S.W. Su. Automatic bearing fault diagnosis using particle swarm clustering and hidden markov model. *Engineering Applications of Artificial Intelligence*, 47: 88–100, 2016.

[106] B. Nayana and P. Geethanjali. Analysis of statistical time-domain features effectiveness in identification of bearing faults from vibration signal. *IEEE Sensors Journal*, 17: 5618–5625, 2017.

[107] A. Zhang, S. Li, Y. Cui, W. Yang, R. Dong and J. Hu. Limited data rolling bearing fault diagnosis with few-shot learning. *IEEE Access*, 7: 110895–110904, 2019.

[108] W. Zhang, G. Peng, C. Li, Y. Chen and Z. Zhang. A new deep learning model for fault diagnosis with good anti-noise and domain adaptation ability on raw vibration signals. *Sensors*, 17: 425, 2017.

[109] Z. Zhuang, H. Lv, J. Xu, Z. Huang and W. Qin. A deep learning method for bearing fault diagnosis through stacked residual dilated convolutions. *Applied Sciences*, 9: 1823, 2019.

Chapter 4

Decision Support System for Complex Systems Risk Assessment with Bayesian Networks

Ayeley Tchangani

1 Introduction

Systems that engineers and scientists face today, whether for their design, modeling, analysis, or management, and in particular for the management of the risks of their dysfunction, are increasingly complex. This complexity is due, among other things, to the need to increase the capacities or performance of these systems by networking them, creating interactions that can lead to unpredictable behavior. Complexity is a word that encompasses a set of concepts whose meaning is highly dependent on the context [3;4;13;22]. The definition of a complex system varies depending on the discipline to which it applies. Nowadays, scientific advances are considerably highlighting this notion of complexity in fields as varied as chemistry, physics, biology, economics, human sciences, etc. In its meaning, complex describes a system or component that, with respect to its design or function, is difficult to understand and verify. Over the past decade, the analysis of complex systems (complexity) has been identified as distinct from studies conducted traditionally in the mathematical and physical sciences [21]. In order to better understand the reactions associated with a phenomenon or mechanism, modeling of behaviors and interactions plays an important role. However, the diversity of systems in terms of architecture, function, environment makes it impossible to formulate general laws to model all of them. In order to best define these systems and model them as closely as possible to reality, understanding and characterization of their complexity is essential. A complex system is made up of many entities whose interactions produce the emergence of a global behavior that cannot be explained solely on the basis of the individual properties of its constituents [10;12]. Often, the interactions of individuals with each other overlap with individual behaviors. Define the interactions for which it is the headquarters is an important key for understanding and controlling the evolution of a complex system. These interactions are first of all temporal, i.e., they evolve over time. They are also multi-scale, i.e., they operate at different levels on the system. In a network, for example, an entity considered elementary may act on a system located at a higher level of which it is a part: this is known as feedback. These feedback phenomena, which are not always

LGP - Université de Toulouse, 47 Avenue d'Azereix, 65016 Tarbes, France.
Email: ayeley.tchangani@iut-tarbes.fr

explicit, lead to global behaviors that are said to be non-linear. The non-linearity means that they are not simply proportional to the individual behaviors of the basic components. This can lead to cascade phenomena, also known as domino effects, and bifurcations in the evolution of the system leading to sudden and difficult qualitative changes to analyze, understand and predict. Complex Systems approach therefore consists in focusing on dynamic interactions in all their diversity. The complexity attributes basically addressed in this chapter are related to the number of components of a system and principally their interactions that may lead to a cascade effect in the case of the failure of one of them; the main interaction considered here is *influence*. Influence is materialized by the fact that components interact in hierarchy to form a system so that it can be described by a directed acyclic graph (DAG). The main purpose of the chapter is to model and analyze complex systems in terms of risk they may face. This task needs to be addressed using sound mathematical tools; given the uncertainty that may affect these systems, graphical probabilistic tools such as Bayesian networks (BN)[14;16;17] and their extentions are well suited for treating the influence. In reality, any human decision is risky in the sense that the outcomes of these decisions are subject to uncertainty of all kinds (random, epistemic, fuzzy, imprecise, etc.). This assertion, confronted with the requirement for transparency, for the scientific quasi-truth of any decision, whether particular or public, on the part of citizens, consumers, or users of the tools made available to them by researchers, calls for a treatment or construction of a decision-making framework that inspires a certain degree of confidence regarding the outcome of the decisions taken. The construction of any framework that should help human beings to make the most appropriate decisions is based on the use of appropriate scientific tools. The choice of these tools is based on the attributes of the decisions to be made and thus of the framework to be built such as:

- the multiplicity of actors involved in the decision-making process;

- the multiplicity of objectives targeted by the decisions;

- the multiplicity of attributes or criteria characterizing the alternatives of decisions in relation to the targeted objectives;

- especially the uncertainty that characterizes both the elements of the decision problem (objectives approximately expressed) and the relationships between these elements (attribute-objective relationships that are uncertain or not clearly defined).

In the perspective of integrating uncertainty into decisions of all kinds in order to minimize the risk that the decision-maker runs, researchers are constantly looking for the most efficient tools for modeling and treating uncertainty. To this end, Bayesian networks, since their introduction in 1988 by Judea Pearl[17], have proven themselves as a tool for modeling and treating uncertainty and thus the possibility of using them to build a decision-making framework where risk is an important dimension. Thus in this chapter we will try to show how the tools built over time and still under construction around Bayesian technology can be effectively exploited in risky decision support processes.

2 Bayesian Technology

A Bayesian Network is a directed acyclic graph (DAG) that represents relationships (in general causal relationships) between elements in a certain knowledge domain; each element represents a random variable associated with a probability table characterizing its parameters, the random variable is also called a node in BN representing. The causal relationship is represented by an adge which is a directed link from one variable called parent to the other variable known as a child. Propagation of local evidence or information through the network relies on Bayes theorem[2], see[17;6]. The strength of relationships called parameters of the BN are collected in conditional probability tables for nodes that do have parents and/or a priori probability tables for nodes without parents. Thanks to their capacity to apprehend uncertainty and complex relationships and to take into account other dimensions involved in risk management, such as time, the large size of the systems to be managed, and multidimensionality, extensions of BNs have been introduced such as:

- dynamic Bayesian networks (DBN) to take into account the effect of time[14],

- object oriented Bayesian networks (OOBN) to apprehend the large size of the systems[7],

- multi-dimensional Bayesian networks or extended object-oriented Bayesian networks (EOOBN)[10].

These are the tools that we will use in a risk management perspective.

3 BN Model for Event Oriented Risk Management

This part is based on[19] and its purpose is to establish a meta-model for risk management where risk is due to the occurence of an udesirable event. The Meta-Model for Risk management consists of an influence diagram (ID) which is an extension of Bayesian networks to allow evaluating alternative decisions and not only relationships as in BN. They are simple visual representations of a decision problem under uncertainty. Influence diagrams offer an intuitive way to identify and display the essential elements, including decisions, uncertainties, and preferences, and how they influence each other. It shows the dependencies among the variables more clearly than a decision tree. The subsequent paragraphs will present all the different variables that will be used by the ultimate influence diagram model in the established framework.

3.1 Variables Identification

To identify and define all the variables to be used in the risk management model (the ultimate influence diagram), we propose to follow the risk management flow chart depicted on Figure 1, which is explained as follow.

- First of all, the analyst or decision maker must identify all the risk factors, in fact all the events that may have a negative impact on the performance of the entity by using risk assessment approaches evoked previously. We consider that this process will lead to a finite discrete set E of events.

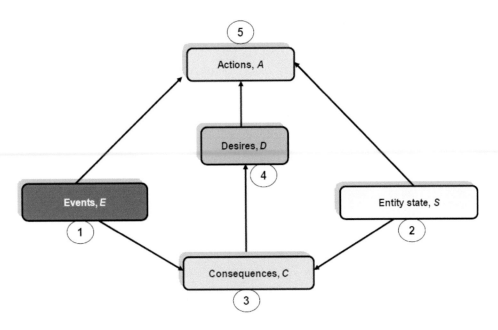

Figure 1: Risk management process flow chart.

- The second stage consists in assessing the variables defining the state of the system that is identifying all the things (economic, social, technological, institutional, cognitive, cultural conditions, etc.) that influence the vulnerability or resiliency (capacity of the entity to resist or not to an adverse event) of the entity given an undesirable event; we consider that a finite discrete set S has been identified.

- In the third stage, one will evaluate the consequences (characterization of negative impact on the entity; complete failure of the system, approximate running of the system, dangerous situation for users, etc.) on the entity if some of the previous events do occur; these consequences depend also on the state of the entity. We consider that a finite discrete set C of consequences is identified.

- The fourth stage is dedicated to defining desires by decision maker; desires are things one wants to affect through management decisions and actions; they define the criteria on which managements decisions will be based and consist most of the time in putting conditions or constraints over consequences (or aggregate indicators) such as damage cost during earthquake must be low, avoid power supply failure during an earthquake, etc. This process will generally lead to identifying the previously mentioned desires set D.

- Finally control variables or management actions are defined; these are things that can be realized in order to achieve desires. Examples: respect anti-seismic norms when constructing, educate population with regard appropriate reaction to adopt during an earthquake, build modern facilities, etc. Once again, we consider that a finite discrete set A of actions is available to decision maker.

3.2   Relationships Identification

To identify all the relationships that may exist between previously defined variables, we propose to use a meta-matrix analysis. The entry (I, J) of such a meta-matrix is a directed acyclic graph describing the influence of variables of set I on the variables of set J. The meta – matrix of our model is a 5×5 matrix of causality, influence, correlation, etc. graphs between previously identified sets E (events), S (entity state), C (consequences), D (desires) and A (actions) as shown by Figure 2, where blank entries mean no direct influence of the corresponding sets.

	E	S	C	D	A
E	E-E graph		E-C graph		
S		S-S graph	S-C graph		
C			C-C graph	C-D graph	
D				D-D graph	
A	A-E graph	A-S graph			A-A graph

Figure 2: Meta-matrix to identify relationships between variables.

These graphs are presented and explained in the following points.

- **Events graph** $(E - Egraph)$: this graph defines causal relationships that may exist between events; to identify these relationships one must answer questions such as: which event may lead to which one ? For instance an earthquake may cause a tsunami or stones falling in mountainous regions.

- **State graph** $(S - Sgraph)$: represents potential influence that may exist between the variables defining the state of the entity.

- **Consequences graph** $(C - Cgraph)$: defines relationships between consequences. For instance, human consequences during an earthquake may be decomposed into economic consequences, infrastructures consequences, cultural consequences, etc. To define this graph one can use a bottom up analysis, going from a particular consequence and identifying all the consequences that lead to it.

- **Desires graph** $(D - Dgraph)$**:** is similar to consequences graph.

- **Actions graph** $(A - Agraph)$**:** this graph defines how one action may influence another one or how the success of an action may depend on another one.

- **Events-Consequences graph** $(E - Cgraph)$**:** defines how uncontrollable variables representing events will impact the consequences.

- **Sate-Consequences graph** $(S - Cgraph)$**:** this graph signifies that the importance of consequences depends on the state of the entity in terms of vulnerability or resiliency.

- **Consequences-Desires graph** $(C - Dgraph)$**:** is straightforward as desires are defined as conditions or constraints over consequences.

- **Actions-Events graph** $(A - Egraph)$**:** this graph represents the risk prevention actions as for some events there may exist actions that reduce their likelihood.

- **Actions-State graph** $(A - Sgraph)$**:** describes how some actions influence the state of the entity; indeed this graph represents the risk mitigation actions effects.

From the meta-matrix, defining a meta-model in terms of meta-Bayesian network is straightforward and is given by Figure 3 to control sequence where we add a constraints graph that has an influence on actions in order to take into account unavoidable resources limitation and other physical and feasibility requirements for actions. Of course when facing a real problem, the meta-model of Figure 3 must be instantiated with knowledgeable variables to obtain a real Bayesian network to support making decision.

3.3   Usage of the Model

The overall model can be used in two senses: *deductive* or *inductive*. In deductive sense, by specifying some local evidence or occurence of an event X in the model, one can propagate it using inference algorithms of Baysian networks to estimate the resultant risk $R_d(X)$ on each desire d and then aggregate them (using appropriate aggregator according to pursued objective) to obtain the overall resultant risk $R(X)$. In the inductive sense, by giving some requirements concerning acceptable risk for each desire, one can back propagate this information to determine the most appropriate actions to set up. One must notice that this model can be used by portion in the sense that the user can be interested in only a subset of variables and do the propagation processes.

3.4   Illustrative Case Study in Natural Risk Management

Let us consider (interested readers can find details of this application in[19]) a problem of developing a model that can be used by authorities of a country or a region (that may face an earthquake events) to support making sound decisions before, during and after an earthquake. Using steps and tools presented previously a Bayesian Meta-Model for Risk Management as sketched by Figure 3 has been obtained arround following variables.

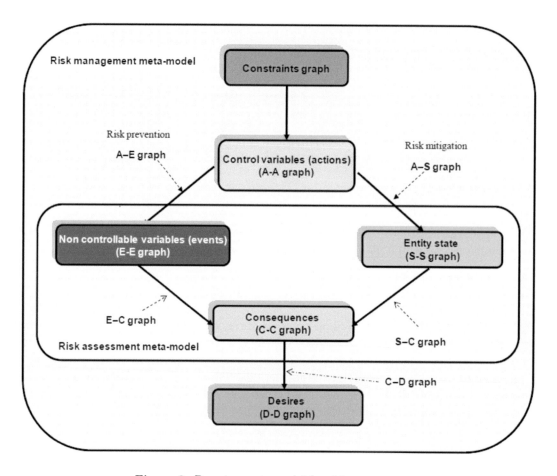

Figure 3: Bayesian meta-model for risk management.

- **Event**: eartnque that can take two status (yes/no)

- **Entity state characterization**: it is characterized through four variables (in practice there may be more variables):

  - *Population awareness of the phenomenon*: this is a qualitative appreciation of how well the concerned population know that an earthquake can occur in the region;

  - *Infrastructure conditions*: a region where infrastructures (buildings, roads, dams, etc.) are built when respecting anti-seismic norms will probably resist better during an earthquake than a region that does not respect these norms;

  - *Emergency systems*: this variable describes the quantity and qualities of resources developed by the region authorities to monitor adverse events (network of sensors to detect tectonic movements, geographic information systems, communication systems, etc.) and to efficiently react during an event (emergency equipment, quality and quantity of emergency trained agents, etc.);

– *Education level*: a well educated population will be more receptive to prescribed behaviour during an earthquake than a non educated one.

- **Consequences characterization**: Consequences taken into account are economic consequences, social consequences, infrastructures consequences, and environmental consequences.

  – Economic consequences: four variables characterize economic consequences

    * *Loss of jobs and know how*: this can be considered to be a mean or long term consequence.

    * *Macro-economic consequences*: destruction of industrial infrastructures and others will lead to negative macro-economic consequences.

    * *Relocation (of population) cost*: this is an immediate consequence that will be influenced by some variables related to emergency systems and infrastructure conditions.

    * *Evacuation (of population) cost*: this is also an immediate consequence as the previous one and will be characterized almost in the same way.

  – Social consequences: five variables were identified as social consequences

    * *Lives loss*: It will depend on some state of the entity variables and other consequences (consequences on buildings for instance).

    * *Impact on the revenue*: economic consequences such as jobs loss will lead to a reduction in revenue of the population that will increase social dependency for instance.

    * *Impact on the social dependency*: reduction in the revenue may increase social dependency among the population.

    * *Impact on education level*: lives loss, revenue reduction and social dependency may lead to a negative impact on the education level.

    * *Post event social consequences*: these consequences could consist in changes in cultural habits (migration of people from rural area to towns that will raise some problems such as criminality) or an impact on the structure of the population (reduction of active members of the population), etc.

  – Infrastructure consequences: three main variables describe these consequences

    * *Loss of energy infrastructures*: this variable, will be a descendant of variables such as dams, power plants, power lines, etc.

    * *Consequences on buildings*: damages caused to buildings will depend on the intensity of the earthquake as well as the nature of the buildings (are the buildings constructed when respecting anti-seismic norms or not?) and they will impact on lives loss that will depend on the usage of the building (office, home, industrial building, etc.).

    * *Loss of communication resources*: the loss of communication infrastructures such as roads, bridges, airports, ports or electronic communication infrastructures will result in negative socioeconomic consequences.

  - Environmental consequences: they are viewed through three variables

    * *Impact on water resources*: contamination of rivers and underground water by dangerous products from an exploded chemical or nuclear plants.

    * *Impact on agriculture resources*: flooded areas may become impracticable for agriculture or crops may be destroyed by fire, floods or a tsunami will ultimately affect economic and social consequences.

    * *Climate consequences*: destruction of forests by fire resulted from an earthquake or by a tsunami can have a long term consequences on the climate.

- **Actions identification**: four main actions have been identified that can be used to manage earthquake risk.

  - *Prepare population*: this action could take different forms: educate the population; inform and train the population to have a good response in the case of an earthquake.

  - *Set up and organize emergency systems*: create a network of sensors to pre-detect an earthquake event in order to alert population by different media for instance.

  - *Prepare after event*: subscribe insurance to face after events problems.

  - *Take legislative decisions*: vote laws and norms to be respected when constructing some infrastructures (buildings, dames, power plants, roads, bridges, etc.).

- **Constraints specification**: contraints may be financial, technical, geographical or time of the day.

  - *Financial constraints*: the considered country or region may face serious financial resources limitation in order to undertake actions defined previously.

  - *Technical constraints*: the region or country may lack technical skills to train emergency agents; to construct and organize an efficiency emergency system.

  - *Geographic constraints*: the accessibility of a region that face a natural disaster by emergency resources may be very difficult (mountains region for instance).

  - *Period of the day*: according to the period of the day an earthquake takes place, it will be more or less easy to organize emergency systems and rescue people.

- **Desires formulation**: desires may be defined by thresholds on consequences level or constraints satisfaction by some consequences (have low level lives loss, prevent infrastructures collapse, prevent occurrence of hunger, etc.).

Once variables are identified and their relationships sketched, one can consider building the entire model. This can be done by implementing existing Bayesian network learning and inference algorithms [17;6] to construct one's own decision support system or one can use existing decision support software based on Bayesian network technology such as that of [5] and [15], the principal ones in our knowledge. Figure 4 shows an extract of a model that could be set up to support decision making and planning regarding risk related to an earthquake event in a building; the focused consequence in this extracted model is human damage. Note that variables in this model can be considered as macro variables that can be decomposed into more

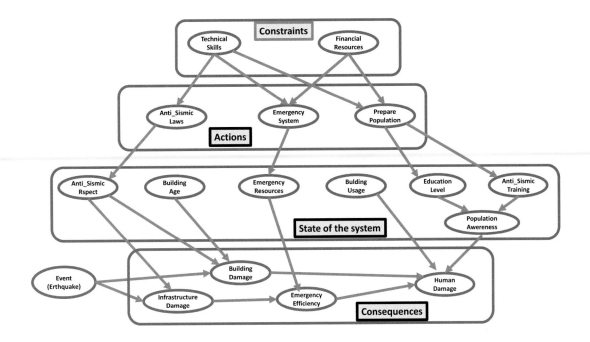

Figure 4: Example of an instance of Bayesian meta-model for risk management.

elementary variables depending on the level of abstraction decision makers accept. We did not find it necessary to consider specifying modalities of variables nor conditional probability tables as this is just an illustration of what can be obtained as structure of a risk management decision model in a particular case using the developed approach. When necessary, by using a team of experts, specification of these parameters can be done without major difficulties and value nodes can be added so that one can optimize or prioritize actions by simulation.

4 BN for Risk Management in Industrial Systems

To illustrate the possibility of using Bayesian networks for risk assessment and management in the industrial field, let us consider (an academic problem that an author uses in his risk management class) the launch monitoring system for an Ariane rocket. The success of an Ariane launch is based on the transmission of flight parameters from the satellite antennas in Libreville to the graphics station or TMAE console at the Kourou space center (see Figure 5 below).

Suppose we are interested in the possibility that the system may fail (i.e., data is not available in Kourou) after 5 years of operation and that the technical data of the elements of the transmission chain are given in the table of Figure 6. It is assumed that each element can take only two modes OK (the element is functionning) or OFF (the element failed). The quantitative data MTTF (Mean Time To Failure, it is assumed that the time to failure follows exponential laws) of the elements are shown in the table of Figure 6. Note that these collected data are just indicative. The Bayesian network model (built using Netica software) of the combinations

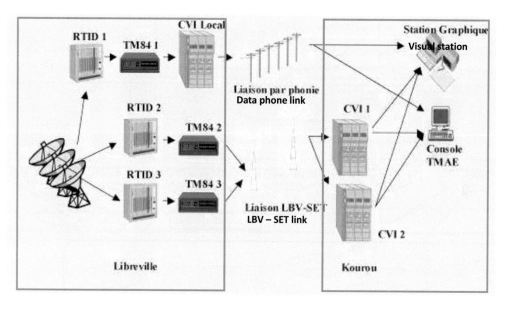

Figure 5: Structure of considered illustrative system.

Elements	MTTF	$Prob(i = OK)(t = 5\ years)$ $= e^{-t/MTTF}$	$Prob(i = OFF)(t = 5\ years)$
SAT	15 years	71.65 %	28.35 %
TM84 1	10 years	60.65 %	39.35 %
TM84 2	10 years	60.65 %	39.35 %
TM84 3	10 years	60.65 %	39.35 %
RTID 1	5 years	36.79 %	63.21 %
RTID 2	5 years	36.79 %	63.21 %
RTID 3	5 years	36.79 %	63.21 %
CVI Local	10 years	60.65 %	39.35 %
CVI 1	5 years	36.79 %	63.21 %
CVI 2	5 years	36.79 %	63.21 %
Liaison par phonie	10 years	60.65 %	39.35 %
Liaison LBV-SET	10 years	60.65 %	39.35 %
Station Graphique	10 years	60.65 %	39.35 %
Console TMAE	10 years	60.65 %	39.35 %

Figure 6: Quantitative parameters of elements of Kourou application.

of the basic events (failure of the elements of the transmission chain) to the dreaded event, which is the absence of flight parameter data at Kourou after 5 years of operation, is given in Figure 7. In terms of risk management, the previous Baysian model of Figure 7 can be used for prediction (determining the probable state of the system given the state of certain basic

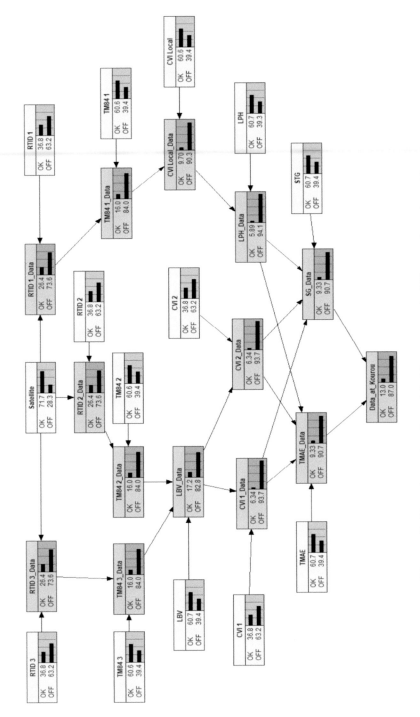

Figure 7: Bayesian network model risk assessment of Kourou launch problem.

elements), diagnosis (determining the probable state of the elements given the observed state of the system) and certain indicators that enable decisions to be made regarding intervention on systems (maintenance, replacement, improvement, predictive maintenance, risk analysis, etc.). To this end let us define following parameters and variables.

- $x_i(t)$ is the inoperability status of component i at time instant t that is binary in this case and given by Equation (1)

$$x_i(t) = \begin{cases} 1 & if \ component \ C_i \ is \ OFF \ at \ time \ t \\ 0 & if \ component \ C_i \ is \ OK \ at \ time \ t \end{cases}, \tag{1}$$

- So that the inoperability status of the overall system can be resumed by its inoperability vector $x(t)$ as shown by Equation (2)

$$x(t) = \begin{bmatrix} x_1(t) & x_2(t) & ... & x_n(t) \end{bmatrix}, \tag{2}$$

- The ultimate analysis goal is to determine $\varphi(x(t))$ that represents the inoperability status of the system at time t defined by Equation (3)

$$\varphi(x(t)) = \begin{cases} 1 & if \ system \ S \ is \ OFF \ at \ time \ t \\ 0 & if \ system \ S \ is \ OK \ at \ time \ t \end{cases}, \tag{3}$$

The main risk indicator $I_S(t)$ in terms of risk management is the probability of faillure of the system (launch faills) given by Equation (4)

$$I_S(t) = \Pr\{\varphi(x(t)) = 1\}, \tag{4}$$

Besides $I_S(t)$ as indicator of risk, some parameters can be useful for risk management such as following ones.

- Criticality of a component: a vector $x(t)$ is critical at time t for component C_i if it verifies Equation (5)

$$\varphi((1_i, x(t))) = 1 \ \ and \ \ \varphi((0_i, x(t))) = 0, \tag{5}$$

where, $(\times_i, x(t))$ means that the component C_i is in its status $\times$ (0 or 1) at time t. It means that if component C_i is inoperable at time instant t then the system will be inoperable and if it is functioning the system will be functioning.

- Risk augmentation factor $RAF_i(t)$ of component i: *relative increase* of the probability of inoperability of the system knowing that the basic component C_i is inoperable given by Equation (6)

$$RAF_i(t) = \frac{I_{S/x_i(t)=1}(t) - I_S(t)}{I_S(t)}, \tag{6}$$

where, $I_{S/x_i(t)=1}$ is the probability of inoperability of the system given that the component C_i is totally inoperable.

- Risk diminution factor $RDF_i(t)$ of component i: *relative decrease* of the probability of inoperability of the system knowing that the component C_i is operating given by following Equation (7)

$$RDF_i(t) = \frac{I_S(t) - I_{S/x_i(t)=0}(t)}{I_S(t)}, \tag{7}$$

where, $I_{S/x_i(t)=0}$ is the probability of inoperability of the system given that the component C_i is totally operable.

- Vessely-Fussel or diagnosis importance factor $VF_i(t)$ of component i: probability that the basic component C_i is inoperable knowing that the system is inoperable defined by Equation (8)

$$VF_i(t) = \Pr\{x_i(t) = 1/\varphi(x(t)) = 1\}, \tag{8}$$

- Birnbaum's factor $BF_i(t)$ of component i: probability that vector $x(t)$ is critical for component C_i at time instant t defined by (9)

$$BF_i(t) = I_{S/x_i(t)=1}(t) - I_{S/x_i(t)=0}(t), \tag{9}$$

- Lambert or critical component factor $LF_i(t)$ (diagnosis) of component i: probability that the vector $x(t)$ is critical for component C_i and the system is inoperable or the probability that the inoperability of component C_i is the cause of the inoperability of the system that is given by Equation (10)

$$LF_i(t) = \Psi_i(t) \Pr\{x_i(t) = 1\}, \tag{10}$$

where $\Psi_i(t)$ is given by (11)

$$\Psi_i(t) = \left(\frac{I_{S/x_i(t)=1}(t) - I_{S/x_i(t)=0}(t)}{I_S(t)}\right), \tag{11}$$

5 DBN for Risk Management of Industrial Systems

5.1 Brief Presentation of DBN

Dynamic Bayesian networks [14] derive from an extension of Bayesian networks (see, [16;17] and references therein) that describe probabilistic relationships between variables of a knowledge domain in order to take into account time behavior. Dynamic Bayesian networks (DBNs) are directed acyclic graphical models of stochastic processes, see [14], and they generalize Hidden Markov Models (HMMs) and Linear Dynamical Systems (LDSs) by representing the hidden and observed state in terms of state variables, which can have complex interdependencies. The graphical structure provides an easy way to specify these conditional interdependencies, and hence to provide a compact parameterization of the model. A dynamic Bayesian networks is completely defined by two components:

- Its structure that is a directed acyclic graph (DAG) where nodes represent variables and directed arcs represents influential relationships between these variables.

- Its parameters that represent conditional probability density (CPD) functions in the case of a continuous variable (the allowed values of the variable belong to a continuous set) or conditional probability table (CPT) in the case of a discrete variable (the allowed values of the variable belong to a discrete set that will be in general a finite set).

A dynamic Bayesian network structure consists of an intra slices directed acyclic graph and an inter slices directed graph; slices represent time instants to describe dynamic behavior of the system. Intra slice graph models the instantaneous relationships of nodes (a Bayesian network) and the inter slice graph represents the dynamics of the nodes. Intra slice parameters are conditional probability density functions and/or conditional probability tables of the corresponding Bayesian network and inter slice parameters represent the dynamics of variables on one hand and their relationships with the variables that influence their behavior on the other hand. The advantage of the Bayesian network model over the Markov chain representation for instance, besides the fact that the model is more compact and/or the possibility to consider the influence of the history up to some complexity, is that the transition matrix P can be learnt (estimated) from the expert knowledge and/or experimental data or parameters depending on external dynamic signals. BN and DBN have been widely used to assist decision making processes in domains such as dependability, product heath management and maintenance, see for instance[10;20] and references therein. Dynamic Bayesian networks are of particular interest for modeling interactions whose effects are delayed as is usually the case for physical systems. Indeed, in this case the interactions are modeled by the inter-slice relations in the Dynamic Bayesian network while the functional relations form the static Bayesian network at the level of a slice. Of course, the indicators or measures of importance defined in the safety of operation literature such as those in Equations (4) to (10) are easily calculable in a DBN model by running the model.

5.2 Illustrative Case Study

Consider a power supply system[18] for a server consisting of a power supplier (P), a circuit breaker (C) and two parallel circuits (active redundancy) each consisting of a cable (C1/2) and a transformer (T1/2) as shown in Figure 8.

The main objective is to model this system in order to prognosis the possibility of inoperability of the server due to a lack of electrical energy. FTA analysis of this system leads to 6 minimal cut sets: two of order 1 (the number of elements in the cut set) in terms of P (main power supplier) and C (circuit bricker) and four of order 2 consisting in $T1T2$ (transformers), $T1C2$ (transformer 1 and cable 2), $T2C1$ (transformer 2 and cable 1) and finally $C1C2$ (cables) and the DBN model of the system is given by Figure 9. Let us consider the following dynamic scenario: it is admitted that nominal failure rate of all components are considered to be $\lambda_i^0 = 10^{-3}/TU$ where TU stands for time unit; but the real failure rate of the two transformers depend on a time varying disturbance signal $w(t)$, with a nominal value w_0, according to the law given by Equation (12)

$$\lambda_{T_i}(t) = \lambda_{T_i}(t-1) + \beta_{T_i}(w(t) - w_0), \ \lambda_{T_i}(0) = \lambda_i^0 \qquad (12)$$

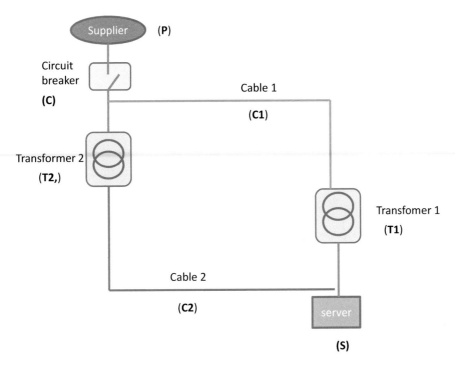

Figure 8: Scheme of illustrative case study.

and the main purpose is to study the influence of this signal on the $I_S(t)$ (see Equation (4)) of the system. Dynamic Bayesian Network model of this system is shown on Figure 9 where $S(t)$ represents the status of whether the server is supplied of power or not. In terms of prognostics, $I_S(t)$ is a good indicator to determine for instance the remaining useful life $RUL^\alpha(t_0)$ at each time instant t_0 at caution or boldness rate α (probability that the system being operational); indeed by setting up the rate α, $RUL^\alpha(t_0)$ is given by Equation (13)

$$RUL^\alpha(t_0) = I_S^{-1}(1-\alpha) - t_0 \tag{13}$$

where $I_S^{-1}(1-\alpha)$ is the inverse of $I_S(t)$ defined by (14)

$$I_S^{-1}(1-\alpha) = \{T : I_S(T) = 1 - \alpha\} \tag{14}$$

the main challenge therefore is to calculate this indicator $I_S(t)$.

Let us denote by $RUL^\alpha_{w_0}(t_0)$ and $RUL^\alpha_{w(t)}(t_0)$ the remaining useful life from time instant t_0 at the caution or boldness index α in nominal behavior of the external signal (w_0) and when transformers are subjected to external signal $w(t)$ respectively. Consider now the following conditions:

- nominal behavior of external signal is $w_0 = 0$,

- $w(t)$ and consequently $\lambda_{T_i}(t)$ behave like the curve shown on Figure 10 (a) and Figure 10 (b) with $\beta_{T_i} = 10^{-3}$.

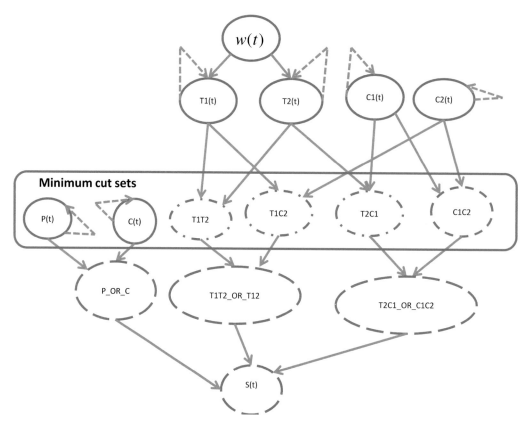

Figure 9: Dynamic Bayesian network model of considered illustrative application.

By running the DBN model given by Figure 9, we obtain result shown on Figure 11 for $I_S(t)$ where the red curve corresponds to perturbed case whereas the blue one corresponds to nominal behavior of external disturbance signal $w(t)$.

From this Figure 11 we can see that at caution or boldness index of $\alpha = 10\%$, the nominal and the disturbed RULs at time instant $t_0 = 20$ are given by $RUL_{w_0}^{0.1}(20) \approx 750 - 20 = 730$ TU and $RUL_{w(t)}^{0.1}(20) \approx 250 - 20 = 230\ TU$. In terms of decision making, given the b ehavior of external signal $w(t)$, decision maker can either maintain the caution or boldness level of 10% and then shorten the mission time from 730 to 230 or maintain the mission time of 730 by diminishing the caution from 10% to almost 0%.

6 EOOBN for Risk Management

Using BN techniques for modelling risk assessment processes becomes increasingly complex when the size of the system increases. For a large-scale system with many interacting elements, constructing a BN to represent its behaviour may be very tricky. Meanwhile, when the size of network grows, the model visibility reduces and the update of parameters becomes burdensome. For this reason, Object Oriented (OO) techniques might be a relevant alternative to reduce

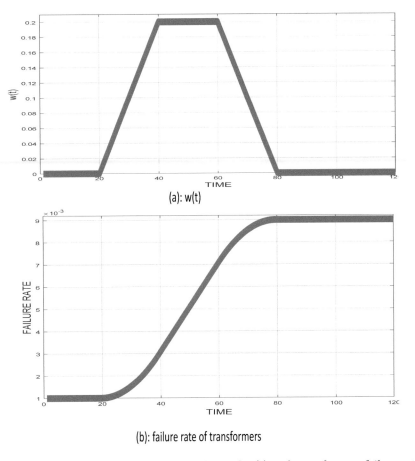

(a): w(t)

(b): failure rate of transformers

Figure 10: Simulated behavior of external signal $w(t)$ and transformers failure rate.

the complexity by highlighting a generic pattern representative of the various dimensions of the problem. An Object Oriented Bayesian Network (OOBN) is a direct application of the object paradigm[1;7]. The OOBN takes advantage of classic BN, but introduces the concept of instance nodes. An instance node is an abstraction of a part of a network that can be used as an elementary component to represent the whole structure. The notion of encapsulation allows the transmission of all properties of the network fragment. An OO network can be viewed as a hierarchical description or model of a problem. This makes the modelling easier since the OOBN fragments at different levels of abstraction are more readable. An OOBN model can be built by asking experts' opinions or using learning techniques. Authors of[8] and[23] give some insights into OOBN structure learning. The construction of such a model can be facilitated by an ontology representation[11]. Once the structure of the system is defined, the CPTs (also called parameters) have to be parameterized. The paper[9] extends the parameters learning algorithm to the objects that have the same structure based on OO assumptions. The parameters being identical reduce the number of parameters to be specified or learnt. Modelling a complex system by an OOBN allows not only reducing the design work but also updating calculations. However, most of the existing works dealing with this topic consider that parameters do not change from an object to another, which most often is not a realistic assumption in a real-world problem modelling

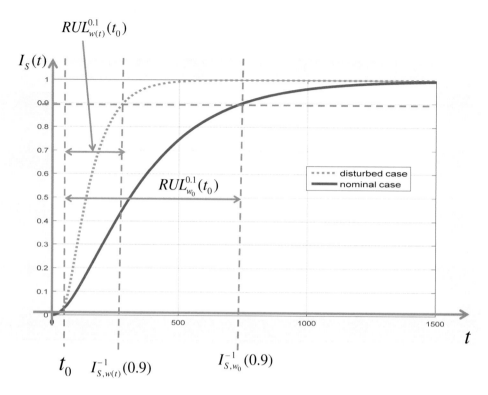

Figure 11: Results obtained by running the DBN model for the considered scenario.

context. As our main goal is to use OOBN for the representation of a large, repeatable and inherited system, this shortcoming must be remedied. In the following section, we will describe a proposed extension of OOBN paradigm that we refer to as EOOBN.

6.1 Extended Object Oriented Bayesian Network

Most of existing works dealing with OOBN consider that parameters do not change from an object to another, which most often is not a realistic assumption in a real world problem modeling context. To overcome this shortcoming the notion of Extended Object Oriented Bayesian Network or multi-dimension BN (MBN) is introduced. The basics of this model are briefly recalled in the following paragraphs, see[10] and[12] for details.

6.1.1 Construction of an EOOBN

In this section, we present an EOOBN approach which introduces much more flexibility, such as the possibility of instantiating parameters according to the considered object and taking into account dynamic behaviour of the system.

Basic Definitions. To overcome the limitations of classical OOBN associated with the structure building mentioned in[23] and[7] and the difficulty to take into account dynamic interactions pointed out in[7], we propose here an extended OOBN to ease parameter variation and dynamic consideration process. The approach is easy to adapt by collaboration mechanism and to propagate observations in a large system. The main components of an EOOBN are listed as follows.

Class, Object, Communication Channel and Virtual Node. Below, we will consider two levels in EOOBN: definition of a class is made at structure level (i.e., the nodes and their connexions in the object) and the object itself will be instantiated both through the input values and with respect to its parameters at the object level, which are likely to evolve with context or time.

- Class: A class (C) is the structure part (S) in a BN independent of the CPT parameters values. It has three kinds of nodes, namely, input nodes, output nodes and internal nodes. Only the input and output nodes are visible from outside the class.

- Object: An object (OS, P) in the EOOBN is an instantiation of the corresponding class. There are two parts in an object: the structure (S) which inherits from the class and the parameters (P) which will be defined by experts or learning processes. Instantiating a class consists in setting its parameters through a learning process or an expert opinion.

- Communication channel: The input and output build the communication channel for an EOOBN. It supports the process of exchanging information within the object and requires the following conditions to be satisfied:

  - Input nodes cannot have parents inside the class.
  - Input node is a reference node which is the projection of an output.
  - Internal nodes cannot have neither parents nor children outside the class.
  - Output nodes cannot have children inside the class.

Figure 12 presents the class which follows the four conditions above for an EOOBN with input nodes V_{in1} and V_{in2}, output nodes V_{out1} and V_{out2}, and internal nodes V_1 and V_2.

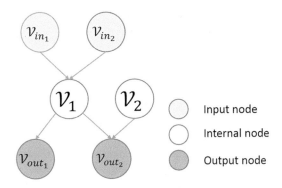

Figure 12: Basic structure of a class in EOOBN.

The class characterizes only the structure of the network. A class can be used only after its instantiation. The EOOBN not only inherits all the advantages of the classical OOBN such as hierarchy or encapsulation, but also offers more flexibility in terms of quantification. The possibility of having different parameter values from an object to another offers the possibility for different objects of the same category to have different parameters. The necessity to follow the behaviour of real-world systems appeals for introducing dynamicity in the model. This can be done by extended classical DBN in OO frame as shown in the following paragraph. Although in[1] a DBN simulation approach is given based on a self-reference node in an object, the dynamic simulation is done by adding a reference link (from dynamic output node to dynamic input node) inside the class; a confusion might appear when trying to add the dynamic part within a large OOBN. To overcome this issue, we introduce the virtual nodes in the EOOBN to simulate the dynamic part.

- Virtual node. The virtual node is a communication channel for the class/object. It usually stands for the temporal node.

  - The virtual node is either an input node or an output node in the class/object.
  - It is associated with the dynamic node in the class/ object as a communication channel with the next time-slice.
  - The transition model represents the parameters between the virtual input and dynamic node; Conditional probabilities between a dynamic node and its virtual output are equalled to 1.

After the instantiation the class one obtain a dynamic object that can be used to study the dynamic behaviour of the considered system.

Construction Method. The construction of a dynamic EOOBN can be done by carrying out the following steps:

- Formalize the structure S of a system (by splitting the system into different classes C).

- Design the structure of each class (C) with respect to S and without considering the dynamic part.

- Identify the dynamic node in class N_{t_i} and add virtual input and output nodes to the time-dependi variables.

- Instantiate the class by introducing the parameters corresponding to the object.

- Connect the objects through their communication channels.

The instantiation of a class requires to be able to quantify its parameters. This can be obtained from expert opinions or learning processes. Due to the spatial characteristics of EOOBN such as the repeatable structure of certain objects, the parameter learning maybe different from the classical learning process. The learning problem for EOOBN will be addressed in a future work. The EOOBN flexibility is mainly explained on one hand by the concepts of class and objects allowing, as previously mentioned, parameter variations but also, in another hand, by its aptitude to accept the introduction of system dynamic behaviour. The definition of class not only enables the independence of its constitutive variables but also local independent computation for each object. The EOOBN models proposed in this article will be always structured according to global and object levels. In order for existing inference algorithms to be used for EOOBN assessment, some adjustments are required that will be presented in the next section.

A specific propagation method has been developed for EOOBN[10]. In terms of usage of this model for risk informed decision making, the following type of decision can be considered:

- *Pre-active decisions:* preparing things to prepare the system to face potential threats; the model can be used to identify weak points with regard to identified threats in a large-scale system to search for appropriate defence mechanism.

- *Reactive decisions:* real-time decision-making when the adverse event takes place. Indeed by simulating, the system decision-makers can deduce what will happen at a particular place knowing that something abnormal does happen somewhere else.

- *Pro-active decisions:* the model can be used to look for actions that may be set up to avoid some catastrophic situations.

6.1.2 Case Study

Main developpments of this part are in[10]. In this section, the construction method has been applied to build an EOOBN within the framework of a cement manufacture process.

The cement production process is made of seven steps:

- 1. Obtaining the raw material from a quarry through a blasting machine.

- 2. Proportioning, blending and grinding.

- 3. Preheating the material in a tower.

- 4. Heating in a kiln.

- 5. Cooling the clinker.

- 6. Grinding finish.

- 7. Bagging thanks to a packaging machine.

Every step of the process is supported by operation machines and operators. It is assumed that every step relies on a single machine and that only the qualified intermediate product can be transferred to the next step. Every machine has its own operation conditions. The fabrication process in each step is a complex physical chemistry dynamic reaction, and the use of an EOOBN is relevant for its simulation. It will enable among other things to take into account of the uncertain environment, considering individually each material or human resource without simplifying the system with too many hypothesis while embracing the whole system whatever its size.

- Step 1: Formalize the structure of a system (by splitting the system into different classes). According to the previous description, the manufacturing process is split into seven blocks corresponding each to the different steps previously defined. A BN-based general machine model is proposed for each asset; the general model will be treated further as a class in the EOOBN.

- Step 2: Design the structure of each class with respect to system and without considering the dynamic part. A machine involves seven basic variables which are listed as follows:

  - Machine state (MS)
  - Upstream state
  - Operator skill (OS)
  - Controller
  - Product quantity
  - Amount of quality product (also called downstream product (DP))

  The machine yield relies on the capacity of the asset to produce a quantity of product with the required quality. Initial quantity of products (P) likely to be generated will depend on the OS, the MS and the upstream product (UP) input. The final quantity or DP will be a proportion of this initial amount of products (P) respecting the quality criteria that will depend not only on OS and MS, but as well on the aptitude of the system to detect possible defects through a control (C).

- Step 3: Identify the dynamic node in the class and add the virtual input and output nodes associated with it around the dynamic variable. this case study, the MS variable is considered as dynamic since it loses efficiency over time. The corresponding virtual input and output nodes are then introduced to obtain the dynamic class.

- Step 4: Instantiate the class by introducing the parameters corresponding to the object. To characterize the specificity of each machine, different parameters are identified and used to instantiate the objects. At this level, the knowledge comes generally from learning processes or expertise; but in the present case, the machine parameters are arbitrarily decided by the authors. To characterize the specificity of each machine, different parameters are identified and used to instantiate the objects. At this level, the knowledge comes generally from learning processes or expertise; but in the present case, the machine parameters are arbitrarily decided by the authors.

- Step 5: Connect the objects through their communication channels. Two communication channels appear in the case study corresponding respectively to the: intermediate product flow and Dynamic of machine state (MS) model.

From the model established (see [10] for details), various key performance indicators can be estimated such as the probability associated with the modalities of the variables of machine 7. In particular, the form of degradation over time of the MS combined with a time-dependent productivity slowdown is observed. The selected case study considered here only few modalities for each variable, but obviously the results could be significantly refined by taking into account more discrete variation intervals for each variable. It is also possible to introduce various evidences whose propagation in the network will help reducing uncertainties and ease the decision-making. The EOOBN simulates the system as a whole without any restrictive assumption. Splitting a big system into different homogeneous sub-models helps reducing the calculation and consequently the computation time while considering the unicity of each asset. As a benefit, one can also consider the advantage of dissociating the different dimensions characterizing the behaviour of a system. Here, the model is based on two dimensions representing the spatio-temporal evolution of a process, but the methodology we propose is not limited and can accept an infinite number of dimensions to be handled simultaneously.

7   Conclusion

This chapter provided an overview of how to use different Bayesian technology tools to model and analyze risk management problems. In terms of Bayesian technology, three main variants have been presented, namely Basic Bayesian Networks (BN), Dynamic Bayesian Networks (DBN), Object Oriented Bayesian Networks (OOBN) and their extension (EOOBN) recently developed in the author's research team. On the applications side, case studies in various domains such as industry, risk management problems in the face of nature have been visited. The work presented in this chapter shows the possibilities of Bayesian technology in the processes of analysis, evaluation and risk management. The models established in this chapter, address the problem of how to obtain the information or knowledge necessary to solve risky decision problems. Risk is a topic of utmost importance for decision makers, whether it is the risk related to unknown diseases, the risk related to industrial activities, the risk related to malicious activities, risk reltated to natural events, etc., and therefore this topic must be considered by scientific methods. This chapter has shown, in some respects, that tools built around Bayesian technology can effectively contribute to understanding these risk-related decision problems. In a decision-making process, there is no worse adversary than uncertainty because it leads to feverishness, fear and apprehension on the part of decision-makers. The adequate treatment of this uncertainty is therefore a commendable contribution to the decision support processes and this chapter has tried to answer this imperative through Bayesian technology.

References

[1] O. Bangso and P.H. Wuillemin. Object oriented Bayesian networks a framework for topdown specification of large Bayesian networks and repetitive structures. *Aalborg: Aalborg Universitetsforlag*, 2000.

[2] T. Bayes. An essay towards solving a problem in the doctrine of chances. *Biometrica*, 46: 293–298, 1958 (reprinted from an original paper of 1763).

[3] M. Gell-Mann. What is complexity. Complexity and industrial clusters. Springer, 13–12, 2002.

[4] N. Goldenfeld and L.P. Kadanoff. Simple lessons from complexity science, 284(15411): 87–3, 1999.

[5] Hugin Expert Software: http://www.hugin.com/.

[6] F.V. Jensen. Lecture notes on Bayesian networks and influence diagrams. *Department of Computer Science*, Aalborg University, 1999.

[7] D. Koller and A. Pfeffer. Object-oriented Bayesian networks. In: *Proceedings of the Thirteenth Conference on Uncertainty in Artificial Intelligence*, Providence, RI. San Mateo, CA: Morgan Kaufmann Publishers, pp. 302–313, 1997.

[8] H. Langseth and T.D. Nielsen. Fusion of domain knowledge with data for structural learning in object oriented domains. *J Mach Learn Res*, 4: 339–368, 2003.

[9] H. Langseth and O. Bangso. Parameter learning in objectoriented Bayesian networks. *Ann Math Artif Intell*, 32(1-4): 221–243, 2001.

[10] Q. Liu, A. Tchangani, F. Pérès and V. Gonzalez-Prida. Object oriented Bayesian network for complex system risk assessment. *Proceedings of the Institution of Mechanical Engineers, Part O: Journal of Risk and Reliability*, 232(4): 340–351, 2018.

[11] Q. Liu, A. Tchangani, B. Kamsu-Foguem and F. Pérès. Modelling a large scale system for risk assessment. In: *Proceedings of International Conference on Industrial Engineering and Systems Management (IESM)*, New York: IEEE, pp. 203–208, 2015.

[12] Q. Liu. Modélisation bayesienne des interactions multidimensionnelles dans un système complexe. Application à la gestion des risques de crues, *PhD Thesis*, Université de Toulouse, 2018.

[13] K. Mainzer. *Thinking in Complexity: The Computational Dynamics of Matter, Mind, and Mankind*. Springer Science & Business Media, 2007.

[14] K.P. Murphy. Dynamic Bayesian Networks: Representation, Inference and Learning, *Ph.D Thesis*, University of California, Berkeley, 2002.

[15] Netica Software: http://www.norsys.com/.

[16] T.D. Nielsen and F.V. Jensen. *Bayesian Networks and Decision Graphs*. Springer Science & Business Media, 2009.

[17] J. Pearl. *Probabilistic Reasoning in Intelligent Systems.* Morgan Kaufmann, 1988.

[18] A. Tchangani and F. Pérès. Modeling interactions for inoperability management: from Fault Tree Analysis (FTA) to Dynamic Bayesian Network (DBN). *4th IFAC Workshop on Advanced Maintenance Engineering, Services and Technologies (A-MEST'20), IFAC PapersOnLine* 53-3, pp. 342–347, 2020.

[19] A. Tchangani. A model to support risk management decision-making. *Studies in Informatics and Control Journal*, 20: 3. 209–220, 2011.

[20] A. Tchangani and D. Noyes. Modeling dynamic reliability using dynamic Bayesian networks. *Journal Européen des Systèmes Automatisés*, 40(8): 911–25, 2006.

[21] G. Weng, U.S. Bhalla and R. Iyengar. Complexity in biological signaling systems. *Science*, 284(15411): 92–5, 1999.

[22] G.M. Whitesides and R.F. Ismagilov. Complexity in chemistry science, 284(15411): 89–4, 1999.

[23] P.H. Wuillemin and L. Torti. Structured probabilistic inference. *Int J Approx Reason*, 53(7): 946–968, 2012.

Chapter 5

Decision Support System using LSTM with Bayesian Optimization for Predictive Maintenance: Remaining Useful Life Prediction

Huu Du Nguyen[1] and Kim Phuc Tran[2,*]

1   Introduction

In the last few years, the rapid development of advanced technologies like cloud computing, the Internet of Things (IoT), big data analytics, and artificial intelligence (AI) had a profound effect on industrial manufacturing, leading to the concept of smart manufacturing. In this process, intelligence has been added to the manufacturing process to drive continuous improvement, knowledge transfer, and data-based decision-making. Thanks to the use of a large number of sensors in equipment, the data from the whole processes have been collected. Then, these data will be then analyzed, processed, and visualized, enabling to manage the manufacturing process more effectively and making better decisions that can bring fruitful business results in the long run.

One of the key factors that makes manufacturing smart is predictive maintenance (PdM). The PdM refers to a prominent strategy to deal with the problem of determining the right time for maintenance activities. In modern industry, maintenance actions involve high costs, ranging from 15% to 70% of total production costs[1]. As a result, maintenance strategies play a very important role to reduce the costs of defective products and equipment inactivity due to system failure. This fact motivates companies and engineerings to develop effective maintenance strategies. PdM is considered a powerful tool to perform the mission. Based on degradation data equipping with condition monitoring instruments such as sensors, the goal of PdM is to determine when specific maintenance is required, allowing to minimize the number of major malfunctions, reduce maintenance costs, and keep the production lines active. In the context of smart manufacturing with advanced technologies, the machinery system has included many components and become more complicated. In such a system, their components work in a

---

[1] International Research Institute for Artificial Intelligence and Data Science, Dong A University, Danang, Vietnam.

[2] Univ. Lille, ENSAIT, ULR 2461 - GEMTEX - Génie et Matériaux Textiles, F-59000 Lille, France.

* Corresponding author: kim-phuc.tran@ensait.fr

common environment and share the same stress, i.e., they are dependent. That means the failure of a specific machine may lead to the breakdown or the disruption of the whole system, and then the whole production line. Therefore, PdM is probably one of the most economical ways to maintain the machinery system in a smart factory. The benefits of PdM have been well documented in the literature like minimizing unplanned downtimes, reducing system faults, increasing efficiency in the use of financial and human resources, diagnosing failures, estimating the lifetime of a machine, and planning the maintenance interventions[2].

One of the important information systems that support businesses in making decisions is the decision support system (DSS). A DSS is an interactive, computer-based information system that integrates multiple functions such as analysis, modeling, diagnosis, prediction, and optimization to facilitate decision making in solving the identified problems[3]. The DSS are nowadays widely used in many fields in real life, such as business[4], medicine[5], and engineering[6]. In the manufacturing industry, the DSS has been applied for maintenance and many other purposes[7;8]. Recently, machine learning (ML) techniques, a set of computer-based algorithms, have emerged as potent tools for analyzing and processing data. ML algorithms can capture complex relationships and important features in the data that are not able recognized by humans or by previous traditional methods. Many ML algorithms have been developed in the literature and applied successfully in many areas in real life. In the PdM topic, researchers have incorporated the power of ML into DSS, making the DSS much more efficient. Thanks to the advanced ML techniques, an ML-based DSS can perform effectively a wide range of tasks with increasingly accurate results such as predicting remaining useful life (RUL), diagnosing failures, and prognosticating malfunctions.

An efficient DSS benefits PdM in particular and business in general. Under recent conditions of manufacturing (i.e., the use of advanced technologies) and the increasing requirements of modern industry, the task of designing such DSS can only be fulfilled by considering advanced algorithms of the machine learning methods. In this chapter, we propose a novel approach to build a DSS using the long short term memory algorithm (LSTM), an important algorithm of the ML method, with Bayesian optimization (BO) for RUL prediction - a crucial topic in PdM. The effectiveness of the proposed method is presented through a case study using a well-known dataset. We also provide a survey about the recent studies on the PdM and related methods in the literature.

The chapter is structured as follows. Section 2 presents an overview of the PdM and RUL. In Section 3, we discuss the ML-based DSS for PdM in the context of smart manufacturing. The LSTM and the BO algorithms have been described in Section 4. The proposed DSS based on the LSTM with BO algorithm is explained in Section 5. A case study to show the performance of the proposed method is given in Section 6. Section 7 is for some concluding remarks and perspectives of the study.

2 Predictive Maintenance and Remaining Useful Life Prediction

As discussed above, applying PdM in manufacturing brings several benefits for industrial production companies. It not only allows manufacturers to find the time for scheduling maintenance by estimating time to failure but also helps them identify the parts of machinery that need to be fixed by pointing out problems in machines. Machines and components degrade during production and their failures may have significant negative effects on the production process, such as scheduling and delivering delays. Without a good maintenance strategy, the company will suffer a lot of damage. For example, it would be a big interruption of the manufacturing process and a remarkable amount of money in lost productivity and charges to repair the failures as the machines are broken before the scheduled maintenance. Meanwhile, a significant delay and another amount of money are wasted in case maintenance is carried out according to a predetermined plan while the machines are still operating stably, not to mention the increase of the failure rate because of installed defective items or human negligence in that unnecessary maintenance operations.

In modern industrial production, especially in smart manufacturing, the role of PdM is becoming increasingly important. The traditional fixed schedule-based maintenance methods are no longer meet the high safety standards of Industry 4.0. As a result, a large number of studies have been carried out to develop advanced methods for PdM. The authors of[9] distinguished three main approaches for PdM, including the physical model-based methods, the knowledge-based methods, and the data-driven methods. The main feature of the physical model-based methods is to describe the condition of the machine using mathematical models. In particular, they use statistical methods for the evaluation end their effectiveness relies strongly on the precision of the condition and measurement of failure[10]. This complexity is reduced in the knowledge-based methods by combining other techniques like expert systems and fuzzy logic[11]. The data-driven methods are the most commonly used in recent times thanks to the development of IoT technology and ML algorithms. Sajid et al.[12] discussed the data science applications for predictive maintenance in context to Industry 4.0. Systematic literature reviews of the methods for PdM can bee seen in[13;14].

Predictive maintenance consists of programs for predicting, diagnosing, and analyzing future maintenance needs. A key idea among many PdM solutions is to estimate RUL - the remaining time before a machine requires a repair or a replacement when it no longer performs well its function. An accurate prognostic of the RUL plays a very important role to perform the PdM operation. It enables the manufacturers to assess accurately an equipment's health status and to optimize the maintenance schedule.

In the literature, there are different expressions for the definition of RUL. For example,[15] defined the RUL at the time t_i, say l_i, as $l_i = t_{EoL} - t_i$ where t_{EoL} is the end of the useful life, namely the RUL of a machine is the length from the current time to the end of its useful life. In some other publications, the RUL is defined as

$$l_i = inf(l : \chi(l + t_i) \geq \gamma)$$

where inf(.) stands for the inferior limit of a variable; $\chi(l + t_i)$ is the health state at the time $l + t_i$ and γ is the failure threshold[16;17]. That means, following this definition, the RUL is considered as the time left before the health states of machinery cross a failure threshold. The failure threshold should be a random variable, but in most studies, the failure threshold is simply considered as a constant line to be easier to apply in practice[18].

Due to its importance, a large number of studies have been devoted to the problem of predicting RUL. The authors of[19] split the current RUL prediction methods into two types: the model-based methods and the data-driven methods. The first type aims to establish mathematical or physical models like the Markov process model[20;21], the Winner process model[22;23], and the Gaussian mixture model[24;25] to describe degradation processes of machines and components. The parameters of the models are updated from measured data, and they can combine both expert knowledge and real-time information. However, many problems are existing for these model-based methods which have been discussed in[26]. The authors also presented the efforts in the literature to deal with these problems. On the contrary, the data-driven methods reach the RUL prediction based on features extracted from monitoring data using statistical and machine learning techniques without relying on any physics or engine degradation mechanics. These data-driven ones can be divided into statistical approaches and machine learning algorithms[27]. The authors of[15] reviewed statistical data-driven approaches for RUL estimation, which rely only on statistical models to estimate the RUL in terms of $f(X_t|Y_t)$, where X_t represents a random variable of the RUL at time t, Y_t represents the available past observed data, and $f(X_t|Y_t)$ is the probability density function of X_t conditional on Y_t. Compared to statistics-based methods, the ML algorithm-based approaches show a stronger capability of capturing the important features of the data. The authors of[28], applied several ML methods like the Linear Regression, Bayesian Linear Regression, Poisson Regression, Neural Network Regression, Boosted Decision Tree Regression and Decision Forest Regression for RUL prediction. The authors of[29] presented a degradation model composed of a multilayer perceptron and a Kalman filter to predict the RUL of a complex system, consisting of an aircraft turbine or turbofan. The authors of[30] proposed a hybrid model that combines support vector machines for the prediction of the RUL of aircraft engines. Recently, deep learning algorithms become more and more widely used for RUL prediction with excellent performances. The authors of[31] used a deep Convolution Neural Networks (CNN) in estimating the RUL. The Recurrent Neural Network (RNN) is used for state-of-charge (SOC) estimation in lithium-ion battery cells in[32;33]. Due to the vanishing and exploding gradient problems, the RNN usually does not perform well in the case of learning long-term dependencies of time series. The Long-Short Term Memory (LSTM) network, a variant of RNN which can overcome its drawback of RNN, is then developed. The authors of[34] used the LSTM network to predict the RUL and to assess the degradation of dental air turbine handpiece in the milling process. It has been shown in[35] that the LSTM outperforms other models like Multilayer Perceptron, RNN, and Gated Recurrent Units. Other variants of the LSTM are also further proposed for RUL prediction under more complex conditions and achieve higher precisions[36;37;38]. Both the CNN and the LSTM techniques belong to supervised learning methods, which require large labeled datasets for training models. The authors of[39] investigated the effect of unsupervised learning in RUL predictions using a semi-supervised setup. The authors have pointed out that semi-supervised learning leads to a higher RUL prediction accuracy compared to supervised learning in several situations. The idea of using a semi-supervised method for the case of less labeled data to predict the RUL of the aero-engine is also proposed in[40]. Due to a large number of publications on a specific method or a specific case study in the literature, several reviews have been published year to year to summarize studies on RUL estimation methods. Table 1 shows the review papers on the topic from 2006 to 2020, which is extended from Table 2 in[18].

Table 1: Review on studies for RUL predictions in the literature.

Refs.	Up to year	Standards related to RUL prediction approaches
41	2006	Statistical approaches, model-based approaches and AI approaches
42	2009	Traditional reliability approaches, physics-based models, data-driven models and integrated approaches
43	2011	Knowledge-based models, aggregate reliability functions, physical models, statistical models, conditional probability models and ANN
44	2010	Model based approaches, data-driven approaches and hybrid prognostic approaches
15	2011	Statistical data driven approaches
11	2015	Model-based methods, data-driven models and combination models
45	2016	Data-driven methods
46	2017	prognostics approaches
18	2018	physics model-based approaches, statistical model-based approaches, AI approaches and hybrid approaches
47	2019	physics based methods, probabilistic methods, AI methods, stochastic methods, and state space methods.
48	2020	Deep learning approaches

3 Machine Learning based Decision Support System for Predictive Maintenance

The era of IoT and Big Data has brought a lot of changes in the way a decision is made in many fields, particularly important areas in industrial manufacturing such as scheduling, quality improvement, and PdM. Instead of purely relying on an expert system, which is a knowledge-based computer program containing experts' knowledge in a specific domain, the important decisions on the process of maintaining machinery now tend to be based on data-driven approaches like ML-based DSS. The development of machine learning algorithms facilitated by the growing capabilities of the hardware and cloud-based solutions has made the DSS a more powerful and effective tool in PdM.

A machine learning-based DSS for PdM can be considered as a complex system consisting of many layers. The physical system in the first layer includes IoT sensors to monitor machines and components. The function of these devices is to collect the data about the current condition of machines from the whole process of manufacturing and then transfer this information to the storing layer. After a pre-processing step, these data have been fed to the AI algorithms to be analyzed in the data mining layer. Important information about the current statuses of the machines and components would be identified, other prognosis-related information like the RUL estimates would be provided. This essential information is the goal of the support system and this is fundamental for the suggestions on PdM tasks at the final step. The main architecture of a DSS for PdM with AI algorithms has been presented in Figure 1. It can be seen from this architecture that the machine learning algorithms play the role of the core of the DSS for PdM.

In the literature, references related to the topic of developing models to apply ML algorithms for PdM are abundant. The author of[49] provided an investigation on the ML-based PdM implementation, comparing the suitable and cost-effective properties between the implementation of ML-based PdM and other strategies. The authors also suggested a mathematical model to

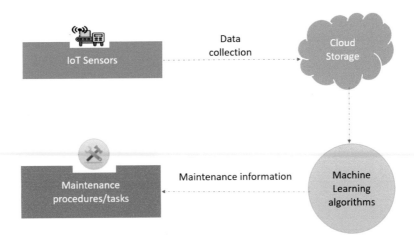

Figure 1: The main architecture of a DSS for PdM with AI algorithms.

build a DSS guiding the PdM implementation. Several ML algorithms such as the decision tree and the random forest algorithms have been used in[50] to present the architecture of a DSS in manufacturing maintenance. An adaptive machine learning-based DSS for flexible PdM is presented in[51]. The authors of[52] developed an integrated neural-network-based DSS for predictive maintenance of rotational equipment. The authors of[53] proposed a generative deep learning model based on the conditional variational autoencoder that enables predictive maintenance integrated production scheduling by operation-specific health prognostics. In this model, the authors have considered both machine degradation modeling and maintenance integrated production scheduling at the same time. A systematic review of the application of ML techniques and ontologies in the context of PdM, highlighting the challenges faced in this topic can be seen in[2].

4 Long Short Term Memory Networks using Bayesian Optimization

In this section, we provide a brief introduction of the proposed algorithms for designing a DSS which is a LSTM network and the BO algorithm.

4.1 Long Short Term Memory Networks

The LSTM network is firstly proposed by[54] based on the Recurrent Neural Network (RNN). In the network, the output at the moment $t-1$ is considered as the input at the next moment, t, and affects the weights of that moment. As a result, it can retain long-term dependencies between data at a given time from many timesteps before. The network can also overcome the vanishing or exploding gradient problem of the RNN architecture. Therefore, LSTM has been widely used to model temporal sequences. The LSTM network structure forms a chain of repeated modules. Each module consists of three control gates:

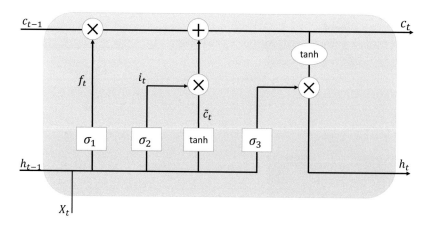

Figure 2: The architecture of a LSTM cell.

the forget gate, the input gate, and the output gate as depicted in Figure 2. In each gate, a sigmoid neural layer and a pointwise multiplication operation are included with the function of outputting numbers in the interval $[0, 1]$ that represents a portion of input information let through.

Let $\mathbf{x} = \{\mathbf{x}_1, \mathbf{x}_2, \ldots, \mathbf{x}_t, \ldots\}$ denote a sequence of input vector, where $\mathbf{x}_t \in \mathbb{R}^m$ represents an m-dimensional vector of readings for m variables at time-instance t. The flow of information in a LSTM cell can be described as following. Given the new information $\mathbf{x}_t$ in state t, firstly, the amount of information from earlier cell state, say h_{t-1}, is controlled in the forget gate by outputing a number within $[0, 1]$:

$$f_t = \sigma_1(\mathbf{W}_f.[h_{t-1}, \mathbf{x}_t] + \mathbf{b}_f), \tag{1}$$

where $\mathbf{W}_f$ and $\mathbf{b}_f$ are the weight matrices and the bias of the forget gate. The value 0 means that all the former information is ignored while the value 1 is for the case of remaining all the information. Then, the input gate determines the amount of new information that can flow into the cell. In this gate, the value i_t and a vector of candidate $\tilde{C}_t$ are generated using a sigmoid function and a tanh layer at the same time. In particular,

$$
\begin{aligned}
i_t &= \sigma_2(\mathbf{W}_i.[h_{t-1}, \mathbf{x}_t] + \mathbf{b}_i), \text{and} & (2)\\
\tilde{C}_t &= tanh(\mathbf{W}_c[h_{t-1}, \mathbf{x}_t] + \mathbf{b}_c, & (3)
\end{aligned}
$$

where $(\mathbf{W}_i, \mathbf{b}_i)$ and $(\mathbf{W}_c, \mathbf{b}_c)$ are the weight matrices and the biases of input gate and memory cell state, respectively. The cell state is updated from these values and the ouput of the forget gate as

$$C_t = f_t * C_{t-1} + i_t * \tilde{C}_t. \tag{4}$$

Finally, the output of current LSTM cell and the new hidden state to the next cell are determined in the output gate as

$$
\begin{aligned}
o_t &= \sigma_3(\mathbf{W}_o.[h_{t-1}, \mathbf{x}_t] + \mathbf{b}_o), & (5)\\
h_t &= o_t * tanh(C_t). & (6)
\end{aligned}
$$

where $\mathbf{W}_o$ and $\mathbf{b}_o$ are the weight matrix and the bias of output gate, determining a part of the cell state being outputed. More detail about advances in the LSTM cell, the structures of LSTM network, and its variant can be seen in [55].

Like in other deep learning methods, it is very important in the use of LSTM to have a suitable optimization algorithm adjusting its hyperparameters. While the model parameters are learned from data during the training process, the model hyperparameters are the set of values that can only be tuned manually. An optimal set of hyperparameters can affect the model performance from 5% to 20% [56]. The methods for optimizing hyperparameters can be classified by manual search methods and automatic search methods. The first kind is sometimes called the trial-and-error-based method, and it depends strongly on the intuition and experience of users. The way to pick up the hyperparameters by this method is normal, not reproducible for different situations. Moreover, there is nothing to be sure that the method can lead to optimal sets of hyperparameters, especially when working with high dimensional data. The second type of method, like the grid search method and the random search method, is then introduced to overcome the problem. The grid search method considers a large number of possible combinations of hyperparameters on the training set to output the one that gives the best performance. It can be computationally expensive when the number of hyperparameters and their corresponding search space is large. Meanwhile, the random search method is based on a principle that there are only a few values possible to be optimal for most data sets [57]. Then it randomly tries combinations of a certain range of possible values. The authors of [58] showed that the random search is more efficient than the grid search, however, it is unreliable in some complex models. In the sequel, we will present an optimization algorithm, namely Bayesian optimization (BO), to overcome the disadvantages of these methods.

4.2 Bayesian Optimization

Relying on the Bayes theorem to search for the maximum or the minimum, BO is an effective tool to optimize an unknown function. Compared to other population-based optimization algorithms, the iterations in BO have been reduced significantly, leading to the capability of quickly finding the optimal values without wasting resources. It has been shown that the BO technique can be effective even in case the optimized function is stochastic, non-convex, or even noncontinuous. In some situations, the BO even outperforms other global optimization algorithms [59]. These features make the BO a critical technique in machine learning and deep learning, and a widely used method in several studies.

In the process of tuning hyperparameters, the objective function, say $f(\mathbf{x})$, serves as an evaluator of hyperparameter combinations by taking in a set of hyperparameters and outputting a score that indicates how well it performs on the validation set. In practice, it is hard to find

$$\mathbf{x}^* = \arg\max_{\mathbf{x} \in \mathcal{A}} f(\mathbf{x})$$

where $\mathcal{A}$ is the space of all possible hyperparameters since $f(\mathbf{x})$ is normally a black-box. The BO techniques deal with the problem by using a surrogate function, the one that is considered as an approximation of the objective function. It is a probabilistic function, built by applying a probabilistic regression model. Its function is to map a set hyperparameters $\mathbf{x}$ to a probability

Table 2: Bayesian Optimization algorithm.

Algorithm: Bayesian Optimization
Input: $f, \mathcal{A}, \mathcal{S}, \mathcal{G}$
Initial sample $\mathcal{D} = \{\mathbf{x}_i, y_i\}_{i=1}^{n}$ $(f, \mathcal{A})$
for $i \leftarrow |\mathcal{D}|$ **to** t **do**
- Build the surrogate model: $p(y|\mathbf{x}, \mathcal{A}) \leftarrow (\mathcal{G}, \mathcal{A})$
- Optimize the acquisition function $\mathcal{S}$ to find $\mathbf{x}_{n+1}$:
$\mathbf{x}_{n+1}$ $\arg\max_{x \in \mathcal{A}} \mathcal{S}(\mathbf{x}, p(y|\mathbf{x}, \mathcal{A}))$
- Sample the objective function: y_{n+1} $f(\mathbf{x}_{n+1})$
- Augment the data: $\mathcal{D}$ $\mathcal{D} \cup (\mathbf{x}_{n+1}, y_{n+1})$
end for

of a score on the objective function, represented by $p(y|\mathbf{x})$. The core principle of the BO method is that it continuously updates the surrogate function (the prior) by combining it with sample information (observed data from the objective function). The updated surrogate function (the posterior) is then optimized according to a criterion. That is to say, BO searches for the optimal set of hyperparameters of the surrogate function by applying a specific criterion rather than optimizing directly the objective function. The criterion applied to the surrogate is defined by an acquisition function (or selection function named by different authors). This is a function used to determine the next set of hyperparameters chosen from the surrogate function. The main steps of the BO algorithm are displayed in Table 2. In this table, $\mathcal{G}$ stands for the probabilistic regression model to build the surrogate function, $\mathcal{S}$ stands for the acquisition function, and a limit t stands for a total number of function evaluations due to a quota on the total resources available. One should consider that in the literature the BO methods are differentiated from the use of different surrogate functions and acquisition functions. The most common choice for them is applying a Gaussian process for the surrogate function and the expected improvement for the acquisition function. More discussion on the possible choices of these two functions can be seen in [60;61;62].

5   Decision Support System for Remaining Useful Life Prediction using LSTM with Bayesian Optimization

In this section, we present an example of an LSTM - BO-based DSS which aims to predict the RUL. We consider the case where the input to LSTM is of the multivariate time series, which is quite popular in practice.

Let $\mathbf{x}_t$ be a multivariate time series with k variables at the time t. That is, $\mathbf{x}_t$ can be expressed as $\mathbf{x}_t = \{x_t^{(1)}, x_t^{(2)}, ..., x_t^{(k)}\}, t = 1, 2, \ldots$. In PdM, $\mathbf{x}_t$ represents the behavior of machines and components at the time t. This kind of data is collected continuously through the manufacturing process and updated to the datasets to be analyzed. The planning to perform maintenance or even deciding to perform maintenance immediately will be made based on analyzing these data. In our case, the data is analyzed using the LSTM - BO and the output is an estimate of the RUL of the machines that help managers to plan to carry out the maintenance.

Suppose that a sequence of N observations $\{\mathbf{x}_1, \mathbf{x}_2, \ldots, \mathbf{x}_N\}$ is used to train the LSTM. Similar to [63], each observation $x_t^{(i)}$ is scaled before being fed to LSTM using the the MinMaxScaler function. We also establish a sliding window of size m, where $m < N$ is chosen based on the nature of data, i.e., it could be considered as a parameter in the use of LSTM. The next value of the characteristic of interest, say $x_*^{(j)}$ where j is a number from 1 to k, is predicted based on the sequence of m observations in each window. Let e_i denote the distance from the true observation $x_i^{(j)}$ to the predicted value $\hat{x}_i^{(j)}$, i.e., $e_i = \|\hat{x}_i^{(j)} - x_i^{(j)}\|$. The parameters of the LSTM network is trained to minimize the loss function $L = \sum_{i=m+1}^{N} e_i$.

In the training process, one should be considered that the LSTM can only learn its parameters. Its hyperparameters, including the learning rate, the number of cells, and the dropout will be tuned automatically using the BO. That is, these hyperparameters are selected as the optimization objects of the Bayesian optimizer. The choice of other parameters like the size of the sliding window is discussed in detail in [63]. The performance of the network is evaluated relying on the loss metric RSME (root mean square error):

$$RMSE = \sqrt{\frac{1}{N-m-1} \sum_{i=m+1}^{N} (\hat{x}_i^{(j)} - x_i^{(j)})^2}. \tag{7}$$

After training, the LSTM network with optimal hyperparameters is used for estimating RUL. The predicted values for RUL of machines and components in the system of study will be the output of the DSS.

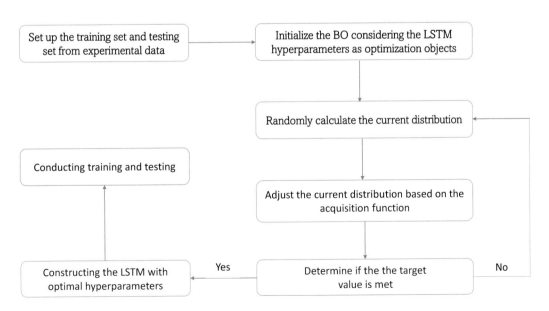

Figure 3: The flow of the LSTM with BO algorithm.

6   A Case Study

In this section, we illustrate the performance of an LSTM-BO based DSS for predicting RUL using the C-MAPSS (Commercial Modular AeroPropulsion System Simulation) datasets. The datasets C-MAPSS are widely used in the study of remaining useful life predictions. For example, several recent deep learning approaches proposed for RUL predictions on the C-MAPSS dataset can be seen in[40]. These are simulated datasets modeling turbofan engine degradation produced and provided by NASA. There are four datasets in C-MAPSS, ranging from FD001 to FD004. More detail in these datasets is presented in[64]. In this study, we utilize only the FD001 dataset to show the effectiveness of the LSTM-BO. Predicting RUL based on this data set is considered to be a challenging task due to not only the inconsistency of the length of condition monitoring data from one engine to another but also its contamination with sensor noises[65].

The C-MAPSS FD001 dataset is divided into two sets, the training set, and the test set. In the training set, the stream data of run-to-failure condition monitoring data for 100 engines of the same type have been included. Meanwhile, the testing set consists of the same type of data of engines that ends sometime before failures appear. Details of the dataset are reproduced in Table 3.

Table 3: The C-MAPSS FD001 dataset.

FD001	Training set	Test set
Number of engines	100	100
Number of data	20631	13096
Minimum running cycle	128	31
Maximum running cycle	362	303
Mean running cycle	206.31	130.96

In the literature, the problem of using the FD001 dataset to demonstrate the efficiency of LSTM in predicting RUL has been conducted in[63] where the authors applied the Grid search to tune the hyperparameters of LSTM. The grid search method could be effective for some situations but not all as the number of models to train exponentially grows when the size of the grid increases. That is to say, the method is inefficient both in saving time and computing power. We overcome this downside by suggesting using the BO for tuning the hyperparameters of LSTM.

The study is conducted as follows. Firstly, the LSTM has been trained based on the data from the training set. The number of cells, dropouts, and the learning rate of the model are optimized by using BO. The obtained results show that using BO leads to the same optimal hyperparameters of LSTM as the Grid search method, but the optimization time is much faster. Using the same platform (i.e., 2.6 GHz Intel(R) Core(TM) i7 and 32GB of RAM as in[63]), the LSTM training process took about 5 hours with the grid search method, but only about half an hour with BO. This time difference is significant when monitoring real-time the status of machines is increasingly becoming important in modern industrial manufacturing. The optimal hyperparameters of the model for this dataset which have been stated in[63] are reproduced in Table 4.

Table 4: The optimal hyperparameters of LSTM for FD001 dataset.

#Best parameters:		
num_cells=50		
dropout_rate=0.1		
lr=0.01		
Layer (type)	Output Shape	Param #
lstm_1 (LSTM)	(None, 30, 50)	13600
dropout_1 (Dropout)	(None, 30, 50)	0
lstm_2 (LSTM)	(None, 50)	20200
dropout_2 (Dropout)	(None, 50)	0
dense_1 (Dense)	(None, 1)	51
activation_1 (Activation)	(None, 1)	0
Total params: 33851		
Trainable params: 33851		
Non-trainable params: 0		

After being trained, the LSTM with optimal hyperparameters is used to predict the RUL of testing engines. As the optimal hyperparameters of LSTM-BO are the same as ones of LSTM with the Grid search method, the performance of the LSTM-BO is also the same. The RSME metric corresponding to LSTM (which is 9.71) is smallest compared to the ones corresponding to other methods in the literature (for example, 12.56 of the RBM-LSTM-FNN method[39], 12.61 of the MTW-BLSTM ensemble method[65], and 15.8 of the LSTM- FW-CatBoost method[66]).

Along with using the regression method for RUL prediction, in this case of study, we also consider the problem of binary classification, i.e., evaluating if a specific machine is going to fail within an anticipated period. In particular, we set up an experiment to predict if the RUL of a machine is greater than 30 cycles or not. Table 5 shows the performance of the proposed LSTM-BO method. It can be seen from the table that the LSTM-BO can bring very high efficiency in estimating the time a machine could fail within a particular time. That means the proposed method has a superior performance both in predicting the RUL and predicting if a machine will fail within a certain time frame.

Table 5: The performance of LSTM - BO for binary classifying with FD001.

Accuracy	Precision	Recall	F1-score
0.971429	0.925926	1.0	0.961538

7 Conclusion and Perspectives

Maintenance plays a very vital role throughout the lifetime of a system and PdM is a very effective way to perform the maintenance mission. The primary goal of PdM is to predict and prevent the failure of equipment before it occurs. In this chapter, we have proposed ML based method to build a DSS using the LSTM with a Bayesian optimization algorithm for predicting RUL. The effectiveness of the proposed method is presented through a case study using a well-known dataset. Our proposed method of using LSTM combined with a BO can reduce training time by more than 10 times but keep the same performance. This makes the DSS more efficient, especially for monitoring systems in real-time.

Several perspectives can be drawn from this study. Firstly, the need to apply advanced ML algorithms in designing a DSS for PdM is indisputable. Among the ML algorithms, the artificial neural networks (ANN) have been very promising methods (our proposed LSTM with BO method in this study also belongs to ANN). Although many studies have been carried out in the literature, leading to the introduction of a large number of ANN-based methods for PdM, there is still a drawback to the existing methods. ANN is sometimes considered as a "black box" since it cannot be explained why the ANN arrived at a specific decision even by the designers. From this point of view, the use of Explainable Machine Learning (XML) could be an alternative solution. Explainable Neural Networks (XNN) refers to methods and techniques in the application of ANN such that the results of the solution can be understood by humans. It is designed to provide explainable insights into the model by eliminating the black-box nature of traditional ANN-based methods. Secondly, many published studies are based on an assumption that the components in a multi-component system are independent. This is not always the case, especially in modern industry and smart manufacturing, since the machines in a production line work in a common environment and share the same stress. Therefore, considering the correlations and investigating the impact of interactions between components could be a novel tendency that makes the DSS for PdM more practical as it reduces significantly the gap between the theory and application of maintenance strategies. Finally, the system structure and the availability of systems have in the past been ignored in the data-driven methods for PdM. The structural function of a system shows the relationship between the state of the system and the state of the components and provides more information about the system while the availability of a system is typically calculated as a function of its reliability, maintainability, and its redundancy. Therefore, these two crucial problems should be considered in the design of a DSS for PdM to be sure of the effectiveness and accuracy of the DSS.

References

[1] M. Bevilacqua and M. Braglia. The analytic hierarchy process applied to maintenance strategy selection. *Reliability Engineering & System Safety*, 70(1): 71–83, 2000.

[2] J. Dalzochio, R. Kunst, E. Pignaton, A. Binotto, S. Sanyal, J. Favilla and J. Barbosa. Machine learning and reasoning for predictive maintenance in industry 4.0: Current status and challenges. *Computers in Industry*, 123(10329): 8, 2020.

[3] L. Romeo, J. Loncarski, M. Paolanti, G. Bocchini, A. Mancini and E. Frontoni. Machine learning-based design support system for the prediction of heterogeneous machine parameters in industry 4.0. *Expert Systems with Applications*, 140(11286): 9, 2020.

[4] N. Antonio, A. de Almeida and L. Nunes. An automated machine learning based decision support system to predict hotel booking cancellations. *An Automated Machine Learning Based Decision Support System to Predict Hotel Booking Cancellations*, 1: 1–20, 2019.

[5] H.M. Zolbanin, D. Delen, D. Crosby and D. Wright. A predictive analytics-based decision support system for drug courts. *Information Systems Frontiers*, pp. 1–20, 2019.

[6] D. Prasad and S. Ratna. Decision support systems in the metal casting industry: An academic review of research articles. *Materials Today: Proceedings*, 5(1): 1298–1312, 2018.

[7] C.J. Turner, C. Emmanouilidis, T. Tomiyama, A. Tiwari and R. Roy. Intelligent decision support for maintenance: an overview and future trends. *International Journal of Computer Integrated Manufacturing*, 32(10): 936–959, 2019.

[8] A. Karmarkar and N. Gilke. Fuzzy logic based decision support systems in variant production. *Materials Today: Proceedings*, 5(2): 3842–3850, 2018.

[9] T. Zonta, C.A. da Costa, R. da Rosa Righi, M.J. de Lima, E.S. da Trindade and G.P. Li. Predictive maintenance in the industry 4.0: A systematic literature review. *Computers & Industrial Engineering*, 1068, 2020.

[10] D. Wu, C. Jennings, J. Terpenny, S. Kumara and R.X. Gao. Cloud-based parallel machine learning for tool wear prediction. *Journal of Manufacturing Science and Engineering*, 140: 4, 2018.

[11] D. Wu, C. Jennings, J. Terpenny and S. Kumara. Cloud-based machine learning for predictive analytics: Tool wear prediction in milling. In *2016 IEEE International Conference on Big Data (Big Data)*, pp. 2062–2069. IEEE, 2016.

[12] S. Sajid, A. Haleem, S. Bahl, M. Javaid, T. Goyal and M. Mittal. Data science applications for predictive maintenance and materials science in context to industry 4.0. *Proceedings, Materials Today*, 2021.

[13] M. Pech, J. Vrchota and J. Bednář. Predictive maintenance and intelligent sensors in smart factory. *Sensors*, 21: 4, 2021.

[14] T.P. Carvalho, F.A. Soares, R. Vita, P. Francisco, J.P. Basto and S.G. Alcala. A systematic literature review of machine learning methods applied to predictive maintenance. *Computers & Industrial Engineering*, 137: 106024, 2019.

[15] X.-S. Si, W. Wang, C.-H. Hu and D.-H. Zhou. Remaining useful life estimation—A review on the statistical data driven approaches. *European Journal of Operational Research*, 213(1): 1–14, 2011.

[16] N.Z. Gebraeel, M.A. Lawley, R. Li and J.K. Ryan. Residual-life distributions from component degradation signals: A bayesian approach. *IEEE Transactions*, 37(6): 543–557, 2005.

[17] N. Li, Y. Lei, J. Lin and S.X. Ding. An improved exponential model for predicting remaining useful life of rolling element bearings. *IEEE Transactions on Industrial Electronics*, 62(12): 7762–7773, 2015.

[18] Y. Lei, N. Li, L. Guo, N. Li, T. Yan and J. Lin. Machinery health prognostics: A systematic review from data acquisition to rul prediction. *Mechanical Systems and Signal Processing*, 104: 799–834, 2018.

[19] J. Liu, W. Wang, F. Ma, Y. Yang and C. Yang. A data-model-fusion prognostic framework for dynamic system state forecasting. *Engineering Applications of Artificial Intelligence*, 25(4): 814–823, 2012.

[20] H. Dui, S. Si, M.J. Zuo and S. Sun. Semi-markov process-based integrated importance measure for multi-state systems. *IEEE Transactions on Reliability*, 64(2): 754–765, 2015.

[21] L. Cui, Y. Xu and X. Zhao. Developments and applications of the finite markov chain imbedding approach in reliability. *IEEE Transactions on Reliability*, 59(4): 685–690, 2010.

[22] X.-S. Si, W. Wang, C.-H. Hu, D.-H. Zhou and M.G. Pecht. Remaining useful life estimation based on a nonlinear diffusion degradation process. *IEEE Transactions on Reliability*, 61(1): 50–67, 2012.

[23] X.-S. Si, W. Wang, M.-Y. Chen, C.-H. Hu and D.-H. Zhou. A degradation path-dependent approach for remaining useful life estimation with an exact and closed-form solution. *European Journal of Operational Research*, 226(1): 53–66, 2013.

[24] J. Yu. Health degradation detection and monitoring of lithium-ion battery based on adaptive learning method. *IEEE Transactions on Instrumentation and Measurement*, 63(7): 1709–1721, 2013.

[25] A.J. Yu. Nonlinear probabilistic method and contribution analysis for machine condition monitoring. *Mechanical Systems and Signal Processing*, 37(1-2): 293–314, 2013.

[26] Y. Lei, N. Li, S. Gontarz, J. Lin, S. Radkowski and J. Dybala. A model-based method for remaining useful life prediction of machinery. *IEEE Transactions on Reliability*, 65(3): 1314–1326, 2016.

[27] K. Javed, R. Gouriveau and N. Zerhouni. State of the art and taxonomy of prognostics approaches, trends of prognostics applications and open issues towards maturity at different technology readiness levels. *Mechanical Systems and Signal Processing*, 94: 214–236, 2017.

[28] O.E. Yurek and D. Birant. Remaining useful life estimation for predictive maintenance using feature engineering. In *2019 Innovations in Intelligent Systems and Applications Conference (ASYU)*, pp. 1–5. IEEE, 2019.

[29] M. Alberto-Olivares, A. Gonzalez-Gutierrez, S. Tovar-Arriaga and E. Gorrostieta-Hurtado. Remaining useful life prediction for turbofan based on a multilayer perceptron and kalman filter. In *2019 16th International Conference on Electrical Engineering, Computing Science and Automatic Control (CCE)*, pp. 1–6. IEEE, 2019.

[30] P.G. Nieto, E. García-Gonzalo, F.S. Lasheras and F.J. de Cos Juez. Hybrid pso–svmbased method for forecasting of the remaining useful life for aircraft engines and evaluation of its reliability. *Reliability Engineering & System Safety*, 138: 219–231, 2015.

[31] X. Li, Q. Ding and J.-Q. Sun. Remaining useful life estimation in prognostics using deep convolution neural networks. *Reliability Engineering & System Safety*, 172: 1–11, 2018.

[32] M. Savargaonkar, A. Chehade, Z. Shi and A.A. Hussein. A cycle-based recurrent neural network for state-of-charge estimation of li-ion battery cells. In *2020 IEEE Transportation Electrification Conference & Expo (ITEC)*, pp. 584–587. IEEE, 2020.

[33] M. Savargaonkar and A. Chehade. An adaptive deep neural network with transfer learning for state-of-charge estimations of battery cells. In *2020 IEEE Transportation Electrification Conference & Expo (ITEC)*, pp. 598–602. IEEE, 2020.

[34] Y.-C. Huang and Y.-H. Chen. Use of long short-term memory for remaining useful life and degradation assessment prediction of dental air turbine handpiece in milling process. *Sensors*, 21: 15, 2021.

[35] Y. Wu, M. Yuan, S. Dong, L. Lin and Y. Liu. Remaining useful life estimation of engineered systems using vanilla lstm neural networks. *Neurocomputing*, 275: 167–179, 2018.

[36] A. Elsheikh, S. Yacout and M.-S. Ouali. Bidirectional handshaking lstm for remaining useful life prediction. *Neurocomputing*, 323: 148–156, 2019.

[37] H. Miao, B. Li, C. Sun and J. Liu. Joint learning of degradation assessment and rul prediction for aeroengines via dual-task deep lstm networks. *IEEE Transactions on Industrial Informatics*, 15(9): 5023–5032, 2019.

[38] Z. Shi and A. Chehade. A dual-lstm framework combining change point detection and remaining useful life prediction. *Reliability Engineering & System Safety*, 205(10725): 7, 2021.

[39] A.L. Ellefsen, E. Bjørlykhaug, V. æsøy, s. Ushakov and H. Zhang. Remaining useful life predictions for turbofan engine degradation using semi-supervised deep architecture, 183: 240–251, 2019.

[40] T. Wang, D. Guo and X.-M. Sun. Remaining useful life predictions for turbofan engine degradation based on concurrent semi-supervised model. *Neural Computing and Applications*, pp. 1–10, 2021.

[41] A.K. Jardine, D. Lin and D. Banjevic. A review on machinery diagnostics and prognostics implementing condition-based maintenance. *Mechanical Systems and Signal Processing*, 20(7): 1483–1510, 2006.

[42] A. Heng, S. Zhang, A.C. Tan and J. Mathew. Rotating machinery prognostics: State of the art, challenges and opportunities. *Mechanical Systems and Signal Processing*, 23(3): 724–739, 2009.

[43] J. Sikorska, M. Hodkiewicz and L. Ma. Prognostic modelling options for remaining useful life estimation by industry. *Mechanical Systems and Signal Processing*, 25(5): 1803–1836, 2011.

[44] J. Lee, F. Wu, W. Zhao, M. Ghaffari, L. Liao and D. Siegel. Prognostics and health management design for rotary machinery systems reviews, methodology and applications. *Mechanical Systems and Signal Processing*, 42(1-2): 314–334, 2014.

[45] L. Wu, X. Fu and Y. Guan. Review of the remaining useful life prognostics of vehicle lithium-ion batteries using data-driven methodologies. *Applied Sciences*, 6: 6, 2016.

[46] C. Su and H.J. Chen. A review on prognostics approaches for remaining useful life of lithium-ion battery. In *IOP Conference Series: Earth and Environmental Science*, volume 93, page 012040. IOP Publishing, 2017.

[47] Y. Hu, S. Liu, H. Lu and H. Zhang. Remaining useful life model and assessment of mechanical products: A brief review and a note on the state space model method. *Chinese Journal of Mechanical Engineering*, 32(1): 1–20, 2019.

[48] Y. Wang, Y. Zhao and S. Addepalli. Remaining useful life prediction using deep learning approaches: A review. *Procedia Manufacturing*, 49: 81–88, 2020.

[49] E. Florian, F. Sgarbossa and I. Zennaro. Machine learning-based predictive maintenance: A cost-oriented model for implementation. *International Journal of Production Economics*, 1081, 2021.

[50] K. Gandhi, B. Schmidt and A.H. Ng. Towards data mining based decision support in manufacturing maintenance. *Procedia Cirp*, 72: 261–265, 2018.

[51] G.A. Susto, J. Wan, S. Pampuri, M. Zanon, A.B. Johnston, P.G. O'Hara and S. McLoone. An adaptive machine learning decision system for flexible predictive maintenance. In *2014 IEEE International Conference on Automation Science and Engineering (CASE)*, pp. 806–811. IEEE, 2014.

[52] S. Wu, N. Gebraeel, M.A. Lawley and Y. Yih. A neural network integrated decision support system for condition-based optimal predictive maintenance policy. *IEEE Transactions on Systems, Man, and Cybernetics-Part A: Systems and Humans*, 37(2): 226–236, 2007.

[53] S. Zhai, B. Gehring and G. Reinhart. Enabling predictive maintenance integrated production scheduling by operation-specific health prognostics with generative deep learning. *Journal of Manufacturing Systems*, 2021.

[54] Hochreiter, Sepp and Schmidhuber, Jürgen. Long short-term memory. *Neural Computation*, 9(8): 1735–1780, 1997.

[55] Y. Yu, X. Si, C. Hu and J. Zhang. A review of recurrent neural networks: Lstm cells and network architectures. *Neural Computation*, 31(7): 1235–1270, 2019.

[56] M. Jun and J.C. Cheng. Selection of target leed credits based on project information and climatic factors using data mining techniques. *Advanced Engineering Informatics*, 32: 224–236, 2017.

[57] J. Bergstra and Y. Bengio. Random search for hyper-parameter optimization. *Journal of Machine Learning Research*, 13: 2, 2012.

[58] J. Bergstra, R. Bardenet, Y. Bengio and B. Kégl. Algorithms for hyper-parameter optimization. *Advances in Neural Information Processing Systems*, 24, 2011.

[59] D.R. Jones. A taxonomy of global optimization methods based on response surfaces. *Journal of Global Optimization*, 21(4): 345–383, 2001.

[60] J. Wu, X.-Y. Chen, H. Zhang, L.-D. Xiong, H. Lei and S.-H. Deng. Hyperparameter optimization for machine learning models based on bayesian optimization. *Journal of Electronic Science and Technology*, 17(1): 26–40, 2019.

[61] B. Alizadeh, A.G. Bafti, H. Kamangir, Y. Zhang, D.B. Wright and K.J. Franz. A novel attention-based lstm cell post-processor coupled with bayesian optimization for streamflow prediction. *Journal of Hydrology*, 601(12652): 6, 2021.

[62] M. Feurer and F. Hutter. Hyperparameter optimization. In *Automated Machine Learning*, pp. 3–33. Springer, Cham, 2019.

[63] H. Nguyen, K.P. Tran, S. Thomassey and M. Hamad. Forecasting and anomaly detection approaches using lstm and lstm autoencoder techniques with the applications in supply chain management. *International Journal of Information Management*, 57(10228): 2, 2021.

[64] A. Saxena and K. Goebel. Turbofan engine degradation simulation data set. *NASA Ames Prognostics Data Repository*, pp. 878–887, 2008.

[65] T. Xia, Y. Song, Y. Zheng, E. Pan and L. Xi. An ensemble framework based on convolutional bi-directional lstm with multiple time windows for remaining useful life estimation. *Computers in Industry*, 115(10318): 2, 2020.

[66] K. Deng, X. Zhang, Y. Cheng, Z. Zheng, F. Jiang, W. Liu and J. Peng. A remaining useful life prediction method with long-short term feature processing for aircraft engines. *Applied Soft Computing*, 1063, 2020.

Chapter 6

Decision Support Systems for Textile Manufacturing Process with Machine Learning

Zaohao Lu,[1] Zhenglei He,[1,2,*] Kim Phuc Tran,[2] Sebastien Thomassey,[2] Xianyi Zeng[2] and Mengna Hong[1]

1 Introduction

With the globally increasing competition in the textile industry, manufacturers are forced to promote the quality, efficiency, and environmental impact simultaneously. These issues refer to dynamically optimizing multiple objective conflicts with multiple conflict constrains and multiple scales, which is a big challenge for the textile manufacturing decision-makers. Due to the intricate interrelationship of a large number of variables from a wide range of textile processes, traditional techniques can hardly deal with the potential complexity. Thus, innovative methods are demanded to tackle these issues.

In the background of Industry 4.0, manufacturing processes are expected to be more intelligent with quick reactivity to the market and adaptation to the big data environment. In this situation, intelligent techniques are regarded as the key techniques simulating human reasoning and perception, permitting to model and analyze with various data, and then leading to smart and fast utilization of IoT (Internet of Things) and cloud computations, as well as data-driven product and market prediction and online traceability. Especially, intelligent techniques in the big data environment will enable to get through the information channel of the whole supply chain from very initial production stages to finished products. Concretely, intelligent manufacturing techniques have been developed to meet variously personalized requirements of customers, deal with quickly and continuously arriving data generated from multiple connected devices, connected materials and connected operators. In general, intelligent manufacturing could be a promising direction to solve the aforementioned problems encountered in textile manufacturing.

Currently, along with the progress of innovative digital technologies, such as Big Data, virtual reality, cloud computing and Internet of Things (IoT), the intelligent manufacturing systems

---

[1] South China University of Technology, China.

[2] Univ. Lille, ENSAIT, ULR 2461 - GEMTEX - Génie et Matériaux Textiles, F-59000 Lille, France.

* Corresponding author: zhenglei.he@ensait.fr

is progressively developed in the textile industry its. In order to meet various personalized requirements of customers and deal with quickly and continuously arriving data generated from multiple connected devices, connected materials and connected operators in the era of Industry 4.0, textile manufacturing needs to be updated to an intelligent level to achieve flexible, smart and reconfigurable manufacturing processes to overcome aforementioned diverse challenges[1]. Certain underpinning technologies with learning capacity from past experiences are needed in this regard. And machine learning techniques, enabling manufacturing systems to efficiently learn from experiences through data, are advantageous to deal with the complexity in the textile manufacturing process with regard to uncertainty and imprecision related to human knowledge on products and processes, thereby allowing problems to be solved and adaptively cooperate with the production optimization in a timely fashion[2].

Machine learning techniques are playing increasingly vital roles in industry development. They have attracted significant attention from both industry and academia. Many successful applications of machine learning techniques for modeling, optimization and decision support of industrial processes have been reported. These techniques are known as efficient data mining tools and can overcome the aforementioned complex problems encountered in the textile industrial processes. The construction of process models and the development of a decision support system upon virtual process models to optimize the textile process solutions remains an open challenge[3].

This chapter aims to inform theory and practice on the modeling and model-based decision support system of the textile manufacturing process through machine learning techniques to enable the manufacturing enterprises to optimize the textile process with trade-off solutions between several conflicting objectives, to be competent to provide collaborative, customizable, flexible and reconfigurable services to end-users. The literature review shows that the modeling and decision-making issues of the textile manufacturing process have been investigated in many subfields. However, in terms of the models, prior investigations either simplify the case by omitting certain non-essential details to achieve manageable equations on the basis of scarification on the accuracy or require prior experts' knowledge and human intervention. More importantly, in terms of the traditional approaches, they can hardly approach the high dimensional computation when the decision-making of the textile manufacturing process is increasingly taking multiple objectives into account. Therefore, dependent on the machine learning techniques, a model-based decision support system was constructed using artificial neural networks (ANN) and reinforcement learning (RL) algorithm, with the collaboration of AHP. It is organized as follows: Section 2 consists of a comprehensive review of the related research. Section 3 presents the problem formulation of decision-making in the textile manufacturing process with a specific case, and Section 4 illustrated the mathematical representation of the problem in the system model. Section 5 shows the application results. Finally, conclusions and future works are discussed in Section 6.

2 Relevant Literatures

In terms of the high degree of variability in materials, processes and parameters as well as the lack of precise control in practice, the textile manufacturers can barely conduct trial and error, and lean on the expertise and experience[4]. There is a strong need to map the intricate relationships between various textile process parameters and performance properties, therefore to assist the decision-makers to find the optimal solutions for the process. The research in process engineering enables it to incorporate more and more specificities of the industrial processes and then become increasingly practical and capable of improving the flexibility of the production operations and productivity. Although process engineering already deals with various generalized practical problems, it is still necessary to consider special ones on the running and cooperation of the textile manufacturing processes.

The next generation of industry, as known as Industry 4.0, holds the promise of increased flexibility in manufacturing, along with mass customization, better quality, and improved productivity. Therefore, it enables the manufacturers to cope with the challenges of producing increasingly individualized products with a shorter manufacturing cycle and higher quality[2]. An intelligent process is one of the basic elements in such a smart manufacturing environment. In order to globally improve the process for the development of an intelligent manufacturing system, it is necessary to properly address the uncertainties and imprecision among process variables in terms of the complex and non-linear relationship between the input process parameters and output performance parameters.

2.1 Intelligent Techniques used for Textile Process Modeling

The model is a simplistic representation of the real phenomenon. It is often used to simulate the performance of a process or a product with various manufacturing solutions, thus the trial and error involved in process design and solution optimization can be eliminated to a certain extent. The analytical models or mathematical models are usually based on certain idealized assumptions, so their applicability is largely governed by the viability of these assumptions[5;6]. Due to the increasing complexity in the development of intelligent textile manufacturing, none of the physical or chemical laws will be available that can figure out the picture of a process taking all the factors into consideration. The application of the textile manufacturing process nowadays incorporates a wide range of variables from the performance assessment and the corresponding effects from the process parameters are unclear, where the practical features cannot be fully reflected by the classical models, and the introduction of data-based intelligent models becomes a necessity.

The process modeling using intelligent techniques has been conducted in many areas, and the applied techniques comprise an artificial neural network (ANN), Fuzzy logic, support vector machine (SVM), gene expression programming (GEP), etc.

2.1.1 Artificial Neural Networks

ANN is a widely investigated artificial intelligence approach in the textile sector[7]. The research of ANN for textile process modeling is very popular, which could be attributed to its excellent capacity to map the extremely nonlinear relationship among the factors and performances of the process. It is developed based on the inspiration of the human brain that interconnects numerous neurons in different hidden layers to process the complex information of a specific input-output relation[8]. A typical structure of ANN is illustrated in Figure 1.

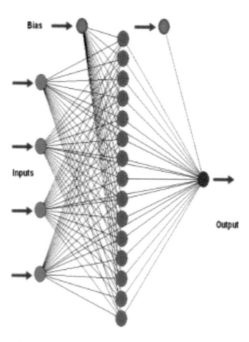

Figure 1: An example of artificial neural network architecture.

2.1.2   Fuzzy Logic

As there are a variety of textile properties that rely on subjective evaluation, and human knowledge may help the interpretation of textile variables and their relationships in certain cases, especially when the data is limited, Fuzzy logic is also very popularly applied in this topic. Fuzzy logic was developed by Prof. Lotfi A. Zadeh in 1965 as an extension of crisp logic[9]. It is built on the structures of qualitative description in approximation rather than exactness. The variables are 1 and 0 or true and false in binary logic, as an example of crisp logic, while the boundaries are not that clear in Fuzzy logic as there are interference Fuzzy sets which contain intermediate states with partial membership ranging from 0 to 1 to define uncertainty. For instance, when the temperature higher than 40°C indicates "hot", as an input and output variable, there would be intermediate states named in linguistic terms like "quite hot", "warm", and "cool" and so on in a Fuzzy inference system by dividing the universe of discourse into a number of sub-regions, rather than only "not hot" is considered for any temperature ≤ 40°C in classic logic. In general, the Fuzzy inference process formulating the mapping from a given input to an output using Fuzzy logic in terms of four steps, namely fuzzification, interference, rule base, and defuzzification. The interpretation of these operations is approachable in[10]. Fuzzy techniques are usually applied in order to solve the control problem by formulating linguistic rules, but they are also frequently used for modeling, optimization and decision-making support in the textile manufacturing industry. As the data and relations among textile process variables are not crisp in this domain, it is dramatically associated with human subjectivity and qualitative descriptions[11].

2.1.3 Fuzzy Inference System

Aside from the ANN and Fuzzy logic, applications of hybrid models combining their fuzzification technique and the learning capability are also widely accessible in textile researches. This is because the compatibility of these hybrid methods on data and human knowledge can well reveal both the subjective and objective factors in the textile manufacturing process. Fuzzification maps an input value to Fuzzy sets in a certain universe of discourse, thus increasing the separability of classes in the feature space and facilitating the training data fitting in the Neuro-Fuzzy model to be more accurate. Neural network techniques help the Fuzzy modeling procedure learn the information from the data and compute the membership function parameters that best allows the associated Fuzzy inference system (FIS) to track the given input-output data. Taking the adaptive-network-based Fuzzy inference system (ANFIS) as an example, it is a hybrid algorithm that transforms the Fuzzy inference system into a functional equivalent adaptive network. It is able to work under uncertain noisy and simulate complex nonlinear mappings which right fits the advantages of both ANN and Fuzzy logic.

2.1.4 Support Vector Machine

Support Vector Regression (SVR) is the most common application form of support vector machine. A typical feature of it is that instead of minimizing the observed training error, SVR minimizes the generalized error bound so as to achieve generalized performance. And it only relies on a subset of the training data due to the cost function for building the model neglects any training data that is close (within a threshold ε) to the model prediction[12;13]. Compared with neural networks, SVR assures more generalization on the foundation of structural risk minimization, and generally performs better with fewer training samples.

2.1.5 Gene Expression Programming

Gene expression programming (GEP) is the development of genetic algorithm (GA) and genetic programming (GP) proposed by[14]. Authors reported that it is not a black-box and explores the inter-relationship between input and output variable[15], and is better than ANN in terms of precision so that the uses of it can be found in certain related studies as well.

2.2 Decision-making of Textile Manufacturing Process

Textile manufacturing originates from the fibers (e.g., cotton) to final products (such as curtain, garment, and composite) through a very long procedure with a wide range of different processes filled with a large number of variables. There are a few criteria which govern the quality of textile process performance and their significance with an overall objective is different. The simultaneous optimization of multiple targets in a textile production scheme from the high dimensional space is challenging.

2.2.1 Classic Methods

A variety of works have been issued on the decision-making of the textile process from the last decades. For example, Sette and Langenhove[16] simulated and optimized the fiber-to-yarn process to balance the conflicting targets of cost and yarn quality. The authors of[17] made a decision on with criteria of ultraviolet protection factors and air permeability to optimize functional clothing.The authors of[18] attempted to balance the parametric combination of injected slub yarn to achieve the least abrasive damage on produced fabrics. The author of[19] takes into account the performances of weaving process, including tensile strength, breaking extension and air permeability, of the cotton woven fabrics by searching optimal parameters of weft yarn count, weave structure, weft yarn density and twist factor.

These works generally used the prior techniques that combine the multiple objectives into a single weighted cost function, the classical approaches such as weighted sum, goal programming, min-max, etc., are not efficient as they cannot find the multiple solutions in a single run but times as many as the number of desired Pareto-optimal solutions. Pareto optimal solutions or non-dominated solutions are equally important in the search space that superior to all the other solutions when multiple objectives are considered simultaneously, and the curve formed by joining Pareto optimal solutions is the well-known Pareto optimal front[20].

2.2.2 Meta-heuristic Methods

The investigations and applications of the related algorithms and computational complexity theory are very popular in the textile manufacturing industry with regard to the multi-criteria decision-making (MCDM) that is feasible to approach the Pareto optimal solutions. Among these, evolutionary algorithms such as genetic algorithms (GA) and gene expression programming (GEP) are the ones that are most often taken into consideration in previous studies in the textile sector. The authors of[21] schedule the flow-shop of a fabric chemical finishing process aiming at minimal make-span and arresting time of machine simultaneously using multi-objective GA. The author of[22] searched optimal solutions about the processing parameters including solution concentration, applied voltage, spinning distance and volume flow rate, to optimize the electrospinning process performance in terms of fiber diameter and its distribution. The electrospinning process parameters were mapped to the performances by the GEP model, and a MCDM method was proposed based on GA to find the optimal average fiber diameter and its distribution. The authors of[23] proposed a nonlinear integer programming framework on the basis of GA to globally optimized the textile dyeing manufacturing process. The results of their case study presented the applicability and suitability of this methodology in a textile dyeing firm and exactly reflected the complexity and uncertainty of application challenges in the multi-criteria decision-making in the textile industry.

2.2.3 Multi-criteria Meta-heuristic Methods

In terms of multi-criteria, the general GA systems developed in the aforementioned works could be not efficient in certain cases as the elitist individuals could be over-reproduced in many generations and lead to early convergence. To this end,[24] proposed a Non-dominated sorting genetic algorithm II (NSGA-II) that introduced a specialized fitness function and fast non-domination sorting as well as crowding distance sorting in the common GA system to promote diversity of the solution in the generations. the modified strategy has been widely applied in related textile studies. For instance, the authors of[25] optimized the yarn strength and the raw material cost of the cotton spinning process simultaneously with NSGA-II on the basis of two objective function models in terms of artificial neural networks and regression equation. Similarly, the authors of[26] described the combined use of NSGA-II with response surface methodology for the design and control of color fast finish process to optimize five quality characteristics, i.e., shade variation to the standard, color fastness to washing, center to selvedge variation, color fastness to light and fabric residual shrinkage. The authors of[27] derived the Pareto optimal solutions using NSGA-II so as to obtain the effective knitting and yarn parameters to engineer knitted fabrics having optimal comfort properties and desired level of ultraviolet protection. The authors of[28] and[29] employed this algorithm with artificial neural networks and Fuzzy logic respectively to optimize the properties of core-spun yarns in the rotor compact spinning process, where the investigated process parameters consist of the filament pre-tension, yarn count and type of sheath fibers, and the objectives were yarn tenacity, hairiness and abrasion resistance for the former but elongation and hairiness for the latter respectively.

Apart from the GA frameworks, applications reported of other heuristic or meta-heuristic algorithms based decision-making in the textile domain also have been presented with synergetic immune clonal selection (SICS), artificial bee colony (ABC) algorithm, ant colony optimization (ACO), and particle swarm optimization (PSO)[30;31], etc. Meanwhile, desirability function[32], in addition to the heuristic or meta-heuristic algorithms, was often proposed in the textile manufacturing process to support multi-criteria decision-making as well[33;34].

These previous researches mostly were realized by using the heuristic methods. Although the general optimization techniques showed their effectiveness, there still exist some drawbacks to coping with the high dimensional decision space about the increasingly complicated multi-inputs and multi-outputs variables as well as multiple objectives in the textile processes. Commonly used heuristic methods like genetic algorithms are time-consuming so that they can hardly be applied in the context of industrial practice when the number of involved variables becomes very large, along with large change intervals[35].

More importantly, as mentioned that the textile manufacturing industry develops rapidly in recent years, reacts quickly to the market and adapts to the big data environment. A developed textile process decision support system could be invalid when the process or applied scenarios vary in the future. These previous works failed to illustrate the capacities of their system for learning from the continuously arriving data to keep updated with the textile process development in this regard, thus are still far from being implemented in the practical applications. It is necessary to investigate on more innovative intelligent methods in this issue.

Model based decision-making of the textile manufacturing process using intelligent techniques is a salient direction for future research, but it is challenging because of the growing complexity in the textile process. The realistic problems in the textile manufacturing industry normally are always related to multi-criteria, which makes this situation to be more knotty. Upon which, the construction of a model-based decision support system was implemented to solve the research questions using artificial neural networks (ANN) and reinforcement learning (RL) algorithm, with the collaboration of AHP. In specific, ANN was applied to model the textile ozonation process, AHP tackled the multi-criteria decision making (MCDM) by structuring a hierarchy of criteria in terms of weights or priorities, RL formulate the decision process of the textile process as the Markov decision process to search the optimal solutions.

3 Case Study: Decision-making of Denim Ozonation

Color fading is an essential finishing process for denim products, but it conventionally was achieved by chemical methods which have a high cost and water consumption, as well as a heavy burden on the environment. Instead, ozone treatment is an advanced finishing process employing ozone gas to bleach or color fade denim without a water bath and consequently it causes fewer environmental issues. However, the complicated and nonlinear relationship between its parameters and color fading effects is still not clearly known, in other words, a model that can predict the engineering application effect is rather necessary.

ANN is the most frequently used one for predicting the denim color properties in related studies. The implementation of it is relatively more manageable, and its high generalization performance can help us simulate more different solutions in the textile ozonation process model, so that it is worth being taken into account in this case study. As the most frequently used and widely discussed MCDM approach from the recently developed discipline of operation research, it has been proven that AHP is to be an extremely useful decision-making method in the textile industry. This may attribute to its involvement of both objective and subjective factors which agree with the characteristic of the textile manufacturing process. RL is a machine learning approach using a relatively well understood and mathematically grounded framework of MDP that has been broadly applied to tackle the practical decision-making issues in the textile industry. Therefore, this case study presents an ANN-AHP-RL based decision support system for the denim ozonation.

3.1 Problem Formulation

Suggest a textile manufacturing process P involves a set of parameter variables $\{v_1, v_2 \dots v_n\}$, and the performance of this process is evaluated by multi-criteria of $\{c_1, c_2 \dots c_m\}$. Decision making needs to figure out how those parameter variables affect the process performances in terms of each criterion, and whether a solution of P $\{v_{1i}, v_{2j} \dots v_{nk}\}$ is good or not relating to $\{c_1, c_2 \dots c_m\}$.

Suppose there is a model map $v_1, v_2 \dots v_n$ of the process to its performance in accordance with $\{c_1, c_2 \dots c_m\}$, then the performance of the specific solution could be presented by:

$$f_i (v_1, v_2 \cdots v_n) |c_i, for \quad i = 1, \dots m \tag{1}$$

$$f (v_1, v_2 \cdots v_n) |C, \quad v_j \in V_j \tag{2}$$

$$argmax_{vj \in Vj}[f(v_1, v_2 \cdots v_n)|C] \tag{3}$$

When the domain of $v_j \in V_i$ is known, and the multi-criteria $\{c_1, c_2 \ldots c_m\}$ problem could be somehow represented by C, and the Equation (1) could be simplified to (2), and so that the objective of decision-makers is to find (3).

Equation (3) aims at searching for the optimal solution of variable settings, while the traditional operation in this area usually relied heavily on trial and error.

3.2 Methodology

3.2.1 ANN Model

In terms of the model construction, 612 sets of experimental data were used, and 75% of the data was divided into the training group and the rest 25% was used to test models. In order to decrease the bias and promote the generalization of applied ANN models in the system, we have trained 4 separate models for predicting 4 outputs ($k/s, L^*, a^*, and\ b^*$) respectively. The final optimized models are tested (25% with unseen data) that can well predict the process performance with accuracy (R-square) of 0.996, 0.938, 0.937, and 0.985 respectively (Figure 2).

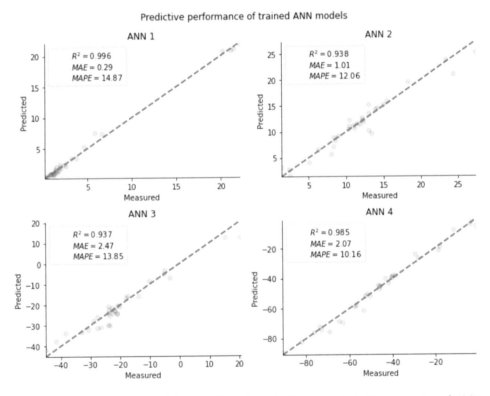

Figure 2: Predictive performance of the models trained in the case study for supporting decision making in textile process.

3.2.2 Determining the Criteria Weights using the AHP

The MCDM problem presented in Equation (3) could be summarized as a single objective optimization problem by structuring a hierarchy of criteria in terms of weights or priorities:

$$argmax_{vj \in Vj}[f(v_1, v_2 \cdots v_n)|C]$$
$$= argmax_{vj \in Vj} \sum_{i=1}^{m} w_i f_i(v_1 v_2 \ldots v_n) \tag{4}$$

where w_1 to w_m are weights of criterion c_1 to c_m respectively.

The AHP is a MCDM method introduced by[36] that uses a typical pair-wise comparison method into extracting relative weights of criteria and alternative scores and turns a multi-criteria problem into the paradigm of Equation (4). Above all, it constructs a pairwise comparison matrix of attributes using a nine-point scale of relative importance, in which number 1 denotes an attribute compared to itself or with any other attribute as important as itself, the numbers of 2, 4, 6 and 8 indicate intermediate values between two adjacent judgments, whereas the numbers 3, 5, 7 and 9 correspond to comparative judgments of 'moderate importance', 'strong importance', 'very strong importance' and 'absolute importance' respectively. A typical comparison matrix (C_m) of $m \times m$ could be established for m criteria as demonstrated below:

$$C_m = \begin{bmatrix} 1 & \cdots & a_{1m} \\ \vdots & \ddots & \vdots \\ a_{m1} & \cdots & 1 \end{bmatrix} \tag{5}$$

where a_{ij} represents the relative importance of criterion c_i regarding criterion c_j. Thus $a_{ij} = \frac{1}{a_{ij}}$ and $a_{ij}=1$ when $i = j$. Note that a consistency index (CI) is introduced in AHP with consistency ratio (CR) on the basis of the principal eigenvector (λ_{max}) to validate the consistency in the pairwise comparison matrix:

$$CI = \frac{\lambda_{max} - m}{m - 1} \text{ and } CR = \frac{CI}{RCI} \tag{6}$$

where RCI is a random consistency index and the values of it are available in[37]. Afterward, the relative weight of the i_{th} criteria (w_i) would be calculated by the geometric mean of the principal eigenvector, i_{th} row (GM_i), of the above matrix, and then normalizing the geometric means of rows:

$$GM_i = \left\{ \prod_{j=1}^{m} a_{ij} \right\}^{\frac{1}{m}} \text{ and } w_i = \frac{GM_i}{\sum_{I=1}^{m} GM_i} \tag{7}$$

By means of combining experts' judgment with our experience, a pairwise comparison matrix of the 4 decision criteria with respect to the overall color performance of ozonation process treated the textile product is provided in Table 1. λ_{max} of this comparison matrix is 4.1042 and known that the RCI for 4 criteria problem is 0.90, as a result, the CR calculated is $0.0386 \leq 0.08$ which implies that the evaluation within the matrix is acceptable.

Table 1: Pairwise comparison matrix of $k/s, L^*, a^*$ and b^* with respect to the overall color performance.

	k/s	L^*	a^*	b^*	GM	w
k/s	1	3	5	5	2.9428	0.556
L^*	1/3	1	3	3	1.3161	0.249
a^*	1/5	1/3	1	2	0.6043	0.114
b^*	1/5	1/3	1/2	1	0.4273	0.081

3.2.3 The Markov Decision Process

Reinforcement learning (RL) is a machine learning algorithm that sorts out the Markov decision process (MDP) in the formula of a tuple: $\{S, A, T, R\}$, where S is a set of environment states, A is a set of actions, T is a transition function, R is a set of rewards or losses. An agent in an MDP environment would learn how to take action from A by observing the environment with states from S, according to corresponding transition probability T and reward R achieved from the interaction. The Markov property indicates that the state transitions are only dependent on the current state and current action is taken, but independent to all prior states and actions[38]. As known that the textile process has a number of parameter variables as $P \{v_1, v_2 \dots v_n\}$, if the probable value of v_j is $p(v_j)$, the parameter of the process defining the environment space φ from $\prod_{j=1}^{n} p(v_j), v_j \in V_j$ impacting the performance of textile process with regards to criteria $\{c_1, c_2 \dots c_m\}$. These parameter variables are independent to each other and obey a Markov process that models the stochastic transitions from a state S_t at time step t to next state S_{t+1}, where the environment state at time step t is:

$$S_t = [s_t^{v_1}, s_t^{v_2} \cdots s_t^{v_n}] \in \varphi \tag{8}$$

RL trains an agent to act optimally in a given environment based on the observation of states and the feedback from their interaction, acquiring rewards and maximizing the accumulative future rewards over time from the interaction[38]. Here, the agent learns in the interaction with the environment by taking actions that can be conducted on the parameter variables $\in$ $P\{v_1, v_2 \dots v_n\}$ at time step t. More specifically, in a time step t, the action of each single variable v_j could be kept (0) or changed up (+) / down (-) in the given range with specific unit u_j. So there are 3^n actions totally in the action space and, for simplicity, the action vector A_t at time step t could be:

$$A_t = [a_t^{v_1}, a_t^{v_2} \cdots a_t^{v_n}], \; where \; a_t^{v_j} \in \{-u_j, 0, +u_j\}, v_j \in V_j \tag{9}$$

The state transition probabilities, as mentions that, are only dependent on the current state S_t and action A_t. It specifies how the reinforcement agent takes action A_t at time step t to transit from S_t to next state S_{t+1} in terms of $T(S_{t+1} \mid S_t, A_t)$. For all $a_t^{v_j} \in \{-u_j, 0, +u_j\}, v_j \in V_j$, $T(S_{t+1} \mid S_t, A_t) > 0$ and $\sum_{S_{t+1} \in \varphi} T(S_{t+1} \mid S_t, A_t) = 1$. The reward achieved by an agent in an environment is specifically related to its transition between states, which evaluates how good the transition agent conducts and facilitates the agent to converging faster to an optimal solution.

3.2.4 The RL Algorithm: Q-learning

Q-learning learns through estimating the sum of rewards r for each state S_t when a particular policy π is being performed. It uses a tabular representation of the $Q^\pi(S_t, A_t)$ value to asign the discounted future reward r of state-action pair at time step t in Q-table. The target of the agent is to maximize accumulated future rewards to reinforce good behavior and optimize the results. In Q-learning algorithm, the maximum achievable $Q^\pi(S_t, A_t)$ obeys Bellman equation on the basis of an intuition: if the optimal value $Q^\pi(S_{t+1}, A_{t+1})$ of all feasible actions A_{t+1} on state S_{t+1} at the next time step is known, then the optimal strategy is to select the action A_{t+1} maximizing the expected value of $r + \gamma \cdot \max_{A_{t+1}} Q^\pi(S_{t+1}, A_{t+1})$.

$$Q^\pi(S_t, A_t) = r + \gamma \cdot \max_{A_{t+1}} Q^\pi(S_{t+1}, A_{t+1}) \tag{10}$$

According to the Bellman equation, the Q-value of the corresponding cell in Q-table is updated iteratively by:

$$
\begin{aligned}
Q^\pi(S_t, A_t) &\leftarrow Q^\pi(S_t, A_t) \\
&+ \alpha[r + \gamma \cdot \max_{A_{t+1}} Q^\pi(S_{t+1}, A_{t+1}) - Q^\pi(S_t, A_t)]
\end{aligned} \tag{11}
$$

where S_t and A_t are the current state and action respectively, while S_{t+1} is the state achieved when executing A_{t+1} in the set of S and A in any given MDP tuples of $\{S, A, T, R\}$. $\alpha \in [0, 1]$ is the learning rate, which indicates how much the agent learned from new decision-making experience $(Q^\pi(S_{t+1}, A_{t+1}))$ would override the old memory $(Q^\pi(S_t, A_t))$. r is the immediate reward, $\gamma \in [0, 1]$ is the discount factor determining the agent's horizon.

3.3 Case Study

We optimize the color performance in terms of k/s, L^*, a^*, and b^* of the textile in the ozonation process by finding a solution including proper parameter variables of water-content, temperature, pH and treating time that minimizes the difference between such specific process treated textile product and the targeted sample. Therefore, the state space φ, in this case, is composed by the solutions with four parameters (water-content, temperature, pH and treating time) in terms of $S_t = [s_t^{v_1}, s_t^{v_2}, s_t^{v_3}, s_t^{v_4}]$. In a time step t, the adjustable units of these parameter variables are 50, 10, 1 and 1 respectively in the range of $[0, 150]$, $[0, 100]$, $[1, 14]$ and $[1, 60]$ respectively. As the action of a single variable v_j could be kept (0) or changed up $(+)$/down $(-)$ in the given range with specific unit u, so there are $3^4 = 81$ actions totally in the action space and the action vector at time step is $A_t = [a_t^{v_1}, a_t^{v_2}, a_t^{v_3}, a_t^{v_4}]$, where $a_t^{v_1} \in \{-50, 0, +50\}$, $v_1 \in [0, 150]$; $a_t^{v_2} \in \{-10, 0, +10\}$, $v_2 \in [0, 100]$; $a_t^{v_3} \in \{-1, 0, +1\}$, $v_3 \in [1, 14]$; $a_t^{v_4} \in \{-1, 0, +1\}$, $v_4 \in [1, 60]$.

The transition probability is 1 for the states in the given range of state space above, but 0 for the states out of it. The reward r at time step t is expected to be in line with how close the agent gets to our target, and as the relative importance of these four performance criteria (0.556, 0.249, 0.114 and 0.081 respectively) is analyzed in AHP, we could set up the reward function as illustrated below to induce the agent to approach our optimization results:

$$r_t = \sum_{i=1}^{m} \sqrt{w_i^2(f_i(s_t) - p_i)^2} - \sum_{i=1}^{m} \sqrt{w_i^2(f_i(s_{t+1}) - p_i)^2} \tag{12}$$

The decisions of the textile ozonation process are functioning the system (p_1, p_2, p_3, p_4, the color performance of the ozonation process in terms of k/s, L^*, a^*, $and\ b^*$), the targeted performance in the present case study would be sampled by experts. In addition to the targets, the parameters of RL such as learning rate α and γ the discount rate, the number of episodes E, number of time steps N, are listed in Table 2.

Table 2: DQN algorithm setting in textile ozonation process application study.

α	γ	$\varepsilon_{increment}$	ε_{max}	E	N
0.01	0.9	0.001	0.9	5	5000

3.3.1 Results and Discussion

As demonstrated in Table 3, there are 5 experimental targets sampled by experts that were used in the present case study.

The simulated color performance of the results in terms of the solutions with minimum error obtained from proposed framework is demonstrated in Table 4 with the targets. And the differences of these results with the targets in terms of the colorimetric values can be seen in Figure 3. It is clear that the presented decision support system has assisted the decision-maker find the solutions.

Table 3: The experimental targets sampled by experts we used in the case study application of proposed decision support system.

	1	2	3	4	5
k/s	0.81	1.00	2.45	1.84	0.41
L^*	15.76	11.63	8.2	9.72	21.6
a^*	-20.84	-24.08	-18.73	-21.09	-36.48
b^*	-70.79	-54.1	-38.17	-42.78	-59.95

Table 4: Simulated results of solutions with minimum errors obtained from DQN based and Q-learning based framework respectively.

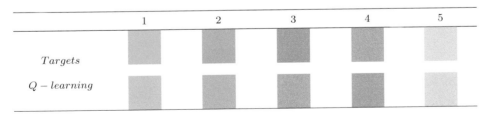

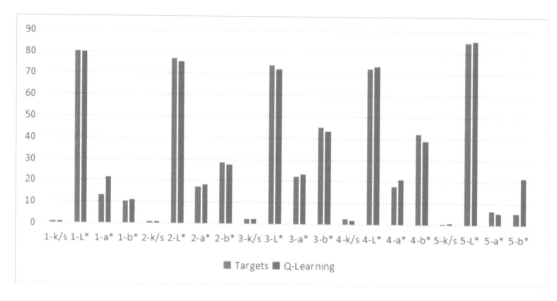

Figure 3: Comparison of the targets with the results.

4 Conclusion

Textile manufacturing is a traditional industry involving high complexities in interconnected processes with limited capacity on the application of modern technologies. Decision-making in this domain generally takes multiple criteria into consideration, which usually arouses more complexity. Traditional classical approaches are no longer efficient owing to the growing complexity with large-scale data and high dimensional decision space in some scenarios. In this chapter, a decision support system combining the ANN model, AHP and Q-learning is proposed for supporting the decision-making of the textile manufacturing process. This developed system tackles the problems with multi-criteria in the textile manufacturing process. It is concluded:

(1) Decision making of the textile manufacturing process could be formulated into the Markov decision process paradigm of $\{S, A, T, R\}$ in the proposed algorithm.

(2) Taking advantage of the ANN models, the proposed framework can effectively exploit the data.

(3) AHP multi-criteria structure benefits the proposed framework to find the optimal textile manufacturing process solution with respect to multiple objectives.

References

[1] W. Shen and D.H. Norrie. Agent-based systems for intelligent manufacturing: A state-of-the-art survey. *Knowl. Inf. Syst.*, 1(2): 129–156, 1999, doi: 10.1007/BF03325096.

[2] R.Y. Zhong, X. Xu, E. Klotz and S.T. Newman. Intelligent manufacturing in the context of industry 4.0: A review. *Engineering*, 3(5): 616–630, 2017, doi: 10.1016/J.ENG.2017.05.015.

[3] K. Suzuki. Artificial Neural Networks: Industrial and Control Engineering, 2011.

[4] J. Fan and L. Hunter. A worsted fabric expert system: Part II: An artificial neural network model for predicting the properties of worsted fabrics. *Text. Res. J.*, 68(10): 763–771, 1998.

[5] P.K. Majumdar and A. Majumdar. Predicting the breaking elongation of ring spun cotton yarns using mathematic. *Text. Res. J.*, 74(7): 652–655, 2004 [Online]. Available: https://journals.sagepub.com/doi/pdf/10.1177/004051750407400717.

[6] A. Moghassem and A. Fallahpour. Processing parameters optimization of draw frame for rotor spun yarn strength using Gene Expression Programming (GEP). *Fibers Polym.*, 12(7): 970–975, 2011, doi: 10.1007/s12221-011-0970-y.

[7] S. Sette and L. Van Langenhove. An overview of soft computing in textiles. *J. Text. Inst.*, 94(1-2): 103–109, 203, doi: 10.1080/00405000308630598.

[8] D.W. Patterson. *Artificial Neural Networks: Theory and Applications*. Prentice Hall PTR, 1998.

[9] L.A. Zadeh. Fuzzy sets. *Inf. Control*, 8(3): 338–353, 1965.

[10] F.M. McNeill and E. Thro. *Fuzzy Logic: A Practical Approach*. Academic Press, 2014.

[11] D. Veit. Fuzzy logic and its application to textile technology. *Simul. Text. Technol. Theory Appl.*, pp. 112–141, 2012, doi: 10.1533/9780857097088.112.

[12] D. Basak, S. Pal and D.C. Patranabis. Support vector regression. *Neural Inf. Process. Rev.*, 11(10): 203–224, 2007.

[13] A. Smola and B. Scholkopf. A tutorial on support vector regression. *Stat. Comput.*, 14: 199–222, 2004, doi: 10.1023/B:STCO.0000035301.49549.88.

[14] C. Ferreira. Gene expression programming: A new adaptive algorithm for solving problems. *arXiv Prepr. cs/0102027*, 2001.

[15] M. Dayik. Prediction of Yarn properties using evaluation programing. *Text. Res. J.*, 79(11): 963–972, 2009, doi: 10.1177/0040517508097792.

[16] S. Sette and L. Van Langenhove. Optimising the fiber-to-yarn production process: Finding a blend of fiber qualities to create an optimal price/quality yarn. *AUTEX Res. J.*, 2(June): 57–64, 2002.

[17] A. Majumdar, S.P. Singh and A. Ghosh. Modelling, optimization and decision making techniques in designing of functional clothing. *Indian J. Fibre Text. Res.*, 36(December): 398–409, 2011.

[18] A. Mukhopadhyay, V.K. Midha and N.C. Ray. Multi-objective optimization of parametric combination of injected slub yarn for producing knitted and woven fabrics with least abrasive damage. *Res. J. Text. Appar.*, 21(2): 111–133, 2017.

[19] A.A. Almetwally. Multi-objective optimization of woven fabric parameters using Taguchi—grey relational analysis multi-objective optimization of woven fabric parameters using Taguchi—grey relational analysis. *J. Nat. Fibers*, 0(0): 1–11, 2019, doi: 10.1080/15440478.2019.1579156.

[20] K. Deb. *Multi-Objective Optimization Using Evolutionary Algorithms*. vol. 16. John Wiley & Sons, 2001.

[21] B. Kordoghli, M. Jmali, S. Saadallah and N. Liouene. Multi-objective scheduling of flow-shop problems in finishing factories using genetic algorithms. *J. Text. Apparel, Technol. Manag.*, 6(3): 1–10, 2010.

[22] D. Nurwaha and X. Wang. Optimization of electrospinning process using intelligent control systems, 24: 593–600, 2013, doi: 10.3233/IFS-2012-0578.

[23] C.C. Wu and N.B. Chang. Global strategy for optimizing textile dyeing manufacturing process via GA-based grey nonlinear integer programming. *Comput. Chem. Eng.*, 27: 833–854, 2003, doi: 10.1016/S0098-1354(02)00270-3.

[24] K. Deb and H. Jain. An evolutionary many-objective optimization algorithm using reference-point-based nondominated sorting approach, Part I: solving problems with box constraints. *IEEE Trans. Evol. Comput.*, 18(4): 577–601, 2013, doi: 10.1109/TEVC.2013.2281535.

[25] S. Das, A. Ghosh, A. Majumdar and D. Banerjee. Yarn engineering using hybrid artificial neural network-genetic algorithm model. *Fibers Polym.*, 14(7): 1220–1226, 2013. doi: 10.1007/s12221-013-1220-2.

[26] K.L. Jeyaraj, C. Muralidharan and T. Senthilvelan. Genetic algorithm based multi-objective optimization of process parameters in color fast finish process—A textile case study. *J. Text. Apparel, Technol. Manag.*, 8(3): 1–26, 2013.

[27] A. Majumdar, P. Mal, A. Ghosh and D. Banerjee. Multi-objective optimization of air permeability and thermal conductivity of Multi-objective optimization of air permeability

and thermal conductivity of knitted fabrics with desired ultraviolet protection. *J. Text. Inst.*, 108(1): 110–116, 2017, doi: 10.1080/00405000.2016.1159270.

[28] P.K. Barzoki, M. Vadood and M.S. Johari. Multi-objective optimization of rotorcraft compact spinning core-spun yarn properties. *J. Text. Polym.*, 6(1): 47–53, 2018.

[29] M. Vadood, P.K. Barzoki and M.S. Johari. Multi objective optimization of rotorcraft compact spinning system using fuzzy-genetic model. *J. Text. Inst.*, 108(12): 2166–2172, 2017, doi: 10.1080/00405000.2017.1316178.

[30] J. Chen, Y. Ding, Y. Jin and K. Hao. A synergetic immune clonal selection algorithm based multi-objective optimization method for carbon fiber drawing process. *Fibers Polym.*, 14(10): 1722–1730, 2013, doi: 10.1007/s12221-013-1722-y.

[31] S. Chakraborty and S. Diyaley. Multi-objective optimization of Yarn characteristics using evolutionary algorithms: A comparative study. *J. Inst. Eng. Ser. E*, 99: 129–140, 2018, doi: 10.1007/s40034-018-0121-8.

[32] G. Derringer and R. Suich. Simultaneous optimization of several response variables. *J. Qual. Technol.*, 12(4): 214–219, 1980.

[33] F.A. Arain, A. Tanwari, T. Hussain and Z.A. Malik. Multiple response optimization of rotor yarn for strength, unevenness, hairiness and imperfections, 13(1): 118–122, 2012, doi: 10.1007/s12221-012-0118-8.

[34] M. Saggiomo, M. Kemper, Y.-S. Gloy and T. Gries. Weaving machine as cyber-physical production system: Multi-objective self-optimization of the weaving process. In *2016 IEEE International Conference on Industrial Technology (ICIT)*, pp. 2084–2089, 2016, doi: 10.1109/ICIT.2016.7475090.

[35] S. Chakraborty, S. Agarwal and S.S. Dandge. Analysis of cotton fibre properties: A data mining approach. *J. Inst. Eng. Ser. E*, 99(2): 163–176, 2018, doi: 10.1007/s40034-018-0125-4.

[36] T.L. Saaty. What is the analytic hierarchy process? *In Mathematical Models for Decision Support*, Springer, pp. 109–121, 1988.

[37] T.L. Saaty. How to make a decision: The analytic hierarchy process. *Eur. J. Oper. Res.*, 48(1): 9–26, 1990.

[38] R.S. Sutton and A.G. Barto. *Introduction to Reinforcement Learning*, vol. 135. MIT Press Cambridge, 1998.

Chapter 7

Anomaly Detection Enables Cybersecurity with Machine Learning Techniques

Truong Thu Huong,[1,]* Nguyen Minh Dan,[1] Le Anh Quang,[1] Nguyen Xuan Hoang,[1] Le Thanh Cong,[1] Kieu-Ha Phung[1] and Kim Phuc Tran[2]

1 Introduction

As we know that Decision Support System (DSS) applications can be used in a vast array of diverse fields, such as making operational decisions, medical diagnosises, and predictive maintenance. This chapter presents recent advancements of research, new methods, and techniques for Machine Learning (ML) based DSS for Cybersecurity of Industrial Systems.

Researchers and practitioners alike will benefit from this chapter to enhance the understanding of ML, and their use in DSS in the context of decision making in Cybersecurity of Industrial Systems. The real-world case studies with guidance and recommendations for the practical applications of these studies are introduced. Status, trends, future directions, and opportunities will be discussed, making it friendly for beginners and young researchers.

This chapter specifically contributes to the world's knowledge of cybersecurity for a cutting-edge system: IoT-based systems that have been thriving in being deployed for various applications nowadays. It gives an overview from the trend of integrating the Internet of Things (IoT) in many systems relating to our society, to IoT-based Industrial systems, to the background of new networking architectures such as Cloud computing and Edge Computing-based architecture that should be deployed in a modern Industry 4.0.

The rest of this chapter will describe the Cybersecurity problem for Industrial systems in general. Then we go over different solutions and designs of anomaly and intrusion detection based on Machine-Learning in different system contexts and applications. Then, we extend our knowledge to a cutting-edge architecture that draws the huge attention of researchers and practitioners of these 2020s: Federated Learning (FL)–based detection schemes. Moreover, pending difficulties, challenges are discussed in order to have a clearer view of the strong points and weak points of currently proposed solutions. Finally, we wrap up all content in the conclusion section.

---

[1] Hanoi University of Science and Technology, Hanoi, Vietnam.
[2] Univ. Lille, ENSAIT, ULR 2461 - GEMTEX - Génie et Matériaux Textiles, F-59000 Lille, France.
* Corresponding author: huong.truongthu@hust.edu.vn

2 Cybersecurity of Industrial Systems

Today, Industry 4.0, or the fourth industrial revolution is characterized by interconnected systems which are also connected in some way to the Internet. Industrial systems have started to merge with the IoT through the introduction of sensing ability in front-end Internet-connected devices to provide services. Thereby, the IoT is providing access to a huge amount of data, collected by the front-end devices over the Internet. However, designing a robust and secured IoT infrastructure is challenging, as the heterogeneous and distributed nature of IoT infrastructure allows numerous attacks such as phishing, spyware, DoS, DDoS, etc. Within that context, computer security becomes a major issue for the industrial world since the industrial systems combined with IoT technology might constitute an open avenue for attackers. Therefore, a reliable IoT system must meet many security requirements such as authentication and access control at the edge layer and attack detection at the network layer[1].

As one specific system of the Industrial systems, we have observed the growing deployment of Industrial Wireless Sensor Networks (IWSN) in a variety of different applications since Wireless Sensor Network (WSN) constitutes one of the most promising third-millennium technologies that can serve a wide range of applications in our surrounding life. The recent integration of WSNs with Internet access capability in sensor nodes has opened new security challenges, especially if they are commissioned for mission-critical tasks such as tactical military (e.g., casualties for the friendly forces on a battlefield) or health-care applications (e.g., exposure of confidential health data).

As a specific and arising case study of IoT-based systems, Smart Manufacturing (SM) is industrial manufacturing that has been profoundly impacted due to the rapid development and wide application of advanced technologies. A SM system is monitored by sensors, controlling operations based on intelligent computing technologies to improve system performance, product quality as well as to minimize costs[2,3]. Such modern Industrial Control Systems (ICS) are critical to the operation of national facilities such as natural gas pipelines, or power grids. However, the fact that a modern ICS is not an isolated system anymore, but connected to the Internet results in a severe consequence if the network is accessed by hackers. Critical data could be stolen or the operating system of a factory could be invaded and destroyed. The control systems of Industrial installations and cyber-physical systems (CPS) can be subject to operating errors or failures, which can lead to a variety of significant operating losses, for example, plant shutdown, or rendering security systems inoperative. Nowadays, the Industrial IoT (IIoT)-based manufacturing systems are now one of the top industries targeted by a variety of attacks. Numerous attacks against SM systems have been reported in[4]. Therefore, the problem of protecting IIoT systems against cyber-attacks is becoming increasingly indispensable and the need of understanding an efficient Cyberattacks detection architecture in ICSs has come into play.

To implement relevant cybersecurity detection solutions, industrial administrators should have a clear understanding of IT systems, communication networks, and control systems. They must also have some knowledge of data generated by benign clients and by attackers, and of the available security solutions.

In this chapter, we present different subjects from the new designs and methods to protect the industrial systems, IoT-based systems, IWSN, in order to give an in-depth overview and to help the reader manage the cybersecurity of their installation. And at most, we focus on elaborating designed solutions for the issue of Cyberattack in ICSs.

2.1 Cyberattack Detection for Industrial Control Systems

Usually, for Cyberattack Detection, we can count a variety of well-known techniques such as firewall, antivirus, or Intrusion Detection Systems (IDS). However, as cyber threats become more and more sophisticated, it arises a need for an AD scheme that can discover anomalies or attacks accurately and in a timely manner while still being lightweight enough for running efficiently on top of IoT devices with limited computing powers in industrial settings. Eventually, it is tougher for network administrators to deal develop dynamic security functions with low complexity in order to afford system response in real-time[5].

The problem of cyberattack detection has been approached from different perspectives: (1) effective Machine-learning-based algorithms, (2) networking paradigm, (3) Distributed or centralized computing.

For the direction of ML-based detection algorithm, we can find a number of researches [6;7;8;9;10;11;12]. In design, a process mining method[6] is designed based on the log data of the devices in the system to make AD more efficient due to the rich source of information log files. We can find also the idea of combining one-class classification algorithms Support Vector Data Description (SVDD) and Kernel Principle Component Analysis (KPCA) in work[7] to deal with intrusion detection in the Supervisory Control and Data Acquisition (SCADA) system. However, this solution may face high computational costs in practice. To solve this, an input dimension reduction technique is added in, with the attack detection algorithm, to reduce the complexity by work[8;9;12]. However, these designs have not considered the problem of live detection, where the task of detecting attacks in ICSs requires fast, accurate, and real-time detection.

For the direction of a new networking paradigm, besides efforts of finding an effective detection algorithm, Cyberattack and AD were also approached from a new networking paradigm perspective - Software Defined Networking (SDN). With the separation of a traditional network into the data plane and the control plane, SDN offers a flexible way to administer the system[13]. An SDN-based architecture was investigated in work[13;14] to solve cybersecurity in IIoT and ICSs. With the SDN networking paradigm, all decisions are centrally made by the SDN controller, possibly leading to slower system response latency issues as well as placing the processing burden on the controller. Moreover, in the AD task, we need to have knowledge of numerous features including additional statistical features of the input data. Unfortunately, it is impossible to get that full knowledge in the SDN environment. Therefore, another distributed architecture should be investigated to solve these limitations: and a distributed system with a detection model at the edge could be a good candidate.

For the direction of distributed/centralized computing, from the beginning of the IoT development, central cloud computing has been always a popular computing method for centralized control and analysis of data collected from a variety of ubiquitous devices. The cloud provides powerful computing capacity and large storage to process Big data. However, offloading intensive computation tasks to a cloud may cause a slower system response due to the delay needed to transmit, process data from those front-end devices to the Cloud. To overcome this limitation, Edge (or distributed) computing came to play to perform computational tasks right at the network edge in a distributed manner. Especially, within the scope of cybersecurity, tasks such as anomaly or attack detection have been more and more preferred to be realized right at the Edge where it is close to anomalies or attack sources. In a traditional method, we usually implement the attack detection module at the network layer, while deploying authentication, limited access, threat hunting, and data encryption at the edge layer, which is expected to have lower computing power. However, as edge devices are getting more and more powerful in terms of computing capacity, the detection task that requires an adequately high computing capability could be now migrated to the edge. Of course, since the computing capacity of an Edge device is still considered limited, detection techniques at the Edge should be implemented in a more light-weighted manner while still maintaining high performance. Light-weigh techniques could comprise data dimension reduction, algorithm running time optimization at the trade-off of sufficiently high complexity. The first benefit of deploying the AD module right at the Edge is that it can obviously reduce the communication time of sending all Big Data to the Cloud for further analysis. Edge-computing-based AD can bring faster system response upon anomaly or attack occurs due to its proximity to end devices (i.e., sources of attacks). For example, in DDoS and Mirai botnet types, sources of attacks are mostly from compromised end devices. The second benefit is that it also reduces the Cloud's workload, which is critical for IoT applications that involve a large number of simultaneous users. For the third benefit, as the network designers ourselves, we prefer local processing to send all raw data directly to the Cloud, from the privacy perspective.

2.2   Anomaly Detection for Time-series Data

In the context of the ICS, we frequently face a type of data so-called time-series data. For this type of data, ML-based detection methods may not always be effective for the multivariate time series data as the network outputs only a single value of the characteristic. From this point of view, effective solutions for forecasting multivariate time series data and for detecting anomalies from these data without using any assumptions for the distribution of prediction errors should be studied.

In the field of AD mechanisms for time-series data, we can find several designs such as [15;16;17;18;19;20;21] to detect anomalies at different times of the system. A common approach for this time-series data is utilizing the Long Short-Term Memory (LSTM) algorithm only [15;21], or Autoencoder (AE) only, or AE in combination with LSTM [18;20]. The hybrid solution can produce a more effective performance on AD.

Besides, the deep generative network is also widely applied in solving time-series AD issues. In particular, networks are composed of symmetric encoders [18;20]. For the water distribution system, a deep architecture based on VAE to detect a cyber-attack as designed in work [20]. VAE's symmetric architecture is used to reproduce the input through encoders and decoders to extract information for AD. However, extracting the sequential information of the time series data is still a limitation of VAE. The best detection performance of this work was observed at 80% at maximum, and only 62.4% for the classification task.

In the same direction, design [15;18] also uses a deep network model with a asymmetrical structure. In that framework, the designers propose a robust time-series AD framework based on a convolutional neural network (CNN) with two symmetrical encoders and decoders. The decomposition in this architecture has an important circular role in handling patterns in the time series data for efficient detection.

The system design in [18] considers the problem of processing centralized data in the cloud that requires a cloud infrastructure with a large storage capacity and strong processing capacity. Nevertheless, using the convolutional structure (i.e., convolutional LSTM such as design [15], or convolutional Encoder-Decoder such as design [18]) can be time-consuming as well as requires a large training dataset.

Opposite to the centralized Cloud-based computing solution, edge computing can be a good remedy for practicing AD at the edge which is supposed to be close to the attack sources. Within that context, implementing a complicated detection algorithm on top may not be afforded by the resource limitation of edge devices. Besides, it was shown in [22] that a model based on neural network (NN) structure does not necessarily need a complex structure to be effective in terms of classification or detection.

In another way, we also can be combining prediction models and unsupervised AD in a hybrid framework to solve the problem of requiring labels of data in AD methods as well as ensuring accurate prediction for time series data. Such designs can be found in some researches such as [17;19;23]. The designers in [17] propose a real-time algorithm to carry out AD for the factory production line.

The combining model of AE and LSTM algorithms can help to detect defective products accurately to minimize time and cost. In fact, the distribution of real-time-series data can be hardly determined because it is a continuous series over time. In that case, using Variational AE (VAE) may be better than AE in terms of representing the extracted data in distribution since it yields more principled and objective probabilities.

We can find such a method presented in [24] which uses VAE for AD. In this design, the designers use the construction error retrieved from the training set to compute heuristically the anomaly threshold by testing different values and choosing the threshold value that gives the highest detection performance. The threshold is chosen in trade-off among the detection performance measures such as precision, recall, and F1-score. Choosing the threshold that way requires network administrators to rerun overall data to find the best threshold, anytime a new training dataset comes.

3 Machine Learning-based Anomaly Detection for Cybersecurity Applications

AD is any process that finds the outliers of a dataset. In the world of distributed systems nowadays, managing and monitoring the system's performance is a necessary issue. With thousands of items to watch, AD can help point out where an error is occurring, enhancing root cause analysis and quickly getting tech support on the issue.

In enterprise IT, AD is commonly used for data cleaning, Intrusion detection, Fraud detection, Systems health monitoring, Event detection in sensor networks, Ecosystem disturbances. The challenge of AD is that there are some drawbacks within: AD systems are either manually built by experts setting thresholds on data or constructed automatically by learning from the available data through ML. Therefore when data changes over time, like fraud, builders need to go back to manually add further security methods. And that's bad because it creates a system that cannot adapt (or is costly and untimely to adapt).

Therefore, AD with ML techniques can make the system work better, be more adaptive and on time, be able to handle large datasets.

In the following sections, we will describe different case studies in the field of AD using ML to solve different problems with Cybersecurity applications.

3.1 Data Driven Hyperparameter Optimization of One-Class Support Vector Machines for Anomaly Detection in Wireless Sensor Networks

The problem of detecting abnormal activities can be reformulated as a One-Class classification problem, where only normal data is used in the training data set. As a result, OCSVM (i.e., One-Class Support Vector Machine) and its variations have been widely adopted in the AD literature. However, OCSVM is often kernelized by Gaussian kernel, which is dependent on the availability of outliers in data. To alleviate this problem, a data-driven hyperparameter optimization algorithm based on OCSVM was proposed for AD in Wireless Sensor Networks (i.e., WSNs).

3.1.1 Anomaly Detection Scheme

Background of OCSVMs and Gaussian Kernel

In this section, we present a brief review of OCSVM[25] and the Gaussian kernel. Consider a data set $\{\mathbf{x}_1, \ldots, \mathbf{x}_N\} \subset \mathcal{R}^D$, in which all data points belong to the same class (target class). The basic idea of OCSVM is to compute a binary discriminant function that maps values from a region containing most of the data point to +1 and other values to –1, by finding a hyperplane that separates the data points from the origin with maximum margin[25]. To deal with nonlinear problems, $\Phi(.)$ is defined to be a nonlinear feature map, which maps the samples into a high-dimensional Hilbert feature space, such that the scalar product $(\Phi(\mathbf{x}).\Phi(\mathbf{y}))$ can be computed by evaluating some kernel $k(\mathbf{x}, \mathbf{y})$. To separate the data set from the origin, the following quadratic program needs to be solved[25]:

$$\underset{\mathbf{w}, \mathbf{a}, \boldsymbol{\xi}, \rho}{\text{Minimize}} \quad \frac{1}{2}||\mathbf{w}||^2 + \frac{1}{\nu N}\sum_{i=1}^{N}\xi_i - \rho \tag{1a}$$

$$\text{Subject to } (\mathbf{w}.\Phi(\mathbf{x}_i)) \geq \rho - \xi_i, \xi_i \geq 0 \quad \forall i = 1 \ldots N \tag{1b}$$

Here, $\mathbf{w}$ is a vector orthogonal to the hyperplane in the feature space, and ρ is the distance to the origin. To account for outliers in the training data, a set of slack variables $\xi = (\xi_1, \xi_2, ..., \xi_N)$ is utilized to allow for some samples to be mapped as negative by the discriminant function

$$f(\mathbf{x}) = \text{sgn}((\mathbf{w}.\Phi(\mathbf{x})) - \rho) \tag{2}$$

while still maximizing the margin. The trade off by the amount of samples in the positive region of $f(\mathbf{x})$ and having a small value for the regularization term $||\mathbf{w}||$ is controlled by the parameter $\nu \in (0, 1]$.

Using multipliers $\alpha_i, \beta_i \geq 0$, a Lagrangian is constructed[25]

$$L = \frac{1}{2}||\mathbf{w}||^2 + \frac{1}{\nu N}\sum_{i=1}^{N}\xi_i - \rho$$

$$- \sum_{i=1}^{N}\alpha_i((\mathbf{w}.\Phi(\mathbf{x}_i)) - \rho + \xi_i) - \sum_{i=1}^{N}\beta_i\xi_i \tag{3}$$

According to[26], the following dual optimization problem is obtained:

$$\alpha_i^\star = \underset{\alpha}{\operatorname{argmin}} \sum_{i=1}^{N}\sum_{j=1}^{N}\alpha_i\alpha_j k(\mathbf{x}_i, \mathbf{x}_j) \tag{4a}$$

$$\text{Subject to } \sum_{i=1}^{N}\alpha_i = 1, 0 \leq \alpha_i \leq \frac{1}{\nu N}, \quad \forall i = 1 \ldots N \tag{4b}$$

Therefore, the value of ρ can be recovered through the observation that for any $\alpha_i^\star$ satisfying the dual optimization problem, the corresponding pattern $\mathbf{x}_i$ satisfies

$$\rho = \langle \mathbf{w}, \Phi(\mathbf{x}_i)\rangle = \sum_{j=1}^{N}\alpha_j^\star k(\mathbf{x}_j, \mathbf{x}_i) \tag{5}$$

It was shown that at the optimum, the inequality constraints (1b) becomes equalities if $0 < \alpha_i^\star < \frac{1}{\nu N}$[25]. Samples $\mathbf{x}_i$ that correspond to $0 < \alpha_i^\star < \frac{1}{\nu N}$ are called *support vectors*. Let N_{SV} being reserved for the number of support vectors. The discriminant function (2) is thus reduced into:

$$f(\mathbf{x}) = \operatorname{sgn}\left(\sum_{i=1}^{N_{\mathrm{SV}}}\alpha_i^\star k(\mathbf{x}, \mathbf{x}_i) - \rho\right) \tag{6}$$

The most commonly used kernel is the radial basis functions (RBF, or Gaussian) kernel:

$$k(\mathbf{x}_i, \mathbf{x}_j) = \exp\left(-\frac{||\mathbf{x}_i - \mathbf{x}_j||^2}{2\sigma^2}\right) \tag{7}$$

where $\sigma > 0$ stands for the kernel width parameter, which controls the flexibility of the kernel. In the feature space, the distance between two mapped samples $\mathbf{x}_i$ and $\mathbf{x}_j$ is:

$$||\phi(\mathbf{x}_i) - \phi(\mathbf{x}_j)||^2 = k(\mathbf{x}_i, \mathbf{x}_i) + k(\mathbf{x}_j, \mathbf{x}_j) - 2k(\mathbf{x}_i, \mathbf{x}_j)$$

$$= 2\left[1 - \exp\left(-\frac{||\mathbf{x}_i - \mathbf{x}_j||^2}{2\sigma^2}\right)\right] \tag{8}$$

This exhibits a positively proportional relation between $||\phi(\mathbf{x}_i) - \phi(\mathbf{x}_j)||$ and $||\mathbf{x}_i - \mathbf{x}_j||$. In other words, the Gaussian kernel preserves the ranking order of the distances between samples in the input and feature spaces.

Anomaly Detection Scheme

In order to improve OCSVM's performance, the following objective function[27] should be maximized:

$$J(\sigma) = \frac{1}{N} \sum_{i=1}^{N} \max_{j} ||\phi(\mathbf{x}_i) - \phi(\mathbf{x}_j)||^2$$

$$- \frac{1}{N} \sum_{i=1}^{N} \min_{j=i} ||\phi(\mathbf{x}_i) - \phi(\mathbf{x}_j)||^2 \tag{9}$$

This performance measure can be further simplified by substituting the Gaussian kernel into (9), yielding:

$$J(\sigma) = \frac{2}{N} \sum_{i=1}^{N} \min_{j=i} k(\mathbf{x}_i, \mathbf{x}_j) - \frac{2}{n} \sum_{i=1}^{N} \max_{j} k(\mathbf{x}_i, \mathbf{x}_j) \tag{10a}$$

$$= \frac{2}{N} \sum_{i=1}^{N} \exp\left(-\frac{\min_{j=i} ||\mathbf{x}_i - \mathbf{x}_j||^2}{2\sigma^2}\right)$$

$$- \frac{2}{N} \sum_{i=1}^{N} \exp\left(-\frac{\max_{j} ||\mathbf{x}_i - \mathbf{x}_j||^2}{2\sigma^2}\right) \tag{10b}$$

Denoting the nearest and farthest neighbors distances respectively as

$$\text{Near}(\mathbf{x}_i) = \min_{j=i} ||\mathbf{x}_i - \mathbf{x}_j||^2 \tag{11a}$$

$$\text{Far}(\mathbf{x}_i) = \max_{j} ||\mathbf{x}_i - \mathbf{x}_j||^2 \tag{11b}$$

Finding the exact values for these distances takes $\mathcal{O}(N^2)$ time. Therefore, approximations or sequential approaches may be desired for large-scale applications. Substituting (11) into (10), we obtain:

$$J(\sigma) = \frac{2}{N} \sum_{i=1}^{N} \exp\left(-\frac{\text{Near}(\mathbf{x}_i)}{2\sigma^2}\right)$$

$$- \frac{2}{N} \sum_{i=1}^{N} \exp\left(-\frac{\text{Far}(\mathbf{x}_i)}{2\sigma^2}\right) \tag{12}$$

Taking the gradient of $J(\sigma)$ with respect to σ:

$$\nabla J(\sigma) = \frac{2}{N} \sum_{i=1}^{N} \exp\left(-\frac{\text{Near}(\mathbf{x}_i)}{2\sigma^2}\right) \frac{\text{Near}(\mathbf{x}_i)}{\sigma^3}$$

$$- \frac{2}{N} \sum_{i=1}^{N} \exp\left(-\frac{\text{Far}(\mathbf{x}_i)}{2\sigma^2}\right) \frac{\text{Far}(\mathbf{x}_i)}{\sigma^3} \tag{13}$$

Note that there is no guarantee that $J(\sigma)$ is convex, which is generally the case in parameters optimization for kernel methods. However, it is still possible to apply conventional gradient-based optimization methods to find $\sigma^\star = \text{argmax}_\sigma J(\sigma)$.

After evaluating the Gaussian kernel parameter σ, we still need to choose the parameter $0 < \nu \ll 1$ and adjust the discriminative threshold ρ by a small amount δ for a more robust AD scheme.

3.1.2 Illustrative Example in WSN Anomaly Detection

Data Description

We consider the WSN data set gathered by Intel Berkeley Research Laboratory (IBRL)[28] with 54 *Mica2Dot* sensor nodes which collect five measurements: light, temperature, temperature corrected relative humidity, voltage, and network topology information at 30-second intervals.

Furthermore, we only utilize two features, namely temperature and humidity.

Gaussian kernel parameter optimization

The objective function $J(\sigma)$ on the given training set is demonstrably strongly convex. After a few iterations of parameter optimization, the MATLAB's® routine *fminunc(·)* provides the kernel parameter $\sigma^\star = 0.2938$.

Detection Performance Results

The OCSVM is computed with $\nu = 0.0001$, $\sigma = 0.2938$, consisting of 9 support vectors, using the LIBSVM library[29]. It was shown that the robustness of OCSVM can be improved by appropriately modifying the discriminative threshold, i.e., the false alarm rate is reduced with an appropriate value for δ[26].

3.2 Real Time Data-Driven Approaches for Credit Card Fraud Detection

In this section, OCSVM[25] and another machine-learning-based algorithm called T^2 control chart[30] are considered together for real-time data. Both algorithms are deployed in a practical scenarios as credit card fraud detection, which tackles the issue of illegally taking holders' credit information without their permission[31;32]. Subsequently, the performance of these two data-driven approaches is assessed on an online e-commerce transactions data set from European credit card holders[33].

3.2.1 Anomaly Detection Scheme

This section presents an AD scheme based on real-time data-driven approaches for credit card fraud, namely OCSVM[25] with the optimal kernel parameter selection and T^2 control chart[30]. The scheme is shown in Figure 1.

For the approach using OCSVM, the idea is similar to the theories elaborated in Section 3.1. A heuristic method, however, is utilized to opt the Gaussian kernel parameters by only using

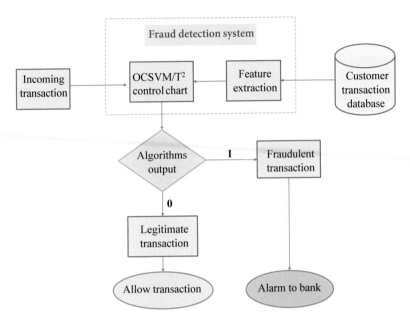

Figure 1: Proposed data-driven approaches for credit card fraud detection.

the knowledge of one class. Here, if the OCSVM decision function of a new data $\mathbf{z}$ $f(\mathbf{z}) > 0$, the observation is placed within the boundary, which causes it to be categorized as a fraud instance.

For the remaining approach, T^2 control chart[30], a tool based on Statistical Process Control (SPC) method[34], is also used to learn one class's characteristics and provide a measure of abnormal behavior of new instances. Hence, T^2 control chart is adopted to solve credit card fraud detection as a data-driven approach. Now, considering a data set $\{\mathbf{x}_1, \ldots, \mathbf{x}_N\} \subset \mathcal{R}^D$, in which all data points belong to the same class (target class), the mean vector μ_0 and the variance-covariance matrix Σ can be evaluated. For a new instance $\mathbf{z}_i$, the T^2 control chart is defined[35]:

$$T_i^2 = (\mathbf{z}_i - \mu_0)^{\mathsf{T}} \Sigma^{-1} (\mathbf{z}_i - \mu_0), \quad i = 1, 2, \ldots \tag{14}$$

The T^2 control chart will emit a fraud signal if $T_i^2 > UCL = H$, where $H > 0$ is selected to achieve a specified in-control Average Run Length (ARL)[36].

3.2.2 Illustrative Example in Credit Card Fraud Detection

Data Description

The data set was gathered from credit-card transactions of cardholders over two days in September 2013, in which there are 284807 non-fraudulent transactions in total. Besides, the principal components analysis (PCA) transformation is applied to the data set to ensure the confidentiality of sensitive information, and then simulations are carried out to create fraudulent transaction data. Next, to experiment with the approaches, 284000 transactions for the training, 200 non-fraudulent, and 200 fraudulent ones for the testing are used.

Detection Performance Results

In the solution, to assess the two-algorithm detection performance, typical measures are used, namely $DR, FPR, Precision, Accuracy, F1-score$, defined in Table 1.

Table 1: Performance metrics.

Performance metrics	Formulas
DR(Recall)	$\frac{TP}{TP+FN}$
FPR	$\frac{FP}{FP+FN}$
Precision	$\frac{TP}{TP+FP}$
Accuracy	$\frac{TP+TN}{TP+TN+FP+FN}$
F-score	$2 \times \frac{Precision \times Recall}{Precision+Recall}$

The results depicted in Table 2 indicate that the OCSVM method outperforms the T^2 control chart in all measures of comparison, but with fast calculation, the T^2 control chart is still effective in detecting frauds. Besides, it is notable that the detection accuracy of both methods is quite high (96.6% for OCSVM, 93.6% for T^2 control chart).

Table 2: Performance metrics of OCSVM and T^2 control chart.

Methods	TP	TN	FP	FN	DR(Recall)	FPR	Precision	Accuracy	F-score
OCSVM	200	283	17	0	1.0000	0.0850	1.0000	0.9660	1.0000
T^2 chart	200	268	32	0	1.0000	0.1600	1.0000	0.9360	1.0000

3.3 Nested One-Class Support Vector Machines for Network Anomaly Detection

3.3.1 Nested OCSVMs and Anomaly Detection Scheme

In nested OCSVM, the set estimates are nested a the parameters controlling the density level. Instead of (4), we consider the following dual optimization[37], where λ is the regularization parameter:

$$\underset{\boldsymbol{\alpha}}{\text{Minimize}} \quad \frac{1}{2\lambda} \sum_{i,j}^{N} \alpha_i \alpha_j k(\mathbf{x}_i, \mathbf{x}_j) - \sum_{i=1}^{N} \alpha_i \tag{15}$$

$$\text{Subject to } 0 \leq \alpha_i \leq \frac{1}{N}, \quad \forall i = 1 \ldots N.$$

The optimal solution is solved with respect to λ, denoted by $\boldsymbol{\alpha}^\star(\lambda) = (\alpha_1^\star(\lambda), \alpha_2^\star(\lambda), \ldots, \alpha_N^\star(\lambda))$. Each $\alpha_i^\star(\lambda)$ is piecewise linear in λ[38]. With this result, a path algorithm was developed[37] and used to generate a family of level set estimates. The set estimate associated with the OCSVM is written as:

$$G_\lambda = \left\{ \mathbf{x} : \sum_{i=1}^{N} \alpha_i^\star(\lambda) k(\mathbf{x}_i, \mathbf{x}) > \lambda \right\}. \tag{16}$$

By substituting $\alpha_i^\star(\lambda)$ with $\alpha_i^\star(\eta\lambda)$, where $\eta > 1$, (16) can result in a consistent estimate of the true level set when using a Gaussian kernel[39]. However, the estimates are not always to be nested[37]. Nested OCSVM solves the following optimization problem:

$$\underset{\boldsymbol{\alpha}_1,\ldots,\boldsymbol{\alpha}_M}{\text{Minimize}} \quad \sum_{m=1}^{M} \left(\frac{1}{2\lambda_m} \sum_{i,j}^{N} \alpha_{i,m}\alpha_{j,m}k(\mathbf{x}_i,\mathbf{x}_j) - \sum_{i=1}^{N} \alpha_{i,m} \right)$$

$$\text{Subject to } 0 \le \alpha_{i,m} \le \frac{1}{N}, \quad \forall i, m \tag{17}$$

$$\frac{\alpha_{i,1}}{\lambda_1} \le \frac{\alpha_{i,2}}{\lambda_2} \le \ldots \le \frac{\alpha_{i,M}}{\lambda_M}, \quad \forall i = 1 \ldots N,$$

where $\lambda_1 > \lambda_2 > \ldots > \lambda_M > 0$ are M different density levels selected as a priori, $\boldsymbol{\alpha}_m = (\alpha_{1,m}, \alpha_{2,m}, \ldots, \alpha_{N,m})$ and each $\alpha_{i,m}$ corresponds to data point $\mathbf{x}_i$ at level λ_m. The optimal solution $\boldsymbol{\alpha}_m^\star = (\alpha_{1,m}^\star, \alpha_{2,m}^\star, \ldots, \alpha_{N,m}^\star)$ defines a level set estimate $\hat{G}_{\lambda_m} = \left\{ \mathbf{x} : \sum_{i=1}^{N} \alpha_{i,m}^\star k(\mathbf{x}_i, \mathbf{x}) > \lambda_m \right\}$. The discrimination function at each level λ_m is $f_{\lambda_m}(x) = \frac{1}{\lambda_m} \sum_{i=1}^{N} \alpha_{i,m}^\star k(\mathbf{x}_i, \mathbf{x})$, which defines a decision boundary. The sample $\mathbf{x}$ is inside the boundary if $f_{\lambda_m}(x) > 1$, on the boundary if $f_{\lambda_m}(x) = 1$ and outside otherwise. Most samples in the high density region will lie inside the boundary whereas most outliers will be outside. The ranking of the sample using the Mean Integrated Decision Function (MIDF)[40] is used to separate the outliers and the samples in the training set:

$$MIDF(\mathbf{x}) = \frac{1}{M} \sum_{i=1}^{M} f_{\lambda_m}(\mathbf{x}). \tag{18}$$

Let us consider two levels $\lambda_1 \le \lambda_2$. The density level set estimate at level $\lambda = \epsilon\lambda_1 + (1-\epsilon)\lambda_2$ which falls between these levels is computed by setting $\alpha_i^\star(\lambda) = \epsilon\alpha_{i,1}^\star + (1-\epsilon)\alpha_{i,2}^\star$ for all i. The level set estimate with respect to λ is

$$\hat{G}_\lambda = \left\{ \mathbf{x} : \sum_{i=1}^{N} \alpha_i^\star(\lambda)k(\mathbf{x}_i, \mathbf{x}) > \lambda \right\}. \tag{19}$$

These generated level set estimates are nested[37], i.e., $\hat{G}_{\lambda_m} \supset \hat{G}_{\lambda_l}$ if $0 < \lambda_m < \lambda_l < \infty$.

A decomposition algorithm was constructed to solve our optimization problem. $\alpha_{i,m}$ is initialized at $1/N$ $\forall i, m$. At each data point $\mathbf{x}_i$, the corresponding coefficients $\{\alpha_{i,m}\}_{m=1:M}$ are updated sequentially. The objective function (17) can be rewritten in term of $\alpha_{i,m}$ as following:

$$\sum_{m=1}^{M} \left(\frac{1}{2\lambda_m} \sum_{i,j}^{N} \alpha_{i,m} \alpha_{j,m} k_{i,j} - \sum_{i=1}^{N} \alpha_{i,m} \right)$$

$$= \sum_{m=1}^{M} \left(\frac{1}{2\lambda_m} \alpha_{i,m}^2 k_{i,i} + \alpha_{i,m} \left(\frac{1}{\lambda_m} \sum_{j=i} \alpha_{j,m} k_{i,j} - 1 \right) \right)$$

$$+ C$$

$$= k_{i,i} \sum_{m=1}^{M} \left(\frac{1}{2\lambda_m} \alpha_{i,m}^2 - \frac{\alpha_{i,m}}{\lambda_m} \left(\alpha_{i,m}^{old} + \frac{\lambda_m(1 - f_{i,m})}{k_{i,i}} \right) \right)$$

$$+ C$$

where $k_{i,j} = k(\mathbf{x}_i, \mathbf{x}_j)$ is the Gaussian kernel, $\alpha_{i,m}^{old}$ is the coefficient from previous iteration and $f_{i,m} = (1/\lambda_m)(\sum_{j=i} \alpha_{j,m} k_{i,j} + \alpha_{i,m}^{old})$. The constant C does not depend on $\alpha_{i,m}$. The optimization problem of M variables is obtained

$$\underset{\alpha_{i,1}, \ldots, \alpha_{i,M}}{\text{Minimize}} \quad \sum_{m}^{N} \left(\frac{1}{2\lambda_m} \alpha_{i,m}^2 - \frac{\alpha_{i,m}}{\lambda_m} \alpha_{i,m}^{new} \right) \tag{20}$$

$$\text{Subject to } 0 \leq \alpha_{i,m} \leq \frac{1}{N}, \quad \forall m = 1 \ldots M$$

$$\frac{\alpha_{i,1}}{\lambda_1} \leq \frac{\alpha_{i,2}}{\lambda_2} \leq \cdots \leq \frac{\alpha_{i,M}}{\lambda_M},$$

with $\alpha_{i,m}^{new} = \alpha_{i,m}^{old} + (\lambda_m(1 - f_{i,m})/k_{i,i})$.

The intrusion detection algorithm here is identical to the algorithm described in 3.1.1, with two differences: Instead of setting the parameter $0 < \nu \ll 1$, we set the regularization levels $\{\lambda_m\}_{m=1}^{M}$. Furthermore, instead of adjusting the discriminative threshold ρ for the decision function, we solve (17) to obtain the Mean Integrated Decision Function MIDF (18). The intrusion detection procedure is demonstrated in Figure 2.

3.3.2 Illustrative Example in Network Anomaly Detection

Data Description

The KDD99 data set collected by Stolfo at Lincoln Laboratory at the Massachusetts Institute of Technology[41] is considered in this case study. The anomaly data containing 4601 observations including 1601 confirmed attacks are used. In the experiment, 2603 normal samples are used for training and the rest of the samples for testing.

Gaussian kernel parameter optimization

The MATLAB's routine *fminunc(·)* is used for parameter optimization, thus providing the kernel parameter $\sigma^\star = 0.2618$ after few iterations.

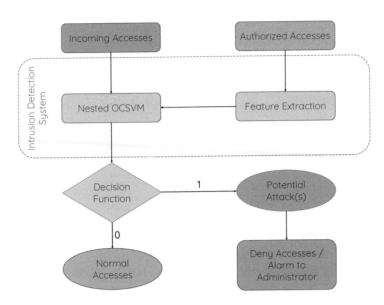

Figure 2: AD system scheme.

Training nested OCSVM and Results

The performance of the nested OCSVM approach for network AD is evaluated in terms of FPR and accuracy (defined in 1). We also investigate the OCSVM approach described in 3.1.

Table 3: Performance metrics of OCSVM and nested OCSVM.

Methods	OCSVM	NOCSVM
FPR	0.0155	0.0012
Accuracy	0.9729	0.9825

Table 3 compares the performance of the OCSVM and nested OCSVM approaches. It is shown that the nested OCSVM method outperforms OCSVM for intrusion detection. For $M = 12$ density levels, the nested OCSVM achieves an accuracy of 98.28% and a lower FPR compared to the OCSVM, while the OCSVM is faster and still gains promising results with an accuracy of 97.29%.

3.4 A Data-Driven Approach for Network Anomaly Detection and Monitoring Based on Kernel Null Space

Another approach for AD based on ML techniques is to employ the Kernel Null Space method[42] and Control Chart–based method - Kernel Quantile Estimato (KQE)r[43]. This mechanism aims for high performance in Novelty Detection with dynamic and efficient detection threshold, adaptive to specific applied data set. In terms of detection performance, this scheme been has shown to outperform current ML techniques used in one-class novelty detection problems, especially in determining network anomalies with real-time constraints.

3.4.1 Anomaly Detection Scheme

In this section, an intrusion detection scheme is formed based on the enhanced Kernel Null Space (EKNS) method and the KQE technique to improve the detection accuracy of IDS/IPS. To be more specific, the scheme is depicted as follows:

- Network traffic is first pre-processed and normalized to get the data suitable for the training phase.

- EKNS is introduced to be the detection model of IDS/IPS. EKNS is proved to be capable of improving the accuracy of detecting novelty samples.

To reform this mechanism regarding the adaptability to changes in data set, a dynamic threshold is computed using KQE[43] for a specified probability q.

EKNS method

Prior to describing the specific AD scheme using EKNS, let us briefly recall the one-class classification method using Kernel Null Space proposed in[42]. Consider a dataset of N training samples $\{x_1, x_2, \ldots, x_N\}$, all belong to a single normal class, with each $x_i \in R^D$ and D is the number of observed features. Similar to OCSVM introduced earlier, the input features $X = [x_1, x_2, \ldots, x_N]$ are separated from the origin in the high-dimensional kernel feature space. As proposed in[42], this method computes a single null projection direction to map all training samples on a single target value s. After the training phase, test sample x^* is projected on the null projection direction to obtain the value s^*, which in turn is used to calculate the novelty score of x^*:

$$NoveltyScore(x^*) = \mid s - s^* \mid .\tag{21}$$

This novelty score is compared with a threshold to determine if the test sample is an anomalous point. Figure 3 illustrates the approach to one-class classification problem with Kernel Null Space.

Based on the Kernel Null Space method, the intrusion scheme uses a so-called EKNS for the AD tasks. EKNS procedure is illustrated in Figure 4, consisting of two phases: the training phase and the detection phase. In the training phase, training data samples $\{x_1, x_2, \ldots, x_N\}$ are first pre-processed as demonstrated earlier, then mapped onto a point s in the Null Space F. Specifically, the commonly used Gaussian kernel (RBF) is selected for Kernel Null Space.

$$k(x, y) = \exp\left(\frac{-\parallel x - y \parallel^2}{2\sigma^2}\right)\tag{22}$$

where σ is the kernel parameter, valued in range [0,1].

Different from the original Kernel Null Space, optimal sigma σ^* is estimated from the data set $\{x_1, x_2, \ldots, x_N\}$ using the method proposed in[26], whereas the optimal σ^* is the parameter

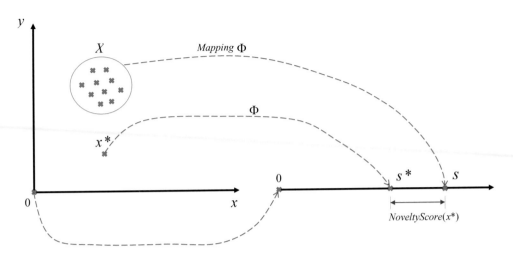

Figure 3: The samples are separated from the origin in the kernel feature space with a mapping Φ, then mapped on a point s, and the novelty score of a testing sample x^* is the distance of its projection s^* to s.

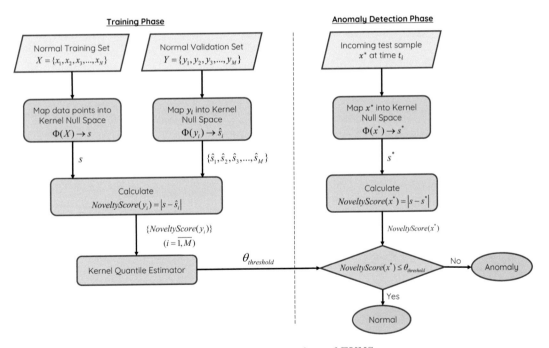

Figure 4: Detection procedure of EKNS.

that maximizes the objective function $J(\sigma)$:

$$J(\sigma) = \frac{2}{N} \sum_{i=1}^{n} \exp\left(-\frac{Near(x_i)}{2\sigma^2}\right) - \frac{2}{N} \sum_{i=1}^{n} \exp\left(-\frac{Far(x_i)}{2\sigma^2}\right) \tag{23}$$

where the nearest and farthest neighbor distances are defined as follows:

$$Near(x_i) = \min_{j \neq i} \| x_i - x_j \|^2$$

$$Far(x_i) = \max_{i} \| x_i - x_j \|^2$$

In [42] and [44], a hard threshold $\theta_{threshold}$ is heuristically defined for the detection task. This method is, to some extent, not optimal, facing trouble, especially when dealing with continuous values since we can not try out all values for threshold determination. Following a different approach, this AD scheme utilizes the KQE technique to obtain a threshold that is adaptive to the constantly changing data set applied to the system, hence a higher detection performance. To get this threshold, the IDS uses another data set called the validation set containing other normal data samples $\{y_1, y_2 \ldots, y_M\}$. Each sample y_i of the validation set is mapped on a point $\hat{s}_i$ in the feature null space, for which $NoveltyScore(y_i)$ is calculated. After mapping all samples of the validation set and calculating Novelty scores for all of them, a set $\{NoveltyScore(y_i)\}$ is formed. With this set of novelty scores, the KQE technique is utilized to derive the threshold $\theta_{threshold}$, which will be discussed further later in this section.

For the detection phase in real-time, when a test sample x^* arrives, the system maps it onto a point s^*, then its $NoveltyScore(x^*)$ is calculated. After that, by comparing the $NoveltyScore(x^*)$ with $\theta_{threshold}$ found in the training phase, x^* can be classified as Normal or Anomaly.

Threshold calculation with KQE

The set of the novelty scores is denoted by $\{NS_1, NS_2, \ldots, NS_M\}$ and investigated for the probability density distribution. In fact, the Novelty Scores set $\{NS_1, NS_2, \ldots, NS_M\}$ can not be approximated by a normal distribution since the underlying distribution of the sample is unknown. In this case, non-parametric methods could be put into use to estimate this unknown distribution. In this scheme, KQE [43] is used to estimate $\theta_{threshold}$ over the set of Novelty Score values.

Let $NS_{(1)} \leq NS_{(2)} \leq \ldots \leq NS_{(M)}$ denote the corresponding order statistics of the novelty scores. Suppose that $K(.)$ is a density function symmetric about Zero and that $h \to 0$ as $n \to \infty$, the KQE can be calculated as follows:

$$KQ_p = \sum_{i=1}^{N} \left[\int_{\frac{i-1}{n}}^{\frac{i}{n}} K_h(t - p)dt \right] NS_{(i)} \qquad (24)$$

where:
$h > 0$ denotes the bandwidth which controls the smoothness of the estimator for a given sample of size n. $K_h(.) = \frac{1}{h}K(\frac{.}{h})$
p is the proportion of the quantile.

Here the standard Gaussian kernel is deployed for the resulting estimate KQ_p which is a smooth unimodal,

$$K(u) = \frac{1}{\sqrt{2\pi}} \exp(-\frac{u^2}{2}) \qquad (25)$$

In this technique, the selection of h is crucial in kernel density estimation: a large h will lead to an over-smoothed density estimate, whereas a small h will produce a ragged density with many spikes at the observations. As described in [43], the bandwidth computed as

$$h_{opt} = \left(\frac{pq}{n+1} \right)^{\frac{1}{2}} \tag{26}$$

where: $q = 1 - p$

For a lot of continuous distributions used in statistics, specific quantiles such as the $p = 0.95$, 0.975, and 0.99 quantiles are tabulated. For that reason, 3 values of q, listing 0.05, 0.025 and 0.01, are to be investigated in experiments with this detection scheme. These three q values corresponds to 3 threshold values $KQ(p = 1 - q)$ (i.e., $\theta_{threshold}$).

3.4.2 Illustrative Example in Network Anomaly Detection

As previously mentioned, the NSL-KDD data set is used to evaluate the detection performance of the solution. The training data set contains 13449 normal samples. After training the system, the system performance is evaluated using 6000 normal as well as anomalous samples of the testing data set. To test performance, all 41 attributes of the data set are utilized.

In the experiments, the performance of the EKNS is compared with the original Kernel Null Space in which the threshold is heuristically selected and fixed at 0.05 [42] and with the OCSVM method [26]. Note that 3 different q values are considered in these experiments: 0.01, 0.025 and 0.05.

In Table 4, it can be seen that with the normalized and pre-processed 41-attribute data set $\{X_1, X_2, \ldots, X_N\}$, the optimal kernel parameter estimated is $\sigma^* = 0.5957$. Subsequently, from the given data set of Novelty scores $\{NS_1, NS_2, \ldots, NS_M\}$, the found threshold is $\theta_{threshold} = 0.0097$, $\theta_{threshold} = 0.0233$, $\theta_{threshold} = 0.0514$ for $q = 0.05$, $q = 0.025$ and $q = 0.001$ respectively.

Particularly in the security context, accuracy is more important than recall when you would like to have fewer False Positives in trade-off to have more False Negatives. Therefore, $q = 0.025$ brings the best performance in terms of Accuracy, FPR among the 3 different values q as shown in Table 4.

From the obtained results, it can also be noted that overall, the EKNS scheme slightly outperforms the OCSVM and the original Kernel Null Space methods in terms of Accuracy,

Table 4: Performance comparison.

$\sigma = 0.5957$	Kernel Null Space			OCSVM	Origin Kernel Null Space with fixed threshold=0.05
	q=0.05 $\theta_{threshold}$= 0.0097	q=0.025 $\theta_{threshold}$= 0.0233	q=0.01 $\theta_{threshold}$= 0.0514		
Accuracy	0.9548	0.9598	0.92	0.9445	0.9212
FPR	0.0443	0.018	0.006	0.0433	0.006
Recall	0.954	0.9377	0.846	0.9323	0.8483
AUC	0.9910	0.9910	0.9910	0.9849	0.9910

AUC, and Recall while marginally inferior to the Original Kernel Null Space method in terms of False Positive Rate (FPR).

4 Federated Learning-based Anomaly Detection for Cybersecurity Applications

FL or collaborative learning is a ML technique that trains a ML algorithm from multiple decentralized local data samples without exchanging them among the distributed areas. Normally, those data are collected from edge devices or servers holding local data samples in a distributed system.

This federated computing scheme contrasts to traditional centralized (i.e., Cloud computing) ML techniques in which all the local datasets are sent to one central Cloud server. Thus, FL could solve critical issues such as data privacy, data security, and faster system response since the detection module can be deployed right at the edge which is in the vicinity of attack sources. Its applications are spread over a number of industries.

In the following subsections, we will describe two case studies of AD architecture using FL architecture to control IoT-based systems: one for an IoT network, and another one for an IoT-based ICS.

4.1 Security System Architecture for IoT Systems

4.1.1 Design of Edge-Cloud System Architecture

There has been a diverse range of proposals for IoT architectures[1], which are intended for a variety of applications. A five-layered architecture was proposed[45], comprising Business Layer, Application Layer, Processing Layer, Transport Layer, and Perception Layer. Another five-layered architecture[46] includes Business Layer, Application Layer, Middleware Layer, Network Layer, and Perception Layer. In the following architecture, one additional architecture, namely the Edge Layer, has been introduced. The Edge Layer can improve the distribution of computing tasks, which in turn improves the near-source intrusion detection, as shown in Figure 5.

Our Edge-Cloud security architecture is designed to: (1) have low complexity in analyzing data, (2) be capable of detecting early attacks right at edge zones, and (3) have accurate attack detection with high reliability. With all these goals, the system not only avoids having been badly damaged before successfully detecting attacks but also adapts quickly to the development trend of IoT network in the future with security and scalability requirements.

This Edge-Cloud security architecture is designed to have: (1) low complexity data analysis, (2) the capability to detect attacks early at edge zones, and (3) a highly accurate attack detection mechanism. With all these goals, the system is not only less susceptible to the damage done before detecting attacks, but also very adaptive to the rapid development of IoT network in the future with security and scalability requirements.

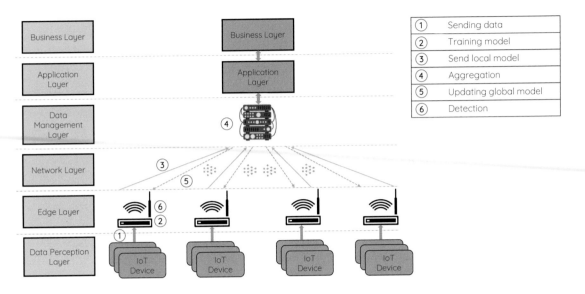

Figure 5: Proposed architecture.

Detailed descriptions of the layers are as follows:

- *Data Perception Layer*: comprises IoT devices with sensors.

- *Edge Layer*: consists of wired or wireless IoT Gateways, each of which is responsible for data processing and multi-attack detection. At the Gateways, a lightweight multi-attack detection module was developed. When an attack is detected, the Gateway traces its source then blocks the malicious connections. In case of an emergency where the source of the attack cannot be determined in time, the Gateway simply blocks all incoming data in its zone to avoid affecting any other legitimate sources of other zones. The Gateway can either send its normalized data to a Cloud Server in the centralized model (i.e., centralized learning), or train the detection module locally and send the weights to the Cloud Server for aggregation in the federated model (i.e., FL). Detecting and mitigating attacks right at each zone will make the system respond faster and more effectively since: (1) near-source attack detection time is smaller; (2) a smaller set of data from one zone only means a reduction in the processing time and computing capacity requirement; and (3) in the worst-case scenario, only the affected zone goes down, the Cloud is still protected and the damage is minimized.

- *Network Layer*: secures data transfer from the lower layer to the higher layer, and thus plays an important role in the general architecture.

- *Data Management Layer*: also known as the Cloud. The Cloud is in charge of analyzing given IoT devices' data sets. The Optimization Module deployed here is responsible for analyzing data, and configuring the NN algorithm. The Cloud periodically sends the configuration information to all gateways.

- *Application Layer*: is responsible for inclusive applications management based on the processed information in the Data Management Layer such as intelligent transportation, smart car, smart health, identity authentication, smart glasses, location, and safety, etc.

- *Business Layer*: covers the whole IoT applications and services management. Business models, flow charts, executive reports, etc., are created based on data received from lower layers and an effective data analysis process.

4.1.2 Data Pre-processing at the Edge

Before the detection phase in which a detection algorithm only takes numerical input, raw traffic needs to be normalized since the data is both categorical and numerical, with numerical data being in vastly different ranges. First, categorical data will be converted to numerical data. Then, all data will be transformed into values in the range between 0 and 1 through the min-max normalization method as follows:

$$z_i = \frac{x_i - min(x)}{max(x) - min(x)} \tag{27}$$

where x_i, z_i $(i = 1, 2 \ldots d)$ are values before and after normalization of one data feature and d is the dimension of data.

In this architecture, 2 learning modes were developed: (1) a centralized-learning-based, (2) a FL-based. The design can be summarized as follows:

- Feature extraction is analyzed in the Cloud to define which features are important to use for detection. It helps the system to reduce complexity for computing the full features of a dataset.

- Centralized learning (CL) in the Cloud to define the number of neurons per hidden layer and the number of layers in order to receive high accuracy and low complexity of the detection phase.

- Design and evaluate the centralized and federated-learning based detection solutions to cope with facts of IoT networks

In the following section, the detection solutions in both aforementioned ways, as well as an elaboration of the reasons to use each of the solutions and perform an evaluation for the two methods, which will be presented.

4.1.3 Detection Mechanism

The detection mechanism, which consists of a feature extraction module and a classification module, is shown in Figure 6. The feature extraction module's purpose is to reduce the dimensionality of the samples that are fed to the classification module. This is especially critical due to the low computational capacity and energy constraints at the edge devices[5]. This extraction phase also increases the efficiency of the detection phase and reduces the time taken for a system to respond and record information. The detection module is implemented with a NN performing multi-class classification to detect different types of attacks at the same time. The NN is

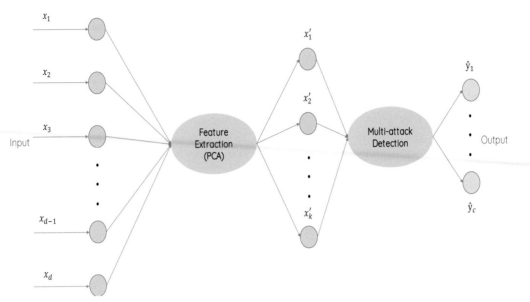

Figure 6: Multi-attack detection mechanism.

optimized in terms of the number of layers as well as the number of neurons in the hidden layers to minimize the algorithm's complexity while still ensuring high detection accuracy.

As shown in Figure 6, normalized data with dimensionality d is passed through the Feature Extraction module to perform feature extraction and the dimensionality of data will be reduced to k features $(k < d)$. These k features are then passed through the NN module to perform multi-class classification.

Feature Extraction Module

There are many techniques in the literature that can reduce data dimensionality, which can be divided into 4 groups[47]: Feature Ranker, Feature Evaluator, Dimensionality Reduction and Clustering Algorithms. Some experimentation was carried out with different algorithms on the BoT-IoT data set[48]. Results showed that PCA[49] is suitable in the proposed architecture, since PCA is fast and computationally cheap, while still able to extract the most important features of data. With PCA, the original data points will be transformed into a new space, where it is possible to differentiate the importance of the components together. The size of data dimensions is decreased from d to k which are k important components of the data in the new space system.

Let's consider the input data matrix including N row vectors $\mathbf{X}=\{x_i\}$ $(i = 1 \ldots N)$ where $x_i=\{x_{i1}, x_{i2}, x_{i3} \ldots x_{id}\}$ with d is the original dimensionality of the data. To extract the principal components of $\mathbf{X}$, we calculate the empirical mean of $\mathbf{X}$: $\bar{x} = N^{-1}\sum_{i=1}^{N} x_i$ and the mean-centered matrix $\mathbf{M}$. Each row vector of $\mathbf{M}$ is given as $m_i = x_i - \bar{x}$. Then, we compute the eigenvalue decomposition of the covariance matrix $V = N^{-1}M^T M$ to get the principal components. The relationship between eigenvalues λ and eigenvectors U of square matrix V satisfies (28)

$$V\lambda = \lambda U \tag{28}$$

where λ is a diagonal matrix, each value λ_i is the i_{th} eigenvalue corresponding eigenvector u_i of matrix U. The eigen decomposition of V is given by:

$$V = \lambda U \lambda^{-1} \tag{29}$$

The principal components of matrix $\mathbf{X}$ are the k vectors of $\mathbf{V}$ that correspond to k largest eigenvalues, denoted by $V_k = \{v_1, v_2, \ldots, v_k\}$. The vectors in V_k form a subspace close to the distribution of the normalized data. To choose k, we can rely on the amount of information retained in the new data point by selecting the first k values of the eigenvalue that capture 90% or 95% of the sum of the eigenvalues. In the experiment with the BoT-IoT data set, $k = 9$ is found to ensure capturing over 95% of the total sum of the eigenvalues. New data with reduced dimensionality is the coordinates of the data projected on the new space.

$$X^{'} = MV_k^T \tag{30}$$

Multi-attack Detection Module

In this module, an NN is deployed to detect multiple types of attacks. The output nodes of the NN correspond to the different attack types. Optimizing the NN's configuration is directly related to the algorithm complexity. To balance the complexity and performance of the multi-attack detection module, the number of layers and neurons per layer was optimized on the BoT-IoT data set.

The function of NN is to perform a nonlinear mapping and convert input information into outputs, which is defined mathematically as $F : R^k \to R^m$. The network input is $x_i^{'} = \{x_{i1}^{'}, x_{i2}^{'} \ldots x_{ik}^{'}\}$ where k is the dimension of data after being processed by the Feature extraction and Dimension reduction Module and W^j is the weight value of jth layer ($j = 1 \ldots l$) with l being the number of hidden layers. The output of each hidden layer is obtained by adding the bias with the products of each input and its corresponding weight W^j, then applying the activation function f, as shown in (31) (define $S_0 = X$)

$$S_j = f(W^j S_{j-1}^T + b^j) \tag{31}$$

In our model, we choose the activation function in hidden layers as ReLU for higher performance and faster convergence[50] and softmax activation function for the Multi-class classification problem. Their mathematical formulae are shown as below:

$$ReLU\ f(x) = \begin{cases} 0 & x \leq 0 \\ x & x \geq 0 \end{cases}, \ Softmax\ \sigma(z_i) = \frac{e^{z_j}}{\sum_{j=1}^{k} e^{z_j}} \tag{32}$$

Accordingly, the input information X passes through each layer and is transformed by (31) until it reaches the output layer with the softmax activation function for the multi-class problem, which is denoted as $\hat{y} = softmax(W^{out} S_l^T)$. This process is called *forward propagation*.

The Detection Algorithm Operation

As mentioned above, the detection module is implemented at the Edge in the IoT system to achieve faster detection near attack sources thereby enabling quicker system response. Detection at the edge also allows the local treatment traffic within a narrowed attacked zone without affecting other edge zones with our security policies.

From the NN's performance perspective, the Loss Function, which calculates the difference between the predicted value $\hat{y}$ and the actual value y, will be used to adjust the training process and learning efficiency of the NN, so that the model can best fit with the data used. In this module, the cross-entropy loss function (33) was chosen for multi-class classification with c classes for c types of attack in the Bot-IoT data set such as DoS – TCP, DDoS – TCP, OS – Fingerprinting.

$$L(\hat{y}, y) = -\sum_{i=1}^{c} y_i log(\hat{y}_i) \tag{33}$$

In the training process, the network is trained by a set of labeled data (x_i, y_i), which is used to reduce the average loss value after each iteration. To get better learning efficiency by adjusting weight (w) and bias (b) in the NN, the loss function (34) needs to be minimized.

$$J_{(w,b)} = \frac{1}{N} \sum_{=1}^{N} L(\hat{y}(x_i^{'}), y(x_i^{'})) \tag{34}$$

In this detection module, the structure of NN (including the number of hidden layers and neurons per hidden layer) is designed at the beginning and will not be changed with the complexity of the system and the model at the edge can be updated in either the centralized or the FL manners. In both scenarios, the subspace matrix V_k (29) of PCA is calculated in the cloud, based on the previously archived data, V_k is then sent to the edge along with the trained detection model in the centralized mode or with the initialized model in the federated model. Each of the manners brings specific pros and cons as we will describe in the next subsections.

CL mode

For CL, all raw data is sent directly to the Cloud, then pre-processed for the training process. The training process is done at the Cloud Server and finished when the loss function converges. The optimized NN parameters are sent to the edge devices to update the local models. This way, the Cloud has an overview of the overall system including multiple different edges. Hence, the detection is potentially more accurate. However, it is obvious that it places a burden on the Cloud Server to compute for a huge bundle of data sent from the edge. Therefore, an efficient optimization technique must be deployed at the Cloud Server.

There are many techniques existing to optimize the loss function[51]. To fasten the convergence in a deep NN-based model, an adaptive learning rate algorithm is needed. In the centralized mode, optimized by Adam's algorithm, the formula (35) shows the rule to calculate and update the parameter of Adam's method described in[52].

$$w^{'} = w - \beta \frac{\hat{m}_t}{\sqrt{\hat{v}_t} + \epsilon}; b^{'} = b - \beta \frac{\hat{m}_t}{\sqrt{\hat{v}_t} + \epsilon} \tag{35}$$

where: β is learning rate, $\hat{m}_t$ and $\hat{v}_t$ is the bias-corrected first (the mean) and the second (the uncentered variance) moment estimates and ϵ is a smoothing term that avoids division by zero. These values will be updated after each iteration, until the value of loss of the function reaches a minimum, this process is called backpropagation.

FL mode

Due to the distributed nature of the IoT ecosystem and the unreliability of wireless transmission, sending all user data to the Cloud for model training may be costly and time-consuming. Furthermore, this approach will also have the risk of exposing private or sensitive user data. All of these problems can be addressed by doing the detection as well as the training phase in the edge. However, as each edge only has access to its own data, which is often small and limited, and the data between the edges can be very different, the quality of the resulting edge-trained model may not be good enough. Using FL, this problem can be ameliorated as the edges can "communicate" with each other through the aggregated weights of the server, while still avoiding sending data directly, saving bandwidth as well as protecting privacy.

FL is a distributed ML technique, in which the training process of a model, as well as the data involved, is divided between multiple parties - or "clients", and no client has access to the data of another. Instead, clients only send the parameters of the local model they train with their own data, either directly with each other in their peer-to-peer model or through a centralized aggregation server in a client-server model. This architecture opts for the centralized model, as it has a faster convergence time.

In the client-server model, the server firstly performs the Feature Extraction phase, as well as choosing the hyperparameters and initializing the parameters of the NN model, then sends this information to all clients. Then, each client will train its model with its own data, using Stochastic Gradient Descent for E local epochs. Afterward, all clients will send the updated weight of their model to the server, which will then calculate the aggregated weight using the following formula[53]:

$$w_t = \sum_{k=1}^{K} \frac{n_k}{n} w_t^k \tag{36}$$

where K is the number of participating clients. The server will then send the calculated weights for all clients to update their model with, completing one communication round. Repeating this process for C communication rounds (with C sufficiently large) and all clients will end up with a well-trained model which is generalized for all the local data, with no data transmission required.

In the FL mode, the detection module utilizes the traditional Stochastic Gradient Descent optimize, which can be written as:

$$w' = w - \eta \nabla_w J_{(w,b)}; b' = b - \eta \nabla_b J_{(w,b)}; \tag{37}$$

with the learning rate $\eta = 0.01$.

4.1.4 Performance Evaluation

In this section, aiming to assess LocKedge, a data set called BoT-IoT[48], gathered from four IoT network scenarios: a smart fridge, a weather station, motion-activated lights, and a smart thermostat[54] is employed. Types of attacks in the data set are shown in Table 5, where the data is split for implementing the training and testing process, with 70% and 30% respectively. In this case, LocKedge is evaluated in terms of complexity, detection performance on both forms of learning (CL and FL), and edge computing capacity.

Table 5: Statistics of the BoT-IoT dataset.

Types of Attack	Number of samples
DoS-HTTP	1485
DoS-TCP	615800
DoS-UDP	1032975
DDoS-HTTP	989
DDoS-TCP	977380
DDoS-UDP	948255
OS Fingerprinting	17914
Server Scanning	73168
Keylogging	73
Data Theft	6
Normal	477
Totals	3668522

Complexity Evaluation

For the feature extraction in the detection module, with given matrices $X, M \in R^{N \times d}$ and $V \in R^{d \times d}$, the time complexity of the PCA algorithm is given by[55]:

$$O(Nd \times min(N, d) + d^3) \tag{38}$$

Next, the data reduced to k dimensions are fed to the only hidden layer of the NN model. For the forward pass from the input layer to the hidden layer, shown in Equation (31), we get $S_{hN} = W_{hk} \times X_{Nk}^T$, where W_{hk} is the weight matrix with h rows (the number of neurons in the hidden layer) and k columns. The complexity of this process is the sum of the time multiplying these two matrices $-O(hkN)$ and applying the activation function $-O(hN)$:

$$O(hkN + hN) = O(hN(k + 1)) = O(hNk)$$

Following that, in the propagation to the output layer, the complexity is given by $O(chN)$, where c is the number of outputs (classes), resulting in the total time complexity of the forward propagation process at each iteration as:

$$O(hNk + chN) = O(N(kh + hc)) \tag{39}$$

In the backward propagation from the output layer to the hidden layer, the error matrix L_{cN} is backward propagated. Adjusting the weight matrix between these layers leads to

$W'_{ch} = W_{ch} - L_{cN} \times S^T_{hN}$, with the time complexity of $O(cNh)$. Similarly, from the hidden layer to the input layer, the complexity is $O(hkN)$. Thus, the total time complexity of the forward and backward propagation for one epoch is $O(N(kh + hc))$, leading to the total complexity of the NN model trained with e epochs as:

$$O(eN(kh + hc)) \qquad (40)$$

So, for a generic NN with many hidden layers, in which h_i is the number of neurons in hidden layer i, the time complexity is determined by the formula:

$$O(eN(dh_1 + \sum_{i=1}^{l-1} h_i h_{i+1} + h_{l-1}c)) \qquad (41)$$

In the worst case, the total time complexity of the entire detection mechanism is:

$$O(Nd \times min(N,d) + d^3 + eN(kh + hc)) \qquad (42)$$

To reduce the time complexity compared to the original NN, the following condition must be met: $O(Nd \times min(N,d) + d^3 + eN(kh + hc)) < eN(dh + hc)$, thus, k must be chosen so that:

$$k < d(1 - \frac{min(N,d)}{eh} - \frac{d^2}{eNh}) \qquad (43)$$

In reality, the input data dimension is often much smaller than the number of samples in security data sets, so $min(N,d) = d$. With the condition $d << N$ and the sufficiently big number of epochs e for d, $\frac{d}{eh} - \frac{d^2}{eNh}$ in (43) will be close to 0. Thus, (43) becomes $k < d$, i.e., the time complexity of the detection mechanism will always outperform more than a multi-layer conventional NN. This is also indicated in Figure 7(a), reproduced from[55], demonstrating the complexity according to the number of neurons in the hidden layer for LocKedge and NN. It can be seen that with the same number of neurons, the LocKedge's complexity is always around two times lower than that of NN. Furthermore, Figure 7(b), reproduced from[55], illustrating training time performance computed by the time from reading the data until the end of the training phase, also shows that the training time of the LocKedge is lower than that of NN in the context of the BoT-IoT data set.

Detection Performance of the Centralized-learning Detection Module

In the centralized scenario, all the data is sent to the Cloud server for training and testing of the model. Figure 8, reproduced from[55], illustrates comparison in terms of accuracy between the centralized approach and the pure NN without the feature processing. The range of neurons in the hidden layer h is from 6 to 46. In general, the accuracy of the centralized detection approach is higher than that of NN. There is the stability of the accuracy of Lockedge and NN, with 0,999 and 0,997, respectively. This suggests that for optimal accuracy, the use of multiple neurons in the hidden layer is not necessary.

In addition, an average detection rate (DR) evaluation is implemented for each attack type between LocKedge, NN, and other Deep Learning (DL) methods: Deep Neural Network (DNN),

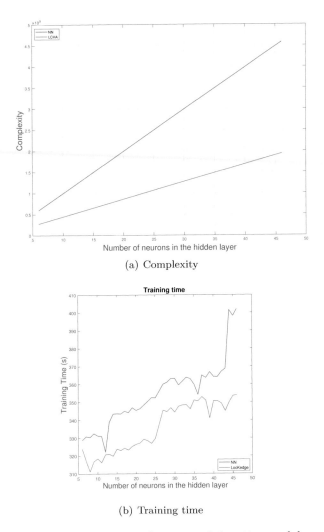

(a) Complexity

(b) Training time

Figure 7: Comparison between the proposed detection module and NN.

Recurrent Neural Network (RNN), and CNN. The results are described in Table 6, taken from the study[56] done on the same Bot-IoT data set. Besides, centralized-learning LocKedge is compared with some popular ML algorithms such as K-Nearest Neighbors (KNN), Decision Tree (DT), Random Forest (RF), and Support Vector Machine (SVM), depicted in Table 7. Generally, the figures indicate that the centralized detection approach has an average DR higher than the other methods in most classes, providing a balanced and more uniform DR between classes. However, in terms of DoS-HTTP and Data Theft attacks, the DR is lower than that of the other methods. The reason is that both of these attacks have a low number of samples, especially Data Theft with only 6 samples, so detecting these two types of attacks precisely requires much more complex detection models. Thus, this lower DR on two out of ten types is an acceptable trade-off for a lightweight model capable of running on edge devices.

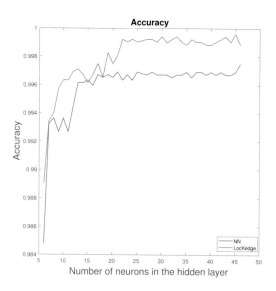

Figure 8: Accuracy comparison between NN and the proposed detection approach.

Table 6: DR of our proposal vs DNN, RNN, CNN, NN.

Attack type	DNN	RNN	CNN	NN	Our proposal
DoS-HTTP	0.96699	0.96868	0.97512	0.76091	0.90862
DoS-TCP	0.96628	0.96772	0.97112	1	1
DoS-UDP	0.96525	0.96761	0.97112	0.99928	0.99928
DDoS-HTTP	0.96616	0.96564	0.97010	0.98662	0.98715
DDoS-TCP	0.96219	0.96650	0.97003	0.99941	0.99965
DDoS-UDP	0.96118	0.9666	0.97006	0.99946	0.99946
OS Fingerprinting	0.96139	0.96762	0.97001	0.98887	0.99258
Server Scanning	0.96428	0.96874	0.97102	0.99947	0.99973
Keylogging	0.96762	0.96999	0.98102	0.98780	0.99268
Data Theft	1	1	1	0.46341	0.56098

Figure 9 reproduced from[55] demonstrates the overall performance of the centralized detection approach and several popular ML algorithms in terms of Precision and F1-score in the classification of multi-attacks detection. In comparison to other solutions for each type of attack, the centralized detection approach is always the highest, which means that the proposed solution can minimize the false positives efficiently. Regarding the F1-score, the proposed approach also outperforms other methods in most attack types, proving to be a good scheme for taking both false positives and false negatives into account.

Finally, the multi-class micro-averaging and macro-averaging ROC Curves for the proposed detection approach in the centralized mode are illustrated in Figure 10, reproduced from[55]. Micro-averaging is plotted by treating each element of the label indicator matrix as a binary prediction, while macro-averaging simply gives equal weight to the classification of each label.

Table 7: DR of our proposal vs. KNN, DT, RF, SVM.

Attack type	KNN	DT	RF	SVM	Our Proposal
DoS-HTTP	0.81690	0.84507	0.76056	0.74647	0.90862
DoS-TCP	1	0.99752	1	1	1
DoS-UDP	0.99851	0.99926	0.99926	0.99554	0.99928
DDoS-HTTP	0.96774	0.82258	0.96774	0.97581	0.98715
DDoS-TCP	0.99173	0.97746	0.99248	0.99624	0.99965
DDoS-UDP	0.99217	1	1	0.96784	0.99946
OS Fingerprinting	0.93478	0.93478	0.89130	0.78261	0.99258
Server Scanning	0.97826	1	1	0.98913	0.99973
Keylogging	1	0.3	0.9	1	0.99268
Data Theft	0	0	0	0	0.56098

The AUC values in both cases reach the most ideal result at 1, indicating that the centralized mode detection approach has uniformity in classifying different labels.

Detection Performance of FL detection approach

With the advantages presented in Section 4.1.3, the FL-driven detection performance of LocKedge is investigated in an IoT network environment with the following scenario:

- The BoT-IoT data set[54] is divided into four smaller client data sets according to the source IP address to simulate an IoT network with 4 distinct zones, where the data from clients are sent to four IoT gateways.

- There are four attacking sources in the BoT-IoT testbed with the range of IP addresses from 192.168.100.147 to 192.168.100.150, assuming that each source attacks a different gateway and all other source IP addresses considered as normal or victim devices in one of the four zones.

- Each data set is split into two sets: a training set and test set, leading to four train sets and four test sets in total. All four training sets are extracted features together via PCA, and then the detection model will be trained with the training sets separately by using the FL approach. Finally, after each communication round, the global model will be evaluated using the four different test sets.

Figure 11 reproduced from[55] shows the accuracy and the loss of the test set after 1000 communication rounds. Based on empirical testing, the number of local epochs was set to one to reduce the training time. As shown in these two figures, the accuracy and the loss are steady after about 350 communication rounds, so this can be a good cut-off point. The accuracy reaches close to 100% for Client 1 and 2, over 90% for Client 4, and about 80% for Client 3.

Moreover, the ROC curves of the Federated mode shown in Figure 12, reproduced in[55], where the macro-averaging AUC is a bit lower compared to the centralized mode because of the different data distribution at nodes or the likelihood without sufficient labels of some nodes. For the micro-averaging AUC results, all values are equal to 1 except for node 3 as 0.99.

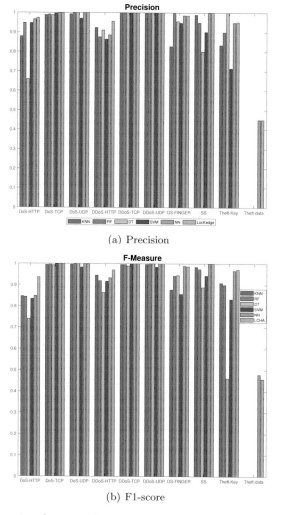

(a) Precision

(b) F1-score

Figure 9: Comparison between the proposed detection module and other solutions.

In addition, a small comparison between the centralized mode and the federated-learning mode in terms of DR, precision, and F1-score is performed, shown in Figure 13, 13(b), and 13(c) respectively, reproduced from[55]. It can be seen that in some types of attacks such as DoS-HTTP, DDoS-HTTP, and theft-data, the results in the FL mode are inferior to its centralized mode counterpart but remains acceptable (greater than 65%). The reason is similar to the case in the macro-averaging AUC evaluation above. In practice, with the FL mode, this is quite normal since different clients will possess their own data sources, and thus some zones may not have enough labels.

Evaluation of Edge Computing Capacity

Finally, to evaluate the Edge-Cloud architecture, the CPU and RAM usage of the edge gateway used to deploy the detection module scheme in different attack volumes is implemented on a

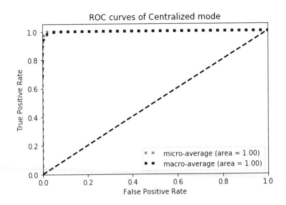

Figure 10: Micro-averaged ROC curve in centralized mode.

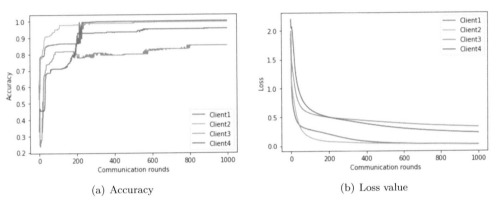

(a) Accuracy (b) Loss value

Figure 11: Detection performance of test set on 1000 communication rounds.

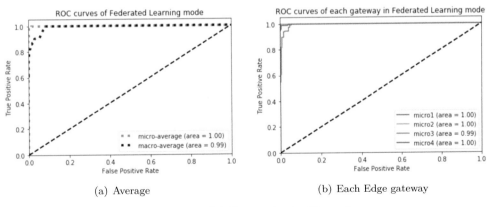

(a) Average (b) Each Edge gateway

Figure 12: ROC curve in the FL mode.

Raspberry Pi 3B+. During deploying the detection module, 400 to 2400 samples per second are loaded to the PI3, shown in Figure 14(a) reproduced from[55]. Over time, the CPU usage fluctuates for each attack rate represented by each line in the figure. Additionally, the average

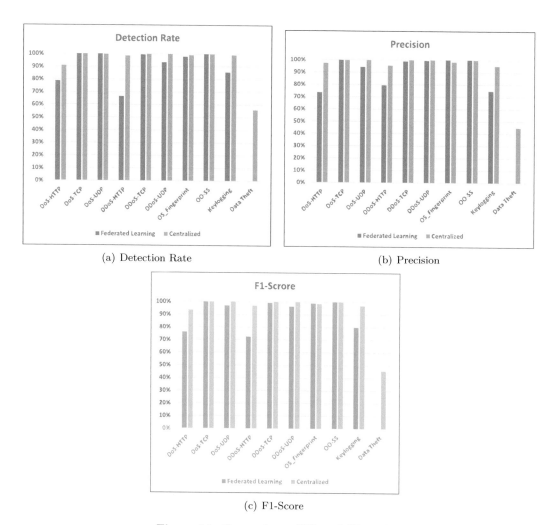

(a) Detection Rate

(b) Precision

(c) F1-Score

Figure 13: Comparison of FL and CL mode.

CPU usage proportion of each different attack rates, represented in Figure 14(b) reproduced from[55]. It can be seen that the CPU usage increases exponentially as the attack rate increases and gets saturated by the attack rate of 2400 samples per second, which means that for the whole quad-core, the Pi3-based edge can tolerate the attack rate of 9.600 samples per second. Similarly, as illustrated in Figure 15, reproduced from[55], the memory usage of the PI3 also increases in direct proportion of attack rates, before reaching stability at the threshold of 1800 samples per second. Therefore, when the sample rate is equal to or higher than 1800 samples per second, up to a certain time, the RAM of PI3 will be used all. In each edge zone, moreover, the sample rates of DDoS-TCP, DDoS-UDP, DoS-TCP, and DoS-UDP are measured, at 3.950, 5086, 1.927, 2.605 samples per second respectively, these figures are below the threshold of PI3 during attack detection. Besides, a more powerful edge device with enough RAM and good clock speed may deploy an edge-cloud architecture better, for example, Raspberry Pi 4 has a faster 1.5GHz processor, and RAM of 2GB which could work better right at the edge.

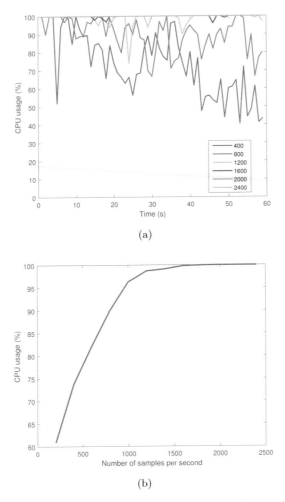

(a)

(b)

Figure 14: CPU usage of a core under rate of 400 to 2400 samples per second.

4.1.5 Summary

In this section, we discuss an Edge-Cloud architecture with a low complexity attack detection mechanism -LocKedge. It can detect multi-attacks faster and take advantage of the edge resources. The evaluation in terms of algorithm complexity, detection performance for both learning modes (centralized and FL mode), and edge computing capacity, using real traffic data set BoT-IoT, demonstrated LocKedge not just has the low complexity and the high accuracy but also outperforms the recent ML models and deep learning models.

4.2 Anomaly Detection in Industrial Control System—Smart Manufacturing

The concept of *Smart Manufacturing* is a paradigm where production processes are supplemented with artificial intelligence (AI) for more accurate and cost-effective decision making

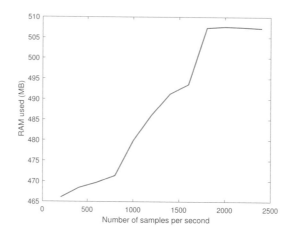

Figure 15: RAM usage with different attack rates.

based on data collected by monitoring sensors, towards an automatic real-time system [2;3]. These data-collecting devices together with gateway devices, control servers, and other actuators constitute an ICS, leading to the definition of Industrial Internet of Things or IIoT.

Over the years, this concept has been adopted in industries of developed countries all over the world. However, this innovation also brings about threats of being targeted by cyber-attacks for sabotage, system exploitation, or more dangerously, confidential information.

This section presents an AD solution based on the FL technique [57], deployed with time-series data in SM context in order to make use of computing resources in edge IoT devices as well as achieve faster detection of anomalies and reduce transmission bandwidth.

4.2.1 Federated Learning-based Architecture for Smart Manufacturing

In the SM context, a new architecture utilizing FL was proposed for AD purposes. In this architecture, AD task is deployed on Edge devices with limited but feasible system resources, grasping the concept of Edge Computing, instead of Cloud Server as in traditional architecture.

Each Edge device serves as a local control unit within a small area, monitoring all data collected and anomalies in that area or even executing immediate decisions if necessary. The FL approach employed in this architecture lets data distributed across different areas be shared via a central Cloud Aggregator. This aggregator helps improve the AD model at each Edge device to have a better performance over a broader as well as more universal dataset without the need of gathering all data in one place.

Moreover, communications among entities in this architecture are based on *Message Queuing Telemetry Transport* or *MQTT* protocol owing to its nature as a lightweight yet reliable publish/subscribe messaging transport and minimal bandwidth required. As a matter of fact, the MQTT protocol is progressively applied in the SM field for communicating purposes.

Figure 16 illustrates proposed hierarchical architecture, consisting three fundamental components as follows:

- **Cloud Server**: The central server aggregates all models received from Edge devices, resulting in a new federated model to be updated for each Edge device.

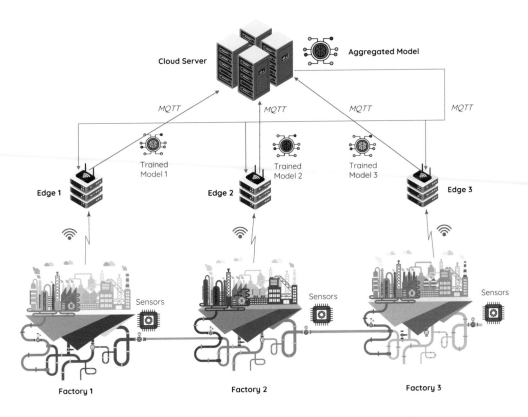

Figure 16: FL–based architecture for Anomaly Detection in Smart Manufacturing.

- **Edge devices**: Those are local administrators in the system, responsible for monitoring data from sensors in a pre-defined restricted area and operating AD function. This very component in the architecture is the key difference between traditional and FL–based architecture. Additionally, Edge devices only send their trained models to Cloud Server instead of all raw data collected to Cloud for further processing. This modification directly facilitates the delay disadvantage of the traditional model.

- **Factory sites**: Production lines are divided into smaller sites, each of which is under the scope of an Edge device (Edge server), comprising various sensors to collect data and actuators to execute decisions issued from servers.

Figure 17 demonstrates comprehensive operation in FL–based architecture proposed. To be more specific,

- First, Cloud Server creates general initial VAE model and LSTM model with random weights. This entity also acts as a Weight Aggregator.

- Cloud Server then subscribe to MQTT topics to which each client sends their its model weights.

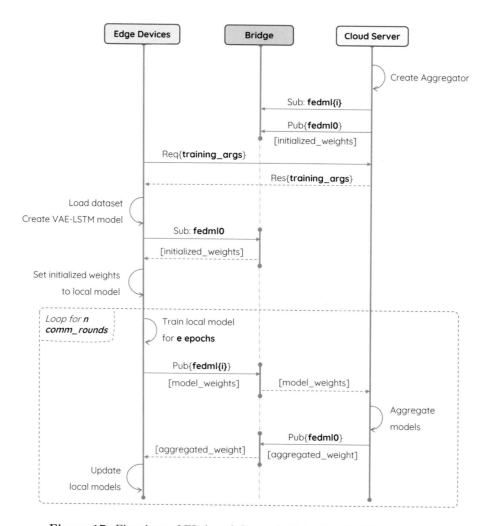

Figure 17: Flowchart of FL–based Anomaly Detection Architecture operation.

- Cloud Server publishes first model's weights to aggregated model topics, then waits for requests of VAE-LSTM model configuration from clients.

- After receiving model configuration replies from the server, Edge devices create local VAE-LSTM models and set initialized weights from subcriptions to aggregated model topics.

- Edge devices train local models with datasets, following by sending trained models' weights w_{t+1}^i to Cloud Server for aggregation. This happens once every communication round.

- Subsequently, Cloud Server computes the weight of aggregated global model by the *FedAvg* formula 44 introduced in[57]:

$$w_{t+1} = \sum_{i=1}^{C} \frac{n_i}{n} w_{t+1}^i \tag{44}$$

where:

C: the number of clients participating in system architecture

n_i: the quantity of data samples that client i holds

n: the total quantity of data samples across system

w_{t+1}^i: the weight of the local model at client i at round $t+1$

w_{t+1}: the weight of the aggregated global model at round $t+1$

- Finally, the weight of the aggregated model is finally sent back to Edge devices for local updates.

4.2.2 Anomaly Detection Algorithm using Hybrid VAE-LSTM Model at Edge Devices

As aforementioned, the proposed AD solution was used with time-series data as input, which is the predominant type of data in ICS. In general, the task of AD for time-series data opposes a number of challenges: noise, concept drift, and contextual information are some which can be taken to account. Furthermore, when deployed in an IIoT environment with an Edge Computing paradigm, requirements such as computing constraints as well as maximum detection time must be met.

To address those issues, in the proposed system, hybrid Variational Autoencoder (VAE) –LSTM model[24] is employed, or VAE-LSTM for short. This particular model was shown to take advantage of robust local features over short windows of VAE. Structural regularities of time series are captured over local windows. LSTM then estimates the long-term correlation in time-series over features produced by the VAE model, leading to a longer-term trend modeled. As a result of the unsupervised learning manner of VAE and LSTM models, this hybrid model is efficient in detecting new anomalous records which it has not encountered before.

To be more detailed, in the deployment of this hybrid model in FL IIoT architecture, the VAE model is formed of a two-Dense-layer encoder and decoder so as to achieve a lightweight operation. This adjustment makes the VAE model more appropriate to be deployed in limited computing capacity Edge devices.

Figure 18 depicts the overall operation of VAE-LSTM model when detecting time-series data anomalies. Specifically,

- First, the time-series data $\{x_1, x_2, \ldots, x_{L_{win}}, x_{L_{win}+1}, \ldots\}$—in which $x_i \in R^D$ is a multivariate data of D-dimensional—is sliced into rolling windows of size L_{win}. Those rolling windows will be used to train VAE model.

- A sequence–s_i, is constructed by concatenating L_{seq} non-overlapping windows, denoted as $\{s_{1,i}, s_{2,i}, \ldots, s_{L_{seq},i}\}$.

- After training phase of VAE model, the sequences $\{s_1, s_2, \ldots, s_i\}$ are fed into the encoder of the VAE module, where each window is compressed into a lower dimensional code. A code sequence e_i comprises multiple codes–$\{e_{1,i}, e_{2,i}, \ldots, e_{L_{seq},i}\}$. Subsequently, the code sequences $\{e_1, e_2, \ldots, e_i\}$ will be the input of the LSTM module.

- The LSTM module applies the first $L_{seq} - 1$ elements from the current code sequence i $(\{e_{1,i}, e_{2,i}, \ldots, e_{L_{seq}-1,i}\})$ to predict the last $L_{seq}-1$ components: $\hat{e}_i = \{\hat{e}_{2,i}, \hat{e}_{3,i}, \ldots, \hat{e}_{L_{seq},i}\}$

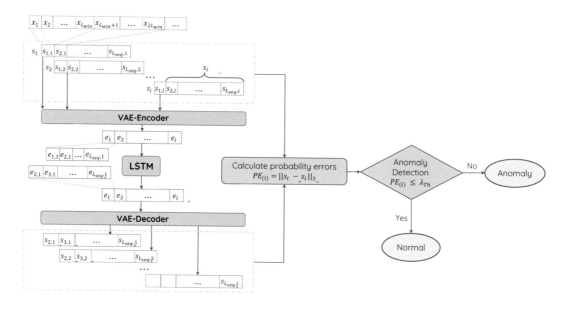

Figure 18: Hybrid VAE-LSTM model Block Diagram.

- Every predicted code sequence $\hat{e}_i$ is then reconstructed by the trained VAE decoder to get predicted sequence value $\hat{s}_i = \{\hat{s}_{2,i}, \hat{s}_{3,i}, \ldots, \hat{s}_{L_{seq},i}\}$.

- Each predicted sequence $\hat{s}_i$ is then compared with $\bar{s}_i$, which is the input sequence s_i excluding the first element, yielding a series of probabilities errors–prediction errors.

$$PE_i = ||\hat{s}_i - \bar{s}_i||_2, \tag{45}$$

- A threshold ζ_{Th} is employed on these errors to detect peculiar data points. This threshold is calculated using KQE[58] method as described in 3.4.1.

Detailed background, as well as operation of VAE and LSTM, will be elaborated in the following sections.

Deployment of VAE

VAE is a variant of AE neural network. In general, an AE is an unsupervised artificial NN aimed to learn an encoding for a set of data effectively. This task is performed by virtue of the symmetric structure of AE. Specifically, it consists of two main parts: an encoder and a decoder with a shared hidden layers with fewer nodes than main parts (a "bottleneck") which describes the code representing input data. This hidden layer is in fact the latent representation of the input data, keeping only the most important information. AE is trained by trying to compress input data to the "bottleneck" layer and subsequently produce output data from this latent representation to be as close as possible as input.

Used in the proposed architecture, VAE[59] is a category of AE which utilizes the Variational Bayesian method. With VAE, the NN describes probability distribution functions instead of deterministic ones. VAE can summarize the local data of a short time window, compressing them into an embedding with lower dimensions as shown in Figure 19. Originally, the AE model will likely result in a fragmented and discontinuous latent representation since its method is mainly minimization of the reproductive loss without considering the state of the middle latent space. VAE is designed to ensure the regularization of the latent space, create continuously distributed encodings, hence the generation of roughly identical data at the output. The structure of a VAE model is shown in Figure 19.

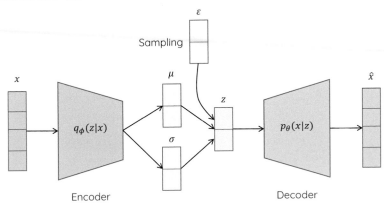

Figure 19: Illustration of VAE structure.

Numerous studies about designing a VAE model have been conducted, proposing different types of layers in its NN layout like recurrent units or Convolutional layers[60]. Nonetheless, these kinds of layers seem to be too complicated to be implemented in edge devices in our IIoT context. Thus, our VAE design only has two Dense layers in each encoder and decoder component, resulting in a lightweight model which can be trained with limited hardware capacity of edge devices. This modification in structure also helps us reduce the cost in communication with a server and vice versa, while achieving a relatively satisfactory detection performance.

Let a latent variable **z** go through a random process with parameters θ in order to generate data **x**. Describe the posterior probability as:

$$p_\theta(z|x) = \frac{p_\theta(x|z)p_\theta(z)}{p_\theta(x)} \tag{46}$$

Both the latent variable and the parameters of the process are not visible. Thus, the posterior probability and the marginal likelihood $p_\theta(x)$ are often intractable. To address this difficulty, a recognition model $q_\phi(z|x)$, which is an approximation of the posterior, is presented. The variational parameters ϕ of this model will be optimized that:

$$q_\phi(z|x) \approx p_\theta(z|x) \tag{47}$$

The marginal log likelihood of the data can be described as:

$$\log p_\theta(x) = D_{KL}(q_\phi(z|x)||p_\theta(z|x)) + \mathcal{L}_{\theta,\phi}(x) \tag{48}$$

where $\mathcal{L}_{\theta,\phi}(x)$ is the *evidence lower bound* (ELBO).

In (48), the first term is the Kullback-Leibler (KL) divergence, non-negative, hence $\log p_\theta(x) \geqslant \mathcal{L}_{\theta,\phi}(x)$. Therefore, optimizing the ELBO with respect to both θ and ϕ will minimize this KL term, yield $q_\phi(z|x)$ closer to the true posterior. The ELBO is defined as:

$$\mathcal{L}_{\theta,\phi}(x) = -D_{KL}(q_\phi(z|x)\|p_\theta(z)) + \mathbb{E}_{q_\phi(z|x)}(\log p_\theta(x|z)) \tag{49}$$

In (49), the first term is the KL divergence of the distribution of the encoding with respect to the normal distribution, ensure that the latent space is continuous while the second term is the reconstruction loss, make sure that the data is being encoded correctly.

An option is having both $q_\phi(z|x)$ and the prior $p_\theta(z)$ be Gaussian. The ELBO to be optimized for each data point i can then be described as:

$$\mathcal{L}_{\theta,\phi}(x^{(i)}) = \sum_{j=1}^{J} \frac{1}{2}\left[1 + \log((\sigma_j^{(i)})^2) - (\sigma_j^{(i)})^2 + (\mu_j^{(i)})^2\right]$$
$$-\frac{1}{L}\sum_{l=1}^{L} \mathbb{E}_{q_\phi(z|x)}\left[\log p_\theta(x^{(i)}|z^{(i,l)})\right] \tag{50}$$

where:
μ and σ are the output mean and standard deviation vectors of the encoder, respectively
J is the size of those vectors
L is the number of times a sample is taken from the latent space

Finally, parameters of the model can be depicted as:

$$(\theta^*, \phi^*) = argmax_{\theta,\phi}\mathcal{L}_{(\theta,\phi)}(x) \tag{51}$$

To obtain the optimal parameters, instead of maximizing $\mathcal{L}$, it is possible to take its negative as a loss function to minimize and apply the gradient descent method. However, due to the sampling of the random variable z in the second term of (50), calculating the gradient is unstable. To overcome this problem, re-parameterization technique introduced in [59] could be used, in which $z = \mu + \sigma \odot \epsilon$ with $\epsilon \sim \mathcal{N}(0,1)$ and sample ϵ instead of latent variable z directly. Following this method, the random sampling is externalized and the gradient descent can be calculated using deterministic nodes as usual.

Deployment of LSTM Networks

Generally, LSTM is a type of RNN, used for learning order-dependence in sequence prediction problems, allowing information to persist. LSTM is specially designed to address the vanishing gradient problem in vanilla RNNs. This is achieved by adding additional cells, input gates, and output gates, yielding a structure as depicted in Figure 20. Those additions allow the gradients to flow through the network without vanishing as quickly.

In this detection system, LSTM receives embeddings that were already computed into low-dimensional by VAE phase and further processes sequential patterns over a longer-term. Despite the fact that many variations of LSTM have been developed, it is shown that some of these appear to have better performance than others only in specific cases [61]. Hence, for the purpose

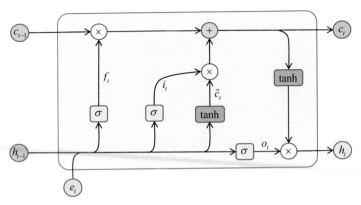

Figure 20: An LSTM cell.

of reduction of the complexity in computation, a simple LSTM network with one cell is utilized in our solution. Figure 20 illustrates the basic structure of one cell in LSTM network at state t.

To be specific, an LSTM cell has input e_t, output h_t (hidden state) and cell state c_t at time t along with c_{t-1} and h_{t-1} which are the output of the cell at the previous step. Different from RNN cell having only one *tanh* function, an LSTM cell has three control stages to remember past data points:

- **The first stage** is the forget gate: the gate decides which information should be kept and which should be forgotten with data point e_t and previous output h_{t-1} as input. This is performed by the function:

$$f_t = \sigma(W_f \times e_t + W_f \times h_{t-1} + b_f) \tag{52}$$

where:
(W_f, b_f): the weight and bias matrices of the forget gate.

- **The second stage** decides how much information should be added to the cell state c which is called the input gate:

$$c_t = c_{t-1} \times f_t + i_t \times \tilde{c}_t \tag{53}$$

in which i_t and $\tilde{c}_t$ are calculated as:

$$i_t = \sigma(W_i \times e_t + W_i \times h_{t-1} + b_i) \tag{54}$$

$$\tilde{c}_t = tanh(W_c \times e_t + W_c \times h_{t-1} + b_c) \tag{55}$$

where (W_i, b_i) and (W_c, b_c) are the weight and the bias matrices of the input gate and cell state, respectively.

In this step, the values i_t is computed by a sigmoid function along with a vector of values $\tilde{c}_t$ generated by a *tanh* function.

- **The last stage** is the output gate stage: The output h_t of LSTM cell depends on input e_t, h_{t-1} as well as the current cell state c_t. The *tanh* function scales down the value range to [1,

1], while the *sigmoid* function filters the information from the cell state being output through the number within [0,1].

$$h_t = O_t \times tanh(c_t) \tag{56}$$

where:

O_t is previously defined in (57)

(W_o, b_o) are the weight matrix and the bias of the output gate

$$O_t = \sigma(W_o \times e_t + W_o \times h_{t-1}+) \tag{57}$$

Overall, c_t acts as a connection between the states of the network. This helps to carry the previous important information to the next states, providing long-term memory for the LSTM model.

In the following sections, we will describe the performance of the proposed architecture in terms of AD and the effectiveness of FL-based Edge computing.

4.2.3 Data Pre-processing

The main case study is SM in a Gas Pipeline Factory, using a realistic time-series data set obtained from the Supervisory Control and Data Acquisition (SCADA) systems[62]. This data set includes 274,628 samples, and each sample contains network information, payload information, etc.[62]

Additionally, other time-series data sets gathered in several different fields, such as electrocardiograms (ECG)[63], respiration[63], power demand[63], gesture[63], space shuttle[63] and NYC taxi[64], are employed to test the model's AD performance in diverse industrial contexts. The short introduction of these data set is shown in the Table 8[65].

Data sets are required as input for all ML models, whether at the Edge or in the cloud. However, those data sets frequently contain several missing feature values and noise, so it is

Table 8: List of the data sets used in our experiments.

Data sets	Description
Gas pipeline (SCADA)[62]	The gas pipeline data set was collected in 2015 by Mississippi State University Lab for AD using their in-house gas pipeline system
ECGs[63]	The data set on Electrocardiograms is a time-series of the electrical signals caused by heartbeats
Respiration[63]	The respiration data set includes information on Patient's respiration measured by thorax extension when waking up
Power demand[63]	The data set provides information on the power consumption of a Dutch research facility in 1997
Gesture[63]	The gesture data set consists of 2 features representing the coordinates of the actor's right hand while performing a variety of actions
Space shuttle[63]	The data set measures the solenoid current of a Marotta MPV-41 series valve cycled on and off
NYC taxi[64]	The data set contains information on The New York taxi passenger data stream from July 2014 to June 2015

Time	Address	Function	Length	Setpoint	Gain	Reset rate	Deadband
1418682163	4	3	16	?	?	?	?
1418682163	4	3	46	?	?	?	?
1418682165	4	16	90	10	115	0.2	0.5
1418682165	4	16	16	?	?	?	?
1418682167	4	3	16	?	?	?	?
1418682167	4	3	46	?	?	?	?
1418682169	4	16	90	10	115	0.2	0.5
1418682169	4	16	16	?	?	?	?

Figure 21: Examples of the missing values in the SCADA data set.

essential to clean and pre-process data before the training process. For example, the SCADA data set is shown in Figure 21 with many missing values (i.e., "?" values).

According to work[66], missing data mechanisms are divided into three categories: missing completely at random (MCAR), missing at random (MAR), and missing not at random (MNAR). MCAR means the missingness of data is unrelated to any values. MAR indicates that the tendency of a value to be missing might depend on the observed data, but not the missing data. In contrast, MNAR denotes that there exists a relationship between the missingness and its value. Considering the missing values as shown in Figure 21 in[65], the SCADA data set is likely to have the characteristic of MAR. As a result, Last Observation Carried Forward (LOCF)[67], a popular method to handle MAR, is applied to process the missing values in the SCADA dataset. In LOCF, the immediately preceding value in the same feature is used to fill in the missing value. If the data set begins with missing values, the first observed value is employed to substitute them.

The following step is data transformation using the mean-standard deviation scale technique as in work (58) to normalize all features to the same scale and arithmetic values.

$$x'_i = \frac{x_i - \mu}{\sigma} \tag{58}$$

In which, μ and σ are the mean and the standard deviation of the listed feature values, respectively. To train and evaluate the model's performance in diverse scenarios, the SCADA data set is split into the training set (160,870 samples) and the testing set (68,657 samples). The training set contains only normal samples for AD purposes.

4.2.4 Detection Performance Evaluation

In this section, the performance of the model is evaluated in various contexts. The assessments were carried on the aforementioned data sets in terms of precision, recall, and F1-score (defined in Table 1 in 3.2.2).

Note that for time series data, an anomaly only occurs in one single time point, but is detected using a window; therefore, all the points in this window are considered as anomalies in the ground truth array. If any components in a window are detected, the whole window is considered detected.

Experiment 1

Experiment 1, as shown in Table 9[65], compares the performance of the FL detection model with the performance of the CL-based VAE-LSTM detection model on top of 7 different data sets. In the CL experiment, 25 different thresholds evenly spread between the smallest and the biggest reconstruction error are evaluated to determine the best heuristic thresholds for each of the 7 data sets[24]. According to work,[65], the application of VAE with multi-layer CNN is unimplementable at Edge devices due to its high computing complexity. Thus, the VAE model of work[24] is implemented with Dense to reduce the number of layers, features, thereby decreasing computing complexity and the matrix of weight at the edge.

In the FL experiment, the proposed threshold optimization using KQE is achieved by varying 9 values of p ranging from 0.1 to 0.9, with the distance of 0.1, in addition to 2 more values of 0.95 and 0.99 for a total of 11 values. Table 9[65] shows that the Hybrid VAE-LSTM module performs well on almost all data sets, except for respiration and gesture data set. Moreover, the FL with KQE approach outperforms the CL VAE-LSTM solution proposed by work[24] in most of the data sets despite the fact that the CL model tends to perform better than their FL counterparts. This demonstrates that an appropriate threshold determined by the KQE technique may significantly enhance the performance of an AD model, and KQE is better and quicker at finding the optimal threshold in most cases.

Table 9: FL approach vs. CL approach over 7 different time-series data sets.

Data set	Test set	Cloud-Centralized-VAE-LSTM[24]			Our FL-based approach		
		Precision	Recall	F1	Precision	Recall	F1
Space shuttle	TEK14	0.5792	0.9990	0.7333	0.8623	0.8431	0.8536
	TEK16	0.9636	0.8881	0.9243	1	1	1
	TEK17	0.8961	0.9637	0.9287	0.9650	1	0.9822
Respiration	nprs43	0.6586	0.4952	0.5653	0.9313	0.5530	0.6939
	nprs44	0.9786	0.2799	0.4353	0.5347	0.5027	0.5182
Gesture	gesture	0.3422	0.9989	0.5098	0.5278	1	0.6910
Nyc taxi	nyc_taxi	0.7711	0.7628	0.7669	0.9606	1	0.9799
ECG	Chfdb_chf01_275	1	1	1	0.9175	1	0.9570
	chfdb_chf13_45590	1	1	1	0.9489	1	0.9738
	chfdbf15	0.6484	0.8968	0.7526	0.9458	1	0.9721
	ltstdb_20221_43	0.9607	1	0.9800	1	1	1
	ltstdb_20321_240	1	1	1	1	1	1
	mitdb__100_180	0.9754	1	0.9876	1	1	1
	qtdbsel102	0.5827	1	0.7364	0.9604	1	0.9797
	stdb_308_0	0.7521	1	0.8585	0.6073	0.6373	0.6220
	xmitdb_x108_0	0.6727	1	0.8043	1	0.7628	0.8654
Power demand	Power_demand	0.2728	0.8948	0.4182	0.7355	0.9100	0.8135
SCADA	Scada	0.9315	1	0.9645	0.9609	0.9982	0.9792

Experiment 2

The heuristic and KQE approaches are tested to identify the best threshold on top of both centralized (e.g., the approach of work[24]) and FL scenarios with SCADA data set to assess the influence of the FL approach and KQE-based threshold optimization on detection performance separately.

Table 9[65] demonstrates that the KQE-based strategy offers a better F1 score and Precision in both centralized and federated cases, with just a small reduction in Recall in the FL approach. With the KQE-based threshold selection method, the cloud-based centralized method proposed by work[24] slightly increases its own detection performance.

The best p found for the SCADA data set is 0.9. The Area under the ROC Curve (AUC) value is also tested for both scenarios because this metric is unaffected by the threshold selection. Moreover, the AUC value of FL is slightly lower than that of the CL model, indicating that the decrease in model quality caused by FL is minor.

Table 10: SCADA centralized vs. federated results.

Learning Approach	Heuristic-based threshold			KQE-based threshold				AUC
	Precision	Recall	F1	Best p	Precision	Recall	F1	
Centralized	0.9315	1	0.9645	0.9	0.9585	1	0.9788	0.8539
Federated	0.9315	1	0.9645	0.9	0.9609	0.9982	0.9702	0.8500

4.2.5 Evaluation on Edge Computing Efficiency

This section describes the performance of real Edge hardware working in the Federated-learning IoT environment to estimate the effectiveness of an Edge-computing architecture in reality with restricted hardware capacity.

The communication efficiency of the FL approach is compared to that of the CL architecture. Furthermore, the concerns of computing resources and energy consumption at each Edge are also covered.

Testbed setup

As illustrated in Figure 22[65], the testbed involves:

- Four Raspberry-Pi-4-Model-B kits acting as edge devices; Raspberry-Pi-4 features a 1.5GHz ARM Quad-core Cortex-A72 processor and 4GB RAM with Raspbian OS 32-bit.

- A Dell Precision 3640 Tower workstation serving as a Cloud Server; the workstation features an Intel Core i7–10700K 3.8GHz (up to 5.1GHz), RAM of 16GB, Arch Linux.

- All Edge devices and Cloud Server are interconnected with a router via their wifi interfaces.

In the Edge devices, the FL-based VAE-LSTM framework is written in Python 3 with the TensorFlow 2 platform, which is built with the support of the FL framework - FedML.

The edge devices and cloud server interchange weights and bias matrices of the VAE-LSTM model via the MQTT protocol, which is standardized for the IoT environment. *EMQ X Broker*[68] is hosted on the cloud server as a MQTT broker for better long-term performance.

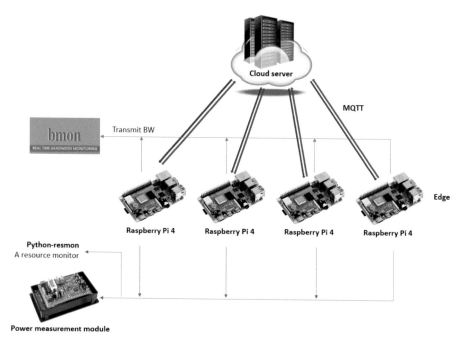

Figure 22: Testbed setup.

Implementation of Bandwidth occupation measurement

To measure bandwidth occupation in the link between each Edge and the cloud server, the tool *bmon*[69] is implemented on the up-streaming direction of the edge devices' WiFi interfaces. *bmon*[69] is a monitoring and debugging networking tool, especially used to capture statistics of a network.

Implementation of Computation resource and Energy consumption measurement

External monitors and peripheral devices are connected to Edge devices via SSH connection to eliminate noise, allowing for more accurate bandwidth occupancy measurements. All measured data are logged into separate text files and processed later to display the measurement results in graphs.

In order to assess the computing occupation level of the Edge devices, *resmon*[70] is applied to measure CPU usage and memory usage during the training task of the FL-based VAE-LSTM model.

The measurement of energy consumption involves using *UM25C USB Tester* to calculate the energy usage of Raspberry Pi.

Experimental Scenarios

Three main scenarios are established to compare the communication efficiency of the proposed FL architecture with the CL architecture utilizing the same type of detection mechanism.

For each scenario, both architectures are tested using the same detection model (i.e., VAE-LSTM) and the same data set (i.e., SCADA of 58MB). Four essential metrics are focused to evaluate the performance of an Edge:

- Bandwidth consumption in the link between the Edge and the cloud

- Power consumption at an Edge during training

- CPU usage at an Edge during training

- Memory usage at an Edge during training

Scenario 1 is for the cloud-based CL architecture, in which all data from clients and sensors are transmitted to the cloud for centralized training and detecting anomalies. Hence, the Edge simply forwards traffic directly to the cloud server.

Scenario 2 is for the FL architecture, in which the training and AD processes are carried out directly at the Edge. As a result, the Edge merely sends its own model to the cloud for global updating (i.e., a matrix of weights).

Scenario 3 is for investigating the behavior of the edge during the detection phase of FL. To set up the experiment, a time-series test set of 2000 samples from the SCADA data set is utilized. This set of data is then fed into the detection module processing one block of 1000 data points at a time. In the detection phase, the output of anomalous points is determined by comparing the reconstruction error with a predefined threshold using the KQE method.

Performance Results and Analysis

Bandwidth Occupation during the training phase

Figure 23[65] demonstrates the bandwidth occupation for Scenario 1. As can be observed, bandwidth occupancy averages about 2000 KiB per second for most of the 45 seconds, peaking at roughly 2600 KiB per second. Meanwhile, as seen in Figure 24[65], there is only an 8-second spike of bandwidth occupation of about 1700 KiB per second over the whole VAE-LSTM training process in FL architecture.

In comparison to the CL architecture, the suggested FL architecture saves 35% bandwidth and only requires 18% of the transmission time (see in Figure 24[65]). Furthermore, in the case of a larger data set, the FL approach will outperform the CL model in terms of Bandwidth occupation since Edge devices only transmitted matrices of weights to the Cloud server.

However, implementing a detection model at each Edge device in a distributed manner may result in a trade-off with resource and energy usage at the Edge. This is a problem since, in order to discover anomalies, all Edge devices must compute and analyze data using their own resources. Thus, it is essential to evaluate the Power, CPU, and Memory consumption of an Edge throughout the training phase.

Power Consumption at the Edge during the training phase

In this experiment, power consumption in each single Edge device during the CL process (i.e., forwarding-traffic process) and the FL process (i.e., training process) are measured.

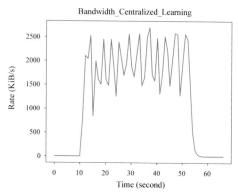

Figure 23: Bandwidth occupied in the Edge-Cloud link for the CL approach.

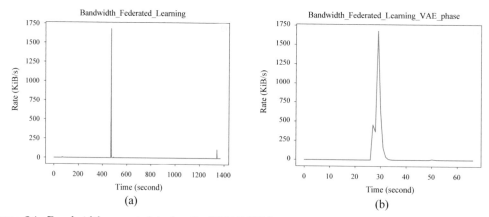

(a)   (b)

Figure 24: Bandwidth occupied during the VAE-LSTM training in the Edge-Cloud link for the FL approach.

As Figure 25(a)[65] illustrated, the power consumption at the edge in the CL scenario is in the range of 2600-3600 mW.

Figure 25(b)[65] shows that the power consumption during the training process in the FL scenario is separated into three continuous stages: the VAE phase, the phase of creating embeddings for the LSTM phase, and the LSTM phase. As measured in the Raspberry-Pi-4 edge device, each cycle of the VAE phase takes around 410 seconds, 850 seconds to produce embeddings and LSTM phase, and 1300 seconds to finish the entire training procedure.

To complete the 15-round VAE-LSTM training process and achieve the high detection performance presented in Table 10[65], the VAE phase is performed 15 times plus one embedding and LTSM phase. It will take an additional 410 seconds for each VAE phase, and the entire training process at the edge will take roughly 2 hours.

It is worth noting that the VAE-LSTM is used for feature extraction in this architecture. In case that network status changes but a long training period is not permitted, the VAE-LSTM trained with the old data without retraining will be utilized to reduce the training time. A new threshold will be recalculated based on both of the prediction scores computed from the old data and new data which is got through the trained VAE-LSTM to provide corresponding prediction scores.

172

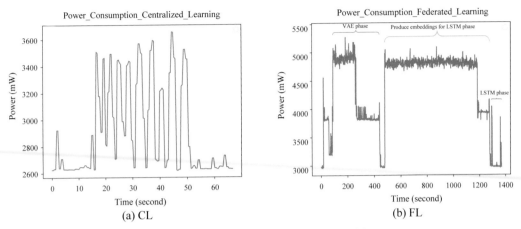

Figure 25: Power consumption at an Edge.

CPU consumption at the Edge during the training phase

CPU usage in a single edge is also measured in the same experimental setting as the Power measurement.

For centralized training scenario, Figure 26(a)[65] elaborates the CPU usage of an Edge during 45 seconds of forwarding data from the sensors to the cloud.

For the FL scenario, Figure 26(b)[65] demonstrates the CPU usage in a single Edge during the training VAE-LSTM process of 1 round of the VAE phase and 1 embeddings and LSTM phase.

As observed, in the CL architecture, the Edge device uses only 5% of the total CPU on average since it is just responsible for passing data from sensors. Whilst, in the FL scenario, the training task takes 80% of the CPU in the worst case. However, Edge's CPU still has 20% left for other application information which may account for another 5%. As a result, the overall CPU usage for AD and other traffic communication tasks is around 85%, illustrating the implementation of this edge-computing architecture in SM.

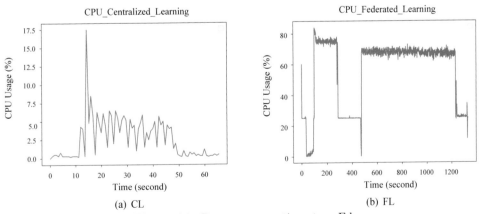

Figure 26: Power consumption at an Edge.

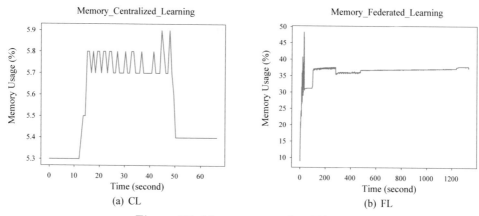

Figure 27: Memory usage of an Edge.

Memory Usage at the Edge during the training phase

The memory usage of an Edge for the CL and FL scenario are presented in the same experimental setting.

Figure 27(a)[65] shows the memory usage of an Edge in CL architecture accounting for less than 6% at a maximum over 45 seconds of the total experiment time. Whilst, in the FL architecture, the memory usage presented in Figure 27(b)[65] accounts for 37% on average during 1300 seconds of the training phase with one round of the VAE phase and one embedding and LSTM phase.

Power Consumption, CPU Usage, Memory Usage at the Edge during the detection phase

In Scenario 3, Power Consumption, CPU, and Memory Usage of the Edge device during the AD phase are presented in Figure 28[65]. As shown in Figure 28(a)[65], power consumption at the Edge during the detection period is typically in the range of 4000–4200 mW, with the Raspberry-Pi-4 edge's baseline power consumption being 2600 mW. The CPU usage during the detection phase takes about 60% on average, and memory usage takes about 11% in the worst case.

Overall, this consumption is lower than that of the training phase, which can be explained as the Edge device no longer required to do complex mathematical computations relating to high dimensional matrices as the training data set. Instead, significantly smaller chunks of data are given as input to the detecting module, resulting in considerable reductions in both power consumption and computational resources utilized.

4.2.6 Summary

In this section, we describe a FL architecture based on Edge Computing for SM application in the context of Big Data. The proposed architecture demonstrates high detection performance, whilst providing the advantage of quick response since AD is implemented close to the attack sources. Furthermore, the system is proved to reduce bandwidth for controlling data in the transmission

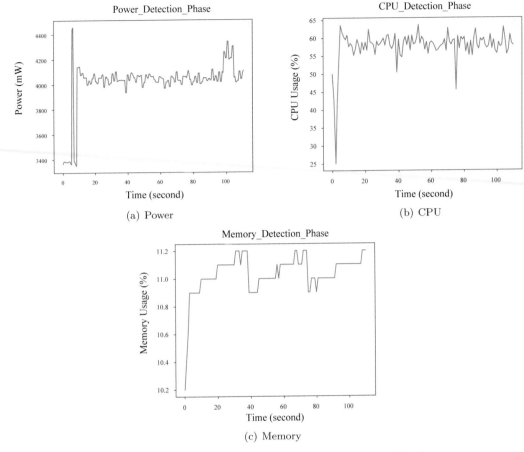

(a) Power

(b) CPU

(c) Memory

Figure 28: Consumption of an Edge device during the AD phase.

link between the edge and the cloud, meanwhile guaranteeing that the edge hardware will not be overloaded in terms of CPU and Memory usage.

5   Difficulties, Challenges, and Perspectives for Machine Learning-based Anomaly Detection for Cybersecurity Applications

After getting through all designs and issues of running an architecture that is resilient and effective for AD within the context of an IoT-based system, we can see that a Federated-Learning architecture based on Edge-computing is a good architecture candidate for smart applications of SM in the context of Big Data. The overall architecture has shown to have high detection performance, whilst giving the advantage of having a fast response since AD is implemented near the attack sources (i.e., the edge). The FL architecture distributes the monitoring and detection task to smaller local areas, so that it can deal with Big Data generated inside a smart factory better. In addition, such a system can reduce bandwidth for controlling data in the transmission link between the edge and the cloud, meanwhile ensuring that the edge hardware will not be overloaded in terms of CPU and Memory usage.

For a future better system design, there are several problems engineers should take into account and consider, as follows:

- To better optimize such distributed systems in terms of weights communicating between the Edge and the Cloud, as well as defining the more suitable training data so that Edge devices take up as little computing resource as possible to be able to carry on more other tasks.

- The limit of the data size and its number of features should be further investigated to ensure the edge computing work in a stable mode.

- Moreover, more aspects of other applications within SM should be covered such as: Predictive maintenance, Quality control, Real-Time Production Optimization in a Smart Factory 4.0.

- To address the change of the normal behaviour over time within an ICS. For example, IoT devices are aging. Hence new behaviour of devices can be classified as an anomaly, which then causes a high false-positive rate. It is a common issue for any AD approach using one-class classification ML in which we use only normal data for training. In fact, there is a research direction in online ML that updates old models with the most up-to-date data. And to the best of our knowledge, this research direction seems not to have been well investigated in the Federated-Learning environment. Within that context, online FL should be an interesting issue to investigate in the future.

- To address a critical aspect when manufacturing sites are not identical, for example, in the number of machines. It raises the issue of imbalanced distributed training for any AI models running on the edge. Since data sets of different sites can be different (i.e., imbalanced data distribution), it increases the bias of pattern learned by the FL server.

Another perspective is the decision interpretability of black-box models, which are based on algorithms related to NNs with tons of parameters. Although the prediction results of these algorithms can achieve high performance, it is problematic for engineers to analyze and investigate them. Explainable Artificial Intelligence (XAI), as a result, can be adopted to overcome this drawback, especially in ICSs where engineers need to closely monitor their IoT systems. The reason is simply that because XAI assists humans to understand the reason why models predict its decision. With state-of-the-art XAI frameworks enabling us to explain and evaluate the reliability of results effectively, in the future, we should employ them to interpret the decisions made by an AD architecture.

In another future direction, quantum AD using quantum machine learning[71] has recently emerged as a hot topic with the advent of quantum computing. Based on some techniques such as quantum matrix, quantum phase estimation and amplitude amplification, Quantum Computing is used to develop quantum algorithms for ML. Since quantum data (in quantum state form) is common in all fields of quantum computation, quantum communication, and quantum simulation, detecting anomalous quantum states is crucial in quantum information processing and communication, especially over the cloud or Quantum Internet.

6 Conclusion

In this chapter, we discussed Cybersecurity for IoT-based Industrial systems, especially for the ICS of a Smart Factory in the new digital era. Machine learning algorithms are shown to be efficient approaches for AD as long as they are chosen, combined, and optimized properly for each system context and characteristic. Moreover, as a reinforcement for those machine-learning-based techniques, a well-designed overall architecture with distributed computing at different sites, with light-weight protocol, with FL could make those AD systems run efficiently in terms of fast system response, bandwidth saving on communication channels, and data privacy. With those cutting-edge AD designs, modern IoT-based Industrial systems or any IoT-based networks could be more resilient and reliable to be deployed for numerous applications and purposes running on top of it.

References

[1] H. Haddadpajouh and R. Parizi. A survey on internet of things security: Requirements, challenges, and solutions. *Internet of Things*, p. 100129, 11, 2019.

[2] Y. Lu, X. Xu and L. Wang. Smart manufacturing process and system automation—A critical review of the standards and envisioned scenarios. *Journal of Manufacturing Systems*, 56: 312–325, 2020.

[3] J. Wang, Y. Ma, L. Zhang, R.X. Gao and D. Wu. Deep learning for smart manufacturing: Methods and applications. *Journal of Manufacturing Systems*, 48: 144–156, 2018, special Issue on Smart Manufacturing.

[4] N. Tuptuk and S. Hailes. Security of smart manufacturing systems. *Journal of Manufacturing Systems*, 47: 93–106, 2018.

[5] M.A. Amanullah, R.A. Ariyaluran Habeeb, F. Nasaruddin, A. Gani, E. Ahmed, A. Nainar, N. Akim and M. Imran. Deep learning and big data technologies for iot security. *Computer Communications*, 151, 02, 2020.

[6] D. Myers, S. Suriadi, K. Radke and E. Foo. Anomaly detection for industrial control systems using process mining. *Computers & Security*, 78: 103–125, 2018.

[7] P. Nader, P. Honeine and P. Beauseroy. l_p-norms in one-class classification for intrusion detection in scada systems. *IEEE Transactions on Industrial Informatics*, 10(4): 2308–2317, 2014.

[8] A. Gumaei, M.M. Hassan, S. Huda, M.R. Hassan, D. Camacho, J. Del Ser and G. Fortino. A robust cyberattack detection approach using optimal features of scada power systems in smart grids. *Applied Soft Computing*, 96: 106658, 2020.

[9] P. Priyanga S, K. Krithivasan, P. S and S. Sriram V S. Detection of cyberattacks in industrial control systems using enhanced principal component analysis and hypergraph-based convolution neural network (EPCA-HG-CNN). *IEEE Transactions on Industry Applications*, 56(4): 4394–4404, July–Aug, 2020, doi: 10.1109/TIA.2020.2977872.

[10] G. Li, Y. Shen, P. Zhao, X. Lu, J. Liu, Y. Liu and S.C. Hoi. Detecting cyberattacks in industrial control systems using online learning algorithms. *Neurocomputing*, 364: 338–348, 2019.

[11] D. Li, K. Paynabar and N. Gebraeel. A degradation-based detection framework against covert cyberattacks on scada systems. *IISE Transactions*, 53(7): 812–829, 2021.

[12] M. Kravchik and A. Shabtai. Efficient cyber attack detection in industrial control systems using lightweight neural networks and pca. *IEEE Transactions on Dependable and Secure Computing*, pp. 1–1, 2021.

[13] F. Adamsky, M. Aubigny, F. Battisti, M. Carli, F. Cimorelli, T. Cruz, A. Di Giorgio, C. Foglietta, A. Galli, A. Giuseppi, F. Liberati, A. Neri, S. Panzieri, F. Pascucci, J. Proenca, P. Pucci, L. Rosa and R. Soua. Integrated protection of industrial control systems from cyber-attacks: The atena approach. *International Journal of Critical Infrastructure Protection*, 21: 72–82, 2018.

[14] R.F. Babiceanu and R. Seker. Cyber resilience protection for industrial internet of things: A software-defined networking approach. *Computers in Industry*, 104: 47–58, 2019.

[15] A. Essien and C. Giannetti. A deep learning model for smart manufacturing using convolutional lstm neural network autoencoders. *IEEE Transactions on Industrial Informatics*, 16(9): 6069–6078, 2020.

[16] A. Luca, M.G.C. Cimino, G. Manco, E. Ritacco and G. Vaglini. Using an autoencoder in the design of an anomaly detector for smart manufacturing. *Pattern Recognition Letters*, 136: 06 2020.

[17] R.-J. Hsieh, J. Chou and C.-H. Ho. Unsupervised online anomaly detection on multivariate sensing time series data for smart manufacturing. In *2019 IEEE 12th Conference on Service-Oriented Computing and Applications (SOCA)*, pp. 90–97, 2019.

[18] J. Gao, X. Song, Q. Wen, P. Wang, L. Sun and H. Xu. Robusttad: Robust time series anomaly detection via decomposition and convolutional neural networks, 2020.

[19] R.-Q. Chen, G.-H. Shi, W.-L. Zhao and C.-H. Liang. A joint model for it operation series prediction and anomaly detection, 2021.

[20] L. Gjorgiev and S. Gievska. Time series anomaly detection with variational autoencoder using mahalanobis distance. In *ICT Innovations 2020. Machine Learning and Applications*, V. Dimitrova and I. Dimitrovski (eds.). Cham: Springer International Publishing, pp. 42–55, 2020.

[21] Y. Liu, S. Garg, J. Nie, Y. Zhang, Z. Xiong, J. Kang and M.S. Hossain. Deep anomaly detection for time-series data in industrial iot: A ommunication-efficient on-device federated learning approach. *IEEE Internet of Things Journal*, 8(8): 6348–6358, 2021.

[22] T.H. Truong, P.B. Ta, M.L. Dao, D.T. Bui, D.L. Tran and T.B. Nguyen. An efficient low complexity edge-cloud framework for security in iot networks. In *2020 IEEE Eighth International Conference on Communications and Electronics (ICCE)*, pp. 533–539, 2021.

[23] H.D. Nguyen, K.P. Tran, S. Thomassey and M. Hamad. Forecasting and anomaly detection approaches using lstm and lstm autoencoder techniques with the applications in supply chain management. *International Journal of Information Management*, 11, 2020.

[24] S. Lin, R. Clark, R. Birke, S. Schönborn, N. Trigoni and S. Roberts. Anomaly detection for time series using vae-lstm hybrid model. In *ICASSP 2020-2020 IEEE International Conference on Acoustics, Speech and Signal Processing (ICASSP)*, pp. 4322–4326, 2020.

[25] B. Schölkopf, J.C. Platt, J. Shawe-Taylor, A.J. Smola and R.C. Williamson. Estimating the support of a high-dimensional distribution. *Neural Computation*, 13(7): 1443–1471, 2001.

[26] V.V. Trinh, K.P. Tran and T.H. Truong. Data-driven hyperparameter optimization of one-class support vector machines for anomaly detection in wireless sensor networks. In *2017 International Conference on Advanced Technologies for Communications (ATC)*, Oct 2017, pp. 6–10, 2017.

[27] Y. Xiao, H. Wang, L. Zhang and W. Xu. Two methods of selecting Gaussian kernel parameters for one-class SVM and their application to fault detection. *Knowledge-Based Systems*, 59: 75–84, 2014 [Online]. Available: http://dx.doi.org/10.1016/j.knosys.2014.01.020.

[28] P. Buonadonna, D. Gay, J.M. Hellerstein, W. Hong and S. Madden. TASK: Sensor network in a box. *Proceedings of the Second European Workshop on Wireless Sensor Networks, EWSN 2005*, vol. 2005, pp. 133–144, 2005.

[29] C.-C. Chang and C.-J. Lin. LIBSVM: A library for support vector machines. *ACM Transactions on Intelligent Systems and Technology*, 2(3): 1–27, 2011 [Online]. Available: http://www.csie.ntu.edu.tw/.

[30] N. Tracy, J. Young and R. Mason. Multivariate control charts for individual observations. *Journal of Quality Technology*, 24(2): 88–95, 1992.

[31] C. Everett. Credit card fraud funds terrorism. *Computer Fraud & Security*, 2003(5): 1, 2003.

[32] T. Bhatla, V. Prabhu and A. Dua. Understanding credit card frauds. *Cards Business Review*, 1(6), 2003.

[33] A. Dal Pozzolo, G. Boracchi, O. Caelen, C. Alippi and G. Bontempi. Credit card fraud detection and concept-drift adaptation with delayed supervised information. In *2015 International Joint Conference on Neural Networks (IJCNN)*. IEEE, 2015.

[34] K.P. Tran, P. Castagliola and G. Celano. Monitoring the ratio of two normal variables using run rules type control charts. *International Journal of Production Research*, 54(6): 1670–1688, 2016.

[35] C.A. Lowry, W.H. Woodall, C.W. Champ and S.E. Rigdon. A multivariate exponentially weighted moving average control chart. *Technometrics*, 34(1): 46, 1992.

[36] K.P. Tran, P. Castagliola, G. Celano and M.B.C. Khoo. Monitoring compositional data using multivariate exponentially weighted moving average scheme: Monitoring compositional data using MEWMA scheme. *Quality and Reliability Engineering International*, 34(3): 391–402, 2018.

[37] G. Lee and C. Scott. Nested support vector machines. *IEEE Transactions on Signal Processing*, 58(3): 1648–1660, 2010.

[38] G. Lee and C.D. Scott. The one class support vector machine solution path. In *Acoustics, Speech and Signal Processing, 2007. ICASSP 2007. IEEE International Conference on*, vol. 2. IEEE, pp. II–521, 2007.

[39] R. Vert and J.-P. Vert. Consistency and convergence rates of one-class svms and related algorithms. *Journal of Machine Learning Research*, 7(May): 817–854, 2006.

[40] K. Sjöstrand, M.S. Hansen, H.B. Larsson and R. Larsen. A path algorithm for the support vector domain description and its application to medical imaging. *Medical Image Analysis*, 11(5): 417–428, 2007.

[41] R. Chetan and D. Ashoka. Data mining based network intrusion detection system: A database centric approach. In *Computer Communication and Informatics (ICCCI), 2012 International Conference on*. IEEE, pp. 1–6, 2012.

[42] P. Bodesheim, A. Freytag, E. Rodner, M. Kemmler and J. Denzler. Kernel null space methods for novelty detection. In *Proceedings of the IEEE Conference on Computer Vision and Pattern Recognition*, pp. 3374–3381, 2013.

[43] S.J. Sheather and J.S. Marron. Kernel quantile estimators. *Journal of the American Statistical Association*, 85(410): 410–416, 1990.

[44] P. Bodesheim, A. Freytag, E. Rodner and J. Denzler. Local novelty detection in multiclass recognition problems. In *Applications of Computer Vision (WACV), 2015 IEEE Winter Conference on*. IEEE, pp. 813–820, 2015.

[45] Miao Wu, Ting-Jie Lu, Fei-Yang Ling, Jing Sun and Hui-Ying Du. Research on the architecture of internet of things. In *2010 3rd International Conference on Advanced Computer Theory and Engineering (ICACTE)*, vol. 5, pp. V5–484–V5–487, 2010.

[46] S. Kraijak and P. Tuwanut. A survey on iot architectures, protocols, applications, security, privacy, real-world implementation and future trends. In *11th International Conference on Wireless Communications, Networking and Mobile Computing (WiCOM 2015)*, pp. 1–6, 2015.

[47] N. Sharma and K. Saroha. Study of dimension reduction methodologies in data mining. In *International Conference on Computing, Communication Automation*, pp. 133–137, 2015.

[48] N. Moustafa. *The Bot-IoT Dataset*, 2020 (accessed February 25, 2020), http://dx.doi.org/10.21227/r7v2-x988.

[49] I.T. Jolliffe. *Principal Component Analysis*. New York, NY: Springer, 2002.

[50] X. Glorot, A. Bordes and Y. Bengio. Deep sparse rectifier neural networks, 15(01), 2010.

[51] S. Ruder. An overview of gradient descent optimization algorithms, 2017.

[52] D.P. Kingma and J. Ba. Adam: A method for stochastic optimization, 2017.

[53] H. McMahan, E. Moore, D. Ramage and B. Agüera y Arcas. Federated learning of deep networks using model averaging. *ArXiv abs/1602.05629, 2016.*, 02, 2016.

[54] N. Koroniotis, N. Moustafa, E. Sitnikova and B. Turnbull. Towards the development of realistic botnet dataset in the internet of things for network forensic analytics: Bot-iot dataset. *Future Generation Computer Systems*, 100: 779–796, 2019.

[55] T.H. Truong, P.B. Ta, M.L. Dao, D.T. Bui, T.B. Nguyen, D.L. Tran and K.P. Tran. Lockedge: Low-complexity cyberattack detection in iot edge computing. *IEEE Access*, 9: 29696–29710, 2021.

[56] M.A. Ferrag, L. Maglaras, S. Moschoyiannis and H. Janicke. Deep learning for cyber security intrusion detection: Approaches, datasets, and comparative study. *Journal of Information Security and Applications*, 50: 12, 2019.

[57] B. McMahan, E. Moore, D. Ramage, S. Hampson and B. A. y Arcas. Communication efficient learning of deep networks from decentralized data. In *Proceedings of the 20th International Conference on Artificial Intelligence and Statistics*, ser. Proceedings of Machine Learning Research, vol. 54. Fort Lauderdale, FL, USA: PMLR, 20–22 Apr 2017, pp. 1273–1282, 2017 [Online]. Available: http://proceedings.mlr.press/v54/mcmahan17a.html.

[58] S.J. Sheather and J.S. Marron. Kernel quantile estimators. *Journal of the American Statistical Association*, 85(410): 410–416, 1990.

[59] D.P. Kingma and M. Welling. Auto-encoding variational bayes, 2014.

[60] L. Gjorgiev and S. Gievska. Time series anomaly detection with variational autoencoder using mahalanobis distance. In *ICT Innovations 2020. Machine Learning and Applications*, V. Dimitrova and I. Dimitrovski (eds.). Cham: Springer International Publishing, pp. 42–55, 2020.

[61] K. Greff, R.K. Srivastava, J. Koutník, B.R. Steunebrink and J. Schmidhuber. Lstm: A search space odyssey. *IEEE Transactions on Neural Networks and Learning Systems*, 28(10): 2222–2232, 2017.

[62] I.P. Turnipseed. A new scada dataset for intrusion detection research, 2015.

[63] E. Keogh, J. Lin and A. Fu. Hot sax: Efficiently finding the most unusual time series subsequence. In *Fifth IEEE International Conference on Data Mining (ICDM'05)*, pp. 8, 2005 [Online]. Available: http://www.cs.ucr.edu/ eamonn/discords/.

[64] Nyc taxi and limousine commission. Last accessed on May, 2021. [Online]. Available: https://www1.nyc.gov/site/tlc/about/tlc-trip-record-data.page.

[65] T.H. Truong, P.B. Ta, M.L. Dao, D.L. Tran, M.D. Nguyen, A.Q. Le, T.C. Le, D.T. Bui and K.P. Tran. Detecting cyberattacks using anomaly detection in industrial control systems: A federated learning approach. *Computers in Industry*, 132: 103509, 2021.

[66] X. Liu. Chapter 14—Methods for handling missing data. In *Methods and Applications of Longitudinal Data Analysis*, X. Liu (ed.). Oxford: Academic Press, pp. 441–473, 2016.

[67] J. Shao and B. Zhong. Last observation carry-forward and last observation analysis. *Statistics in Medicine*, 22(15): 2429–2441, 2003.

[68] [Online]. Available: https://docs.emqx.io/en/broker/v4.3/.

[69] [Online]. Available: https://github.com/tgraf/bmon.

[70] [Online]. Available: https://github.com/xybu/python-resmon.

[71] N. Liu and P. Rebentrost. Quantum machine learning for quantum anomaly detection. *Physical Review A*, 97(4), Apr 2018. [Online]. Available: http://dx.doi.org/10.1103/PhysRevA.97.042315.

Chapter 8

Machine Learning for Compositional Data Analysis in Support of the Decision Making Process

Thi Thuy Van Nguyen,[1,2] Cédric Heuchenne[1,*] and Kim Phuc Tran[3]

1 Introduction

In recent years, data has played an important role in the business world. The development of advanced technologies such as Artificial Intelligence, Big Data, Internet of Things, etc., makes data analysis more and more indispensable in all fields of life. As a result, companies are beginning to strengthen their digital transformations and this leads to an ever-increasing demand for data analysis. In business, knowing the right customers' demands is a crucial step before making specific business strategies decisions. For example, based on data from customers such as demographics, consumption history, attitudes, etc., the banks analyze data and categorize customers into different segments to come up with specific strategies such as offering loans, granting credit cards, etc. By properly assessing customer needs, companies can make effective business decisions that can help them save time and costs, increase operational efficiency. Besides, the right data analysis also helps companies avoid making wrong decisions, thereby limiting possible risks and making better decisions in the future. The results from data analysis provide insight into the decision making process, and enhance the quality of decision-based. Companies can use data analysis to develop an efficient decision making process in order to increase profit, reduce risks and operate more effectively.

Although data analysis has a crucial role in the support of decision making, traditional analysis methods can not be used directly on compositional data (CoDa) due to its constrained structure: it has only positive components and the sum of these components is a constant. Unlike normal data, there are not many studies on applying machine learning (ML) to CoDa. The common way when dealing with CoDa is transforming it into normal data by some popular transformation methods such as additive log-ratio, center log-ratio[4], isometric log-ratio[21]

---

[1] HEC Liège - Management School of the University of Liège, Belgium.
[2] International Research Institute for Artificial Intelligence and Data Science, Dong A University, Danang, Vietnam.
[3] Univ. Lille, ENSAIT, ULR 2461 - GEMTEX - Génie et Matériaux Textiles, F-59000 Lille, France.
* Corresponding author: C.Heuchenne@uliege.be

transformation before analyzing it. In[68], the authors proposed a more general transformation method involving one single parameter, named α-transformation. The choice of α depends on the goals of the analysis and when α tends to 0, this method converges to the isometric log-ratio transformation. Besides the existing parametric distributions for describing CoDa over simplex space such as Dirichlet class, additive logistic-normal class (see[1;7]), several approaches for describing CoDa using kernel density estimation methods also have been proposed, see, for example,[6;15]. In[56], the authors proposed a new method named Deep Compositional Data Analysis (DeepCoDA) for analyzing and interpreting a high-dimensional CoDa. The proposed method can perform well without hyperparameter tuning and can be used for personalized interpretability of CoDa. Due to the importance of ML in data analysis as well as its limited researches on CoDa, this chapter will summarize the most popular ML techniques on CoDa and propose an efficient method to transform this special data into normal form. An anomaly detection method using Support Vector Data Description (SVDD) and a simulation example applying this method is also presented. The organization of the chapter is as follows: Section 1 will briefly introduce the importance of data analysis in decision making and its role in support of the decision making process. Modeling of CoDa and Aitchison geometry on Simplex space will be presented in Section 2. In Section 3, we will summarize the most popular ML techniques on Coda, including principal component analysis (PCA), clustering, classification, and regression. An anomaly detection method using SVDD and a simulation example will be presented in Section 4. Finally, Section 5 provides the summary of the chapter with some comments.

2 Modeling of Compositional Data

In statistics, CoDa are vectors whose components are strictly positive and they often represent proportions, percentages, concentrations, or frequencies of some whole. Their applications can be found in many domains such as chemical researches, econometric and survey data analyses, and food industry, see[4;64;26].

By definition, a (row) vector, $\mathbf{x} = (x_1, x_2, \ldots, x_D)$, is a D-part composition when its components are strictly positive numbers and carry only relative information, see[4;53]. The relative information here refers only to the proportions between components of the composition, regardless of its numerical values. The sum of the components of $\mathbf{x}$, $\sum_{i=1}^{D} x_i$, is a constant κ. For instance, $\kappa = 1$ means that the measurements are made in proportion while $\kappa = 100$ refers to measurements in percentage. Each composition can be considered as an equivalent class made of proportional factors due to the fact that multiplication of a vector of positive components by a positive constant does not change the ratios between its components. In this case, i.e., if $\mathbf{x} = \lambda \mathbf{y}$ where $\mathbf{x}, \mathbf{y}$ are compositions, λ is a constant, we say that $\mathbf{x}, \mathbf{y}$ are compositionally equivalent. Equivalently, if we define the closure of a D-part composition $\mathbf{x} = (x_1, x_2, \ldots, x_D)$ to $\kappa > 0$ by

$$\mathcal{C}(\mathbf{x}) = \left(\frac{\kappa \cdot x_1}{\sum_{i=1}^{D} x_i}, \frac{\kappa \cdot x_2}{\sum_{i=1}^{D} x_i}, \ldots, \frac{\kappa \cdot x_D}{\sum_{i=1}^{D} x_i} \right) \tag{1}$$

then two D-part compositions are compositionally equivalent if $\mathcal{C}(\mathbf{x}) = \mathcal{C}(\mathbf{y})$, for every positive constant κ. The sample space of CoDa is the simplex

$$S^D = \left\{ \mathbf{x} = (x_1, x_2, \dots, x_D) \mid x_i > 0, i = 1, \dots, D; \sum_{i=1}^{D} x_i = \kappa \right\} \tag{2}$$

In the real space, we can add vectors or multiply vectors by scalar using Euclidean geometry to obtain their properties or compute the distance between vectors. But this geometry can not apply directly to CoDa in S^D because of its special structure. Instead, the author of[4] introduced the Aitchison geometry, with two basic operations required for a vector space structure of the simplex S^D: Perturbation and powering operators, which are equivalent to the addition and multiplication by a scalar operations in the real space. The perturbation (denoted by $\oplus$) of $\mathbf{x} \in S^D$ by $\mathbf{y} \in S^D$ is defined by

$$\mathbf{x} \oplus \mathbf{y} = \mathcal{C}(x_1 y_1, \dots, x_D y_D) \in S^D$$

and the powering (denoted by $\odot$) of $x \in S^D$ by a constant $\alpha \in \mathbb{R}$ is

$$\alpha \odot \mathbf{x} = \mathcal{C}(x_1^\alpha, \dots, x_D^\alpha) \in S^D$$

The simplex S^D with the perturbation operation and the power transformation, denoted by $(S^D, \oplus, \odot)$, is a vector space. To obtain a linear vector space structure in this vector space, the Aitchison inner product, Aitchison norm, and Aitchison distance between vectors on S^D are defined as follows:

Let $\mathbf{x}, \mathbf{y}$ be two vectors in S^D. The Aitchison inner product of $\mathbf{x}, \mathbf{y}$, denoted by $\langle \mathbf{x}, \mathbf{y} \rangle_a$ is

$$\langle \mathbf{x}, \mathbf{y} \rangle_a = \frac{1}{2D} \sum_{i=1}^{D} \sum_{j=1}^{D} \ln \frac{x_i}{x_j} \ln \frac{y_i}{y_j} \tag{3}$$

The Aitchison norm of $\mathbf{x}$, denoted by $\|\mathbf{x}\|_a$ is

$$\|\mathbf{x}\|_a = \sqrt{\frac{1}{2D} \sum_{i=1}^{D} \sum_{j=1}^{D} \left(\ln \frac{x_i}{x_j} \right)^2} \tag{4}$$

The Aitchison distance between $\mathbf{x}, \mathbf{y}$, denoted by $d_a(\mathbf{x}, \mathbf{y})$, is

$$d_a(\mathbf{x}, \mathbf{y}) = \sqrt{\frac{1}{2D} \sum_{i=1}^{D} \sum_{j=1}^{D} \left(\ln \frac{x_i}{x_j} - \ln \frac{y_i}{y_j} \right)^2} \tag{5}$$

Here, we use the subindex "a" to refer to the Aitchison geometry.

In practice, instead of directly using composition data and deploying the model on the Simplex space, CoDa are often transformed to vectors in the Euclidean space. The goal of the transformations is to remove the constraints of CoDa. The two first transformation methods were proposed by[4], namely, additive log-ratio transformation (alr) and centered log-ratio transformation (clr). The alr : $S^D \to \mathbb{R}^{D-1}$ transformation is an isomorphism which transforms

D-part composition $\mathbf{x} = (x_1, \ldots, x_D) \in S^D$ to a real vector in $\mathbb{R}^{D-1}$ while considering x_D as a reference part, defined by

$$\text{alr}(\mathbf{x}) = \left(\ln \frac{x_1}{x_D}, \ln \frac{x_2}{x_D}, \ldots, \ln \frac{x_{D-1}}{x_D} \right) = \zeta \tag{6}$$

The inverse of alr from Euclidean space to Simplex space recovers $\mathbf{x}$ from $\zeta = (\zeta_1, \ldots, \zeta_{D-1})$ by $\text{alr}^{-1}(\zeta) = \mathbf{x} = (x_1, \ldots, x_D)$ where $x_i = \dfrac{\exp(\zeta_i)}{1 + \sum_{j=1}^{D-1} \exp(\zeta_j)}$ for $i = 1, \ldots, D-1$ and $x_D = \dfrac{1}{1 + \sum_{j=1}^{D-1} \exp(\zeta_j)}$.

The clr transformation is an isometry from the Simplex space S^D to a subspace $U \subset \mathbb{R}^D$, defined by

$$\text{clr}(\mathbf{x}) = \left(\ln \frac{x_1}{g_m(\mathbf{x})}, \ln \frac{x_2}{g_m(\mathbf{x})}, \ldots, \ln \frac{x_D}{g_m(\mathbf{x})} \right) = (\xi_1, \xi_2, \ldots, \xi_D) \tag{7}$$

where $g_m(\mathbf{x}) = \left(\prod_{i=1}^{D} x_i \right)^{\frac{1}{D}} = \exp\left(\frac{1}{D} \sum_{i=1}^{D} x_i \right)$ is the component-wise geometric mean of the composition and $\sum_{i=1}^{D} \xi_i = 0$. The inverse of clr recovers $\mathbf{x}$ from $\xi = (\xi_1, \ldots, \xi_D)$ by

$$\text{clr}^{-1}(\xi) = \mathcal{C}(\exp(\xi)) = \mathcal{C}(\exp(\xi_1), \exp(\xi_2), \ldots, \exp(\xi_D)).$$

The authors of[21] introduced a new transformation that is directly associated with an orthogonal coordinate system in the Simplex space, namely isometric log-ratio transformation (irl), avoiding the drawbacks of both alr and clr methods. Isometric log-ratio transform (ilr) is an isometry from S^D to $\mathbb{R}^{D-1}$. Let $\mathbf{e}_1, \mathbf{e}_2, \ldots, \mathbf{e}_{D-1}$ be an orthonormal basis of the simplex S^D. A composition $\mathbf{x} \in S^D$ can be expressed as

$$\mathbf{x} = \bigoplus_{i=1}^{D-1} x_i^* \odot \mathbf{e}_i, \quad x_i^* = \langle \mathbf{x}, \mathbf{e}_i \rangle_a = \langle \text{clr}(\mathbf{x}), \text{clr}(\mathbf{e}_i) \rangle \tag{8}$$

where $\langle , \rangle_a$ denotes the Aitchison inner product. Hence, the ilr transformation of $\mathbf{x} \in S^D$ is $\text{ilr}(\mathbf{x}) = \mathbf{x}^* = [x_1^*, x_2^*, \ldots, x_{D-1}^*]$. Let Ψ be a $(D-1 \times D)$ matrix whose i^{th} row is $\psi_i = \text{clr}(\mathbf{e}_i)$, $i = 1, \ldots, D-1$. This matrix is known as a contrast matrix associated with the orthonormal basis $\mathbf{e}_1, \mathbf{e}_2, \ldots, \mathbf{e}_{D-1}$. The ilr transformation $\mathbf{x}^*$ of composition $\mathbf{x}$ can be computed by

$$\mathbf{x}^* = \text{ilr}(\mathbf{x}) = \text{clr}(\mathbf{x}) \cdot \Psi^T$$

From its coordinate $\mathbf{x}^*$, $\mathbf{x}$ can be recovered by firstly constructing the contrast matrix Ψ, computing $\mathbf{x}^* \Psi$ and then obtaining $\mathbf{x}$ by $\mathbf{x} = \mathcal{C}(\exp(\mathbf{x}^* \Psi))$ For more detail, see[53], Chapter 4.

3 Machine Learning for Multivariate Compositional Data

ML algorithms such as PCA, clustering, classification, regression, etc., have been developed and applied in many domains of life for decades. Besides researches applied to normal data, ML methods on CoDa have also received a lot of attention recently. The most common methods to handling the constraints of CoDa are transforming them into a normal form using some popular transformation methods such as additive log-ratio (alr), centered log-ratio (clr) (see[4]) or isometric log-ratio (ilr) (see[21]) transformations. This section will briefly summarize the researches related to popular ML methods applying to CoDa, including PCA, clustering, classification, and regression. Some examples on the simulation and the real data using those methods are also presented at the end of each subsection.

3.1 Principal Component Analysis

PCA is a well-known method for reducing the dimension of data while preserving as much of variance of the dataset as possible. PCA was firstly introduced by Karl Pearson[41] in 1901 and independently studied and developed later by Hotelling[38] in 1933 and has become one of the most valuable results of applied algebra nowadays. Due to its simplicity and robust ability to extract relevant information from confusing data, PCA is widely used in many domains such as neuroscience, quantitative finance, facial recognition, image compression, etc., see, for example,[50;48;49;36] among many others for more details.

Although researches and techniques related to PCA have been developed and widely used in many domains for decades, most of them are applied to normal data in the Euclidean space. Due to the special structure of CoDa, traditional PCA techniques can not be applied directly. Some authors proposed to transform CoDa into real data before applying PCA techniques: In[2;3;5], the authors applied PCA to clr-transformation data; the robust PCA based on ilr-transformation data was discussed in[23;24]. A novel PCA modeling procedure for CoDa vectors to handle some drawbacks of previous methods was proposed in[71]. In[9], the authors proposed combining log-ratio transformation and exponential family PCA to attain the benefits of both methods. The rest of the subsection will present briefly the PCA method on multivariate CoDa.

Suppose there is a multivariate compositional sample of size n and suppose the ith individual is characterized by p D-part features, denoted by $(\mathbf{x}_{i1}, \mathbf{x}_{i2}, \ldots, \mathbf{x}_{ip})$. Let $\mathbf{X}$ denote the multivariate CoDa matrix,

$$\mathbf{X} = (\mathbf{X}_1, \mathbf{X}_2, \ldots, \mathbf{X}_p) = \begin{pmatrix} \mathbf{Z}_1^T \\ \mathbf{Z}_2^T \\ \vdots \\ \mathbf{Z}_n^T \end{pmatrix} = \begin{pmatrix} \mathbf{x}_{11} & \mathbf{x}_{12} & \cdots & \mathbf{x}_{1p} \\ \mathbf{x}_{21} & \mathbf{x}_{22} & \cdots & \mathbf{x}_{2p} \\ \vdots & \vdots & \ddots & \vdots \\ \mathbf{x}_{n1} & \mathbf{x}_{n2} & \cdots & \mathbf{x}_{np} \end{pmatrix} \tag{9}$$

where $\mathbf{X}_i = (\mathbf{x}_{1i}, \mathbf{x}_{2i}, \ldots, \mathbf{x}_{ni})^T, i = 1, \ldots, p$ is the ith compostional feature, $\mathbf{Z}_j = (\mathbf{x}_{j1}, \mathbf{x}_{j2}, \ldots, \mathbf{x}_{jp})^T, j = 1, \ldots, n$ is the jth CoDa vector, $\mathbf{x}_{lk} = (x_{lk1}, x_{lk2}, \ldots, x_{lkD}) \in S^D$ for $l = 1, \ldots, n$ and $k = 1, \ldots, p$. For n observations of random compositional variable $\mathbf{X}_i$, the authors of[52] defined the sample mean by

$$E(\mathbf{X}_i) = \bar{\mathbf{x}}_i = \mathcal{C}\left(g(\mathbf{L}_{i1}), g(\mathbf{L}_{i2}), \ldots, g(\mathbf{L}_{iD})\right) \tag{10}$$

where g is the geometric mean, $\mathbf{L}_{ik} = (x_{1ik}, x_{2ik}, \ldots, x_{nik})^T$, $k = 1, \ldots, D$. The authors of[71] defined the sample variance $Var(\mathbf{X}_i)$ by

$$Var(\mathbf{X}_i) = \frac{1}{n} \sum_{j=1}^{n} \|\mathbf{x}_{ji} \ominus \bar{\mathbf{x}}_i\|_{S^D}^2 \tag{11}$$

where $\|\cdot\|_{S^D}$ denotes the norm defined on the Simplex space S^D, $\mathbf{x}_{ki} \ominus \bar{\mathbf{x}}_i = \mathbf{x}_{ki} \oplus ((-1) \odot \bar{\mathbf{x}}_i)$. The covariance of any random compositional vectors $\mathbf{X}_i, \mathbf{X}_j$ defined by[71] is as follows

$$Cov(\mathbf{X}_i, \mathbf{X}_j) = \frac{1}{n} \sum_{k=1}^{n} \langle \mathbf{x}_{ki} \ominus \bar{\mathbf{x}}_i, \mathbf{x}_{kj} \ominus \bar{\mathbf{x}}_j \rangle_{S^D} \tag{12}$$

where $\langle , \rangle_{S^D}$ denotes the inner product in S^D.

The PCA algorithm on multivariate CoDa proposed by[71] is summarized as follows: Suppose there is a compositional sample of size n, described by p multivariate compositional variables $\mathbf{X}_1, \mathbf{X}_2, \ldots, \mathbf{X}_p$ as in (9). The ith principal component $\mathbf{V}_i$ of $\mathbf{X}$ is defined by

$$\mathbf{V}_i = \bigoplus_{j=1}^{p} e_{ij} \odot \mathbf{X}_j \tag{13}$$

where $\mathbf{e}_i = (e_{i1}, e_{i2}, \ldots, e_{ip})^T \in \mathbb{R}^p$ is chosen such that $Var(\mathbf{V}_i)$ attains its maximum value, $\|\mathbf{e}_i\| = 1$ and $\langle \mathbf{e}_i, \mathbf{e}_j \rangle = 0$ for all $j \neq i, j = 1, \ldots, p$. Suppose $\mathbf{X}_1, \mathbf{X}_2, \ldots, \mathbf{X}_p$ have been centralized. The sample variance $Var(\mathbf{V}_i)$ can be expressing by

$$Var(\mathbf{V}_i) = Var(\bigoplus_{j=1}^{p} e_{ij} \odot \mathbf{X}_j)$$
$$= \sum_{k=1}^{p} \sum_{l=1}^{p} e_{ik} e_{il} Cov(\mathbf{X}_k, \mathbf{X}_l)$$
$$= \mathbf{e}_i^T \mathbf{S} \mathbf{e}_i \tag{14}$$

where $\mathbf{S}$ is the variance-covariance matrix of $\mathbf{X}_1, \mathbf{X}_2, \ldots, \mathbf{X}_p$. The first k principal components of the PCA problem can be found through the solutions of the problem

$$\max_{\mathbf{e}_i} \sum_{i=1}^{k} \mathbf{e}_i^T \mathbf{S} \mathbf{e}_i \tag{15}$$

subject to
$$\|\mathbf{e}_i\| = 1, \quad i = 1, \ldots, k$$
$$\langle \mathbf{e}_i, \mathbf{e}_j \rangle = 0, \quad j = 1, \ldots, k, \ j \neq i$$
$$\mathbf{e}_1^T \mathbf{S} \mathbf{e}_1 \geq \mathbf{e}_2^T \mathbf{S} \mathbf{e}_2 \geq \ldots \geq \mathbf{e}_k^T \mathbf{S} \mathbf{e}_k, \quad k \leq p$$

The solution of this problem is the first k eigenvectors of $\mathbf{S}$ corresponding to the first k eigenvalues $\lambda_1, \ldots, \lambda_k$ with $\lambda_1 \geq \lambda_2 \geq \ldots \geq \lambda_k > 0$. The authors of[71] applied this PCA method on two real sets of CoDa and the results showed that this proposed method is an effective approach to CoDa.

Figure 2 illustrates the explained variance proportions according to the number of principal components when applying the PCA method on the CoDa set "HITChip Atlas dataset" (see[42]). This set contains data from 1006 healthy people from 15 western countries with the information of the 130 major known bacterias in the human intestine. Figure 1 illustrates the ternary diagram of three components named "Actinomycetaceae", "Xanthomonadaceae", and "Yersinia" from this set. As can be seen from Figure 2, the first 80 principal components cover 97.5% amount of information (variance) of projected data after using the PCA method. The code of this example can be found on ML for compositional data analysis.

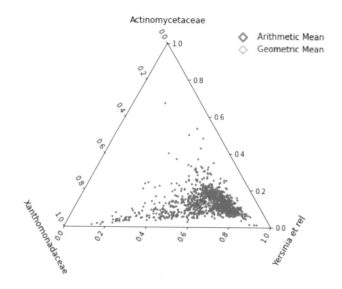

Figure 1: Ternary diagram of three components of Atlas dataset.

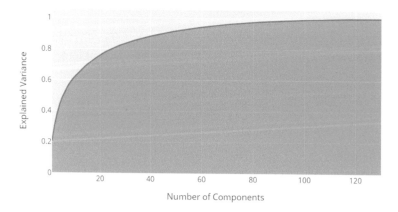

Figure 2: Explained variance versus number of components.

3.2 Clustering

In ML, clustering (or cluster analysis) is an unsupervised learning method with the aim to segment the set of data points into different groups such that similar points (in some sense) belong to the same group, and differ from other points in other groups. Clustering was firstly introduced in [20] to describe the cultural relationship and has become a popular technique in statistical analysis nowadays. It has been used in many domains, such as biology, medicine, marketing, social sciences, etc., see, for example, [19;47;31;8], and [60] among many others for references. There are many clustering methods existing in the literature, some of them could be mentioned as Partitional clustering, Density-Based clustering, Model-Based clustering, Hierarchical clustering, Fuzzy clustering. This subsection will briefly present a popular algorithm in the Partitioning clustering group: the K-means clustering algorithm. Firstly, we will present the K-means algorithm in normal data, then move to its application on CoDa. The goal of K-means clustering is to partition the set of data points into K clusters such that each point is allocated into the cluster with the nearest cluster centroid (the middle of a cluster). The particular K-means algorithm is as follows.

Given a set of n observations $\mathbf{x}_1, \mathbf{x}_2, \ldots, \mathbf{x}_n$, $\mathbf{x}_i \in \mathbb{R}^d, i = 1, \ldots, n$ and we want to segment these observations into K clusters, denoted by $C_1, C_2, \ldots, C_K$ for $K < n$. Let μ_i denote the sample mean of cluster C_i,

$$\mu_i = \frac{1}{|C_i|} \sum_{\mathbf{x}_j \in C_i} \mathbf{x}_j$$

where $|C_i|$ denotes the number of observations in cluster C_i. The aim of K-means clustering is to minimize the sum of squares error (SSE) on all clusters, thus the K-means optimization problem would be

$$\underset{C_1, \ldots, C_K}{\operatorname{argmin}} \sum_{i=1}^{K} \sum_{\mathbf{x} \in C_i} \|\mathbf{x} - \mu_i\|^2 \tag{16}$$

Many works have been proposed to solve K-means optimization problem (16), see, for example, [35;54;32] and [14] among many others.

Although there are large numbers of methods proposed for clustering, similar to many other ML methods, most of them are developed and applied to the normal data in Euclidean space. These techniques can not be applied directly to CoDa due to its special structure. So far, according to our knowledge, the number of researches related to clustering on CoDa is still small. The common approach to handle constraints of CoDa when using clustering methods is to transform it by log-ratio transformation methods (see [44;76]). In [59], the author proposed a fast and effective algorithm for clustering CoDa named Diluvian Clustering and showed that this method is well suited to a large set of noisy CoDa. In [27], the authors used centered log-ratio and its novel extension named the log centered log-ratio to transform CoDa, and then using the K-means algorithm for clustering and illustrating the performance of proposed methods on both RNA-sequencing and bicycle sharing data. A convex clustering method for grouping CoDa based on isometric log-ratio transformation had been proposed in [72] and the numerical simulation results of clustering on ilr-transformed data showed a higher accuracy comparing with directly clustering on original data. The rest of this subsection will present briefly K-means clustering on a sample of CoDa by using center log-ratio transformation and its novel extension, proposed by the authors of[27], named the log centered log ratio transformation.

Given a set of n compositional observations $\mathbf{x}_1, \mathbf{x}_2, \ldots, \mathbf{x}_n$, $\mathbf{x}_i \in S^D$, $\mathbf{x}_i = (x_{i1}, x_{i1}, \ldots, x_{iD})$, $i = 1, \ldots, n$ and suppose that we want to divide these observations into K clusters, denoted by $C_1, C_2, \ldots, C_K$ for $K < n$. If the center log-ratio transformation is applied on $\mathbf{x}_1, \mathbf{x}_2, \ldots, \mathbf{x}_n$, then the new transformed data $\mathbf{x}_i$, $i = 1, \ldots, n$ would be

$$\text{clr}(\mathbf{x}_i) = \left(\ln \frac{x_{i1}}{g_m(\mathbf{x}_i)}, \ln \frac{x_{i2}}{g_m(\mathbf{x}_i)}, \ldots, \ln \frac{x_{iD}}{g_m(\mathbf{x}_i)} \right)$$

where g_m is the geometric mean function. Let $\mu_{i,clr}$ denote the sample mean of clr-transformed data of cluster C_i,

$$\mu_{i,clr} = \frac{1}{|C_i|} \sum_{\text{clr}(\mathbf{x}_j) \in C_i} \text{clr}(\mathbf{x}_j)$$

where $|C_i|$ is the number of observations in C_i. The K-means optimization problem for the transformed data would be

$$\underset{C_1, \ldots, C_K}{\operatorname{argmin}} \sum_{i=1}^{K} \sum_{\text{clr}(\mathbf{x}) \in C_i} \|\text{clr}(\mathbf{x}) - \mu_{i,clr}\|_2^2 \tag{17}$$

For CoDa with a large number of components having very small proportions, the clr-transformation seems to be sensitive to small fluctuations and can bring undesired clustering results (see[27]). To overcome this problem, the authors of[27] proposed a new extension of the clr-transformation, named the log centered log-ratio, denoted by logCLR and defined as follows

$$\text{logCLR}(\mathbf{x}_i) = (\text{logCLR}(x_{i1}), \text{logCLR}(x_{i2}), \ldots, \text{logCLR}(x_{iD})) \tag{18}$$

where

$$\text{logCLR}(x_{ik}) = \begin{cases} -\left[\ln \left(1 - \ln \frac{x_{ik}}{g_m(\mathbf{x}_i)} \right) \right]^2 & \text{if} \quad \frac{x_{ik}}{g_m(\mathbf{x}_i)} \leq 1 \\ \left(\ln \frac{x_{ik}}{g_m(\mathbf{x}_i)} \right)^2 & \text{otherwise.} \end{cases}$$

The number of clusters K can be found by the method proposed by[25],

$$K = \underset{K < n}{\operatorname{argmin}} \sum_{k=1}^{K} \sum_{\mathbf{x}_i \in C_k} \|t(\mathbf{x}_i) - \mu_{k,t}\|_2^2 + pen(K) \tag{19}$$

where $t(\mathbf{x}_i)$ denotes the transformation method, $\mu_{k,t}$ is the sample mean of cluster C_k under transformation method t, $pen(K) = \alpha\sqrt{KnD}$ is a penalty function, α is a constant. The authors of[27] applied both type of transformation on three sets of compostional data: mouse RNA-seq data, fly embryonic RNA-seq data, and Velib bicycle sharing system data. The results indicated that logCLR-transformation yielded satisfactory results comparing to clr-transformation.

Figure 3 illustrates an example of applying the K-means clustering method to a simulated CoDa set. This set contains 3200 data points generated from three different Dirichlet distributions. The isometric log-ratio is used to transform CoDa into the normal form. As can be seen

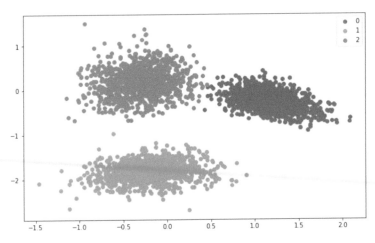

Figure 3: Three clusters corresponding to three different data sets.

from this figure, after applying the K-means method with the number of clusters $K = 3$, the original data are segmented and presented in different colors (blue, orange, and green). The code of this example can be found on ML for compositional data analysis.

3.3 Classification

In ML, classification refers to the process of predicting the class label of given input data and it is one of the most important subjects in supervised learning. For example, classifying customers having ability of default or not default when they apply for a new loan is a type of classification problems in the bank. Another popular example is filtering spam email to classify whether a new email is a spam or not spam. Classification has many applications in many domains, such as loan approval, marketing strategy, medical diagnosis, biometric identification, etc. Building classification model corresponds to approximate a predictive mapping f from input variable $\mathbf{x}$ (explanatory variable) to discrete output y (response variable). The training data will include both input data and its label (output). Classification algorithms will utilize information from both input and output to "learn" their relations and estimate the predictive mapping f. Mathematically, the classification model will have the form

$$y = f(\mathbf{x}) \quad \text{where } y \text{ is categorical.}$$

There are many well-known classification algorithms, such as Logistic regression, Support Vector Machine (SVM), Linear discriminant analysis, Naïve Bayes, Decision trees, etc. Each algorithm has its own advantages and disadvantages, depends on particular problems. They have been studied and developed for many years and have been applied in many domains of finance, medicine, industry, etc., see, for example,[13;65;74] and[43].

Although researches related to classifications in ML have been developed and widely used for many decades, most of them are developed for using on normal data in Euclidean space; so they can not be applied directly to CoDa. The difficulty when dealing with CoDa is that it contains only positive parts and is restricted by constant constraint. When analyzing CoDa, researchers often use some popular transformation methods like clr, ilr to transform CoDa from

193

the Simplex space S^D to Euclidean space $\mathbb{R}^D$ or $\mathbb{R}^{D-1}$. Under these transformations, the transformed data is no longer restricted by the constant constraint and the relative information of the original data is preserved. However, besides its advantage of removing the constant constraint of CoDa, these transformation methods have some drawbacks. For example, when building a classification model on CoDa based on ilr- transformation, some common methods often used are linear discrimination analysis, logistic regression. If the distribution of ilr-transformed data is not normal (Gaussian), the linear discrimination analysis seems not to be an appropriate method, see [55;40]. When two classes follow two separate Dirichlet distributions, the Bayes decision boundary on ilr-transformed data is not polynomial, hence logistic regression can not be applied in this case, see [40]. In [69], the authors used α- transformation proposed by [68] to transform CoDa: Given compositional vector $\mathbf{x} \in S^P$, the α- transformation $\mathbf{z}_\alpha(\mathbf{x})$ of $\mathbf{x}$ defined by

$$\mathbf{z}_\alpha(\mathbf{x}) = \mathbf{H} \cdot \left(\frac{D\mathbf{u}_\alpha(\mathbf{x}) - \mathbf{1}_D}{\alpha} \right) \tag{20}$$

where

$$\mathbf{u}_\alpha(\mathbf{x}) = \left(\frac{x_1^\alpha}{\sum_{i=1}^P x_i}, \frac{x_2^\alpha}{\sum_{i=1}^P x_i}, \dots, \frac{x_P^\alpha}{\sum_{i=1}^P x_i} \right)^T,$$

$\mathbf{1}_D = (1, \dots, 1)^T \in \mathbb{R}^D$, $\mathbf{H}$ is a $(P \times D)$-matrix consisting of P orthonormal rows, each row is orthogonal to $\mathbf{1}_D$. Using this α-transformation, the authors of [69] built linear discriminant analysis and k-nearest neighbors models for CoDa and showed that this approach is well defined even when the dataset contains observations with some zero components.

Among many classification algorithms, SVM becomes one of the most popular ones since it does not require any assumption on the distribution of data. This section will present two classification approaches using the SVM algorithm on CoDa: One with ilr-transformation and one with Dirichlet feature embedding method proposed by Gu et al. [29].

3.3.1 Support Vector Machine Classification using Ilr—Transformation

In ML, SVM proposed by Cortes et al. [17] is a supervised learning method, often used in classification problems. SVM can perform linear classification that separates a positive sample of data from negatives ones as much as possible by a hyperplane. Besides, SVM can also perform non-linear classifications by implicitly mapping inputs into high-dimensional features spaces by using Kernel functions, see [70;61]. In this subsection, we will present briefly the SVM model with the real data, and then apply this model to CoDa based on ilr - transformation.

Suppose we have a training set of size n: $\{(\mathbf{x}_1, y_1), (\mathbf{x}_2 . y_2), \dots, (\mathbf{x}_n, y_n)\}$ where $\mathbf{x}_i \in \mathbb{R}^p$ is the features vector, $y_i \in \{-1, +1\}$ is the binary response and we want to obtain a hyperplane that separates data with label -1 from data with label 1 as much as possible. Let $\mathbf{w}^T\mathbf{x} + b = 0$ denote the separated hyperplane, then the SVM optimization problem will be

$$(\mathbf{w}, \mathbf{b}, \xi) = \operatorname*{argmin}_{\mathbf{w}, \mathbf{b}, \xi} \frac{1}{2} \|\mathbf{w}\|_2^2 + C \sum_{i=1}^n \xi_i \tag{21}$$

$$\text{subject to} \quad 1 - \xi_i - y_i(\mathbf{w}^T\mathbf{x}_i + b) \le 0 \quad i = 1, \dots, n$$
$$-\xi_i \le 0, \quad i = 1, \dots, n$$

The parameter C controls the balance between the maximization of classification margin and the minimization of errors. Introducing two Lagrange multipliers α_i, γ_i (note that γ_i is omitted during the solving process), the dual problem of the problem (21) becomes

$$\alpha = \underset{\alpha}{\arg\min} \quad \frac{1}{2} \sum_{i=1}^{n} \sum_{j=1}^{n} \alpha_i \alpha_j y_i y_j \mathbf{x}_i^T \mathbf{x}_j - \sum_{i=1}^{n} \alpha_i \tag{22}$$

$$\text{subject to} \qquad \sum_{i=1}^{n} \alpha_i y_i = 0 \quad i = 1, \ldots, n$$

$$0 \leq \alpha_i \leq C, \quad i = 1, \ldots, n$$

Solving this problem, we obtain

$$\mathbf{w} = \sum_{m \in S} \alpha_m y_m \mathbf{x}_m \tag{23}$$

$$b = \frac{1}{|\mathcal{M}|} \sum_{i \in \mathcal{M}} \left(y_i - \sum_{m \in S} \alpha_m y_m K(\mathbf{x}_m, \mathbf{x}_i) \right) \tag{24}$$

and then the decision function of problem

$$D(\mathbf{x}) = sign(\mathbf{w}^T \mathbf{x} + b)$$
$$= sign \left[\sum_{m \in S} \alpha_m y_m K(\mathbf{x}_m, \mathbf{x}) + \frac{1}{|\mathcal{M}|} \sum_{i \in \mathcal{M}} \left(y_i - \sum_{m \in S} \alpha_m y_m K(\mathbf{x}_m, \mathbf{x}_i) \right) \right] \tag{25}$$

where S is the set of support vectors, $\mathcal{M} = \{m : 0 < \alpha_m < C\}$ and $|\mathcal{M}|$ is the number of elements in $\mathcal{M}$. Note that in the solution $\mathbf{w}, b$ and the decision function (25), we use the kernel function $K(\mathbf{x}_m, \mathbf{x})$ instead of inner product of $\mathbf{x}_m, \mathbf{x}$ to obtain a more flexible solution. To classify a new object $\mathbf{z}$, we just need to compute the sign of the decision function $D(\mathbf{z})$: If $D(\mathbf{z}) \geq 0$ then $\mathbf{z}$ belongs to the positive class and vice versa.

Now, suppose we have a compositional sample of size n: $(\mathbf{x}_1, y_1)$, $(\mathbf{x}_2, y_2)$, ..., $(\mathbf{x}_n, y_n)$, where $\mathbf{x}_i \in S^D$ is the compositional features vector, $y_i \in \{-1, +1\}$ is the binary response. Let $E = \{\mathbf{e}_1, \mathbf{e}_2, \ldots, \mathbf{e}_{D-1}\}$ be an orthonormal basis of the simplex S^D and $\mathbf{x}_i^*$ denote the coordinates of $\mathbf{x}_i, i = 1, \ldots, n$ with respect to basis E, i.e.,

$$\mathbf{x}_i^* = ilr_E(\mathbf{x}_i) = (x_{i1}^*, x_{i2}^*, \ldots, x_{i,D-1}^*) \in \mathbb{R}^{D-1}$$

where ilr_E denotes the isometric log-ratio transformation based on the orthonormal basis E. Since the new transformed data are vectors in $\mathbb{R}^{D-1}$ and no longer restricted by a constant sum, it can be applied directly on SVM model (21). The new sample would be $S = \{(\mathbf{x}_i^*, y_i), i = 1, \ldots, n\}$ and the new decision function would be

$$D(\mathbf{x}^*) = sign(\mathbf{w}^{*T} \mathbf{x}^* + b)$$
$$= sign \left[\sum_{m \in S} \alpha_m y_m K(\mathbf{x}_m^*, \mathbf{x}^*) + \frac{1}{|\mathcal{M}|} \sum_{i \in \mathcal{M}} \left(y_i - \sum_{m \in S} \alpha_m y_m K(\mathbf{x}_m^*, \mathbf{x}_i^*) \right) \right] \tag{26}$$

To classify a new compositional object $\mathbf{z}$, we just need to transfer $\mathbf{z}$ into its ilr- form, $\mathbf{z}^*$, and then compute the sign of decision function for $\mathbf{z}^*$: If $D(\mathbf{z}^*) \geq 0$ then $\mathbf{z}$ belongs to the positive class and vice versa. Based on the ilr-transformation method, the authors of [40] showed that SVM model outperforms others (linear discriminant analysis, quadratic discriminant analysis, logistic regression model) in both simulation and real Hydrochem data.

3.3.2 Support Vector Machine Classification using Dirichlet Feature Embedding Transformation

In [22], the authors have shown that the marginal density ratio is the most powerful classifier for the univariate classification problems. Using the independence assumption of Naïve Bayes, this idea can be extended to multivariate classification problems: the marginal density ratios can also be used as the features in multivariate classifiers to obtain a powerful model. Specifically, each feature will be transformed independently by its marginal density ratio and concatenated together to create the transformed data using in the multivariate classification problem. The decision boundary under study (with the log-version of marginal density ratios) can be described as:

$$\mathcal{D} = \left\{ \mathbf{x} : \beta_0 + \sum_{i=1}^{p} \beta_i \log \frac{f_i(x_i)}{g_i(x_i)} = 0, \quad \beta_0, \beta_1, \ldots, \beta_p \in \mathbb{R} \right\}$$

where $\mathbf{x} = (x_1, \ldots, x_p)^T$ is $p-$dimensional scalar feature vector, f_i, g_i are the class conditional densities for class 1 and class -1 of ith feature, respectively, β_i is the coefficient used to capture the correlation between features. Thus, the log-version of the density ratios,

$$\log \frac{f(\mathbf{x})}{g(\mathbf{x})} = \left(\log \frac{f_1(x_1)}{g_1(x_1)}, \log \frac{f_2(x_2)}{g_2(x_2)}, \ldots, \log \frac{f_p(x_p)}{g_p(x_p)} \right)^T$$

is much more informative than the original data $\mathbf{x} = (x_1, \ldots, x_p)^T$. Hence, using $\log \frac{f(\mathbf{x})}{g(\mathbf{x})}$ as the features in the multivariate classification problem can bring a much more powerful model, see [22] for more detail.

However, this method can not be applied directly to CoDa due to the constraints of CoDa. To handle this problem, the authors of [29] proposed to use the Dirichlet feature embedding method to transform CoDa before building the SVM classification model. As it is well-known, the Dirichlet distribution is well-defined on the Simplex spaces. Recall that, the Dirichlet distribution of order p with the parameter $\kappa = (\kappa_1, \ldots, \kappa_p)$ has the probability density function f given by

$$f(\mathbf{x}) = \frac{\Gamma(\kappa_+)}{\prod_{i=1}^{p} \Gamma(\kappa_i)} \prod_{i=1}^{p} x_i^{\kappa_i - 1}, \tag{27}$$

where $\mathbf{x} = (x_1, x_2, \ldots, x_p) \in S^p, \kappa = (\kappa_1, \ldots, \kappa_p)^T \in \mathbb{R}_+^p, \kappa_+ = \sum_{i=1}^{p} \kappa_i$ and Γ denotes the gamma function.

Using the idea of [22] and knowing that Dirichlet distribution is well-defined on the Simplex spaces, the authors of [29] proposed to use Dirichlet density ratios for multivariate CoDa to remove the constant constraint, reduce the data dimension and improve the quality of data. Specifically, let

$$S_p^D = \{\mathbf{X} = (\mathbf{x}_1^T, \mathbf{x}_2^T, \ldots, \mathbf{x}_p^T) : \mathbf{x}_i \in S^D\}$$

denote the set of multiple D-part compositional vectors of dimension p and suppose we have a compositional sample of n observations: $S = \{(\mathbf{X}_i, Y_i), i = 1, \ldots, n\}$ where $\mathbf{X}_i$ is the multivariate compositional predictor,

$$\mathbf{X}_i = (\mathbf{x}_{i1}^T, \mathbf{x}_{i2}^T, \ldots, \mathbf{x}_{ip}^T) \in S_p^D$$

and $Y_i \in \{-1, 1\}$ is the binary response, $i = 1, \ldots, n$. Let $f_j(\mathbf{x}_{ij}), g_j(\mathbf{x}_{ij}), j = 1, \ldots, p$ denote the class conditional densities for class 1 and -1, respectively, with $\mathbf{x}_{ij}$ being the jth compositional feature of the predictor vector $\mathbf{X}_i$. As stated before, the $\log \dfrac{f_j(\mathbf{x}_{ij})}{g_j(\mathbf{x}_{ij})}$ would be used as new feature instead of $\mathbf{x}_{ij}$ to obtain a more powerful classification model. From the available data $S = \{(\mathbf{X}_i, Y_i), i = 1, \ldots, n\}$, the procedure to estimate the class conditional densities $f_j, g_j, j = 1, \ldots, p$ is as follows

- **Step 1. Splitting data:** Randomly split the full training set S into two mutually exclusive subsets S_1, S_2 of size M, N, respectively, where $S_1 \equiv (\mathbf{X}^{(1)}, Y^{(1)})$, and $S_2 \equiv (\mathbf{X}^{(2)}, Y^{(2)})$; $S = S_1 \cup S_2$ and $S_1 \cap S_2 = \emptyset$.

- **Step 2. Estimating Dirichlet density:** Let

$$\mathbf{X}^{1+} = (\mathbf{x}_1^{1+}, \mathbf{x}_2^{1+}, \ldots, \mathbf{x}_p^{1+}) = \{\mathbf{X}_i^{(1)} \in S_p^D | Y_i^{(1)} = 1, i = 1, \ldots, M\}$$

be the set of compositional predictors coressponding to $Y_i^{(1)} = 1$ in S_1 and

$$\mathbf{X}^{1-} = (\mathbf{x}_1^{1-}, \mathbf{x}_2^{1-}, \ldots, \mathbf{x}_p^{1-}) = \{\mathbf{X}_i^{(1)} \in S_p^D | Y_i^{(1)} = -1, i = 1, \ldots, M\}$$

be the set of compositional predictors coressponding to $Y_i^{(1)} = -1$ in S_1 such that $\mathbf{X}^{1+} \cup \mathbf{X}^{1-} = \mathbf{X}^{(1)}, \mathbf{X}^{1+} \cap \mathbf{X}^{1-} = \emptyset$. Using maximum likelihood estimation method to estimate the Dirichlet densities $\hat{f}_j, \hat{g}_j$ based on $\mathbf{x}_j^{1+}, \mathbf{x}_j^{1-}$, respectively, $j = 1, \ldots, p$.

- **Step 3. Transforming data:** Using the estimated Dirichlet densities $\hat{f}_j, \hat{g}_j$ to transform compositional features of individuals in S_2 into new real features:

$$\hat{x}_{ij}^{(2)} = \log \hat{f}_j(\mathbf{x}_{ij}^{(2)}) - \log \hat{g}_j(\mathbf{x}_{ij}^{(2)}), i = 1, \ldots, N; j = 1, \ldots, p$$

where $\mathbf{x}_{ij}^{(2)})$ is the jth compositional feature of individual i^{th} in S_2. Thus, the new transformed features of individual i^{th} in S_2 would be $\hat{\mathbf{X}}_i^{(2)} = (\hat{x}_{i1}^{(2)}, \hat{x}_{i2}^{(2)}, \ldots, \hat{x}_{ip}^{(2)}) \in \mathbb{R}^p$ and the new transformed data would be

$$\hat{S}_2 = \{(\hat{\mathbf{X}}_i^{(2)}, Y_i^{(2)}), \quad i = 1, \ldots, N\}.$$

With this transformation method (Dirichlet feature embedding method), we can remove the constraints (non-negative and unit-sum) on each multivariate compositional predictor vector, and reduce its dimension from $(D \cdot p)$ to p. The new transformed sample $\hat{S}_2$ with a much smaller dimension would be used directly to train SVM classification. This type of SVM classification model is called D-CoDaSVM. The authors of[29] compared D-CoDaSVM model with CoDaSVM, ALR-CoDaSVM and ILR-CoDaSVM (CoDaSVM refers to SVM model on original CoDa, and ALR-CoDaSVM and ILR-CoDaSVM refer to SVM model on CoDa based on alr, ilr transformations, respectively), and showed that D-CoDaSVM outperforms three others.

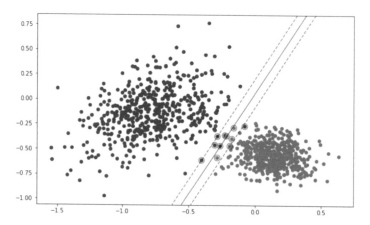

Figure 4: Hyperplane separating data with different classes.

Figure 4 illustrates an example of applying the SVM method to a simulated CoDa set. This set contains 1000 data points with different labels 1 and -1, generated from two different Dirichlet distributions. The isometric log-ratio is used to transform CoDa into normal form. As can be seen from this figure, the black line (hyperplane) separating two classes (marked by green and blue colors) has the maximum margin. The code of this example can be found on ML for compositional data analysis.

3.4 Regression

In statistics, linear regression is a popular technique that is used to model the relationship between scalar responses and the explanatory variables (predictors). The purpose of linear regression is to estimate a linear model from the data that can be used to predict the response based on the value of explanatory variables. Mathematically, assume we have a sample of n observations: $(\mathbf{x}_1, y_1), (\mathbf{x}_2, y_2), \ldots, (\mathbf{x}_n, y_n)$, where $\mathbf{x}_i = (x_{i1}, \ldots, x_{ik})^T \in \mathbb{R}^k$ is the vector of k explanatory variables, $y_i \in \mathbb{R}$ is the scalar response. The linear regression model assumes that the relation between the response and the explanatory variables is linear and this relation is modeled through the noise $\epsilon_i, i = 1, \ldots, n$. Specifically, we try to fit the model of the form

$$y_i = \beta_0 + \beta_1 x_{i1} + \ldots + \beta_k x_{ik} + \epsilon_i = \beta^T \mathbf{x}_i + \epsilon_i, \qquad i = 1, \ldots, n$$

where $\beta = (\beta_0, \beta_1, \ldots, \beta_k)^T \in \mathbb{R}^{k+1}$ is parameter vector of model that we will try to estimate, $\mathbf{x}_i = (1, x_{i1}, \ldots, x_{ik})^T \in \mathbb{R}^{k+1}$. Combining n equations together, we get the model of the form

$$Y = \mathbf{X}\beta + \epsilon, \tag{28}$$

where

$$Y = \begin{bmatrix} y_1 \\ y_2 \\ \vdots \\ y_n \end{bmatrix}, \mathbf{X} = \begin{bmatrix} 1 & x_{11} & \cdots & x_{1k} \\ 1 & x_{21} & \cdots & x_{2k} \\ \vdots & \vdots & \ddots & \vdots \\ 1 & x_{n1} & \cdots & x_{nk} \end{bmatrix}, \quad \epsilon = \begin{bmatrix} \epsilon_1 \\ \epsilon_2 \\ \vdots \\ \epsilon_n \end{bmatrix}$$

The most common method to fit the linear regression model (28) is the least squares technique. Denoting the predicted response by $\hat{y}_i, \hat{y}_i = \beta^T \mathbf{x}_i, i = 1, \ldots, n$ then fitting a linear regression model to a given dataset would correspond to estimate the parameters $\beta_i, i = 0, \ldots, k$ such that the error $\epsilon_i = y_i - \beta^T \mathbf{x}_i$ between the real response y_i and its predicted value $\hat{y}_i$ is smallest and that happens for all observations. Finding the best model that fits the data then becomes finding the parameters β such that the loss function reaches its minimum value. The problem becomes

$$\beta = \underset{\beta}{\mathrm{argmin}} \quad \frac{1}{2n} \sum_{i=1}^{n} (y_i - \beta^T \mathbf{x}_i)^2.$$

Linear regression is one of the most popular fields in statistics and has been analyzing and developing for decades, see, for example,[58;73] and [18] for more detail. Although techniques related to linear regression have been developed and widely used in many statistical applications, most of them are applied to the normal data; the responses are scalar and the explanatory variables are real vectors and obey Euclidean geometry in the real space. In case the responses or predictors are CoDa, we should notice that all operations like the difference, the distance between compositional vectors must be done using Aitchison geometry of the Simplex space. There are some types of linear regression models with CoDa have been studied so far, including linear regression with compositional responses, linear regression with compositional predictors (see, for example,[4;39;11] and [53]) and linear regression with both responses and predictors are compositional (see, for example,[11] and [63]). In[66], the authors proposed to use a new method to transform data, namely α-transformation, to perform regression. The major advantage of this transformation method comparing with the traditional ones is that it can handle the zero values existing in the data. The kernel-based semi-parametric regression method was proposed by Chen et al.[16] to test the effect of microbiome compositions on the continuous or binary responses. In[57], the authors applied kernel-based approaches into penalized regression models to analyze microbiome data. Their developed models have contributed a supervised learning counterpart to the unsupervised learning of principal coordinate analysis (PCoA). In addition to these approaches, Dirichlet regression for CoDa also has been received some attention. In[30], a Dirichlet multivariable regression model for CoDa had been described in order to assess the effects of covariates on the contribution of components in CoDa. In[37], the authors developed the maximum likelihood estimation methods in Dirichlet regression to model CoDa in the occurrence of a covariate and used the total variability and the goodness of fit measurements to evaluate the performance of the proposed models in analyzing CoDa. The adjusted Dirichlet regression model based on modifying the log-likelihood of the Dirichlet distribution had been proposed in[67] in order to handle the appearance of zero values in the components of CoDa.

The rest of this subsection will present briefly how regression models are built on the Simplex space and the formula of these models under isometric log-ratio transformation. Three cases according to the types of response and predictors data will be considered.

- **Case 1: The responses are compositional and the predictors are real**

Suppose we have a compositional sample of n observations $(\mathbf{x}_i, \mathbf{y}_i), i = 1, \ldots, n$ where $\mathbf{y}_i \in S^D$ are compositional responses and $\mathbf{x}_i \in \mathbb{R}^{k+1}$ $i = 1, \ldots, n$ are real predictors, $\mathbf{x}_i = (1, x_{i1}, \ldots, x_{ik}) \in \mathbb{R}^{k+1}$. Let $\hat{\mathbf{y}}(\mathbf{x}_i)$ denote the predicted response, then the linear regression model has the form

$$\hat{\mathbf{y}}(\mathbf{x}_i) = (x_{i0} \odot \boldsymbol{\beta}_0) \oplus (x_{i1} \odot \boldsymbol{\beta}_1) \oplus \ldots \oplus (x_{ik} \odot \boldsymbol{\beta}_k)$$

$$= \bigoplus_{j=0}^{k} (x_{ij} \odot \boldsymbol{\beta}_j) \tag{29}$$

where $\boldsymbol{\beta}_i \in S^D$ are the compositional coefficients of model (29), which will be estimated from data. Least squares is one of the most popular methods using to fit the model (29). Note that in this model, the response $\mathbf{y}_i$ and its estimator $\hat{\mathbf{y}}(\mathbf{x}_i)$ are compositional. The difference between the estimated response and the real value is defined by $(\hat{\mathbf{y}}(\mathbf{x}_i) \ominus \mathbf{y}_i)$ and is measured by the square of Aitchison distance $d_a^2(\hat{\mathbf{y}}(\mathbf{x}_i), \mathbf{y}_i)$. Thus, the fitting problem becomes finding coefficient $\boldsymbol{\beta}_i \in S^D$ such that the Aitchison distance between every n couple $(\hat{\mathbf{y}}(\mathbf{x}_i), \mathbf{y}_i)$ is minimized. Mathematically, the problem becomes

$$\boldsymbol{\beta} = \underset{\boldsymbol{\beta}}{\operatorname{argmin}} \quad \sum_{i=1}^{n} \|\hat{\mathbf{y}}(\mathbf{x}_i) \ominus \mathbf{y}_i\|_a^2$$

$$= \underset{\boldsymbol{\beta}}{\operatorname{argmin}} \quad \sum_{i=1}^{n} \left\| \left(\bigoplus_{j=0}^{k} (x_{ij} \odot \boldsymbol{\beta}_j) \right) \ominus \mathbf{y}_i \right\|_a^2 \tag{30}$$

This model has $k+1$ compositional coefficients $\boldsymbol{\beta}_0, \boldsymbol{\beta}_1, \ldots, \boldsymbol{\beta}_k \in S^D$, each coefficient has D parts, and note that the last part can be inferred from (D–1) previous parts, hence the total coefficients to be estimated is $(k+1) \cdot (D-1)$. The authors of[53] used isometric logratio transformation (ilr) method to transfer this problem into $D-1$ ordinary least squares problem. Let $\{\mathbf{e}_1, \mathbf{e}_2, \ldots, \mathbf{e}_{D-1}\}$ be an orthonormal basis of the simplex S^D and $\mathbf{y}_i^*, \hat{\mathbf{y}}^*(\mathbf{x}_i)$, and $\boldsymbol{\beta}_j^*$ denote the coordinates of $\mathbf{y}_i, \hat{\mathbf{y}}(\mathbf{x}_i)$, and $\boldsymbol{\beta}_j$, i.e.,

$$\mathbf{y}_i^* = \operatorname{ilr}(\mathbf{y}_i) = (y_{i1}^*, y_{i2}^*, \ldots, y_{i,D-1}^*) \in \mathbb{R}^{D-1}$$
$$\hat{\mathbf{y}}^*(\mathbf{x}_i) = (\hat{y}_1^*(\mathbf{x}_i), \hat{y}_2^*(\mathbf{x}_i), \ldots, \hat{y}_{D-1}^*(\mathbf{x}_i)) \in \mathbb{R}^{D-1}$$
$$\boldsymbol{\beta}_j^* = (\beta_{j1}^*, \beta_{j2}^*, \ldots, \beta_{j,D-1}^*) \in \mathbb{R}^{D-1}$$

where ilr denotes the isometric log-ratio transformation based on orthonormal basis $\mathbf{e}_1, \mathbf{e}_2, \ldots, \mathbf{e}_{D-1}$ and $i = 1, \ldots, n; j = 0, \ldots, k$. With this transformation, the perturbation and powering in S^D space become the sum and product by scalar in $\mathbb{R}^{D-1}$; the Aitchison distance becomes the distance in $\mathbb{R}^{D-1}$. Hence, the model (29) becomes

$$\hat{\mathbf{y}}^*(\mathbf{x}_i) = \boldsymbol{\beta}_0^* x_{i0} + \boldsymbol{\beta}_1^* x_{i1} + \ldots + \boldsymbol{\beta}_k^* x_{ik}, \quad i = 1, \ldots, n \tag{31}$$

and each coordinate $\hat{y}_r^*(\mathbf{x}_i)$ of $\hat{\mathbf{y}}^*(\mathbf{x}_i)$ will be

$$\hat{y}_r^*(\mathbf{x}_i) = \beta_{0r}^* x_{i0} + \beta_{1r}^* x_{i1} + \ldots + \beta_{kr}^* x_{ik}, \quad r = 1, \ldots, D-1. \tag{32}$$

Thus, the fitting model problem will become

$$\boldsymbol{\beta}^* = \underset{\boldsymbol{\beta}^*}{\operatorname{argmin}} \quad \sum_{i=1}^{n} \|\hat{\mathbf{y}}^*(\mathbf{x}_i) - \mathbf{y}_i^*\|^2$$

$$= \underset{\boldsymbol{\beta}^*}{\operatorname{argmin}} \quad \sum_{j=1}^{D-1} \left(\sum_{i=1}^{n} \left(\hat{y}_j^*(\mathbf{x}_i) - y_{ij}^* \right)^2 \right) \tag{33}$$

In the loss function of problem (33), for each $j, j = 1, \ldots, D-1$, the sum $\sum_{i=1}^{n} \left(\hat{y}_j^*(\mathbf{x}_i) - y_{ij}^* \right)^2$ is non-negative, hence solving (33) is corresponding to minimize each sum $\sum_{i=1}^{n} \left(\hat{y}_j^*(\mathbf{x}_i) - y_{ij}^* \right)^2$ of the outer sum. Hence, the fitting model becomes

$$\bar{\beta}_r^* = \underset{\bar{\beta}_r^*}{\operatorname{argmin}} \quad \sum_{i=1}^{n} \left(\hat{y}_r^*(\mathbf{x}_i) - y_{ir}^* \right)^2, \quad r = 1, \ldots, D-1 \tag{34}$$

where $\bar{\beta}_r^* = (\beta_{0r}^*, \beta_{1r}^*, \ldots, \beta_{kr}^*)$. With this conclusion, the original problem (30) with $(k+1) \cdot (D-1)$ unknown coefficients becomes $D-1$ least squares problems, each problem is easy to solve and analyze by many known techniques in the linear regression literature. For more detail, see, for example,[4;11;53].

- **Case 2: The predictors are compositional and the responses are real**

  Suppose we have a compositional sample of n observations $(\mathbf{x}_i, y_i), i = 1, \ldots, n$ where $\mathbf{x}_i \in S^D$ are compositional predictors and $y_i \in \mathbb{R}$, $i = 1, \ldots, n$ are real responses. Let $\hat{y}(\mathbf{x}_i)$ denote the predicted response, then the regression model for this case has the form:

  $$\hat{y}(\mathbf{x}_i) = \beta_0 + \langle \boldsymbol{\beta}, \mathbf{x}_i \rangle_a, \quad i = 1, \ldots, n \tag{35}$$

  where $\boldsymbol{\beta} \in S^D$ is the gradient of $\hat{y}(\mathbf{x}_i)$ with respect to $\mathbf{x}_i$, $\beta_0 \in \mathbb{R}$ is the intercept of the model, and $\langle, \rangle_a$ denotes the Aitchison inner product. Recall that, if $\mathbf{x}, \mathbf{y} \in S^D$ then

  $$\langle \mathbf{x}, \mathbf{y} \rangle_a = \langle \operatorname{clr}(\mathbf{x}), \operatorname{clr}(\mathbf{y}) \rangle = \langle \operatorname{ilr}(\mathbf{x}), \operatorname{ilr}(\mathbf{y}) \rangle \in \mathbb{R}$$

  (see[53]). Let $\mathcal{L}(\beta_0, \boldsymbol{\beta})$ be the loss function of the regression model (35), i.e., the function that is minimized with respect to $(\beta_0, \boldsymbol{\beta}))$, then

  $$\mathcal{L}(\beta, \boldsymbol{\beta}) = \sum_{i=1}^{n} \left(y_i - \beta_0 - \langle \boldsymbol{\beta}, \mathbf{x}_i \rangle_a \right)^2$$

  $$= \sum_{i=1}^{n} \left(y_i - \beta_0 - \langle \operatorname{clr}(\boldsymbol{\beta}), \operatorname{clr}(\mathbf{x}_i) \rangle \right)^2 \tag{36}$$

  $$= \sum_{i=1}^{n} \left(y_i - \beta_0 - \langle \operatorname{ilr}(\boldsymbol{\beta}), \operatorname{ilr}(\mathbf{x}_i) \rangle \right)^2 \tag{37}$$

If the center log-ratio transformation (clr) or isometric log-ratio transformation (ilr) method is used, then the problem becomes the ordinary least squares problem and easy to solve. For example, using ilr transformation, $\text{ilr}(\boldsymbol{\beta}) = (\beta_1^*, \beta_2^*, \ldots, \beta_{D-1}^*)$, $\text{ilr}(\mathbf{x}_i) = (x_{i1}^*, x_{i2}^*, \ldots, x_{i,D-1}^*)$, the fitting problems will become

$$\beta_0, \boldsymbol{\beta}^* = \underset{\beta_0, \boldsymbol{\beta}^*}{\arg\min} \sum_{i=1}^{n} \left[y_i - \beta_0 - \left(\beta_1^* x_{i1}^* + \ldots + \beta_{D-1}^* x_{i,D-1}^* \right) \right]^2 \tag{38}$$

This problem, again, can be solved efficiently by the least squares method.

- **Case 3: Both responses and predictors are compositional**

Suppose we have a compositional sample of n observations $(\mathbf{x}_i, \mathbf{y}_i), i = 1, \ldots, n$ where $\mathbf{y}_i = (y_{i1}, \ldots, y_{iQ}) \in S^Q$ is the compositional response and $\mathbf{x}_i = (x_{i1}, \ldots, x_{iP}) \in S^P$ is the compositional predictor, $i = 1, \ldots, n$. Let $\hat{\mathbf{y}}_i$ denote the predicted response, then the linear regression model proposed by Tolosana-Delgado et al.[63] has the form:

$$\hat{\mathbf{y}}_i = \mathbf{b}_0 \oplus B\mathbf{x}_i, \quad \mathbf{y}_i = \hat{\mathbf{y}}_i \oplus \boldsymbol{\epsilon}_i \tag{39}$$

where B is a linear application from S^P to S^Q, $\mathbf{b}_0$ is the intercept of model, $\boldsymbol{\epsilon}_i \in S^Q$ is the error of estimation of $\mathbf{y}_i$.

Let $E = \{\mathbf{e}_1, \mathbf{e}_2, \ldots, \mathbf{e}_{P-1}\}$ and $E' = \{\mathbf{e}_1', \mathbf{e}_2', \ldots, \mathbf{e}_{Q-1}'\}$ be orthonormal bases of the simplex S^P and S^Q, respectively, and $\text{ilr}_P, \text{ilr}_Q$ denote the ilr-transformations with respect to basis E, E', respectively. Using the ilr- transformation, the model (39) becomes

$$\text{ilr}_Q(\hat{\mathbf{y}}_i) = \text{ilr}_Q(\mathbf{b}_0) + \text{ilr}_P(\mathbf{x}_i) \cdot \mathbf{B} \tag{40}$$

where $\mathbf{B}$ is the matrix representation of the application B with respect to two bases E, E'. Assuming that under the ilr-transformation, the transformed data are jointly normally distributed, then the classical multivariate regression methods can be used to obtain the parameters of the model (40). For more detail, see[63;12].

Figure 5 shows the relations between the mass of Arctic fish and two morphometric measurements named "Hw" and "Bg". These relations are plotted from the "FishMorphology" dataset used in the book of Greenacre[28]. This dataset contains 75 observations on 26 morphometric measurements in millimeters of Arctic charr fish. To analyze this dataset, Greenacre[28] considered it as CoDa by expressing these 26 morphometric measurements as the proportions of their respective sum. As can be seen from this figure, the mass of Arctic fish is proportional with their morphometric measurements "Hw" and "Bg". Considering "FishMorphology" dataset as CoDa and using isometric log-ratio transformation method, the regression model presenting the relation between the mass and the morphometric measurements of Arctic fish would be:

$$\begin{aligned} Y_i &= \beta_0 + \langle \mathbf{b}, \mathbf{X}_i \rangle_a + \epsilon_i \\ &= \beta_0 + \langle \text{ilr}(\mathbf{b}), \text{ilr}(\mathbf{X}_i) \rangle + \epsilon_i \\ &= \beta_0 + \sum_{k=1}^{25} \text{ilr}_k(\mathbf{b}) \, \text{ilr}_k(\mathbf{X}_i) + \epsilon_i \\ &= \beta_0 + \sum_{k=1}^{25} \beta_k \, \text{ilr}_k(\mathbf{X}_i) + \epsilon_i, \quad i = 1, \ldots, 75 \end{aligned}$$

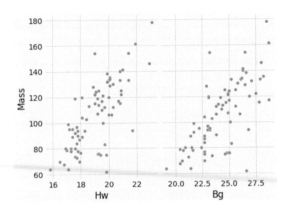

Figure 5: Relations between mass of Arctic fish and two morphometric measurements.

where Y_i denotes the mass and $\mathbf{X}_i$ denotes the vector of 26 morphometric measurements of ith Arctic fish in the dataset, $\mathrm{ilr}_k(\mathbf{X}_i)$ denotes the kth coordinate of $\mathbf{X}_i$ under the ilr-transformation. The variance score of this regression model is 0.78 and the explained variance score between the real mass and predicted mass using this model is 0.96. The code of this example can be found on ML for compositional data analysis.

4   Anomaly Detection using Support Vector Data Description

In ML, SVDD is a well-known algorithm in detecting anomalies (outliers). SVDD was firstly introduced by Tax and Duin[62], and widely used in anomaly detection due to its free assumption about the distribution of the observed data (see, for example,[10;51], and[75], among many others). Although there have been many researches related to SVDD and its applications, most of them were developed for using in normal data. Due to the constraints on the CoDa, these researches can not be applied directly without handling these constraints. This section will briefly present the main idea of the SVDD algorithm and propose a promising method to transform CoDa based on Dirichlet density estimation before using it to train the SVDD anomaly detection model.

4.1   Support Vector Data Description

SVDD is a one-class classification algorithm that allows us to detect abnormal observations by modeling the normal ones. This algorithm obtains a spherical shaped boundary around the dataset, specified by its center $\mathbf{a}$ and the radius R. The volume of this sphere is minimized by minimizing the squared radius R^2, demanding that the sphere contains most of the training objects. In practice, SVDD is widely used to detect novel data or outliers.

Suppose we have an unlabeled training set of size n: $S = \{\mathbf{x}_1, \mathbf{x}_2, \ldots, \mathbf{x}_n\}$ where $\mathbf{x}_i \in \mathbb{R}^p$ are feature vectors, and we want to obtain a description of this dataset. The SVDD optimization problem is

$$\min_{R,\mathbf{a}} R^2 + C \sum_{i=1}^{n} \xi_i$$

subject to $\|\mathbf{x}_i - \mathbf{a}\|^2 \leq R^2 + \xi_i, \quad i = 1, \ldots, n; \ \xi_i \geq 0$

The parameter C controls the balance between the volume of the sphere and the errors. Solving this problem by introducing Lagrange multipliers α_i, γ_i (note that γ_i are omitted during solving process), we obtain the center $\mathbf{a}$ as the linear combination of the support vectors, $\mathbf{a} = \sum_{SV} \alpha_s \mathbf{x}_s$, where SV is the index set of the support vectors and

$$R^2 = \langle \mathbf{x}_k, \mathbf{x}_k \rangle - 2 \sum_{i=1} \alpha_i \langle \mathbf{x}_i, \mathbf{x}_k \rangle + \sum_{i,j} \alpha_i \alpha_j \langle \mathbf{x}_i, \mathbf{x}_j \rangle$$

for any $\mathbf{x}_k \in SV_{<C}$, the set of support vectors having $\alpha_k < C$. To test a new object $\mathbf{z}$, we calculate the distance between $\mathbf{z}$ and the center $\mathbf{a}$ of the sphere. $\mathbf{z}$ is considered as in-class (normal point) when this distance is smaller than or equal to the radius R

$$\|\mathbf{z} - \mathbf{a}\|^2 = \langle \mathbf{z}, \mathbf{z} \rangle - 2 \sum_{i=1} \alpha_i \langle \mathbf{z}, \mathbf{x}_i \rangle + \sum_{i,j} \alpha_i \alpha_j \langle \mathbf{x}_i, \mathbf{x}_j \rangle \leq R^2$$

Instead of using the inner product in the above formulas, we often use the Kernel functions to obtain a more flexible data description. The authors of [70;61] have proposed some kernel functions for the Support Vector Classifier. In the above problem, if a Gaussian kernel function, $K(\mathbf{x}_i, \mathbf{x}_j) = \exp(-\|\mathbf{x}_i - \mathbf{x}_j\|^2 / s^2)$, is used as the distance function over two data points then we would consider a test object $\mathbf{z}$ as in-class if

$$\sum_i \alpha_i \exp\left(\frac{-\|\mathbf{z} - \mathbf{x}_i\|^2}{s^2}\right) \geq -\frac{R^2}{2} + C_R$$

where C_R depends only on the support vectors and not on $\mathbf{z}$.

4.2 Anomaly Detection using SVDD with Dirichlet Density Estimation

As stated before, most SVDD anomaly detection methods so far have been developed for use on normal data; they can not be applied directly to CoDa due to its special structure. This section will introduce a method to transform CoDa into normal form based on Dirichlet density estimation before using it to train the SVDD model.

4.2.1 Transform CoDa using Dirichlet Density Estimation

According to [22], the marginal density ratios are the most powerful for solving the univariate binary classification problems and this idea can be extended to multivariate classification problems based on the independence assumptions between feature variables of Naïve Bayes. In particular, each feature will be transformed independently by its corresponding marginal density ratio and then concatenated together to train the classifier model. Recall that, in this case, the decision boundary under study can be described as

$$\mathcal{D} = \left\{ \mathbf{x} : \beta_0 + \sum_{i=1}^p \beta_i \log \frac{f_i(x_i)}{g_i(x_i)} = 0, \quad \beta_0, \beta_1, \dots, \beta_p \in \mathbb{R} \right\}$$

where $\mathbf{x} = (x_1, \dots, x_p)^T$ is $p-$dimensional scalar feature vector, f_i, g_i are class conditional densities for class 1 and class -1 of ith feature, respectively, $\beta_i, i = 1, \dots, p$ are coefficients used to capture the correlation between the features, and β_0 is the intercept of the model. In this subsection, we will extend this idea to the multivariate one-classification problems. The marginal density of each feature will be used instead of the original one and then combined together to train the classification problem.

However, as mentioned before, the sum of the components in a CoDa vector is constrained by a constant and each component carries only relative information; therefore, we cannot treat CoDa in the same way as normal data. To handle this problem, we will implement the Dirichlet density estimation method (based on the idea of the Dirichlet feature embedding method proposed by Gu et al.[29]) on CoDa to remove this constraint before using SVDD algorithm to design anomaly detection model. As stated before, the Dirichlet distribution is well defined on the Simplex spaces. The properties of Dirichlet distribution and its applications can be found in many works, see[34;33;45] and[46], for example. The estimated Dirichlet density will be used to transform the CoDa in order to remove the constant constraint and improve the quality of data before training the SVDD model. The particular procedures of the proposed method are as follows.

Suppose we have n normal observations $\mathbf{X}_i, i = 1, \ldots, n$, each observation is characterized by l CoDa vectors. Without loss of generality, we can assume that the constant constraint on each CoDa vector $\mathbf{x} = (x_1, x_2, \ldots, x_D) \in S^D$ is equal to 1, i.e., $\sum_{i=1}^{D} x_i = 1$. We also suppose that each of these l CoDa vectors can have different number of parts $p_1, p_2, \ldots, p_l$. Hence, each $\mathbf{X}_i$ can be expressed by $\mathbf{X}_i = \left[x_{i1}^{(1)}, x_{i2}^{(1)}, \ldots, x_{ip_1}^{(1)}, \ldots, x_{i1}^{(l)}, x_{i2}^{(l)}, \ldots, x_{ip_l}^{(l)} \right]$. The summary procedure for transforming CoDa data using the Dirichlet density estimation method is as follows:

- **Step 1. Spliting data:** Randomly split the data into two mutually exclusive subsets, denoted by $S_1 \equiv \mathbf{X}^{(1)}$, with the sample size M and $S_2 \equiv \mathbf{X}^{(2)}$, with the sample size N; $S_1 \cup S_2 = S$ denotes the full training dataset $(S_1 \cap S_2 = \emptyset)$. Note that, in $\mathbf{X}^{(1)}$ (or $\mathbf{X}^{(2)}$), we can consider individuals with different compositional features with different dimensions. More precisely,

$$
\mathbf{X}^{(1)} = \begin{bmatrix} x_{11}^{(1)}, x_{12}^{(1)}, \ldots, x_{1p_1}^{(1)} & \cdots & x_{11}^{(l)}, x_{12}^{(l)}, \ldots, x_{1p_l}^{(l)} \\ \vdots & \ddots & \vdots \\ x_{M1}^{(1)}, x_{M2}^{(1)}, \ldots, x_{Mp_1}^{(1)} & \cdots & x_{M1}^{(l)}, x_{M2}^{(l)}, \ldots, x_{Mp_l}^{(l)} \end{bmatrix} \tag{41}
$$

  and similarly for $\mathbf{X}^{(2)}$. Each of the l compositional features could have a different number of parts, here denoted by $p_1, \ldots, p_l$. Therefore $x_{ih}^{(j)}$ is the hth part of the jth compositional feature for the ith individual.

- **Step 2. Estimating Dirichlet density:** Based on the independence assumption of Naïve Bayes, we will use the maximum likelihood method for each of the l compositional variables in the set S_1. Thus, the Dirichlet probability density function $\hat{f}(\mathbf{x}_k^{(j)})$ based on the estimates computed from $\mathbf{X}^{(1)}$ for the kth individual and the jth compositional variable will be

$$
\hat{f}(\mathbf{x}_k^{(j)}) = \frac{\Gamma(\hat{\kappa}_+^{(j)})}{\prod_{i=1}^{p_j} \Gamma(\hat{\kappa}_i^{(j)})} \prod_{i=1}^{p_j} (x_{ki}^{(j)})^{\hat{\kappa}_i^{(j)} - 1}, \tag{42}
$$

where $\hat{\kappa}_i^{(j)}$, $i = 1, \ldots, p_j$, are the maximum likelihood estimates of $\kappa_i^{(j)}$, the parameters of the Dirichlet distribution for the jth compositional variable, $\hat{\kappa}_+^{(j)} = \sum_{i=1}^{p_j} \hat{\kappa}_i^{(j)}$.

- **Step 3. Transforming data:** each individual in S_2 will be transformed into its estimated probability density (or its logarithmic version), thus the transformed data will not be constrained by the unit sum. This transformed dataset, denoted by $\hat{\mathbf{X}}^{(2)}$, would include N data of dimension l, more precisely,

$$\hat{\mathbf{X}}^{(2)} = \begin{bmatrix} \hat{f}(\mathbf{x}_1^{(1)}) & \hat{f}(\mathbf{x}_1^{(2)}) & \cdots & \hat{f}(\mathbf{x}_1^{(l)}) \\ \vdots & \ddots & & \vdots \\ \hat{f}(\mathbf{x}_N^{(1)}) & \hat{f}(\mathbf{x}_N^{(2)}) & \cdots & \hat{f}(\mathbf{x}_N^{(l)}) \end{bmatrix} \tag{43}$$

and could be used to train the SVDD algorithm.

In summary, by using the Dirichlet density estimation method to transform the original multivariate CoDa vector, we can not only remove the constraint (non-negative and unit-sum on each CoDa vector), but also reduce its dimension from $(p_1 + \ldots + p_l)$ to l.

4.2.2 Anomaly Detection using SVDD with Dirichlet Density-transformed Data

In this subsection, we will describe the procedure for designing an SVDD anomaly detection model using the Dirichlet density transformation method. As mentioned before, CoDa vector has special structure, as its components are non-negative and constrained by unit sum; thus, we can not apply the traditional SVDD directly on CoDa. Instead, we will transform this special data into normal data before applying further technologies. As stated above, applying the Dirichlet density transformation method on CoDa would bring us the transformed data without constant constraint and with a really low dimension. Next, an SVDD classification model will be built using this newly transformed data and finally, an SVDD anomaly detection model for multivariate CoDa with different parts will be built.

1. **Data transformation**

   As suggested in Section 4.2.1, Dirichlet density transformation is a great method to transform CoDa vector from Simplex space to a real numerical vector in Euclidean space. This method not only removes the constraints on CoDa but also reduces the dimension of data. As can be seen in Section 4.2.1, the dimension in multivariate CoDa is quite high. For example, each individual in the set S_2 is characterized by l CoDa vectors $\mathbf{x}^{(1)}, \ldots, \mathbf{x}^{(l)}$, each of these l vectors has different parts, i.e., $\mathbf{x}^{(1)} \in S^{p_1}, \ldots, \mathbf{x}^{(l)} \in S^{p_l}$, thus, the total dimensions in our data is $p_1 + \ldots + p_l$. Using the Dirichlet density estimation method brings us newly transformed data with much lower dimension l. The traditional transformation method like center log-ratio (clr) and isometric log-ratio (ilr) transformation do not have this property. Thus, this method enables us to use the transformed data directly on classification algorithms, reduce the training complexity and increase the training speed.

2. SVDD classification model for multivariate CoDa

After using the Dirichlet density estimation method on the original CoDa set, the newly transformed data would be used directly to train the SVDD algorithm to obtain the SVDD classifier model. The summary procedure for building the SVDD classifier on the multivariate CoDa is as follows:

- **Step 1.** Transforming original multivariate CoDa into normal data using the Dirichlet density estimation method. The new transformed data is no longer constrained by a constant sum and has lower dimension. Let $\hat{\mathbf{x}}_1, \ldots, \hat{\mathbf{x}}_N$ denote the new transformed data, then $\hat{\mathbf{x}}_1$ would be

$$\hat{\mathbf{x}}_i = (\hat{f}(\mathbf{x}_i^{(1)}), \hat{f}(\mathbf{x}_i^{(2)}), \ldots, \hat{f}(\mathbf{x}_i^{(l)})) \in \mathbb{R}^l, \qquad i = 1, \ldots, n$$

  where $\hat{f}(\mathbf{x}_i^{(j)})$ is the estimated Dirichlet density function for the jth compositional variable of the ith individual.

- **Step 2.** Using transformed data $\hat{\mathbf{x}}_1, \ldots, \hat{\mathbf{x}}_n$ to train the SVDD model. The SVDD optimization problem based on new transformed data would be

$$\min_{R,\hat{\mathbf{a}}} R^2 + C \sum_{i=1}^n \xi_i$$

subject to $\qquad \|\hat{\mathbf{x}} - \hat{\mathbf{a}}\|^2 \le R^2 + \xi_i, \quad i = 1, \ldots, n; \ \xi_i \ge 0$

  where R is the radius and $\hat{\mathbf{a}}$ is the center of the sphere. Solving this problem, we obtain the center of the sphere $\hat{\mathbf{a}} = \sum_{SV} \alpha_s \hat{\mathbf{x}}_s$, where SV is the index set of the support vectors and

$$R^2 = \langle \hat{\mathbf{x}}_k, \hat{\mathbf{x}}_k \rangle - 2 \sum_{i=1}^n \alpha_i \langle \hat{\mathbf{x}}_i, \hat{\mathbf{x}}_k \rangle + \sum_{i,j} \alpha_i \alpha_j \langle \hat{\mathbf{x}}_i, \hat{\mathbf{x}}_j \rangle$$

  for any $\hat{\mathbf{x}}_k \in SV_{<C}$, the set of support vectors having $\alpha_k < C$.

- **Step 3.** Model prediction: To test a new object $\mathbf{z}$, we need to transform this CoDa object by its estimated Dirichlet density $\hat{\mathbf{z}}$, and then, we calculate the distance between $\hat{\mathbf{z}}$ and center $\hat{\mathbf{a}}$ of the sphere. $\mathbf{z}$ is considered as in-class when this distance is smaller or equal to the radius R:

$$\|\hat{\mathbf{z}} - \hat{\mathbf{a}}\|^2 = \langle \hat{\mathbf{z}}, \hat{\mathbf{z}} \rangle - 2 \sum_{i=1}^n \alpha_i \langle \hat{\mathbf{z}}, \hat{\mathbf{x}}_i \rangle + \sum_{i,j} \alpha_i \alpha_j \langle \hat{\mathbf{x}}_i, \hat{\mathbf{x}}_j \rangle \le R^2$$

4.2.3 An Example of Anomaly Detection using SVDD

In this part, we will design an SVDD model to detect anomalies on a simulation CoDa set, using the transformation method proposed in subsection 4.2.1. Our simulation will include two CoDa sets:

- Training data: Including 1000 CoDa vectors in S_2^3, randomly generated from Dirichlet distributions with parameters $\alpha_{0N} = (10, 1, 30)$, $\alpha_{1N} = (4, 9, 1)$, respectively. Denote this set by $\mathbf{X}_1$, hence each data point in $\mathbf{X}_1$ has form

$$\mathbf{x}_i = [(a_1, a_2, a_3), (b_1, b_2, b_3)]$$

where $(a_1, a_2, a_3) \in S^3$ follows a Dirichlet distribution with parameter $\alpha_{0N} = (10, 1, 30)$ and (b_1, b_2, b_3) follows a Dirichlet distribution with parameter $\alpha_{1N} = (4, 9, 1)$.

- Testing data: Including 100 CoDa vectors in S_2^3, randomly generated from Dirichlet distributions with parameters $\alpha_{0N} = (10, 1, 30)$, $\alpha_{1N} = (4, 9, 1)$, respectively, and 10 CoDa vectors in S_2^3 generated from other Dirichlet distributions with parameters $\alpha_{0A} = (50, 100, 20)$, $\alpha_{1A} = (44, 90, 1)$, respectively. We assume that these later 10 CoDa vectors are anomalies. Denote this set by $\mathbf{X}_2$

The procedure of designing model is as follows:

- Step 1: Transforming data in $\mathbf{X}_1$ into their estimated Dirichlet densities by maximum likelihood estimation method and formula (42). Denote the new data set by $\hat{\mathbf{X}}_1$.

- Step 2: Building an SVDD model using data $\hat{\mathbf{X}}_1$.

The testing data $\mathbf{X}_2$ will be used to test the performance of the SVDD model. Before testing, we will transform data in $\mathbf{X}_2$ by using Dirichlet distributions with parameters $\alpha_{0N} = (10, 1, 30)$, $\alpha_{1N} = (4, 9, 1)$. Defining the accuracy of the model by the ratio of the correct predictions to the total number of samples, then the accuracy of the testing model in this simulation example is 97.3% and we detect 8 anomaly points (over 10 points), as illustrated in Figure 6. The performance of this SVDD model is illustrated by the ROC curve in Figure 7. The area under the curve is quite high 0.947, showing that this method would be a promising approach for building classification models as well as anomaly detection models on CoDa.

The Python code to run this example can be found on ML for compositional data analysis.

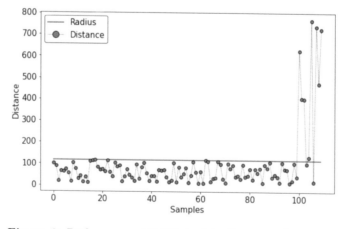

Figure 6: Performance of SVDD in detecting anomaly points.

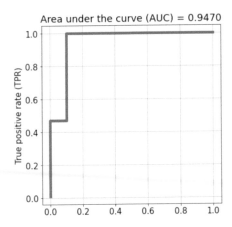

Figure 7: The ROC curve showing the performance of SVDD model.

5 Conclusion

In this chapter, we have summarized the context of modeling CoDa in the Simplex space and popular ML methods applied to this special data including PCA, clustering, classification, and regression. Besides, we proposed a method based on Dirichlet density estimation to transform multivariate CoDa data before applying to SVDD algorithm to build an anomaly detection model. As a result, this method is not only removing the constraint of CoDa, but also reducing its dimension, and hence enabling the transformed data to be used directly on classification algorithms, reducing the training complexity and increasing the training speed. On the applications side, we applied this proposed transformation method on a simulation CoDa set and used transformed data to build the SVDD anomaly detection model. Combining the benefit of the transformed method and the free assumption on the distribution of data in SVDD algorithm, this would be a promising method on data pre-processing topics, which enable us to remove the outliers and increase the accuracy of models. Based on known knowledge on ML for CoDa and this result, our next research direction will focus on developing new ML techniques for compositional time series data analysis.

References

[1] J. Aitchison. The statistical analysis of compositional data. *Journal of the Royal Statistical Society. Series B (Methodological)*, pp. 139–177, 1982.

[2] J. Aitchison. Principal component analysis of compositional data. *Biometrika*, 70(1): 57–65, 1983.

[3] J. Aitchison. Reducing the dimensionality of compositional data sets. *Mathematical Geology*, 70(1): 617–635, 1984.

[4] J. Aitchison. *The Statistical Analysis of Compositional Data (Monographs on Statistics and Applied Probability)*. Chapman & Hall Ltd., London, (Reprinted in 2003 with Additional Material by the Blackburg Press), 1986.

[5] J. Aitchison and M. Greenacre. Biplots of compositional data. *Journal of the Royal Statistical Society: Series C (Applied Statistics)*, 51(4): 375–392, 2002.

[6] J. Aitchison and I.J. Lauder. Kernel density estimation for compositional data. *Journal of the Royal Statistical Society, Series C (Applied Statistics)*, 34(2): 129–137, 1985.

[7] J. Aitchison and S.M. Shen. Logistic-normal distributions: Some properties and uses. *Biometrika*, 67(2): 261–272, 1980.

[8] H. Alashwal, M. El Halaby, J.J. Crouse, A. Abdalla and A.A. Moustafa. The application of unsupervised clustering methods to alzheimer's disease. *Frontiers in Computational Neuroscience*, 13: 31, 2019.

[9] M. Avalos, R. Nock, C.S. Ong, J. Rouar and K. Sun. Representation learning of compositional data. In *Advances in Neural Information Processing Systems*, volume 31. Curran Associates, Inc., 2018.

[10] A. Banerjee, P. Burlina and R. Meth. Fast hyperspectral anomaly detection via svdd. In *2007 IEEE International Conference on Image Processing*, volume 4, pp. IV-101–IV-104, 2007.

[11] K.G. Boogaart and R. Tolosana-Delgado. *Analyzing Compositional Data with R*. Springer-Verlag Berlin Heidelberg, 2013.

[12] K.G. Boogaart, P. Filzmoser and K. Hron. Classical and robust regression analysis with compositional data. *Mathematical Geosciences*, 53: 823–858, 2021.

[13] Y. Ccoicca. Applications of support vector machines in the exploratory phase of petroleum and natural gas: A survey. *International Journal of Engineering and Technology*, 2: 113–125, 2013.

[14] M.E. Celebi, H.A. Kingravi and P.A. Vela. A comparative study of efficient initialization methods for the k-means clustering algorithm. *Expert Systems with Applications*, 40(1): 200–210, 2013.

[15] J. Chacon, G. Figueras and J. Martin-Fernandez. Gaussian kernels for density estimation with compositional data. *Computers and Geosciences*, 37: 702–711, 2011.

[16] J. Chen and H. Li. Kernel methods for regression analysis of microbiome compositional data. *Springer Proceedings in Mathematics and Statistics*, 55: 191–201, 2013.

[17] C. Cortes and V. Vapnik. Support-vector networks. *Machine Learning*, 20: 273–297, 1995.

[18] A.F. David. *Statistical Models: Theory and Practice*. Cambridge University Press, 2 edition, 2009.

[19] J.K. David and L.S. Christopher. The application of cluster analysis in strategic management research: An analysis and critique. *Strategic Management Journal*, 17(6): 441–458, 1996.

[20] H.E. Driver and A.L. Kroeber. Quantitative expression of cultural relationships. In *University of California Publications in American Archaeology and Ethnology*, pp. 211–256. Berkeley: University of California Press, 1932.

[21] J.J. Egozcue, V. Pawlowsky-Glahn, G. Mateu-Figueras and C. Barceló-Vidal. Isometric logratio transformations for compositional data analysis. *Mathematical Geology*, 35(3): 279–300, 2003.

[22] J. Fan, Y. Feng, J. Jiang and X. Tong. Feature augmentation via nonparametrics and selection (fans) in high dimensional classification, 2016.

[23] P. Filzmoser. Robust principal component and factor analysis in the geostatistical treatment of environmental data. *Environmetrics*, 10(4): 363–375, 1999.

[24] P. Filzmoser, K. Hron and C. Reimann. Principal component analysis for compositional data with outliers. *Environmetrics*, 20(6): 621–632, 2009.

[25] A. Fischer. On the number of groups in clustering. *Statistics and Probability Letters*, 81(12): 1771–1781, 2011.

[26] F.S. Zaidi, P. Castagliola, K.P. Tran and M.B.C. Khoo. Performance of the hotelling t 2 control chart for compositional data in the presence of measurement errors. *Journal of Applied Statistics*, 46(14): 2583–2602, 2019.

[27] A. Godichon-Baggioni, C. Maugis-Rabusseau and A. Rau. Clustering transformed compositional data using k-means, with applications in gene expression and bicycle sharing system data. *Journal of Applied Statistics*, 46(1): 47–65, 2019.

[28] M. Greenacre. *Compositional Data Analysis in Practice*. Chapman and Hall/CRC, 2018.

[29] J. Gu, B. Cui and S. Lu. A classification framework for multivariate compositional data with dirichlet feature embedding. *Knowledge-Based Systems*, 212: 106614, 2021.

[30] R. Gueorguieva, R. Rosenheck and D. Zelterman. Dirichlet component regression and its applications to psychiatric data. *Computational Statistics & Data Analysis*, 52: 5344–5355, 2008.

[31] P.H. Guzzi, E. Masciari, G.M. Mazzeo and C. Zaniolo. A discussion on the biological relevance of clustering results. In *Information Technology in Bio- and Medical Informatics*, pp. 30–44. Springer International Publishing, 2014.

[32] G. Hamerly and C. Elkan. Alternatives to the k-means algorithm that find better clusterings. pp. 600–607, 2002.

[33] R.K.S. Hankin. A generalization of the dirichlet distribution. *Journal of Statistical Software*, 33, 2010.

[34] H.S. Hariharan and R.P. Velu. On estimating dirichlet parameters—A comparison of initial values. *Journal of Statistical Computation and Simulation*, 48: 47–58, 1993.

[35] J.A. Hartigan and M.A. Wong. Algorithm as 136: A k-means clustering algorithm. *Journal of the Royal Statistical Society. Series C (Applied Statistics)*, 28(1): 100–108, 1979.

[36] W. Hernandez and A. Mendez. Application of principal component analysis to image compression. In *Statistics*, Turkmen Goksel (ed.). Chapter 7. IntechOpen, Rijeka, 2018.

[37] R. Hijazi and R. Jernigan. Modelling compositional data using dirichlet regression models. *Journal of Applied Probability and Statistics*, 4: 77–91, 2009.

[38] H. Hotelling. Analysis of a complex of statistical variables into principal components. *Journal of Educational Psychology*, 24(6): 417–441, 1933.

[39] K. Hron, P. Filzmoser and K. Thompson. Linear regression with compositional explanatory variables. *Journal of Applied Statistics*, 39(5): 1115–1128, 2012.

[40] J.Y. Joo and S. Lee. Binary classification on compositional data. *Communications for Statistical Applications and Methods*, 28(1): 89–97, 2021.

[41] F.R.S. Karl Pearson. Liii on lines and planes of closest fit to systems of points in space. *The London, Edinburgh, and Dublin Philosophical Magazine and Journal of Science*, 2(11): 559–572, 1901.

[42] L. Lahti, J. Salojarvi, A. Salonen, M. Scheffer and W.M. de Vos. Tipping elements in the human intestinal ecosystem. *Nature Communications*, 5(4344), 2014.

[43] Q. Li and T. Li. Research on the application of naive bayes and support vector machine algorithm on exercises classification. *Journal of Physics: Conference Series*, 1437: 012071, 2020.

[44] J.A. Martin-Fernandez, C. Barcelo-Vidal and V. Pawlowsky-Glahn. A critical approach to non-parametric classification of compositional data. pp. 49–56, 1998.

[45] K.W. Ng, G.L. Tian and M.L. Tang. *Dirichlet and Related Distributions: Theory, Methods and Applications*. John Wiley & Sons, 2011.

[46] A. Ongaro and S. Migliorati. A generalization of the dirichlet distribution. *Journal of Multivariate Analysis*, 114: 412–426, 2013.

[47] J. Oyelade, O. Oladipupo and I. Obagbuwa. Application of k means clustering algorithm for prediction of students academic performance. *International Journal of Computer Science and Information Security*, 7, 2010.

[48] R. Pang, B.J. Lansdell and A.L. Fairhall. Dimensionality reduction in neuroscience. *Current Biology*, 26(14): R656–R660, 2016.

[49] G. Pasini. Principal component analysis for stock portfolio management. *International Journal of Pure and Apllied Mathematics*, 115, 2017.

[50] L. Paul and A. Suman. Face recognition using principal component analysis method. *International Journal of Advanced Research in Computer Engineering and Technology (IJARCET)*, 1: 135–139, 2012.

[51] E.J. Pauwels and O. Ambekar. One class classification for anomaly detection: Support vector data description revisited. In *Advances in Data Mining. Applications and Theoretical Aspects*, Petra Perner (ed.). pp. 25–39, 2011, Berlin, Heidelberg. Springer Berlin Heidelberg.

[52] V. Pawlowsky-Glahn and J.J. Egozcue. Blu estimators and compositional data. *Mathematical Geology*, 34: 259–274, 2002.

[53] V. Pawlowsky-Glahn, J.J. Egozcue and R. Tolosana-Delgado. *Modeling and Analysis of Compositional Data*. John Wiley & Sons, 2015.

[54] D. Pelleg and A. Moore. Accelerating exact k-means algorithms with geometric reasoning. *Proceedings of the Fifth ACM SIGKDD International Conference on Knowledge Discovery and Data Mining*, pp. 277–281, 1999.

[55] S. Pospiech, K.G. Tolosana-Delgado and R. van den Boogaart. Discriminant analysis for compositional data incorporating cell-wise uncertainties. *Mathematical Geosciences*, 53: 1–20, 2021.

[56] T. Quinn, D. Nguyen, S. Rana, S. Gupta and S. Venkatesh. Deepcoda: Personalized interpretability for compositional health data. In *ICML*, 2020.

[57] T.W. Randolph, S. Zhao, W. Copeland, M. Hullar and A. Shojaie. Kernel-penalized regression for analysis of microbiome data. *The Annals of Applied Statistics*, 12(1): 540–566, 2018.

[58] A.B. Richard. *Regression Analysis: A Constructive Critique.* SAGE Publications, Inc., 2004.

[59] N.W.M. Ritchie. Diluvian clustering: A fast, effective algorithm for clustering compositional and other data. *Microscopy and Microanalysis*, 21(5): 1173–1183, 2015.

[60] R. Saha, M.T. Tariq, M. Hadi and Y. Xiao. Pattern recognition using clustering analysis to support transportation system management, operations, and modeling. *Journal of Advanced Transportation*, 2019: 1–12, 12, 2019.

[61] A. Smola, B. Scholkopf and K. Muller. The connection between regularization operators and support vector kernels. *Neural Networks*, pp. 637–649, 1998.

[62] D.M.J. Tax and R.P.W. Duin. Support vector data description. *Machine Learning*, 54(1): 45–66, 2004.

[63] R. Tolosana-Delgado and K. Boogaart. Regression between compositional data sets. *Proceedings of the 5th International Workshop on compositional Data Analysis CoDaWork*, Vorau, Austria, 2013.

[64] K.P. Tran, P. Castagliola, G. Celanoi and M.B.C. Khoo. Monitoring compositional data using multivariate exponentially weighted moving average scheme. *Quality and Reliability Engineering International*, 34(3): 391–402, 2018.

[65] G. Trovato, G. Chrupala and A. Takanishi. Application of the naive bayes classifier for representation and use of heterogeneous and incomplete knowledge in social robotics. *Robotics*, 5, 2016.

[66] M. Tsagris. Regression analysis with compositional data containing zero values. *Chilean Journal of Statistics*, 6(2): 47–57, 2015.

[67] M. Tsagris and C. Stewart. A dirichlet regression model for compositional data with zeros. *Lobachevskii Journal of Mathematics*, 39: 398–412, 2018.

[68] M. Tsagris, S. Preston and A.T.A. Wood. A data-based power transformation for compositional data. *Proceedings of the 4th Compositional Data Analysis Workshop*, 2011.

[69] M. Tsagris, S.P. Preston and A.T.A. Wood. Improved classification for compositional data using the -transformation. *Journal of Classification*, 33: 243–261, 2016.

[70] V.N. Vapnik. *Statistical Learning Theory.* John Wiley & Sons, 1998.

[71] H. Wang, L. Shangguan, R. Guan and L. Billard. Principal component analysis for compositional data vectors. *Computational Statistics*, 30, 2015.

[72] X. Wang, H. Wang and Z. Wang. Convex clustering method for compositional data modeling. *Soft Computing*, 25: 2965–2980, 2021.

[73] X. Yan and X.G. Su. Linear regression analysis. *World Scientific*, 2009. Doi: 10.1142/6986.

[74] C. Zangmo and M. Tiensuwan. Application of logistic regression models to cancer patients: A case study of data from jigme dorji wangchuck national referral hospital (JDWNRH) in bhutan. *Journal of Physics: Conference Series*, 1039: 012031, 2018.

[75] Z. Zhang and X. Deng. Anomaly detection using improved deep svdd model with data structure preservation. *Pattern Recognition Letters*, 148: 1–6, 2021.

[76] D. Zhou, H. Chen and Y. Lou. The logratio approach to the classification of modern sediments and sedimentary environments in northern south china sea. *Mathematical Geology*, 23: 157–165, 2013.

Chapter 9

Decision Support System with Genetic Algorithm for Economic Statistical Design of Nonparametric Control Chart

Alejandro Marcos Alvarez,[1] Cédric Heuchenne,[2,*] Phuong Hanh Tran[3,4] and Alireza Faraz[3]

1 Introduction

From the 1920s to the present, control charts have been considered as useful tools of Statistical Process Monitoring (SPM) that have been widely applied in business and industry areas. Moreover, this statistical approach has also been considered as an effective method for anomaly detection (AD) in different areas[1;2;3;4]. Early detecting of an abnormality helps practitioners not only solve problems in an easier way but also save costs by monitoring and reducing variations in the process. It is important to note that there exists many different control charts that can be used to detect unwanted changes in the distribution parameters of the process. Usually, these charts assume that the quality characteristic follows a specific distribution, for instance, a normal distribution. In this case, we talk about a parametric control chart. However, when the quality characteristic follows a distribution different from the assumed one, the performance of the parametric charts may deteriorate dramatically. Hence, developing nonparametric (or distribution-free) control charts that do not depend on any parametric distributional assumption is an important issue.

According to[5], classical and modern approaches are considered as two distinct methodologies for nonparametric control charts. The classical approach refers to nonparametric statistical tests while the modern approach connects with smoothing techniques. The former is based on ranks rather than raw data while the latter estimates the form of a model relationship/distribution

[1] Akka Technologies, Belgium.

[2] HEC Liège-Management School of the University of Liège; Centre for Quantitative methods and Operations Management (QuantOM), Belgium & Institute of Statistics, Biostatistics and Actuarial Sciences, Université catholique de Louvain, Belgium.

[3] HEC Liège-Management School of the University of Liège; Centre for Quantitative methods and Operations Management (QuantOM), Belgium.

[4] Univ. Lille, ENSAIT, ULR 2461 - GEMTEX - Génie et Matériaux Textiles, F-59000 Lille, France.

* Corresponding author: C.Heuchenne@ulg.ac.be

from a smooth curve. In the nonparametric framework with the statistical tests, a variety of control charts have been investigated widely in the science community, most commonly including the sign, the Wilcoxon signed-rank, and the Wilcoxon rank-sum methods,[6;7;8;9;10]. It is known that the sign test is commonly applied because of its simplicity. However, this test only focuses on the difference sign between each observation and the median value without considering the magnitude of the observations. The Wilcoxon signed-rank test is a useful tool to fix this gap. It is noted that both the sign test and the Wilcoxon signed-rank tests are considered as useful nonparametric alternatives to the one-sample and paired t-tests. Furthermore, Wilcoxon rank-sum test, which is also known as the Mann - Whitney U (i.e., Mann - Whitney - Wilcoxon test or U - test), has been viewed as a nonparametric alternative to treat the unpaired t-test. Since the past few decades, the community has witnessed the development of numerous nonparametric approaches in SPM because of the limited knowledge about the distribution of the underlying processes[11;12;13;14].

Besides the type of a control chart being nonparametric or parametric, the behavior of a control chart is controlled by three main parameters included in the sample size n, the sampling interval h, and the position of the upper control limit (UCL) that must be carefully chosen in order to maximize its performance. In the earliest times, the parameters were chosen based on some heuristics that were known to perform acceptably well in practice. Later on, more sophisticated methods were designed to choose the good parameter values. These approaches are referred to as statistical design (SD)[15] and economic design (ED)[16]. These methods find the values of the parameters in such a way that some SD or cost ED guarantees are ensured, respectively. A more recent approach, called Economic Statistical Design (ESD)[17], combines both ideas in a single method. An ESD for a given control chart allows it to find the design parameters that minimize the expected cost of operating the process, while imposing statistical constraints on the ability of the chart to detect deviations of the quality characteristic from the parameter under study (for example, the mean or the median). Because of those advantages and the lack of knowledge about underlying process distributions, many efforts in the statistical community have been devoted to applying either SD or ESD approaches in various types of nonparametric control charts[7;6;8;18;10;9].

It is clear that the practitioners need to make decisions regarding the optimization of process parameters when they apply these above approaches to design control charts. In order to deal with this issue, it can be relied on a decision aid, namely Decision Support System (DSS). DSS is defined as an information system that analyses data which is generated by applications or collected from various sources such as internal or external organizations and presents it so that the practitioners can make decisions at higher performance and lower cost[19]. There have been several algorithms based on this issue such as Genetic Algorithm (GA), neural networks, logistic regression, classification trees, and fuzzy logic[20]. GA was first presented by John Holland in 1975 and then it has been highlighted as the main technique for parameter identification[21]. Numerous studies have shown the effective role of GA methods in optimization application with ED and ESD of control charts[22;23;24]. Getting inspiration from principles of natural selection in Darwinism, GA approach allows one to find out the optimal solution or best generation which is the result of the pairing of randomly selected individuals from the population over generations. From the initial population which consists of individuals that represent solutions, individuals will be randomly selected to become parents to produce the next generation. These new generations include individuals including which ones have the best characteristics of the previous parent and others are mutations. This process is repeated over generations until the population converges to a solution of the optimization problem or the computational budget is exhausted.

From the above discussions, our study, therefore, tackles the problem of finding optimal design parameters for Shewhart charts using the sign statistic (hereafter denoted by SN charts) and the Wilcoxon signed-rank statistic (hereafter denoted by SR charts). Our aim is to detect location shifts (for example the median), but it can also be extended to other nonparametric control charts (to control scale shifts for example). In comparison with the studies of[18] and[9], we propose a method that uses ESD with constraints on both Type I and Type II errors to find the parameters that optimize the operating cost of the process when the SN and SR charts are applied. Moreover, our cost function is independent of the out-of-control (OC) distribution and in particular of the location shift between the in control (IC) and OC states. This is made possible by using the nonparametric properties of the involved statistical tests. In practice, this allows the user to avoid making assumptions about the underlying quality characteristics and especially about the parameters (location shift) of the process which are often difficult to estimate and not often constant over time. We then run some experiments to compare the parametric and nonparametric ESD in a realistic setting. The experiments show promising results in particular in terms of robustness against OC distribution changes and reliability of guarantees in practice about $\mathrm{ARL_{ic}}$ and $\mathrm{ARL_{oc}}$. To our knowledge, this is the first time that ESD is applied in a fully nonparametric setting with Type I and Type II constraints based on the Sign and the Wilcoxon signed-rank tests, and a fortiori with such a cost function independent of the OC distribution.

The chapter is organized as follows. A brief review about SPM, parametric and nonparametric control charts; particular about the Shewhart $\bar{x}$, SN and SR charts, and recent related works are presented in Section 2. The cost model and the statistical constraints are provided in Section 3. We outline the experimental framework in Section 4, while, in Section 5, we discuss the results and compare the performance of the Shewhart $\bar{x}$, SN and SR charts. Finally, concluding remarks are given in Section 6.

2 Background

In this section, we provide the most important quantities and notations related to the control charts we use in this chapter. Some recently related works are also presented.

2.1 Statistical Process Monitoring with Control Chart

Control chart has been viewed as an important tool of SPM that offers an elegant way to control a process which is in IC or OC state[25]. Specifically, control chart monitors a quality characteristic whose value is observed from the process output over time. The value x_{ij} of the quality characteristic of a certain number n of times is measured at given time steps ($i = 1, 2, \ldots$) separated by h time units. From each sample $x_i = (x_{i1}, x_{i2}, \ldots, x_{in})$, a 'statistic' $y_i = f_c(x_i)$ is computed and then plotted on the control chart versus the corresponding sample number or versus time. The process is declared OC in case the statistic computed at a given moment is larger than a chosen threshold k, called the upper control limit (UCL). From a practical point of view, the use of control charts is split into two stages. First, a so-called phase I is applied to gather data in order to better understand the considered process when it is in the IC state. Once gathered, the data is used to estimate the IC distribution of the quality characteristic. Once the IC distribution is known, the so-called phase II is applied. The primary objective of phase II is to detect changes in the distribution of the quality characteristic with respect to the assumed correct distribution, i.e., the IC distribution estimated during phase I[26].

The efficiency of control charts can be analyzed in terms of Type I and Type II error probabilities, denoted α and β, respectively. The concept of average run length (ARL) is also often used as a performance measure for control charts. The ARL represents the average number of samples after which a signal is raised by the control chart. The IC ARL is computed according to $\text{ARL}_{\text{ic}} = \frac{1}{\alpha}$, while the OC ARL is given by $\text{ARL}_{\text{oc}} = \frac{1}{1-\beta}$. The IC ARL represents the average number of samples before a false alarm, while the OC ARL corresponds to the average number of samples before a signal is raised when the process is out of control. A good control chart design will maximize ARL_{ic}, while minimizing ARL_{oc}.

2.2 Parametric and Nonparametric Control Charts

There are two different approaches for control charts depending on the process distributional assumptions: parametric and nonparametric charts. Due to the space limitation of the chapter, we focus hereunder on a brief review of control charts related to our study such as the $\bar{x}$ chart, the SN chart, and the SR chart.

2.2.1 The $\bar{x}$ Chart

The Shewhart $\bar{x}$ chart is a parametric control chart that is traditionally used to control the mean of a process. It assumes that the quality characteristic follows a normal distribution with mean μ_{ic} and standard deviation σ_{ic} in the IC state. When the process is out of control, the distribution of the quality characteristic is still assumed to be a normal distribution but with parameters μ_{oc} and σ_{oc}. Let $(x_{i1}, x_{i2}, \ldots, x_{in})$ be the ith sample of size n, then the statistic is computed according to

$$y_i = f_C(x_i) = \bar{x}_i = \frac{x_{i1} + x_{i2} + \ldots + x_{in}}{n},$$

Type I and Type II error probabilities can be computed (thanks to the normality assumption), for a given sample size n and a given upper control limit UCL with:

$$\alpha = \frac{1}{2}\left[1 - \text{erf}\left(\frac{\text{UCL} - \mu_{\text{ic}}}{\sigma_s^{\text{ic}}\sqrt{2}}\right)\right], \text{ and } \beta = \frac{1}{2}\left[1 + \text{erf}\left(\frac{\text{UCL} - \mu_{\text{oc}}}{\sigma_s^{\text{oc}}\sqrt{2}}\right)\right],$$

where $\sigma_s^{\text{ic}} = \frac{\sigma_{\text{ic}}}{\sqrt{n}}$, $\sigma_s^{\text{oc}} = \frac{\sigma_{\text{oc}}}{\sqrt{n}}$, and $\text{erf}(\cdot)$ is the so-called error function defined by $\text{erf}(z) = \frac{2}{\sqrt{\pi}}\int_0^z e^{-t^2}\,dt$.

2.2.2 The SN Chart

The SN chart is a nonparametric chart based on the sign test. This test can be used to check statistical hypotheses about any quantile, and in particular the median, of any continuous distribution. More specifically, it requires continuity in the assumed median only. This test has a large variety of applications since it may be applied even if the distribution is not symmetric.

In the case of the median, the statistic of the SN chart is computed as follows

$$y_i = f_{\mathcal{C}}(x_i) = \mathrm{SN}_i^{\theta_{\mathrm{ic}}} = \sum_{j=1}^{n} \mathrm{sign}\,(x_{ij} - \theta_{\mathrm{ic}}),$$

where θ_{ic} is the IC median of the quality characteristic, and $\mathrm{sign}(\cdot)$ is the sign function that returns -1, 0, or 1, when its argument is strictly less, equal, or greater than 0, respectively. For the sake of simplicity in the exposition, we consider that all x_{ij} are different from the median θ_{ic}. There exists a relationship between the sign statistic $\mathrm{SN}_i^{\theta_{\mathrm{ic}}}$ and the 'traditional' sign statistic defined by $\mathrm{K}_i^{\theta_{\mathrm{ic}}} = \sum_{j=1}^{n} \mathbf{1}_{\mathbb{R}_0^+}(x_{ij} - \theta_{\mathrm{ic}})$, where $\mathbf{1}_{\mathbb{R}_0^+}(\cdot)$ is an indicator function that returns 1 if its argument is strictly positive, and 0 otherwise. The $\mathrm{SN}_i^{\theta_{\mathrm{ic}}}$ and $\mathrm{K}_i^{\theta_{\mathrm{ic}}}$ statistics obey the following relation

$$2\mathrm{K}_i^{\theta_{\mathrm{ic}}} = \mathrm{SN}_i^{\theta_{\mathrm{ic}}} + n,$$

that permits to compute the distribution of $\mathrm{SN}_i^{\theta_{\mathrm{ic}}}$ from that of $\mathrm{K}_i^{\theta_{\mathrm{ic}}}$, which is distributed according to a binomial distribution. When the process is in control, the distribution of the statistic $\mathrm{SN}_i^{\theta_{\mathrm{ic}}}$ to control the median is given by

$$P_{\mathrm{SN}_i^{\theta_{\mathrm{ic}}}}[z|\,\mathrm{IC}] = P_{\mathrm{K}_i^{\theta_{\mathrm{ic}}}}\left[\left.\frac{z+n}{2}\right|\mathrm{IC}\right] = \frac{n!}{\left(\frac{n+z}{2}\right)!\left(\frac{n-z}{2}\right)!}(0.5)^{\left(\frac{n+z}{2}\right)}(0.5)^{\left(\frac{n-z}{2}\right)}, \qquad (1)$$

with Equation (1) valid as long as both n and z have the same parity. Note that, due to the above definition of the SN chart statistic, the distribution (1) is valid for any statistic $\mathrm{SN}_i^{\theta'}$ as long as the median of the distribution of the observations is θ'. In particular, this is true for θ_{oc} when the process is out of control such that $P_{\mathrm{SN}_i^{\theta_{\mathrm{ic}}}}[z|\,\mathrm{IC}] = P_{\mathrm{SN}_i^{\theta_{\mathrm{oc}}}}[z|\,\mathrm{OC}]$.

Type I error probability of the sign statistic $\mathrm{SN}_i^{\theta_{\mathrm{ic}}}$ for a given control limit k can finally be obtained by summing over the possible values that $\mathrm{SN}_i^{\theta_{\mathrm{ic}}}$ can have:

$$\alpha = \sum_{z=k}^{n} P_{\mathrm{SN}_i^{\theta_{\mathrm{ic}}}}[z|\,\mathrm{IC}], \qquad (2)$$

where the sum is over all z that have the same parity as n. Type II error probability is more complicated to compute, see Section 3.

2.2.3 The SR Chart

The SR chart is a nonparametric chart based on the so-called Wilcoxon signed-rank statistic and is used to detect drifts of a given location parameter, for instance, the median, from its IC value. Unlike the SN chart, we assume in SR charts that the distribution of the quality characteristic is continuous symmetric.

When we are interested in controlling the deviations of the median of the quality characteristic from its IC value θ_{ic}, the statistic of the SR chart is given by

$$y_i = f_{\mathcal{C}}(x_i) = \mathrm{SR}_i^{\theta_{\mathrm{ic}}} = \sum_{j=1}^{n} \mathrm{sign}\,(x_{ij} - \theta_{\mathrm{ic}})\,R_{ij},$$

where R_{ij} is the rank of $x_{ij} - \theta_{ic}$ when we sort the set $\{|x_{i1} - \theta_{ic}|, |x_{i2} - \theta_{ic}|, \ldots, |x_{in} - \theta_{ic}|\}$ in ascending order. Similarly to the SN chart, all x_{ij} are assumed to be different from the median θ_{ic}.

The $\mathrm{SR}_i^{\theta_{ic}}$ statistic depends on the simpler statistic

$$\mathrm{W}_i^{\theta_{ic}} = \sum_{j=1}^{n} \mathbf{1}_{\mathbb{R}_0^+}\left(x_{ij} - \theta_{ic}\right) R_{ij}$$

through the relation:

$$\mathrm{SR}_i^{\theta_{ic}} = 2\mathrm{W}_i^{\theta_{ic}} - \frac{n(n+1)}{2},$$

where $\mathbf{1}_{\mathbb{R}_0^+}(\cdot)$ is the indicator function that is equal to 1 when the argument belongs to $\mathbb{R}_0^+$ and is 0 otherwise. When the process is in control, the statistic $\mathrm{W}_i^{\theta_{ic}}$ is distributed according to a recursively determinable probability distribution given by

$$P_{\mathrm{W}_i^{\theta_{ic}}}\left[z|\,\mathrm{IC}\right] = \frac{u_n(z)}{2^n},$$

where $u_n(z)$ represents the number of vectors c composed of zeros and ones such that the dot product of c with the vector composed of the integers $\{1, \ldots, n\}$ is equal to z. The value of $u_n(z)$ can be obtained through the recursive formula

$$u_n(z) = u_{n-1}(z - n) + u_{n-1}(z),$$

which can be initialized for $n = 2$ with $u_2(0) = u_2(1) = u_2(2) = u_2(3) = 1$.

In the end, the probability distribution of $\mathrm{SR}_i^{\theta_{ic}}$ can be found from that of $\mathrm{W}_i^{\theta_{ic}}$ with a simple transformation:

$$P_{\mathrm{SR}_i^{\theta_{ic}}}\left[z|\,\mathrm{IC}\right] = P_{\mathrm{W}_i^{\theta_{ic}}}\left[\frac{z}{2} + \frac{n(n+1)}{4}\middle|\,\mathrm{IC}\right]. \tag{3}$$

Note that, due to the definition of the Wilcoxon signed-rank statistic, the distribution (3) is valid for any $\mathrm{SR}_i^{\theta'}$ as long as the median of the symmetric distribution of the observations is θ'. In particular, this is true for θ_{oc} when the process is out of control, such that $P_{\mathrm{SR}_i^{\theta_{ic}}}\left[z|\,\mathrm{IC}\right] = P_{\mathrm{SR}_i^{\theta_{oc}}}\left[z|\,\mathrm{OC}\right]$.

Type I error probability for a control limit k is given by

$$\alpha = \sum_{z=k}^{\frac{n(n+1)}{2}} P_{\mathrm{SR}_i^{\theta_{ic}}}\left[z|\,\mathrm{IC}\right],$$

where the sum is over the z having the same parity as $\frac{n(n+1)}{2}$. Type II error probability is more complicated to compute, see Section 3.

2.3 Related Works

The authors of[7] presented an ED of two-sided Exponentially Weighted Moving Average (EWMA) chart based on the sign test for detecting location parameter changes. From their numerical results, they showed that the sample size and the loss cost drop when the process shift rises. Using the same framework as the sign test with ED,[6] combined the one-sided Shewhart chart and the minimized cost function to detect abrupt shifts in the location parameter. Their study however assumes that the shape of the quality characteristic distribution does not change between the IC and OC states. Then,[8] proposed to develop a two-sided Shewhart chart based on the two-sample Wilcoxon rank-sum statistic with parameters obtained through Duncan's economic model[16;27]. This minimization problem does not involve statistical constraints. In addition, in the unpublished doctoral dissertation of[18], Shewhart one-sided control charts based on the sign and the Wilcoxon rank-sum tests are used for location changes while the Ansari-Bradley statistic is applied for scale changes. The ESD with some constraints on Type I error (not Type II) are added. Furthermore, in the same idea as[6;10] studied an ED of the Shewhart chart based on the sign scheme using the technique of minimization of loss cost per unit time. The study shown that the performance of the sign chart can be improved for moderate shifts and the loss cost is nearly robust to the changes in all input parameters. Based on the same tests for tracking location parameters in the study of[18;9] recently proposed the sign and the Wilcoxon rank-sum tests for one-sided Shewhart charts with restricted false alarm probability included in their cost minimization problem (ESD). However, they do not study consequences on ARL_{oc}.

3   Economic Statistical Design of SN & SR Control Charts

In order to implement a control chart, we have to determine the values of the sample size n, the sampling interval h, and the value k (or UCL) of the upper control limit. We describe the ESD method[17] that is used to find optimal values for those design parameters and adapt it to our nonparametric context.

The ESD method consists in finding the values (k, n, h) such that the expected cost of operating the process per time unit is minimized and that statistical guarantees are ensured. We describe here the cost model developed by[16], where $Q_{exp}(k, n, h)$ is the expected cost of a cycle, $T_{exp}(k, n, h)$, the expected cycle time and ESD tries to minimize $Q_{exp}(k, n, h)/T_{exp}(k, n, h)$.

When the process is first assumed to be in control, the expected cycle time $T_{exp}(k, n, h)$ is composed of four components (see Figure 1):

1. The mean time before an assignable cause occurs, which is equal to $\frac{1}{\lambda}$ (the time difference between two causes is assumed to follow an exponential distribution of mean $\frac{1}{\lambda}$).

2. The adjusted average time to signal (AATS)[22] composed of:

   (a) the expected time between the occurrence of an assignable cause and the next sample, which is given by $h - \tau(h)$, where $\tau(h) = \frac{1-\exp(-\lambda h)(1+\lambda h)}{\lambda(1-\exp(-\lambda h))}$ is the average amount of time after which an assignable cause occurs given that it occurs between samples j and $j + 1$;

   (b) the expected amount of time, from the first sample after the occurrence of the cause, required by the chart to signal an OC state, which is given by $h\left(\text{ARL}_{oc}(k, n, h) - 1\right)$ where $\text{ARL}_{oc}(k, n, h) = \frac{1}{1-\beta(k,n,h)}$.

3. The expected time to take a sample of n measurements and to interpret the results, which is equal to nE, where E denotes the expected time to take and analyze one observation.

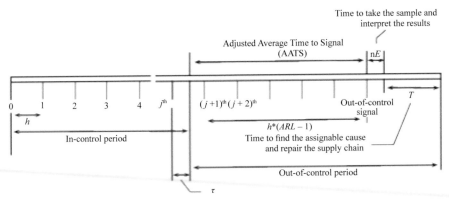

Figure 1: Expected cycle time $T_{exp}(k, n, h)$ and its components for the economic design of control charts.

4. The expected time to identify and correct the assignable cause, denoted by T.

The expected cost $Q_{exp}(k, n, h)$ of a cycle is composed of three terms:

1. The expected cost of operating the process when it is both in control and out of control. This cost is given by

$$\frac{C_0}{\lambda} + C_1 \left(h\text{ARL}_{oc}(k, n, h) - \tau(h) + nE + T \right),$$

where C_0 represents the IC cost per time unit, and C_1 denotes the OC cost per time unit.

2. The expected cost of investigating both true and false alarms. This cost is given by $W\alpha(k, n, h)\frac{\exp(-\lambda h)}{1 - \exp(-\lambda h)} + Y$, where W is the cost of investigating false alarms, $\alpha(k, n, h)$ is Type I error probability, and Y is the cost of investigating a true alarm and repairing the process.

3. The expected cost of sampling per cycle. This cost is given by

$$\frac{S}{h}T_{exp}(k, n, h) = \frac{S}{h}\left(\frac{1}{\lambda} - \tau(h) + \frac{h}{1 - \beta(k, n, h)} + nE + T\right),$$

where S denotes the sampling cost per sample.

ESD also includes some statistical guarantees on ARL_{ic} and ARL_{oc} as originally proposed by [15]: $\text{ARL}_{ic}(k, n, h) \geq L_{ic}$ and $\text{ARL}_{oc}(k, n, h) \leq L_{oc}$ or, equivalently, $\alpha(k, n, h) \leq \alpha_0 = \frac{1}{L_{ic}}$ and $\beta(k, n, h) \leq \beta_0 = 1 - \frac{1}{L_{oc}}$.

Given these definitions, ESD consists in finding the values (k^*, n^*, h^*) that solve the following optimization problem:

$$(k^*, n^*, h^*) = \arg\min_{k, n, h} \frac{Q_{exp}(k, n, h)}{T_{exp}(k, n, h)} \tag{4}$$

$$\text{subject to} \quad h > nE,$$
$$\alpha(k, n, h) \leq \alpha_0,$$
$$\beta(k, n, h) \leq \beta_0,$$
$$k > 0,$$
$$n \in \mathbb{N}_0^+, \ h > 0,$$

where the constraint $h > nE$ is added to make sure that the sampling interval is not shorter than the amount of time needed to actually take and analyze a sample.

Next, we adapt this ESD to nonparametric control charts; that consists in calculating $\alpha(k, n, h)$ and $\beta(k, n, h)$ in the above context. Since the IC distributions of $\mathrm{SN}_i^{\theta_{ic}}$ and $\mathrm{SR}_i^{\theta_{ic}}$ are fully known, it is easy to obtain

$$\alpha(k, n) = \sum_{z=k}^{n} P_{\mathrm{SN}_i^{\theta_{ic}}}[z|\,\mathrm{IC}], \tag{5}$$

for different values of k and n and equivalently for $\mathrm{SR}_i^{\theta_{ic}}$. Next, we focus on β. We could consider a known value for θ_{oc} and the resulting shift $\theta_{oc} - \theta_{ic}$ from the IC to the OC states; adding some assumptions on the IC/OC distribution of the data, for example, the same IC and OC distributions except for the median ($\theta_{ic} \neq \theta_{oc}$) would lead to an estimated approximate expression for β[9]. Another similar idea is provided at the end of the Appendix.

However, the above shift is often not known in practice and is not constant over time: it results from a sometimes rough evaluation, which influences the above expected cost per time unit. In addition, the other parameters (λ, E, C_0, $C_1 \ldots$) of this objective function in (4) are also averages or approximations that make small differences between two cost values not fully relevant.

We propose in this chapter to consider the inequality $\beta \leq 1 - \alpha$ and to replace β by $1 - \alpha$ in the optimization problem (4). This inequality naturally comes from the properties of the sign and the Wilcoxon tests statistics. The proof for the SR chart follows the lines of the one for the SN chart hereafter. In the case of the SN chart, Type I error probability for a given control limit k can easily be computed with Equation (2) and Type II error probability corresponding to this control limit k is given by

$$\beta = \sum_{z=-n}^{k-1} P_{\mathrm{SN}_i^{\theta_{ic}}}[z|\,\mathrm{OC}]. \tag{6}$$

Unfortunately, the discrete probability distribution $P_{\mathrm{SN}_i^{\theta_{ic}}}[z|\,\mathrm{OC}]$ is unknown. However, since $\mathrm{SN}_i^{\theta_{oc}} \leq \mathrm{SN}_i^{\theta_{ic}}$ and $P_{\mathrm{SN}_i^{\theta_{ic}}}[z|\,\mathrm{IC}] = P_{\mathrm{SN}_i^{\theta_{oc}}}[z|\,\mathrm{OC}]$ for all possible values of z, it is clear that

$$\beta \leq \sum_{z=-n}^{k-1} P_{\mathrm{SN}_i^{\theta_{oc}}}[z|\,\mathrm{OC}] = 1 - \alpha. \tag{7}$$

The optimization problem (4) thus provides the optimal design (k^*, n^*, h^*) for the "worst" shift that might arise ($\theta_{oc} - \theta_{ic} = 0$). This cost interpretation is not possible with parametric charts without additional assumptions about the OC distribution. Obviously, (k^*, n^*, h^*) can then be introduced into another (real) cost function with a corresponding evaluation of the true β. For the SN and SR charts, the former cost is denoted by Exp. Cost while the latter (but simulated) cost is denoted by Cost in the tables in the Appendix. If this real cost is not too far from the cost obtained by an $\bar{x}$ chart (which is the benchmark in the Appendix) with known θ_{oc} when the $\bar{x}$ chart assumptions are valid, we can conclude that our methodology fosters reasonable costs with less Type II errors and thus detects OC states more quickly. Next, more importantly, when the (IC/OC) distributional assumptions of the classical/parametric control charts are not satisfied, their optimized cost is not reliable anymore and the resulting design may lead to high amounts of real Type II errors; in such situations, our procedures that do not assume any (IC/OC) distributional assumption (except continuity, symmetricity as explained above) become even more relevant. For all those reasons, we will finally claim that it is more secure to use a nonparametric control chart of our type which at least, beyond a reasonable cost, provides stable Type I and Type II errors (and often substantially lower Type II errors). Those statements are tested in Section 4 through extensive simulations. It is important to note that the optimization problem of this chapter is solve by GA method[24].

4   Experiments

In this work, we compare parametric and nonparametric ESD control charts by simulating a delivery chain process and by implementing the different schemes to monitor that process. The simulated operating costs, false positives and false negatives rates then allow for fairly comparison between the parametric and nonparametric charts in different situations. We adopt the following experimental framework.

- **Step 1: the distribution of the quality characteristic**

  We consider quality characteristics distributed according to different distributions: the normal, Cauchy, and double exponential distributions (see Table 1). In our experiments, we work with so-called 'experimental configurations'. An experimental configuration is composed of a distribution type and two sets of parameters that characterize the IC and OC distributions of the quality characteristic. The set of experimental configurations is reported in Table 2. Additional configurations are also added at the end the chapter and in the Appendix for specific purposes developed below. The values of the means, standard deviations and medians of the above distributions needed to implement the control charts are computed from the parameters of the distributions. For each distribution type, the experimental configurations are numbered to be referred to more easily. For example, for the normal distribution, experimental configuration # 14 corresponds to a quality characteristic following a normal distribution in IC and OC states with parameters $(\mu_{ic} = 10, \sigma_{ic} = 4)$ and $(\mu_{oc} = 17.5, \sigma_{oc} = 4)$, respectively.

  In the case of the Cauchy distribution, it is not possible to theoretically compute the mean and standard deviation since those quantities are not defined. However, the $\bar{x}$ chart still

Table 1: Different distributions considered in this work.

Normal	parameters	the mean $\mu \in \mathbb{R}$
		the standard deviation $\sigma \in (0; +\infty)$
	pdf	$pdf(x) = \frac{1}{\sigma\sqrt{2\pi}} \exp -\frac{(x-\mu)^2}{2\sigma^2}$
Cauchy	parameters	the location $\theta \in \mathbb{R}$
		the scale $\gamma \in (0; +\infty)$
	pdf	$pdf(x) = \frac{1}{\pi\gamma\left[1+\left(\frac{x-\theta}{\gamma}\right)^2\right]}$
Double exponential	parameters	the location $\mu \in \mathbb{R}$
		the scale $b \in (0; +\infty)$
	pdf	$pdf(x) = \frac{1}{2b} \exp\left(-\frac{|x-\mu|}{b}\right)$

Table 2: Description of the experimental configurations for the normal, the Cauchy, and the double exponential distributions.

#	Normal distribution Parameters				Cauchy distribution Parameters				Double exponential distribution Parameters			
	μ_{ic}	σ_{ic}	μ_{oc}	σ_{oc}	θ_{ic}	γ_{ic}	θ_{oc}	γ_{oc}	μ_{ic}	b_{ic}	μ_{oc}	b_{oc}
1	10	1	12.5	1	10	1	12.5	1	10	$1/\sqrt{2}$	12.5	$1/\sqrt{2}$
2	10	2	12.5	2	10	2	12.5	2	10	$2/\sqrt{2}$	12.5	$2/\sqrt{2}$
3	10	3	12.5	3	10	3	12.5	3	10	$3/\sqrt{2}$	12.5	$3/\sqrt{2}$
4	10	4	12.5	4	10	4	12.5	4	10	$4/\sqrt{2}$	12.5	$4/\sqrt{2}$
5	10	5	12.5	5	10	5	12.5	5	10	$5/\sqrt{2}$	12.5	$5/\sqrt{2}$
6	10	1	15	1	10	1	15	1	10	$1/\sqrt{2}$	15	$1/\sqrt{2}$
7	10	2	15	2	10	2	15	2	10	$2/\sqrt{2}$	15	$2/\sqrt{2}$
8	10	3	15	3	10	3	15	3	10	$3/\sqrt{2}$	15	$3/\sqrt{2}$
9	10	4	15	4	10	4	15	4	10	$4/\sqrt{2}$	15	$4/\sqrt{2}$
10	10	5	15	5	10	5	15	5	10	$5/\sqrt{2}$	15	$5/\sqrt{2}$
11	10	1	17.5	1	10	1	17.5	1	10	$1/\sqrt{2}$	17.5	$1/\sqrt{2}$
12	10	2	17.5	2	10	2	17.5	2	10	$2/\sqrt{2}$	17.5	$2/\sqrt{2}$
13	10	3	17.5	3	10	3	17.5	3	10	$3/\sqrt{2}$	17.5	$3/\sqrt{2}$
14	10	4	17.5	4	10	4	17.5	4	10	$4/\sqrt{2}$	17.5	$4/\sqrt{2}$
15	10	5	17.5	5	10	5	17.5	5	10	$5/\sqrt{2}$	17.5	$5/\sqrt{2}$
16	10	1	20	1	10	1	20	1	10	$1/\sqrt{2}$	20	$1/\sqrt{2}$
17	10	2	20	2	10	2	20	2	10	$2/\sqrt{2}$	20	$2/\sqrt{2}$
18	10	3	20	3	10	3	20	3	10	$3/\sqrt{2}$	20	$3/\sqrt{2}$
19	10	4	20	4	10	4	20	4	10	$4/\sqrt{2}$	20	$4/\sqrt{2}$
20	10	5	20	5	10	5	20	5	10	$5/\sqrt{2}$	20	$5/\sqrt{2}$

requires a mean and a standard deviation in order to compute Type I and Type II error probabilities. As a result, and even if the characteristics do not exist, we estimate these values through the traditional phase I method, using $m = 25$ samples of size $n = 5$, as usual[25]. Note that the OC mean and standard deviation are computed through the same phase I approach with samples generated from the OC distribution.

With the samples at hand, the estimates $\tilde{\mu}$ of the mean, $\tilde{\sigma}$ of the standard deviation, and $\tilde{\theta}$ of the median are computed with the following formula

$$\tilde{\mu} = \frac{\overline{x}_1 + \ldots + \overline{x}_m}{m}, \text{ with } \overline{x}_i = \frac{x_{i1} + \ldots + x_{in}}{n},$$

$$\tilde{\sigma} = \frac{s_1 + \ldots + s_m}{m} \left(\sqrt{\frac{2}{n-1}} \frac{\Gamma\left(\frac{n}{2}\right)}{\Gamma\left(\frac{n-1}{2}\right)} \right)^{-1},$$

$$\text{with } s_i = \sqrt{\frac{\sum_{j=1}^{n} (x_{ij} - \overline{x}_i)^2}{n-1}},$$

$$\tilde{\theta} = \frac{\theta'_1 + \ldots + \theta'_m}{m}, \text{ with } \theta'_i = \text{median}(x_{i1}, \ldots, x_{in}).$$

For the Cauchy distribution, since the mean and standard deviation are approximated, we estimate the median as well, in order to fairly compare the parametric and nonparametric charts.

Table 3: Parameters of the delivery chain process.

$\lambda = 0.003$	$C_0 = 3,150$	$C_1 = 29,637$
$W = 250$	$Y = 10,375$	$S = 10$
$E = 0.23$	$T = 0.62$	

- **Step 2: ESD problem and control chart implementation**

To create the ESD problem, it suffices to introduce the $\alpha(k, n, h)$ and $\beta(k, n, h)$ functions of the corresponding control chart into Problem (4), and to give specific values to the parameters describing the cost model. We consider the problem studied by[22]. They focus on the control of a delivery chain process. We use the set of values presented in their paper (see Table 3 for the constraints). Next, problem (4) is solved with genetic algorithms, see[22], with population size set to 2,000 and maximum number of generations to 1,000. Once the optimization terminates, the optimal values (k^*, n^*, h^*) of the parameters are collected to implement the control chart.

We set the values of α_0 and β_0 to 0.1 and 0.99, respectively. These values are chosen to render the problem easier to solve. Indeed, due to the combinatorial nature of the problem, setting aggressive statistical constraints might prevent the optimization algorithm from finding a solution. In this first study, we avoid such issues by choosing large values for α_0 and β_0. Furthermore, note that, because of the way Type II error probability is computed for the nonparametric charts, the following relation must hold: $\beta_0 \geq 1 - \alpha_0$.

In the nonparametric control charts, medians of the distributions are computed theoretically from the parameters of the distributions except for the Cauchy distribution, see Step 1.

- **Step 3: performing the experiments and analyzing the experimental results**

Once the control chart is implemented, we simulate the delivery chain process with delivery times distributed according to the chosen distributions (experimental configurations). The arrival times of the assignable causes are drawn from an exponential distribution with parameter $\lambda = 0.003$. The process starts in control, and we randomly generate the time of occurrence of the first assignable cause before the first IC sample is taken. This time indicates after how long the process will go out of control. Before the state switches to OC, all the samples are drawn from the IC distribution corresponding to the experimental configuration that we selected. For each sample, the traditional procedure is applied: first compute the statistic, and then compare the statistic to the control limit. If the computed statistic falls outside the limits, an OC signal is raised. Of course, this corresponds to a false alarm, since the process is in control.

After a certain amount of time, the switch occurs and the process goes out of control. In this state, the procedure is the same, except that the sample is drawn from the chosen OC distribution. Here, the number of false negatives corresponds to the number of samples between the first sample after the process went out of control and the sample at which the chart gives an OC signal. After the OC signal, the process takes some time to be repaired and then returns to the IC state. The procedure then starts all over again.

A time horizon is fixed to avoid running the process for ever. This time horizon corresponds to 10,000 time units. The number of samples is given by $\frac{10,000}{h^*}$. Once the time horizon is exhausted, the experimental run terminates and results about the states, false and true alarms are collected in order to evaluate how well the chart performed for that particular experimental configuration. This simulation procedure is applied repeatedly 1,000 times for each experimental configuration and finally, the operating cost of the process, the observed Type I and Type II errors, computed as averages over all those runs (1,000), are listed in the tables and fully analyzed.

Finally, our analysis of the experiments mostly focuses on the operating cost of the process, and the observed Type I and Type II errors.

5   Results Discussion

In this section, we briefly analyze the experimental results. The entirety of the results is available in the Appendix. The simulation results for each distribution and each experimental configuration are illustrated in Figures 2 to 4 and Table 2, respectively. In these figures, three performance measures are reported: the average cost per time unit observed during the simulations, and the frequency of occurrence, observed during the simulations, of false positives and false negatives. The graphs show that the results, for all charts, deteriorate when the variabilities increase and when the OC distribution gets closer to the IC distribution. Moreover, in the case of the normal and double exponential distributions, the nonparametric charts yield a lower FN (false negatives) rate, while the FP (false positives) rate increases due to the small values of k^*. If we take a closer look at the simulated operating costs in the case of the normal distribution, we see that the costs obtained with the nonparametric ESD and the bounded β are close to those obtained by the $\bar{x}$ chart that uses the real β. These are surprisingly good results that show that the nonparametric charts remain competitive compared to the expected winner (the $\bar{x}$ chart used on normal distributions). For the other distributions, the parametric and nonparametric costs are always close to each other (sometimes better, sometimes worse), except in the case of the Cauchy distribution where the $\bar{x}$ chart becomes very expensive in the complicated situations (large scale parameter). A clear advantage of nonparametric charts is that the number of situations in which the expected values of α and β given by the model match the experimental results is larger than for parametric charts. More precisely, the false positives and negatives rates being a main concern, using nonparametric charts is a wise choice, since parametric charts do not guarantee, in general, false positives nor false negatives rates. We illustrate this with an experiment where the IC distribution is different from the OC distribution. More specifically, we focus here on the situation where the IC distribution is normal and the OC distribution is a shifted exponential (λ_{oc} is the parameter of the exponential and δ_{oc} is the upward shift). The ESD is carried out with the assumption that the IC and OC means are known and that the standard deviation is the same in and out of control. These choices are often made in practice and they impact the ESD of the $\bar{x}$ chart, but they do not influence the design of the nonparametric charts. Table 4 reports the experimental operational costs obtained with the three designs when the parameters of the OC distribution (λ_{oc} and δ_{oc}) vary. The results show that there are situations in which using the $\bar{x}$ chart becomes very expensive, while the operating costs of the nonparametric charts remain constant. In general, the parametric

Table 4: Additional experiments with an IC normal distribution (μ_{ic}, σ_{ic}) and an OC shifted exponential distribution (λ_{oc} is the parameter of the exponential and δ_{oc} is the upward shift). This table reports the experimental operational costs for all charts and the considered parameters configurations.

IC: Normal		OC: expo.		Experimental operational costs		
μ_{ic}	σ_{ic}	λ_{oc}	δ_{oc}	$\overline{x}$	SN	SR
10	2	0.1	10	3,302.6	3,293.7	3,321.9
10	2	0.1	12	3,295.1	3,293.7	3,321.9
10	2	0.1	15	3,285.0	3,293.7	3,321.9
10	2	0.1	20	3,272.1	3,293.7	3,321.9
10	2	0.2	10	3,300.3	3,293.7	3,321.9
10	2	0.2	12	3,304.3	3,293.7	3,321.9
10	2	0.2	15	3,279.6	3,293.7	3,321.9
10	2	0.2	20	3,269.1	3,293.7	3,321.9
10	2	0.5	10	3,367.4	3,293.7	3,321.9
10	2	0.5	12	3,292.1	3,293.7	3,321.9
10	2	0.5	15	3,274.1	3,293.7	3,321.9
10	2	0.5	20	3,270.7	3,293.7	3,321.9
10	2	1	10	3,581.0	3,293.7	3,321.9
10	2	1	12	3,307.5	3,293.7	3,321.9
10	2	1	15	3,277.5	3,293.7	3,321.9
10	2	1	20	3,270.7	3,293.7	3,321.9
10	2	2	10	8,539.6	3,293.7	3,321.9
10	2	2	12	3,326.5	3,293.7	3,321.9
10	2	2	15	3,279.6	3,293.7	3,321.9
10	2	2	20	3,270.1	3,293.7	3,321.9

chart does not suffer too much from its wrong assumptions when the shift of the exponential (δ_{oc}) is large, i.e., the parametric chart is good in the easy case. On the other hand, when the problem becomes more complicated, i.e., when the shift is rather small, the parametric chart behaves somewhat badly. For instance, in the extreme case when $\lambda_{oc} = 2$ and $\delta_{oc} = 10$, the $\overline{x}$ chart suffers from a false negative rate of 0.994, which is prohibitive and explains the dramatic rise in the operational cost that achieves 8,539.6. To better understand this effect, we report in Table 5 additional results for increasing values of λ_{oc}. The table shows that increasing λ_{oc} has a huge impact on the false negative rate and indirectly on the operational costs of the $\overline{x}$ chart that increase importantly when λ_{oc} increases a bit. It is not the case for the nonparametric charts that are not influenced by the parameters of the distributions and exhibit a very low operational cost in all situations. This again shows the superiority of the nonparametric charts over the $\overline{x}$ chart when the problem is subject to uncertainty. The full experimental results are reported in Tables 15–17. Another advantage of the bounded β approach that we propose is that the statistical constraints as well as the design parameters remain valid for any OC distribution as well (as long as it is continuous in the case of the SN chart, and continuous and symmetric in the case of the SR chart). Here also, the OC distribution and its parameters (in particular the location shift) may change over time without too much impacting the results.

As explained in Section 3, we could have chosen to assume more known information about the OC distribution as for example in the study of[9]. We could also have decided to only introduce one known (or estimable) parameter for the OC distribution without any additional assumption. More precisely, we could have assumed a known probability $P[x_{ij} > \theta_{ic}]$ for all ij, where x_{ij} denotes the jth random variable of the ith sample. This would have been sufficient

Table 5: Additional experiments with an IC normal distribution (μ_{ic}, σ_{ic}) and an OC shifted exponential distribution (λ_{oc} is the parameter of the exponential and δ_{oc} is the upward shift). This table reports additional experimental results in a difficult case where the shift of the OC distribution is small. The table reports the false positives, false negatives, and experimental costs for the considered charts.

IC: Norm.		OC: exp.		$\bar{x}$			SN			SR		
μ_{ic}	σ_{ic}	λ_{oc}	δ_{oc}	FP	FN	cost	FP	FN	cost	FP	FN	cost
10	2	1	10	0.1	0.875	3581.0	0.062	0.000	3293.7	0.098	0.000	3321.9
10	2	1.25	10	0.1	0.958	3902.0	0.062	0.000	3293.7	0.098	0.000	3321.9
10	2	1.5	10	0.1	0.978	4377.6	0.062	0.000	3293.7	0.098	0.000	3321.9
10	2	1.75	10	0.1	0.988	5180.5	0.062	0.000	3293.7	0.098	0.000	3321.9
10	2	2	10	0.1	0.994	8539.6	0.062	0.000	3293.7	0.098	0.000	3321.9

to fully know the OC distribution of $SN_i^{\theta_{ic}}$ and legitimate in comparison with the $\bar{x}$ chart for which all the quantities (parameters, distributions) are specified. Nonetheless, for the sake of robustness (and therefore in order to provide designs that can be applied to a class of problems as wide as possible), we preferred to avoid assumptions; the results show that there is almost no loss of performance even with respect to the restricted (by assumptions) $\bar{x}$ chart, and even when its strong assumptions are perfectly fulfilled. On the contrary, in situations where these assumptions are not valid, the gain of performance of the nonparametric ESD can be very high.

Finally, it can be interesting to observe the behavior of the control charts when the quality characteristic is uniformly distributed. Indeed, we can have in that way an overview of the charts performance from distributions with no tail (uniform) up to distributions with heavy tails (Cauchy). The results are displayed in Tables 18 and 19. We consider uniform distributions on the intervals $[a_{ic} - b_{ic}, a_{ic} + b_{ic}]$ and $[a_{oc} - b_{oc}, a_{oc} + b_{oc}]$ for the IC and OC cases respectively, $a_{ic} = 10$ and $b_{ic} = b_{oc}$. IC and OC distributions have the same means and variances as in the normal case: Table 6 is thus also valid for uniform experiments with $\mu_{oc} = a_{oc}$ in the second column and $b_{oc} = 1.73; 3.46; 5.20; 6.93; 8.66$ replacing $\sigma_{oc} = 1; 2; 3.4; 5$ in the third column.

Results for the uniform and the normal distributions are close. Indeed, the distribution of a sum of independent uniform random variables with the same support is symmetric. FP and FN rates are quite similar to the theoretical α and β obtained with the normal distribution, except when the threshold k^* corresponds to a point far on the right of the IC distribution, there where the tails of the normal distribution and the distribution of the average of independent uniform random variables are quite different. Since the last distribution can be zero, it is possible to find nul FP and/or FN rates for many simulations (6, 11, 16, 17 for example for the $\bar{x}$ chart); since the design does not depend on the data distributions, FP rate is never nul in the nonparametric charts but FN rate is in many cases (1, 6, 7, 11, 12, 13, 14, 16, 17, 18, 19, 20). It is interesting to see that in simulation 12 for the $\bar{x}$ chart, both FP and FN rates could be zero but the threshold is chosen too large (with the normal assumption) so as to make nonzero FN rate. Again, the nonparametric charts exhibit stable FP rates in line with their theoretical value, whereas in comparison with distributions with infinite support and heavier tails, many of their FN rates are zeros. In general, the heavier the tails of the considered distributions, the higher the FN rates (see the simulations with the Cauchy distribution) and the impact on the average operating costs, although as already seen, the OC distribution characteristics also influence the performance of the control charts: for example, the uniform distribution having no tails, FN rate (for the SN and SR charts) is zero in many cases but for some IC and OC distributions that overlap more, FN rate is lower for the normal than for the uniform distribution. However, in any case, the design of nonparametric control charts as well as their Type I error do not depend on the data distribution (under the continuity and/or symmetry assumptions) and can provide through the idea of bounded Type II error, reasonable FN rate and average operating cost, which is clearly not always the case for parametric control charts.

6 Conclusions

In this work, we have applied the ESD to nonparametric control charts. To this end, we have developed bounds for Type II error probability, i.e., the FN rates, that have been used within the ESD model. We implemented the optimization problem defining this model and used it to find the optimal design parameters of nonparametric control charts. Later, we compared the behavior of parametric and nonparametric ESD on different probability distributions with different values of the distribution parameters.

The simulation results show that the ESD of nonparametric control charts compares favorably with traditional methods. The average operating cost is roughly equal to the one obtained when parametric charts are used. A main difference is that the statistical guarantees offered by the ESD are overall met with the nonparametric ESD, unlike the parametric one. This is a strong superiority over parametric charts since statistical guarantees are usually one of the most important criteria in the design of control charts.

As further research, SN and SR charts could be constructed with constraints on both Type I and Type II errors and the use of a known location shift in the cost function. We can expect from our study that their performance would be between the $\bar{x}$ charts and the proposed SN and SR charts. In practice, the advantages of the charts proposed in this chapter should also be observed but their interest in specific cases (situations with known location shifts for example) could be pointed out. Also, the extension to the two-sample Wilcoxon signed-rank test is also of great interest when we have reliable in-control samples.

Acknowledgements

Research activities of Phuong Hanh Tran have been supported by Univ. Lille, ENSAIT, ULR 2461 - GEMTEX - Engineering and Textile Materials, Roubaix, France and HEC Liège - Management School of the University of Liège, Liège, Belgium under grant 2020/MOB/000504.

References

[1] F. Kadri, F. Harrou, S. Chaabane, Y. Sun and C. Tahon. Seasonal arma-based spc charts for anomaly detection: Application to emergency department systems. *Neurocomputing*, 173: 2102–2114, 2016.

[2] R. Noorossana, S.S. Hosseini and A. Heydarzade. An overview of dynamic anomaly detection in social networks via control charts. *Quality and Reliability Engineering International*, 34(4): 641–648, 2018.

[3] P.H. Tran, K.P. Tran, T.H. Truong, C. Heuchenne, H. Tran and T.M.H. Le. Real time data-driven approaches for credit card fraud detection. In *Proceedings of the 2018 International Conference on E-business and Applications*, pp. 6–9, 2018.

[4] P.H. Tran, C. Heuchenne, H.D. Nguyen and H. Marie. Monitoring coefficient of variation using one-sided run rules control charts in the presence of measurement errors. *Journal of Applied Statistics*, 48(12): 2178–2204, 2021.

[5] A. Pagan and A. Ullah. *Nonparametric Econometrics*. Cambridge University Press, 1999.

[6] C. Li, A. Mukherjee, Q. Su and M. Xie. Robust algorithms for economic designing of a nonparametric control chart for abrupt shift in location. *Journal of Statistical Computation and Simulation*, 86(2): 306–323, 2016.

[7] S.H. Patil and T.D. Shirke. Economic design of a nonparametric ewma control chart for location. *Production*, 26(4): 698–706, 2016.

[8] C. Li, A. Mukherjee, Q. Su and M. Xie. Optimal design of a distribution-free quality control scheme for cost-efficient monitoring of unknown location. *International Journal of Production Research*, 54(24): 7259–7273, 2016.

[9] C. Li and A. Mukherjee. Nonparametric cost-minimized shewhart-type process monitoring with restricted false alarm probability. *Quality and Reliability Engineering International*, 35(6):1846–1865, 2019.

[10] S.H. Patil and D.T. Shirke. Economic design of non parametric sign control chart. *Communications in Statistics-Theory and Methods*, 46(18): 8987–8998, 2017.

[11] L. Liu, F. Tsung and J. Zhang. Adaptive nonparametric CUSUM scheme for detecting unknown shifts in location. *International Journal of Production Research*, 52(6): 1592–1606, 2014.

[12] M.A. Graham, S. Chakraborti and A. Mukherjee. Design and implementation of cusum exceedance control charts for unknown location. *International Journal of Production Research*, 52(18): 5546–5564, 2014.

[13] G. Celano, P. Castagliola, S. Chakraborti and G. Nenes. The performance of the shewhart sign control chart for finite horizon processes. *International Journal of Advanced Manufacturing Technology*, pp. 1–16, 2015.

[14] P. Qiu. Some perspectives on nonparametric statistical process control. *Journal of Quality Technology*, 50(1): 49–65, 2018.

[15] W.H. Woodall. The statistical design of quality control charts. *Journal of the Royal Statistical Society. Series D (The Statistician)*, 34(2): 155–160, 1985.

[16] A.J. Duncan. The economic design of X charts used to maintain current control of a process. *Journal of the American Statistical Association*, 51(274): 228–242, 1956.

[17] E.M. Saniga. Economic statistical control-chart designs with an application to X and R charts. *Technometrics*, 31(3): 313–320, 1989.

[18] C. Li. Economic modeling and performance investigation of quality control charts. Unpublished doctoral dessertation. *City University of Hong Kong, Hong Kong, China*, 2017.

[19] S.B. Eom, S.M. Lee, E.B. Kim and C. Somarajan. A survey of decision support system applications (1988–1994). *Journal of the Operational Research Society*, 49(2): 109–120, 1998.

[20] V. García-Díaz. Algorithms in decision support systems, 2021.

[21] J.H. Holland. *Adaptation in Natural and Artificial Systems: An Introductory Analysis with Applications to Biology, Control, and Artificial Intelligence*. MIT press, 1992.

[22] A. Faraz, C. Heuchenne, E. Saniga and E. Foster. Monitoring delivery chains using multivariate control charts. *European Journal of Operational Research*, 228(1): 282–289, 2013.

[23] A. Faraz, C. Heuchenne and E. Saniga. Optimal t2 control chart with a double sampling scheme–an alternative to the mewma chart. *Quality and Reliability Engineering International*, 28(7): 751–760, 2012.

[24] A. Faraz and E. Saniga. Multiobjective genetic algorithm approach to the economic statistical design of control charts with an application to bar and s2 charts. *Quality and Reliability Engineering International*, 29(3): 407–415, 2013.

[25] D.C. Montgomery. *Introduction to Statistical Quality Control*. John Wiley & Sons, 2007.

[26] G. Vining. Technical advice: Phase I and phase II control charts. *Quality Engineering*, 21(4): 478–479, 2009.

[27] T.J. Lorenzen and L.C. Vance. The economic design of control charts: A unified approach. *Technometrics*, 28(1): 3–10, 1986.

Appendix

This appendix reports the complete experimental results that we obtained during our experiments. Each line of the experimental results tables corresponds to an experimental configuration detailed in Table 2.

The following table summarizes the results tables appearing in this appendix grouped by distribution and result type.

	Optimization results		Simulation results FP and FN rate		Simulation results Exp. vs. true cost	
	Table #	Page #	Table #	Page #	Table #	Page #
Normal	6	235	7	236	8	237
Cauchy	9	238	10	239	11	240
Double exponential	12	241	13	242	14	243

The experimental procedure is split in two parts: the optimization part to find the optimal parameters k, n, and h; and the simulation part where the control chart is indeed implemented and used on a simulated process.

The results are presented in three different tables for each distribution type. The first table gives the optimal values k^*, n^*, and h^*, found by the optimization algorithm to minimize the expected cost of the model. The second table reports the expected values of α and β corresponding to the optimal values (k^*, n^*, h^*), and compares those values to the real false positives and false negatives rates observed during the experiments. The third table shows the discrepancies between the expected cost predicted by the model for the current value of the parameters and the truly experienced cost.

Additionally, we report some results where the IC distribution is different from the OC distribution. Those results are reported in Tables 15–17. Finally, Tables 18 and 19 report results for data uniformly distributed with the same means and variances in Table 6. These tables should be read as the previous ones.

Table 6: Normal distribution. Results of the optimization of the economic statistical design for every considered control chart. This table gives the optimal values of k, n, and h, for every experimental configuration. The column 'Opt' indicates whether the optimization algorithm found a feasible solution ($\circ$), or not ($\times$).

#	Param.		Opt	$\bar{x}$			Opt	SN			Opt	SR		
	μ_{oc}	σ_{oc}		k^*	n^*	h^*		k^*	n^*	h^*		k^*	n^*	h^*
1	12.5	1	$\circ$	11.72	2	0.48	$\circ$	3	4	0.92	$\circ$	20	8	1.84
2	12.5	2	$\circ$	12.4	2	0.46	$\circ$	3	4	0.92	$\circ$	20	8	1.84
3	12.5	3	$\circ$	12.96	2	0.46	$\circ$	3	4	0.92	$\circ$	20	8	1.84
4	12.5	4	$\circ$	13.62	2	0.46	$\circ$	3	4	0.92	$\circ$	20	8	1.84
5	12.5	5	$\circ$	14.53	2	0.46	$\circ$	3	4	0.92	$\circ$	20	8	1.84
6	15	1	$\circ$	13	1	0.5	$\circ$	3	4	0.92	$\circ$	20	8	1.84
7	15	2	$\circ$	13.43	2	0.48	$\circ$	3	4	0.92	$\circ$	20	8	1.84
8	15	3	$\circ$	14.17	2	0.46	$\circ$	3	4	0.92	$\circ$	20	8	1.84
9	15	4	$\circ$	14.79	2	0.46	$\circ$	3	4	0.92	$\circ$	20	8	1.84
10	15	5	$\circ$	15.37	2	0.46	$\circ$	3	4	0.92	$\circ$	20	8	1.84
11	17.5	1	$\circ$	14.09	1	0.5	$\circ$	3	4	0.92	$\circ$	20	8	1.84
12	17.5	2	$\circ$	15.01	1	0.49	$\circ$	3	4	0.92	$\circ$	20	8	1.84
13	17.5	3	$\circ$	15.15	2	0.48	$\circ$	3	4	0.92	$\circ$	20	8	1.84
14	17.5	4	$\circ$	15.91	2	0.46	$\circ$	3	4	0.92	$\circ$	20	8	1.84
15	17.5	5	$\circ$	16.58	2	0.46	$\circ$	3	4	0.92	$\circ$	20	8	1.84
16	20	1	$\circ$	15.25	1	0.5	$\circ$	3	4	0.92	$\circ$	20	8	1.84
17	20	2	$\circ$	16	1	0.5	$\circ$	3	4	0.92	$\circ$	20	8	1.84
18	20	3	$\circ$	17.06	1	0.47	$\circ$	3	4	0.92	$\circ$	20	8	1.84
19	20	4	$\circ$	16.86	2	0.48	$\circ$	3	4	0.92	$\circ$	20	8	1.84
20	20	5	$\circ$	17.65	2	0.46	$\circ$	3	4	0.92	$\circ$	20	8	1.84

Table 7: Normal distribution. Results of the simulation experiments where the expected probabilities of Type I (α) and Type II (β) errors are compared to the probabilities observed during the experiments. 'FP' represents the false positives rates (Type I errors), and 'FN' represents the false negatives rates (Type II errors) observed during the simulations. The values between brackets are the corresponding standard deviations.

#	Param. μ_{oc}	σ_{oc}	$\bar{x}$ α	β	FP	FN	SN α	β	FP	FN	SR α	β	FP	FN
1	12.5	1	0.008	0.134	0.008 (0.001)	0.134 (0.043)	0.062	0.938	0.063 (0.002)	0.024 (0.028)	0.098	0.902	0.098 (0.004)	0.000 (0.000)
2	12.5	2	0.045	0.471	0.045 (0.001)	0.465 (0.057)	0.062	0.938	0.063 (0.002)	0.355 (0.074)	0.098	0.902	0.098 (0.004)	0.027 (0.029)
3	12.5	3	0.081	0.586	0.081 (0.002)	0.581 (0.053)	0.062	0.938	0.063 (0.002)	0.587 (0.058)	0.098	0.902	0.098 (0.004)	0.192 (0.066)
4	12.5	4	0.1	0.655	0.100 (0.002)	0.651 (0.042)	0.062	0.938	0.063 (0.002)	0.704 (0.048)	0.098	0.902	0.098 (0.004)	0.367 (0.072)
5	12.5	5	0.1	0.717	0.100 (0.002)	0.714 (0.041)	0.062	0.938	0.063 (0.002)	0.763 (0.040)	0.098	0.902	0.098 (0.004)	0.491 (0.068)
6	15	1	0.001	0.023	0.001 (0.000)	0.023 (0.019)	0.062	0.938	0.063 (0.002)	0.000 (0.000)	0.098	0.902	0.098 (0.004)	0.000 (0.000)
7	15	2	0.008	0.134	0.008 (0.001)	0.134 (0.043)	0.062	0.938	0.063 (0.002)	0.024 (0.028)	0.098	0.902	0.098 (0.004)	0.000 (0.000)
8	15	3	0.025	0.347	0.025 (0.001)	0.342 (0.057)	0.062	0.938	0.063 (0.002)	0.173 (0.065)	0.098	0.902	0.098 (0.004)	0.002 (0.007)
9	15	4	0.045	0.471	0.045 (0.001)	0.465 (0.057)	0.062	0.938	0.063 (0.002)	0.355 (0.074)	0.098	0.902	0.098 (0.004)	0.027 (0.029)
10	15	5	0.064	0.541	0.064 (0.002)	0.539 (0.050)	0.062	0.938	0.063 (0.002)	0.491 (0.066)	0.098	0.902	0.098 (0.004)	0.099 (0.052)
11	17.5	1	0	0	0.000 (0.000)	0.000 (0.002)	0.062	0.938	0.063 (0.002)	0.000 (0.000)	0.098	0.902	0.098 (0.004)	0.000 (0.000)
12	17.5	2	0.006	0.107	0.006 (0.001)	0.107 (0.039)	0.062	0.938	0.063 (0.002)	0.000 (0.003)	0.098	0.902	0.098 (0.004)	0.000 (0.000)
13	17.5	3	0.008	0.134	0.008 (0.001)	0.134 (0.043)	0.062	0.938	0.063 (0.002)	0.024 (0.028)	0.098	0.902	0.098 (0.004)	0.000 (0.000)
14	17.5	4	0.018	0.287	0.018 (0.001)	0.287 (0.053)	0.062	0.938	0.063 (0.002)	0.116 (0.053)	0.098	0.902	0.098 (0.004)	0.000 (0.002)
15	17.5	5	0.031	0.397	0.031 (0.001)	0.395 (0.056)	0.062	0.938	0.062 (0.002)	0.233 (0.069)	0.098	0.902	0.098 (0.004)	0.005 (0.012)
16	20	1	0	0	0.000 (0.000)	0.000 (0.000)	0.062	0.938	0.063 (0.002)	0.000 (0.000)	0.098	0.902	0.098 (0.004)	0.000 (0.000)
17	20	2	0.001	0.023	0.001 (0.000)	0.023 (0.019)	0.062	0.938	0.063 (0.002)	0.000 (0.000)	0.098	0.902	0.098 (0.004)	0.000 (0.000)
18	20	3	0.009	0.163	0.009 (0.001)	0.160 (0.045)	0.062	0.938	0.063 (0.002)	0.002 (0.008)	0.098	0.902	0.098 (0.004)	0.000 (0.000)
19	20	4	0.008	0.134	0.008 (0.001)	0.134 (0.043)	0.062	0.938	0.063 (0.002)	0.024 (0.028)	0.098	0.902	0.098 (0.004)	0.000 (0.000)
20	20	5	0.015	0.253	0.015 (0.001)	0.254 (0.051)	0.062	0.938	0.063 (0.002)	0.084 (0.047)	0.098	0.902	0.098 (0.004)	0.000 (0.001)

Table 8: Normal distribution. Results of the simulation experiments for every considered control chart. This table compares the expected cost of operating the process given by the cost model and the actual average cost obtained during the experiments. The values between brackets are the corresponding standard deviations.

#	Param. μ_{oc}	σ_{oc}	$\bar{x}$ Exp. cost	Cost	SN Exp. cost	Cost	SR Exp. cost	Cost
1	12.5	1	3,316.1	3,280.6 (19.9)	4,405.5	3,296.8 (21.7)	4,723.9	3,321.8 (28.6)
2	12.5	2	3,363	3,326.1 (25.8)	4,405.5	3,334.4 (30.9)	4,723.9	3,325.1 (30.5)
3	12.5	3	3,401.6	3,365.7 (29.0)	4,405.5	3,400.2 (48.6)	4,723.9	3,357.1 (37.2)
4	12.5	4	3,428.9	3,394.3 (33.3)	4,405.5	3,468.7 (64.4)	4,723.9	3,406.1 (49.6)
5	12.5	5	3,451.9	3,416.9 (41.2)	4,405.5	3,533.4 (81.8)	4,723.9	3,462.3 (66.0)
6	15	1	3,289.7	3,271 (19.1)	4,405.5	3,294.6 (21.5)	4,723.9	3,321.8 (28.6)
7	15	2	3,316.1	3,280.6 (19.9)	4,405.5	3,296.8 (21.7)	4,723.9	3,321.8 (28.6)
8	15	3	3,339.1	3,302.5 (22.8)	4,405.5	3,309.9 (25.9)	4,723.9	3,320.1 (27.8)
9	15	4	3,363	3,326.1 (25.8)	4,405.5	3,334.4 (30.9)	4,723.9	3,325.1 (30.5)
10	15	5	3,384	3,347.7 (28.4)	4,405.5	3,367.9 (39.4)	4,723.9	3,334.6 (32.9)
11	17.5	1	3,288.2	3,268.5 (18.0)	4,405.5	3,294.6 (21.5)	4,723.9	3,321.8 (28.6)
12	17.5	2	3,295.9	3,276.9 (19.1)	4,405.5	3,294.2 (21.4)	4,723.9	3,321.8 (28.6)
13	17.5	3	3,316.1	3,280.6 (19.9)	4,405.5	3,296.8 (21.7)	4,723.9	3,321.8 (28.6)
14	17.5	4	3,330.9	3,294.6 (21.1)	4,405.5	3,303.2 (23.0)	4,723.9	3,319.3 (28.1)
15	17.5	5	3,347.2	3,310.3 (23.6)	4,405.5	3,317.9 (28.3)	4,723.9	3,321 (29.8)
16	20	1	3,288.1	3,269.1 (18.1)	4,405.5	3,294.6 (21.5)	4,723.9	3,321.8 (28.6)
17	20	2	3,289.7	3,271 (19.1)	4,405.5	3,294.6 (21.5)	4,723.9	3,321.8 (28.6)
18	20	3	3,300.4	3,281.4 (18.6)	4,405.5	3,293.3 (21.4)	4,723.9	3,321.8 (28.6)
19	20	4	3,316.1	3,280.6 (19.9)	4,405.5	3,296.8 (21.7)	4,723.9	3,321.8 (28.6)
20	20	5	3,326.9	3,290.8 (21.2)	4,405.5	3,300.4 (23.8)	4,723.9	3,320.7 (29.0)

237

Table 9: Cauchy distribution. Results of the optimization of the economic statistical design for every considered control chart. This table gives the optimal values of k, n, and h, for every experimental configuration. The column 'Opt' indicates whether the optimization algorithm found a feasible solution (○), or not (×).

#	Param.		$\bar{x}$				SN				SR			
	θ_{oc}	γ_{oc}	Opt	k^*	n^*	h^*	Opt	k^*	n^*	h^*	Opt	k^*	n^*	h^*
1	12.5	1	○	12.09	17	3.92	○	3	4	0.92	○	20	8	1.84
2	12.5	2	○	12.62	50	11.5	○	3	4	0.92	○	20	8	1.84
3	12.5	3	×	14.48	44	28.88	○	3	4	0.92	○	20	8	1.84
4	12.5	4	×	15.24	50	18.88	○	3	4	0.92	○	20	8	1.84
5	12.5	5	×	16.54	50	13.78	○	3	4	0.92	○	20	8	1.84
6	15	1	○	14.06	4	0.92	○	3	4	0.92	○	20	8	1.84
7	15	2	○	14.18	17	3.92	○	3	4	0.92	○	20	8	1.84
8	15	3	○	14.18	43	9.9	○	3	4	0.92	○	20	8	1.84
9	15	4	○	15.24	50	11.5	○	3	4	0.92	○	20	8	1.84
10	15	5	○	16.6	49	11.29	○	3	4	0.92	○	20	8	1.84
11	17.5	1	○	15.71	3	0.69	○	3	4	0.92	○	20	8	1.84
12	17.5	2	○	16.72	6	1.38	○	3	4	0.92	○	20	8	1.84
13	17.5	3	○	16.27	17	3.92	○	3	4	0.92	○	20	8	1.84
14	17.5	4	○	16.41	31	7.18	○	3	4	0.92	○	20	8	1.84
15	17.5	5	○	16.54	50	11.5	○	3	4	0.92	○	20	8	1.84
16	20	1	○	17.78	2	0.61	○	3	4	0.92	○	20	8	1.84
17	20	2	○	18.13	4	0.92	○	3	4	0.92	○	20	8	1.84
18	20	3	○	18.82	8	1.86	○	3	4	0.92	○	20	8	1.84
19	20	4	○	18.36	17	3.92	○	3	4	0.92	○	20	8	1.84
20	20	5	○	18.37	28	6.51	○	3	4	0.92	○	20	8	1.84

Table 10: Cauchy distribution. Results of the simulation experiments where the expected probabilities of Type I (α) and Type II (β) errors are compared to the probabilities observed during the experiments. 'FP' represents the false positives rates (Type I errors), and 'FN' represents the false negatives rates (Type II errors) observed during the simulations. The values between brackets are the corresponding standard deviations.

#	Param. θ_{oc}	γ_{oc}	$\bar{x}$ α	β	FP	FN	SN α	β	FP	FN	SR α	β	FP	FN
1	12.5	1	0.1	0.395	0.142 (0.007)	0.368 (0.071)	0.062	0.938	0.044 (0.002)	0.410 (0.070)	0.098	0.902	0.065 (0.003)	0.182 (0.065)
2	12.5	2	0.1	0.793	0.208 (0.014)	0.509 (0.067)	0.062	0.938	0.044 (0.002)	0.644 (0.054)	0.098	0.902	0.065 (0.003)	0.432 (0.070)
3	12.5	3	0.08	0.989	0.188 (0.024)	0.679 (0.057)	0.062	0.938	0.044 (0.002)	0.761 (0.039)	0.098	0.902	0.065 (0.003)	0.603 (0.058)
4	12.5	4	0.1	0.994	0.208 (0.019)	0.685 (0.054)	0.062	0.938	0.044 (0.002)	0.821 (0.031)	0.098	0.902	0.065 (0.003)	0.698 (0.050)
5	12.5	5	0.1	0.998	0.208 (0.016)	0.709 (0.053)	0.062	0.938	0.044 (0.002)	0.856 (0.025)	0.098	0.902	0.065 (0.003)	0.758 (0.040)
6	15	1	0.1	0.297	0.077 (0.003)	0.250 (0.068)	0.062	0.938	0.044 (0.002)	0.226 (0.069)	0.098	0.902	0.066 (0.003)	0.059 (0.041)
7	15	2	0.1	0.395	0.142 (0.007)	0.368 (0.071)	0.062	0.938	0.044 (0.002)	0.410 (0.070)	0.098	0.902	0.065 (0.003)	0.182 (0.065)
8	15	3	0.1	0.47	0.198 (0.013)	0.407 (0.075)	0.062	0.938	0.044 (0.002)	0.548 (0.063)	0.098	0.902	0.065 (0.003)	0.313 (0.068)
9	15	4	0.1	0.793	0.208 (0.014)	0.509 (0.067)	0.062	0.938	0.044 (0.002)	0.644 (0.054)	0.098	0.902	0.065 (0.003)	0.432 (0.070)
10	15	5	0.1	0.934	0.207 (0.014)	0.591 (0.061)	0.062	0.938	0.044 (0.002)	0.713 (0.045)	0.098	0.902	0.066 (0.003)	0.527 (0.065)
11	17.5	1	0.056	0.153	0.055 (0.002)	0.162 (0.063)	0.062	0.938	0.044 (0.002)	0.157 (0.058)	0.098	0.902	0.066 (0.003)	0.028 (0.030)
12	17.5	2	0.1	0.444	0.092 (0.003)	0.372 (0.074)	0.062	0.938	0.044 (0.002)	0.300 (0.075)	0.098	0.902	0.065 (0.003)	0.094 (0.049)
13	17.5	3	0.1	0.395	0.142 (0.007)	0.368 (0.071)	0.062	0.938	0.044 (0.002)	0.410 (0.070)	0.098	0.902	0.065 (0.003)	0.182 (0.065)
14	17.5	4	0.1	0.474	0.178 (0.010)	0.406 (0.071)	0.062	0.938	0.044 (0.002)	0.507 (0.066)	0.098	0.902	0.065 (0.003)	0.271 (0.071)
15	17.5	5	0.1	0.555	0.208 (0.014)	0.427 (0.070)	0.062	0.938	0.044 (0.002)	0.587 (0.059)	0.098	0.902	0.066 (0.003)	0.357 (0.071)
16	20	1	0.037	0.142	0.041 (0.002)	0.133 (0.042)	0.062	0.938	0.044 (0.002)	0.117 (0.056)	0.098	0.902	0.066 (0.003)	0.017 (0.023)
17	20	2	0.1	0.297	0.077 (0.003)	0.25 (0.068)	0.062	0.938	0.044 (0.002)	0.226 (0.069)	0.098	0.902	0.066 (0.003)	0.059 (0.041)
18	20	3	0.1	0.435	0.105 (0.004)	0.372 (0.072)	0.062	0.938	0.044 (0.002)	0.323 (0.072)	0.098	0.902	0.066 (0.003)	0.114 (0.053)
19	20	4	0.1	0.395	0.142 (0.007)	0.368 (0.071)	0.062	0.938	0.044 (0.002)	0.410 (0.070)	0.098	0.902	0.065 (0.003)	0.182 (0.065)
20	20	5	0.1	0.433	0.172 (0.010)	0.393 (0.071)	0.062	0.938	0.044 (0.002)	0.486 (0.069)	0.098	0.902	0.066 (0.003)	0.248 (0.069)

Table 11: Cauchy distribution. Results of the simulation experiments for every considered control chart. This table compares the expected cost of operating the process given by the cost model and the actual average cost obtained during the experiments. The values between brackets are the corresponding standard deviations.

#	Param. θ_{oc}	Param. γ_{oc}	$\bar{x}$ Exp. cost	$\bar{x}$ Cost	SN Exp. cost	SN Cost	SR Exp. cost	SR Cost
1	12.5	1	3,889.3	3,578.9 (91.8)	4,405.5	3,342.3 (34.9)	4,723.9	3,349 (38.3)
2	12.5	2	7,324.3	4,538.4 (332.6)	4,405.5	3,422.9 (55.5)	4,723.9	3,429 (59.9)
3	12.5	3	26,636.7	7,851 (1050.5)	4,405.5	3,523.9 (78.6)	4,723.9	3,541.5 (88.2)
4	12.5	4	27,078.8	6,600.8 (818.3)	4,405.5	3,633.3 (105.1)	4,723.9	3,657.6 (116.0)
5	12.5	5	28,296.4	6,052.8 (698.9)	4,405.5	3,723.5 (128.1)	4,723.9	3,778.7 (145.5)
6	15	1	3,407.3	3,322 (28.2)	4,405.5	3,309 (27.3)	4,723.9	3,324.5 (32.1)
7	15	2	3,889.3	3,578.9 (91.8)	4,405.5	3,342.3 (34.9)	4,723.9	3,349 (38.3)
8	15	3	4,978.7	4,120.9 (235.2)	4,405.5	3,379.1 (44.7)	4,723.9	3,383.3 (45.9)
9	15	4	7,324.3	4,538.4 (332.6)	4,405.5	3,422.9 (55.5)	4,723.9	3,429 (59.9)
10	15	5	12,381	4,869.6 (404.3)	4,405.5	3,472.9 (66.7)	4,723.9	3,481.4 (69.5)
11	17.5	1	3,356.4	3,302.4 (22.1)	4,405.5	3,303.6 (25.6)	4,723.9	3,318.6 (29.5)
12	17.5	2	3,504.2	3,374.6 (41.5)	4,405.5	3,322.9 (28.8)	4,723.9	3,332.6 (32.4)
13	17.5	3	3,889.3	3,578.9 (91.8)	4,405.5	3,342.3 (34.9)	4,723.9	3,349 (38.3)
14	17.5	4	4,528.8	3,887.2 (164.0)	4,405.5	3,367.1 (40.5)	4,723.9	3,371.5 (45.1)
15	17.5	5	5,518	4,312.3 (271.9)	4,405.5	3,393.7 (47.3)	4,723.9	3,397.1 (50.2)
16	20	1	3,330.1	3,295.4 (19.7)	4,405.5	3,299.1 (23.8)	4,723.9	3,320 (30.0)
17	20	2	3,407.3	3,322 (28.2)	4,405.5	3,309 (27.3)	4,723.9	3,324.5 (32.1)
18	20	3	3,577.1	3,413 (51.1)	4,405.5	3,325.9 (30.5)	4,723.9	3,337.2 (33.7)
19	20	4	3,889.3	3,578.9 (91.8)	4,405.5	3,342.5 (34.9)	4,723.9	3,349 (38.3)
20	20	5	4,346.7	3,816.7 (150.5)	4,405.5	3,361 (39.5)	4,723.9	3,365.1 (42.3)

Table 12: Double exponential distribution. Results of the optimization of the economic statistical design for every considered control chart. This table gives the optimal values of k, n, and h, for every experimental configuration. The column 'Opt' indicates whether the optimization algorithm found a feasible solution ($\circ$), or not ($\times$).

#	Param.		$\bar{x}$				SN				SR			
	μ_{oc}	b_{oc}	Opt	k^*	n^*	h^*	Opt	k^*	n^*	h^*	Opt	k^*	n^*	h^*
1	12.5	$1/\sqrt{2}$	$\circ$	11.72	2	0.48	$\circ$	3	4	0.92	$\circ$	20	8	1.84
2	12.5	$2/\sqrt{2}$	$\circ$	12.4	2	0.46	$\circ$	3	4	0.92	$\circ$	20	8	1.84
3	12.5	$3/\sqrt{2}$	$\circ$	12.96	2	0.46	$\circ$	3	4	0.92	$\circ$	20	8	1.84
4	12.5	$4/\sqrt{2}$	$\circ$	13.62	2	0.46	$\circ$	3	4	0.92	$\circ$	20	8	1.84
5	12.5	$5/\sqrt{2}$	$\circ$	14.53	2	0.46	$\circ$	3	4	0.92	$\circ$	20	8	1.84
6	15	$1/\sqrt{2}$	$\circ$	13	1	0.5	$\circ$	3	4	0.92	$\circ$	20	8	1.84
7	15	$2/\sqrt{2}$	$\circ$	13.43	2	0.48	$\circ$	3	4	0.92	$\circ$	20	8	1.84
8	15	$3/\sqrt{2}$	$\circ$	14.17	2	0.46	$\circ$	3	4	0.92	$\circ$	20	8	1.84
9	15	$4/\sqrt{2}$	$\circ$	14.79	2	0.46	$\circ$	3	4	0.92	$\circ$	20	8	1.84
10	15	$5/\sqrt{2}$	$\circ$	15.37	2	0.46	$\circ$	3	4	0.92	$\circ$	20	8	1.84
11	17.5	$1/\sqrt{2}$	$\circ$	14.09	1	0.5	$\circ$	3	4	0.92	$\circ$	20	8	1.84
12	17.5	$2/\sqrt{2}$	$\circ$	15.01	1	0.49	$\circ$	3	4	0.92	$\circ$	20	8	1.84
13	17.5	$3/\sqrt{2}$	$\circ$	15.15	2	0.48	$\circ$	3	4	0.92	$\circ$	20	8	1.84
14	17.5	$4/\sqrt{2}$	$\circ$	15.91	2	0.46	$\circ$	3	4	0.92	$\circ$	20	8	1.84
15	17.5	$5/\sqrt{2}$	$\circ$	16.58	2	0.46	$\circ$	3	4	0.92	$\circ$	20	8	1.84
16	20	$1/\sqrt{2}$	$\circ$	15.25	1	0.5	$\circ$	3	4	0.92	$\circ$	20	8	1.84
17	20	$2/\sqrt{2}$	$\circ$	16	1	0.5	$\circ$	3	4	0.92	$\circ$	20	8	1.84
18	20	$3/\sqrt{2}$	$\circ$	17.06	1	0.47	$\circ$	3	4	0.92	$\circ$	20	8	1.84
19	20	$4/\sqrt{2}$	$\circ$	16.86	2	0.48	$\circ$	3	4	0.92	$\circ$	20	8	1.84
20	20	$5/\sqrt{2}$	$\circ$	17.65	2	0.46	$\circ$	3	4	0.92	$\circ$	20	8	1.84

Table 13: Double exponential distribution. Results of the simulation experiments where the expected probabilities of Type I (α) and Type II (β) errors are compared to the probabilities observed during the experiments. 'FP' represents the false positives rates (Type I errors), and 'FN' represents the false negatives rates (Type II errors) observed during the simulations. The values between brackets are the corresponding standard deviations.

#	Param.		$\bar{x}$				SN				SR			
	μ_{oc}	b_{oc}	α	β	FP	FN	α	β	FP	FN	α	β	FP	FN
1	12.5	$1/\sqrt{2}$	0.008	0.134	0.013 (0.001)	0.116 (0.040)	0.062	0.938	0.063 (0.002)	0.055 (0.040)	0.098	0.902	0.098 (0.004)	0.000 (0.002)
2	12.5	$2/\sqrt{2}$	0.045	0.471	0.045 (0.001)	0.459 (0.057)	0.062	0.938	0.063 (0.002)	0.293 (0.073)	0.098	0.902	0.098 (0.004)	0.033 (0.032)
3	12.5	$3/\sqrt{2}$	0.081	0.586	0.073 (0.002)	0.602 (0.050)	0.062	0.938	0.063 (0.002)	0.481 (0.067)	0.098	0.902	0.098 (0.004)	0.149 (0.060)
4	12.5	$4/\sqrt{2}$	0.1	0.655	0.088 (0.002)	0.681 (0.044)	0.062	0.938	0.063 (0.002)	0.597 (0.060)	0.098	0.902	0.098 (0.004)	0.285 (0.074)
5	12.5	$5/\sqrt{2}$	0.1	0.717	0.088 (0.002)	0.748 (0.037)	0.062	0.938	0.063 (0.002)	0.672 (0.050)	0.098	0.902	0.098 (0.004)	0.399 (0.069)
6	15	$1/\sqrt{2}$	0.001	0.023	0.007 (0.001)	0.028 (0.022)	0.062	0.938	0.063 (0.002)	0.001 (0.006)	0.098	0.902	0.098 (0.004)	0.000 (0.000)
7	15	$2/\sqrt{2}$	0.008	0.134	0.013 (0.001)	0.116 (0.040)	0.062	0.938	0.063 (0.002)	0.055 (0.040)	0.098	0.902	0.098 (0.004)	0.000 (0.002)
8	15	$3/\sqrt{2}$	0.025	0.347	0.029 (0.001)	0.316 (0.054)	0.062	0.938	0.063 (0.002)	0.171 (0.063)	0.098	0.902	0.098 (0.004)	0.005 (0.013)
9	15	$4/\sqrt{2}$	0.045	0.471	0.045 (0.001)	0.459 (0.057)	0.062	0.938	0.063 (0.002)	0.293 (0.073)	0.098	0.902	0.098 (0.004)	0.033 (0.032)
10	15	$5/\sqrt{2}$	0.064	0.541	0.061 (0.002)	0.549 (0.049)	0.062	0.938	0.063 (0.002)	0.393 (0.069)	0.098	0.902	0.098 (0.004)	0.083 (0.049)
11	17.5	$1/\sqrt{2}$	0	0	0.002 (0.000)	0.004 (0.008)	0.062	0.938	0.063 (0.002)	0.000 (0.001)	0.098	0.902	0.098 (0.004)	0.000 (0.000)
12	17.5	$2/\sqrt{2}$	0.006	0.107	0.014 (0.001)	0.086 (0.035)	0.062	0.938	0.063 (0.002)	0.010 (0.018)	0.098	0.902	0.098 (0.004)	0.000 (0.000)
13	17.5	$3/\sqrt{2}$	0.008	0.134	0.013 (0.001)	0.116 (0.040)	0.062	0.938	0.063 (0.002)	0.055 (0.040)	0.098	0.902	0.098 (0.004)	0.000 (0.002)
14	17.5	$4/\sqrt{2}$	0.018	0.287	0.024 (0.001)	0.255 (0.053)	0.062	0.938	0.063 (0.002)	0.129 (0.059)	0.098	0.902	0.098 (0.004)	0.002 (0.008)
15	17.5	$5/\sqrt{2}$	0.031	0.397	0.035 (0.001)	0.368 (0.055)	0.062	0.938	0.063 (0.002)	0.214 (0.068)	0.098	0.902	0.098 (0.004)	0.011 (0.018)
16	20	$1/\sqrt{2}$	0	0	0.000 (0.000)	0.001 (0.003)	0.062	0.938	0.063 (0.002)	0.000 (0.000)	0.098	0.902	0.098 (0.004)	0.000 (0.000)
17	20	$2/\sqrt{2}$	0.001	0.023	0.007 (0.001)	0.028 (0.022)	0.062	0.938	0.063 (0.002)	0.001 (0.006)	0.098	0.902	0.098 (0.004)	0.000 (0.000)
18	20	$3/\sqrt{2}$	0.009	0.163	0.018 (0.001)	0.122 (0.040)	0.062	0.938	0.063 (0.002)	0.018 (0.024)	0.098	0.902	0.098 (0.004)	0.000 (0.000)
19	20	$4/\sqrt{2}$	0.008	0.134	0.013 (0.001)	0.116 (0.040)	0.062	0.938	0.063 (0.002)	0.055 (0.040)	0.098	0.902	0.098 (0.004)	0.000 (0.002)
20	20	$5/\sqrt{2}$	0.015	0.253	0.021 (0.001)	0.217 (0.050)	0.062	0.938	0.063 (0.002)	0.110 (0.055)	0.098	0.902	0.098 (0.004)	0.001 (0.007)

Table 14: Double exponential distribution. Results of the simulation experiments for every considered control chart. This table compares the expected cost of operating the process given by the cost model and the actual average cost obtained during the experiments. The values between brackets are the corresponding standard deviations.

#	Param. μ_{oc}	Param. b_{oc}	$\bar{x}$ Exp. cost	$\bar{x}$ Cost	SN Exp. cost	SN Cost	SR Exp. cost	SR Cost
1	12.5	$1/\sqrt{2}$	3,316.1	3,282.7 (18.4)	4,405.5	3,299.5 (23.4)	4,723.9	3,322.2 (29.0)
2	12.5	$2/\sqrt{2}$	3,363	3,324.7 (25.8)	4,405.5	3,325.2 (29.0)	4,723.9	3,326 (30.4)
3	12.5	$3/\sqrt{2}$	3,401.6	3,365 (30.9)	4,405.5	3,364.2 (37.4)	4,723.9	3,346.5 (34.9)
4	12.5	$4/\sqrt{2}$	3,428.9	3,394.1 (35.1)	4,405.5	3,406 (48.4)	4,723.9	3,379.6 (44.0)
5	12.5	$5/\sqrt{2}$	3,451.9	3,426.1 (42.5)	4,405.5	3,447.1 (60.7)	4,723.9	3,421 (53.6)
6	15	$1/\sqrt{2}$	3,289.7	3,274.5 (18.0)	4,405.5	3,293.5 (21.0)	4,723.9	3,321.2 (28.9)
7	15	$2/\sqrt{2}$	3,316.1	3,282.7 (18.4)	4,405.5	3,299.5 (23.4)	4,723.9	3,322.2 (29.0)
8	15	$3/\sqrt{2}$	3,339.1	3,301.7 (21.4)	4,405.5	3,309 (25.1)	4,723.9	3,321.8 (27.7)
9	15	$4/\sqrt{2}$	3,363	3,324.7 (25.8)	4,405.5	3,325.2 (29.0)	4,723.9	3,326 (30.4)
10	15	$5/\sqrt{2}$	3,384	3,346.4 (28.7)	4,405.5	3,343.2 (32.5)	4,723.9	3,335.1 (31.7)
11	17.5	$1/\sqrt{2}$	3,288.2	3,269.8 (18.5)	4,405.5	3,294.4 (21.6)	4,723.9	3,321.2 (28.9)
12	17.5	$2/\sqrt{2}$	3,295.9	3,281 (18.6)	4,405.5	3,296.5 (22.0)	4,723.9	3,321.2 (28.9)
13	17.5	$3/\sqrt{2}$	3,316.1	3,282.7 (18.4)	4,405.5	3,299.5 (23.4)	4,723.9	3,322.2 (29.0)
14	17.5	$4/\sqrt{2}$	3,330.9	3,296.1 (21.0)	4,405.5	3,305.1 (23.3)	4,723.9	3,322.2 (29.4)
15	17.5	$5/\sqrt{2}$	3,347.2	3,309.4 (22.1)	4,405.5	3,314.5 (26.5)	4,723.9	3,324 (28.6)
16	20	$1/\sqrt{2}$	3,288.1	3,270.2 (19.2)	4,405.5	3,294.4 (21.6)	4,723.9	3,321.2 (28.9)
17	20	$2/\sqrt{2}$	3,289.7	3,274.5 (18.0)	4,405.5	3,293.5 (21.0)	4,723.9	3,321.2 (28.9)
18	20	$3/\sqrt{2}$	3,300.4	3,284.4 (19.0)	4,405.5	3,295.7 (21.4)	4,723.9	3,321.2 (28.9)
19	20	$4/\sqrt{2}$	3,316.1	3,282.7 (18.4)	4,405.5	3,299.5 (23.4)	4,723.9	3,322.2 (29.0)
20	20	$5/\sqrt{2}$	3,326.9	3,292.8 (19.3)	4,405.5	3,303.2 (22.6)	4,723.9	3,319.4 (29.4)

Table 15: Additional experiments for the $\bar{x}$ chart with an IC normal distribution and an OC shifted exponential distribution. k^*, n^*, and h^* are the optimal parameters of the chart found by the ESD. α and β are the expected Type I and Type II error probabilities. FP and FN are the real (observed) Type I and Type II error probabilities. 'Exp. cost' represents the expected cost given by the model, while 'Cost' represents the real (observed) cost.

IC Normal		OC Expo.		Opt	k^*	n^*	h^*	α	β	$\bar{x}$ chart results		Exp. cost	Cost
μ_{ic}	σ_{ic}	λ_{oc}	δ_{oc}							FP	FN		
10	2	0.1	10	○	16.00	1	0.5	0.001	0.023	0.001 (0)	0.449 (0.057)	3,289.7	3,302.6 (25.4)
10	2	0.1	12	○	16.84	1	0.5	0	0.005	0 (0)	0.379 (0.054)	3,288.5	3,295.1 (23.5)
10	2	0.1	15	○	18.17	1	0.5	0	0	0 (0)	0.27 (0.052)	3,288.2	3,285.0 (20.8)
10	2	0.1	20	○	20.50	1	0.5	0	0	0 (0)	0.047 (0.027)	3,288.1	3,272.1 (19.0)
10	2	0.1	25	○	22.87	1	0.5	0	0	0 (0)	0 (0)	3,288.1	3,270.3 (18.4)
10	2	0.2	10	○	13.43	2	0.48	0.008	0.134	0.008 (0.001)	0.399 (0.055)	3,316.1	3,300.3 (23.2)
10	2	0.2	12	○	14.83	1	0.48	0.008	0.139	0.008 (0.001)	0.429 (0.054)	3,298.4	3,304.3 (25.3)
10	2	0.2	15	○	16.00	1	0.5	0.001	0.023	0.001 (0)	0.181 (0.048)	3,289.7	3,279.6 (20.8)
10	2	0.2	20	○	18.17	1	0.5	0	0	0 (0)	0 (0)	3,288.2	3,269.1 (19.1)
10	2	0.2	25	○	20.50	1	0.5	0	0	0 (0)	0 (0)	3,288.1	3,269.9 (18.4)
10	2	0.5	10	○	12.15	2	0.46	0.064	0.541	0.064 (0.002)	0.627 (0.048)	3,384.0	3,367.4 (32.6)
10	2	0.5	12	○	13.06	2	0.46	0.015	0.253	0.015 (0.001)	0.281 (0.055)	3,326.9	3,292.1 (20.9)
10	2	0.5	15	○	14.83	1	0.48	0.008	0.139	0.008 (0.001)	0 (0)	3,298.4	3,274.1 (17.7)
10	2	0.5	20	○	16.84	1	0.5	0	0.005	0 (0)	0 (0)	3,288.5	3,270.7 (18.3)
10	2	0.5	25	○	19.09	1	0.5	0	0	0 (0)	0 (0)	3,288.1	3,270.7 (18.8)
10	2	1	10	○	11.81	2	0.46	0.1	0.717	0.1 (0.002)	0.875 (0.02)	3,451.9	3,581.0 (77.1)
10	2	1	12	○	12.63	2	0.46	0.031	0.397	0.031 (0.001)	0.356 (0.054)	3,347.2	3,307.5 (23.0)
10	2	1	15	○	14.46	1	0.46	0.013	0.221	0.013 (0.001)	0 (0)	3,305.5	3,277.5 (18.0)
10	2	1	20	○	16.41	1	0.5	0.001	0.011	0.001 (0)	0 (0)	3,288.9	3,270.7 (18.1)
10	2	1	25	○	18.63	1	0.5	0	0	0 (0)	0 (0)	3,288.2	3,270.1 (18.1)
10	2	2	10	○	11.81	2	0.49	0.1	0.823	0.1 (0.002)	0.994 (0.001)	3,535.8	8,539.6 (1,226.7)
10	2	2	12	○	12.40	2	0.46	0.045	0.471	0.045 (0.001)	0.466 (0.056)	3,363.0	3,326.5 (25.9)
10	2	2	15	○	14.28	1	0.45	0.016	0.271	0.016 (0.001)	0 (0)	3,310.5	3,279.6 (18.6)
10	2	2	20	○	16.20	1	0.5	0.001	0.016	0.001 (0)	0 (0)	3,289.3	3,270.1 (18.4)
10	2	2	25	○	18.40	1	0.5	0	0	0 (0)	0 (0)	3,288.2	3,270.2 (18.6)

Table 16: Additional experiments for the SN chart with an IC normal distribution and an OC shifted exponential distribution. k^*, n^*, and h^* are the optimal parameters of the chart found by the ESD. α and β are the expected Type I and Type II error probabilities. FP and FN are the real (observed) Type I and Type II error probabilities. 'Exp. cost' represents the expected cost given by the model, while 'Cost' represents the real (observed) cost.

IC Normal		OC Expo.		Opt	k^*	n^*	h^*	SN chart results					
μ_{ic}	σ_{ic}	λ_{oc}	δ_{oc}					α	β	FP	FN	Exp. cost	Cost
10	2	0.1	10	○	3	4	0.92	0.062	0.938	0.062 (0.002)	0.000 (0.000)	4,405.5	3,293.7 (21.9)
10	2	0.1	12	○	3	4	0.92	0.062	0.938	0.062 (0.002)	0.000 (0.000)	4,405.5	3,293.7 (21.9)
10	2	0.1	15	○	3	4	0.92	0.062	0.938	0.062 (0.002)	0.000 (0.000)	4,405.5	3,293.7 (21.9)
10	2	0.1	20	○	3	4	0.92	0.062	0.938	0.062 (0.002)	0.000 (0.000)	4,405.5	3,293.7 (21.9)
10	2	0.1	25	○	3	4	0.92	0.062	0.938	0.062 (0.002)	0.000 (0.000)	4,405.5	3,293.7 (21.9)
10	2	0.2	10	○	3	4	0.92	0.062	0.938	0.062 (0.002)	0.000 (0.000)	4,405.5	3,293.7 (21.9)
10	2	0.2	12	○	3	4	0.92	0.062	0.938	0.062 (0.002)	0.000 (0.000)	4,405.5	3,293.7 (21.9)
10	2	0.2	15	○	3	4	0.92	0.062	0.938	0.062 (0.002)	0.000 (0.000)	4,405.5	3,293.7 (21.9)
10	2	0.2	20	○	3	4	0.92	0.062	0.938	0.062 (0.002)	0.000 (0.000)	4,405.5	3,293.7 (21.9)
10	2	0.2	25	○	3	4	0.92	0.062	0.938	0.062 (0.002)	0.000 (0.000)	4,405.5	3,293.7 (21.9)
10	2	0.5	10	○	3	4	0.92	0.062	0.938	0.062 (0.002)	0.000 (0.000)	4,405.5	3,293.7 (21.9)
10	2	0.5	12	○	3	4	0.92	0.062	0.938	0.062 (0.002)	0.000 (0.000)	4,405.5	3,293.7 (21.9)
10	2	0.5	15	○	3	4	0.92	0.062	0.938	0.062 (0.002)	0.000 (0.000)	4,405.5	3,293.7 (21.9)
10	2	0.5	20	○	3	4	0.92	0.062	0.938	0.062 (0.002)	0.000 (0.000)	4,405.5	3,293.7 (21.9)
10	2	0.5	25	○	3	4	0.92	0.062	0.938	0.062 (0.002)	0.000 (0.000)	4,405.5	3,293.7 (21.9)
10	2	1	10	○	3	4	0.92	0.062	0.938	0.062 (0.002)	0.000 (0.000)	4,405.5	3,293.7 (21.9)
10	2	1	12	○	3	4	0.92	0.062	0.938	0.062 (0.002)	0.000 (0.000)	4,405.5	3,293.7 (21.9)
10	2	1	15	○	3	4	0.92	0.062	0.938	0.062 (0.002)	0.000 (0.000)	4,405.5	3,293.7 (21.9)
10	2	1	20	○	3	4	0.92	0.062	0.938	0.062 (0.002)	0.000 (0.000)	4,405.5	3,293.7 (21.9)
10	2	1	25	○	3	4	0.92	0.062	0.938	0.062 (0.002)	0.000 (0.000)	4,405.5	3,293.7 (21.9)
10	2	2	10	○	3	4	0.92	0.062	0.938	0.062 (0.002)	0.000 (0.000)	4,405.5	3,293.7 (21.9)
10	2	2	12	○	3	4	0.92	0.062	0.938	0.062 (0.002)	0.000 (0.000)	4,405.5	3,293.7 (21.9)
10	2	2	15	○	3	4	0.92	0.062	0.938	0.062 (0.002)	0.000 (0.000)	4,405.5	3,293.7 (21.9)
10	2	2	20	○	3	4	0.92	0.062	0.938	0.062 (0.002)	0.000 (0.000)	4,405.5	3,293.7 (21.9)
10	2	2	25	○	3	4	0.92	0.062	0.938	0.062 (0.002)	0.000 (0.000)	4,405.5	3,293.7 (21.9)

Table 17: Additional experiments for the SR chart with an IC normal distribution and an OC shifted exponential distribution. k^*, n^*, and h^* are the optimal parameters of the chart found by the ESD. α and β are the expected Type I and Type II error probabilities. FP and FN are the real (observed) Type I and Type II error probabilities. 'Exp. cost' represents the expected cost given by the model, while 'Cost' represents the real (observed) cost.

IC Normal		OC Expo.		Opt	k^*	n^*	h^*	α	β	SR chart results			
μ_{ic}	σ_{ic}	λ_{oc}	δ_{oc}							FP	FN	Exp. cost	Cost
10	2	0.1	10	○	20	8	1.84	0.098	0.902	0.098 (0.004)	0.000 (0.000)	4,723.9	3,321.9 (28.7)
10	2	0.1	12	○	20	8	1.84	0.098	0.902	0.098 (0.004)	0.000 (0.000)	4,723.9	3,321.9 (28.7)
10	2	0.1	15	○	20	8	1.84	0.098	0.902	0.098 (0.004)	0.000 (0.000)	4,723.9	3,321.9 (28.7)
10	2	0.1	20	○	20	8	1.84	0.098	0.902	0.098 (0.004)	0.000 (0.000)	4,723.9	3,321.9 (28.7)
10	2	0.1	25	○	20	8	1.84	0.098	0.902	0.098 (0.004)	0.000 (0.000)	4,723.9	3,321.9 (28.7)
10	2	0.2	10	○	20	8	1.84	0.098	0.902	0.098 (0.004)	0.000 (0.000)	4,723.9	3,321.9 (28.7)
10	2	0.2	12	○	20	8	1.84	0.098	0.902	0.098 (0.004)	0.000 (0.000)	4,723.9	3,321.9 (28.7)
10	2	0.2	15	○	20	8	1.84	0.098	0.902	0.098 (0.004)	0.000 (0.000)	4,723.9	3,321.9 (28.7)
10	2	0.2	20	○	20	8	1.84	0.098	0.902	0.098 (0.004)	0.000 (0.000)	4,723.9	3,321.9 (28.7)
10	2	0.2	25	○	20	8	1.84	0.098	0.902	0.098 (0.004)	0.000 (0.000)	4,723.9	3,321.9 (28.7)
10	2	0.5	10	○	20	8	1.84	0.098	0.902	0.098 (0.004)	0.000 (0.000)	4,723.9	3,321.9 (28.7)
10	2	0.5	12	○	20	8	1.84	0.098	0.902	0.098 (0.004)	0.000 (0.000)	4,723.9	3,321.9 (28.7)
10	2	0.5	15	○	20	8	1.84	0.098	0.902	0.098 (0.004)	0.000 (0.000)	4,723.9	3,321.9 (28.7)
10	2	0.5	20	○	20	8	1.84	0.098	0.902	0.098 (0.004)	0.000 (0.000)	4,723.9	3,321.9 (28.7)
10	2	0.5	25	○	20	8	1.84	0.098	0.902	0.098 (0.004)	0.000 (0.000)	4,723.9	3,321.9 (28.7)
10	2	1	10	○	20	8	1.84	0.098	0.902	0.098 (0.004)	0.000 (0.000)	4,723.9	3,321.9 (28.7)
10	2	1	12	○	20	8	1.84	0.098	0.902	0.098 (0.004)	0.000 (0.000)	4,723.9	3,321.9 (28.7)
10	2	1	15	○	20	8	1.84	0.098	0.902	0.098 (0.004)	0.000 (0.000)	4,723.9	3,321.9 (28.7)
10	2	1	20	○	20	8	1.84	0.098	0.902	0.098 (0.004)	0.000 (0.000)	4,723.9	3,321.9 (28.7)
10	2	1	25	○	20	8	1.84	0.098	0.902	0.098 (0.004)	0.000 (0.000)	4,723.9	3,321.9 (28.7)
10	2	2	10	○	20	8	1.84	0.098	0.902	0.098 (0.004)	0.000 (0.000)	4,723.9	3,321.9 (28.7)
10	2	2	12	○	20	8	1.84	0.098	0.902	0.098 (0.004)	0.000 (0.000)	4,723.9	3,321.9 (28.7)
10	2	2	15	○	20	8	1.84	0.098	0.902	0.098 (0.004)	0.000 (0.000)	4,723.9	3,321.9 (28.7)
10	2	2	20	○	20	8	1.84	0.098	0.902	0.098 (0.004)	0.000 (0.000)	4,723.9	3,321.9 (28.7)
10	2	2	25	○	20	8	1.84	0.098	0.902	0.098 (0.004)	0.000 (0.000)	4,723.9	3,321.9 (28.7)

Table 18: Uniform distribution. Results of the simulation experiments where the expected probabilities of Type I (α) and Type II (β) errors are compared to the probabilities observed during the experiments. 'FP' represents the false positives rates (Type I errors), and 'FN' represents the false negatives rates (Type II errors) observed during the simulations. The values between brackets are the corresponding standard deviations.

#	Param.		$\bar{x}$				SN				SR			
	a_{oc}	b_{oc}	α	β	FP	FN	α	β	FP	FN	α	β	FP	FN
1	12.5	1.73	0.008	0.134	1.2×10^{-4} (0.000)	0.146 (0.038)	0.062	0.938	0.063 (0.002)	0	0.098	0.902	0.098 (0.004)	0
2	12.5	3.46	0.045	0.471	0.047 (0.001)	0.471 (0.054)	0.062	0.938	0.063 (0.002)	0.450 (0.068)	0.098	0.902	0.098 (0.004)	0.033 (0.028)
3	12.5	5.20	0.081	0.586	0.092 (0.003)	0.585 (0.049)	0.062	0.938	0.063 (0.002)	0.696 (0.057)	0.098	0.902	0.098 (0.004)	0.246 (0.062)
4	12.5	6.93	0.1	0.655	0.114 (0.003)	0.649 (0.041)	0.062	0.938	0.063 (0.002)	0.786 (0.049)	0.098	0.902	0.098 (0.004)	0.429 (0.073)
5	12.5	8.66	0.1	0.717	0.114 (0.003)	0.707 (0.040)	0.062	0.938	0.063 (0.002)	0.827 (0.041)	0.098	0.902	0.098 (0.004)	0.542 (0.069)
6	15	1.73	0.001	0.023	0	0	0.062	0.938	0.063 (0.002)	0	0.098	0.902	0.098 (0.004)	0
7	15	3.46	0.008	0.134	1.2×10^{-4} (0.000)	0.146 (0.037)	0.062	0.938	0.063 (0.002)	0	0.098	0.902	0.098 (0.004)	0
8	15	5.20	0.025	0.347	0.020 (0.001)	0.352 (0.052)	0.062	0.938	0.063 (0.002)	0.070 (0.045)	0.098	0.902	0.098 (0.004)	0.000 (0.000)
9	15	6.93	0.045	0.471	0.047 (0.001)	0.471 (0.054)	0.062	0.938	0.063 (0.002)	0.451 (0.071)	0.098	0.902	0.098 (0.004)	0.033 (0.023)
10	15	8.66	0.064	0.541	0.071 (0.002)	0.542 (0.049)	0.062	0.938	0.063 (0.002)	0.615 (0.067)	0.098	0.902	0.098 (0.004)	0.134 (0.049)
11	17.5	1.73	0	0	0	0	0.062	0.938	0.063 (0.002)	0	0.098	0.902	0.098 (0.004)	0
12	17.5	3.46	0.006	0.107	0	0.140 (0.030)	0.062	0.938	0.063 (0.002)	0	0.098	0.902	0.098 (0.004)	0
13	17.5	5.20	0.008	0.134	1.5×10^{-4} (0.000)	0.147 (0.041)	0.062	0.938	0.063 (0.002)	0	0.098	0.902	0.098 (0.004)	0
14	17.5	6.93	0.018	0.287	0.010 (0.001)	0.299 (0.049)	0.062	0.938	0.063 (0.002)	0	0.098	0.902	0.098 (0.004)	0
15	17.5	8.66	0.031	0.397	0.028 (0.002)	0.401 (0.050)	0.062	0.938	0.063 (0.002)	0.238 (0.067)	0.098	0.902	0.098 (0.004)	0.002 (0.010)
16	20	1.73	0	0	0	0	0.062	0.938	0.063 (0.002)	0	0.098	0.902	0.098 (0.004)	0
17	20	3.46	0.001	0.023	0	0	0.062	0.938	0.063 (0.002)	0	0.098	0.902	0.098 (0.004)	0
18	20	5.20	0.009	0.163	0	0.221 (0.043)	0.062	0.938	0.063 (0.002)	0	0.098	0.902	0.098 (0.004)	0
19	20	6.93	0.008	0.134	1.4×10^{-4} (0.000)	0.146 (0.042)	0.062	0.938	0.063 (0.002)	0	0.098	0.902	0.098 (0.004)	0
20	20	8.66	0.015	0.253	0.007 (0.001)	0.267 (0.049)	0.062	0.938	0.063 (0.002)	0	0.098	0.902	0.098 (0.004)	0

Table 19: Uniform distribution. Results of the simulation experiments for every considered control chart. This table compares the expected cost of operating the process given by the cost model and the actual average cost obtained during the experiments. The values between brackets are the corresponding standard deviations.

#	Param.		$\bar{x}$		SN		SR	
	a_{oc}	b_{oc}	Exp. cost	Cost	Exp. cost	Cost	Exp. cost	Cost
1	12.5	1.73	3,316.1	3,276.6 (18.2)	4,405.5	3,297.1 (18.7)	4,723.9	3,323.3 (25.7)
2	12.5	3.46	3,363	3,327.8 (24.8)	4,405.5	3,353.4 (30.2)	4,723.9	3,327.3 (29.5)
3	12.5	5.20	3,401.6	3,372.0 (31.0)	4,405.5	3,461.2 (47.9)	4,723.9	3,368.9 (35.3)
4	12.5	6.93	3,428.9	3,399.3 (36.2)	4,405.5	3,558.7 (66.8)	4,723.9	3,429.7 (46.6)
5	12.5	8.66	3,451.9	3,420.3 (42.2)	4,405.5	3,635.4 (82.8)	4,723.9	3,490.9 (65.0)
6	15	1.73	3,289.7	3,255.2 (18.1)	4,405.5	3,296.6 (18.5)	4,723.9	3,323.1 (25.2)
7	15	3.46	3,316.1	3,278.2 (17.9)	4,405.5	3,297.1 (18.7)	4,723.9	3,323.8 (25.3)
8	15	5.20	3,339.1	3,298.5 (22.8)	4,405.5	3,310.9 (24.7)	4,723.9	3,323.9 (27.8)
9	15	6.93	3,363	3,328.0 (22.4)	4,405.5	3,353.4 (28.9)	4,723.9	3,327.6 (29.5)
10	15	8.66	3,384	3,351.0 (25.7)	4,405.5	3,412.9 (40.4)	4,723.9	3,345.5 (31.8)
11	17.5	1.73	3,288.2	3,265.5 (16.7)	4,405.5	3,295.8 (18.5)	4,723.9	3,323.8 (25.6)
12	17.5	3.46	3,295.9	3,268.9 (17.1)	4,405.5	3,295.8 (18.4)	4,723.9	3,323.8 (25.8)
13	17.5	5.20	3,316.1	3,275.6 (16.9)	4,405.5	3,296.1 (18.7)	4,723.9	3,323.9 (26.1)
14	17.5	6.93	3,330.9	3,291.3 (20.1)	4,405.5	3,296.3 (19.0)	4,723.9	3,324.3 (26.1)
15	17.5	8.66	3,347.2	3,308.4 (23.1)	4,405.5	3,319.9 (28.3)	4,723.9	3,324.6 (28.7)
16	20	1.73	3,288.1	3,269.7 (17.7)	4,405.5	3,295.8 (18.5)	4,723.9	3,323.1 (24.6)
17	20	3.46	3,289.7	3,270.5 (18.7)	4,405.5	3,295.9 (18.4)	4,723.9	3,323.3 (24.6)
18	20	5.20	3,300.4	3,280.4 (18.2)	4,405.5	3,295.9 (18.3)	4,723.9	3,323.7 (25.1)
19	20	6.93	3,316.1	3,277.4 (17.1)	4,405.5	3,296.3 (18.7)	4,723.9	3,323.8 (25.6)
20	20	8.66	3,326.9	3,288.2 (19.2)	4,405.5	3,296.3 (18.8)	4,723.9	3,324.1 (25.7)

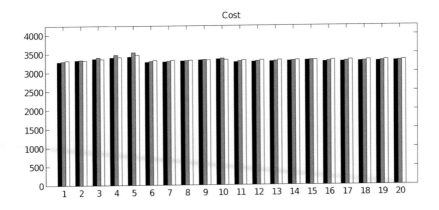

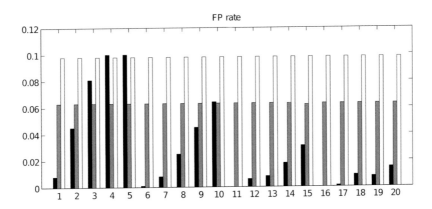

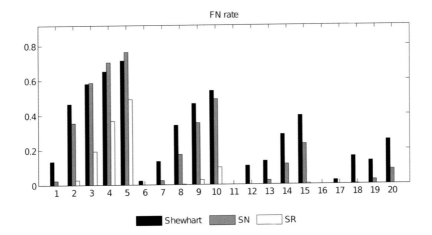

Figure 2: Results for normal distribution.

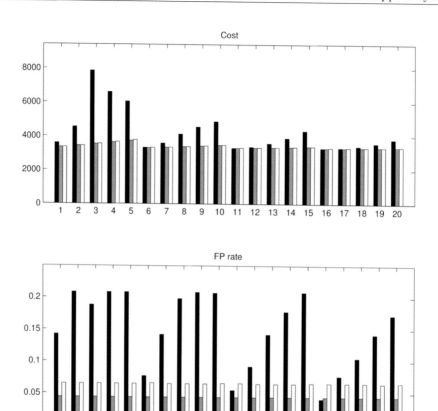

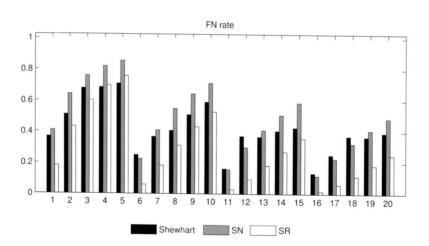

Figure 3: Results for Cauchy distribution.

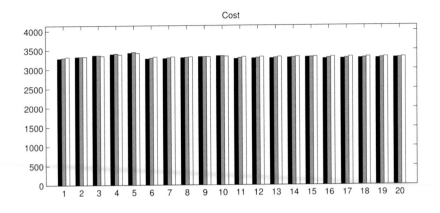

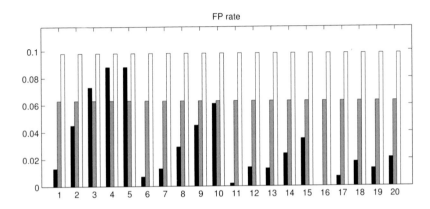

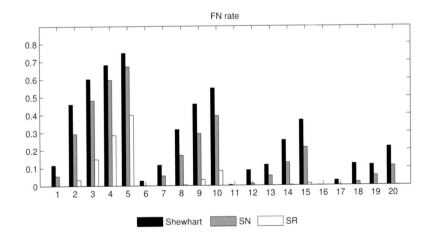

Figure 4: Results for double exponential distribution.

Chapter 10

Jamming Detection in Electromagnetic Communication with Machine Learning: A Survey and Perspective

Jonathan Villain,* Virginie Deniau and Christophe Gransart

1 Introduction

For Wireless communications, whether it is satellite networks, cellular networks, Wi-Fi networks, bluetooth networks or different protocols with lower rates such as LoRaWan or SigFox, communications are established through radio waves. Wireless communication technologies continue to undergo rapid advancement and its use is more and more common like border surveillance, health care applications, environmental monitoring, home intelligence, etc. However, challenges remain to be addressed in issues relating to coverage and deployment, scalability, quality-of-service, size, computational power, energy efficiency and security. But Wireless communication signals intrinsically have a great ability to spread in all directions. The main consequence of this "wild propagation" of radio waves is the possibility that for an unauthorized person to listen to the network, possibly outside the location where the wireless network is supposed to be deployed and confined. The risks of poor protection of a wireless network are various. It is possible to interact with the communications whether to scramble video surveillance, to interrupt calls, to retrieve personal information or to induce themselves into a secure system.

Cybersecurity is about protecting computers, servers, mobile devices, electronic systems, networks and data against malicious attacks. It is also called computer security or information systems security. You can encounter it in many contexts, from corporate IT to mobile devices. It can be divided into several categories which are network security for protecting the computer network against intruders, application security which aims to protect software and devices against threats, information security which ensures data integrity and confidentiality, operational security which includes the processes and decisions related to the processing and the protection of data and others like disaster recovery and User training.

University Gustave Eiffel, IFSTTAR, COSYS-LEOST F-59650 Villeneuve d'Ascq, France.
Emails: virginie.deniau@univ-eiffel.fr, christophe.gransart@univ-eiffel.fr
* Corresponding author: jonathan.villain@univ-eiffel.fr

From an electromagnetic point of view it is possible to identify profiles in the evolution of the electromagnetic signal to identify attacks on wireless communication systems. Considering the vulnerability of wireless communication physical layers, the types of attack most often studied are jamming attacks, which provoke DDoS on the applications linked to the communication.

With the strong growth in the use of wireless communication networks brought about by the use of the IoT, new access points appear regularly for people with malicious intention. We can list for example some "man in the middle" attacks like ARP spoofing, DNS poisonning, trafic analysis or customers tracking. We can also highlight some use of jamming signal like muting surveillance systems, make autonomous vehicles unable to communicate, silence alarms, make maintenance communications impossible, etc.

In this context, ML techniques are in common use for self-learning, reliant systems to handle cybersecurity tasks such as identifying malicious URLs, spam email detection, intrusion detection, network protection, and tracking user and process behavior. For example, key ML algorithms such as clustering, gradient boosting, random forest, and XGBoos are implement to detect attacks and identify the countermeasure to be implemented.

In this chapter we describe what are the jamming attacks, make a point on the use of ML for attack detection, highlight the difficulties and the challenges encountered in this context then we illustrate with a practical case study.

2 Electromagnetic Waves Communication Jamming

Transmitted information jamming in electronic warfare is a form of electronic attack where jammers radiate interfering signals toward a communication system, blocking the receiver capability to interpret the information transmited in the wireless communication signals. The purpose of information jamming is to interfere with the effective use of the electromagnetic spectrum like a Denial of service attack. There are several ways to shoot down a communication signal using jamming signals which are more or less smart and their effects have to be studied.

2.1 Susceptibility of the Physical Layer in Presence of a Jamming Signal

Communications can be vulnerable to different types of EM interference, unintentional or intentional. The use of wireless communication is considered for different critical applications (video monitoring, location, maintenance, etc.). The EM interference can corrupt the communication signals and cause denial of service for these different applications. EM interferences can be generated intentionally by using communication jammers. Jammers are small radio frequency generators that emit electromagnetic signals in the frequency bands normally reserved for different communication standards. The EM signals emanating from the jammer are superimposed on the communication signal at the input of the communication receivers that are in the jammer's action area. This superposition distorts the communication signals at the input of the receivers which are thus unable to interpret them.

A mean is to make the communication signal more robust to jamming signals, one solution is to decrease the data rate. Indeed, reducing the bit rate generally means opting for a modulation that is more robust to interference and for an information redundancy that allows errors to be detected and corrected at reception. However, this solution is only valid if the interfering signal is not too powerful. When the power of the jamming signal is comparable to those of the communication signal, the only one countermeasure is to turn off the jamming signal transmitter or to shift the communication signal over an other frequency band not affected by the jamming signal. However, each communication protocol is associated with specific frequency bands set by the standards and it is therefore not allowed to change the frequency band of the communication signal at will.

A recent example has taken place in Nantes Atlantique Airport. A person left a jammer operating in his car, while he took a flight to Africa in April 2017. The jamming signal interfered with the tracking systems of planes arriving and taking off from the airport, leading to delays on several flights.The French national frequency agency (ANFR) was therefore contacted to solve the problem. By performing spectral analysis in different frequency bands and moving around the airport area, the ANFR team recognized a spectral occupation characteristic of the presence of a jammer. Then, moving to maximize the power received from the jamming signal, the ANFR team converged on the position of the vehicle in which the jammer had been left behind, and finally turn off the jammer.

In order to automatically detect jamming attacks, certain studies focus on studying the data link layer and the physical layer. On the data link layer, the jamming can be detected by studying the loss of communication and the transfer rate. In fact, the transfer rate of a communication depends on the noise level present on the channel, a loss in transfer rate can be induced by the presence of a jamming signal. An other approach is to detect an inspected rate by attempting to retry to send a communication frame. Detection based on the analysis of the physical layer needs to consider the radio frequency characteristics of the jamming signals. The vast majority of commercial jammers uses a frequency-sweeping interference signal, which sweeps a frequency band $[f_1, f_2]$ in a time duration T which implies a difference in the measured power on the channel.

In this context, studies[1;2;3] analyze different types of denial of service attacks. All those studies agree that a more efficient attack requires protocol-aware jamming. However, these studies also indicate that jamming attacks can also be efficient with comparable power to that of the communication signals and they do not require synchronization or consideration of the protocol details. To study the impact of such jammers on the communications, some works[4;5] study the impact of intentional EM interferences on the performance of Wi-Fi communications. They analyze the susceptibility of OFDM signals to understand how certain parameters of the jamming interference signal act on the degradation of the communication. In their studies, they use devices which can degrade network performance by transmitting jamming signals either in the uplink or in the downlink frequency bands and show that the sweep period of the jamming signal can significantly changes the impact on the communication. They noticed that the impact of the interfering signal greatly depends on the relationship between its sweep period and the time-window duration of receiver signal process. Then, they show that by adapting the width of the observation time windows of the reception stage, they could reduce the impact of the interference signal. However, in the different communication protocols, the time-window duration of receiver signal process is fixed by the standards and can not be modified at will.

Using this vulnerability, it is possible to shot down communication. The more the jamming signal is filled with knowledge of the communication protocol, harder it is to detect this jamming signal.

2.2 Smart Jamming

A smart jammer is a jammer that only emits when communication is taking place. The advantage of this type of jammer is that it is not detectable when no communication is established. We focus, in this subsection, on a jammer that keeps track of attempts to retransmit the packet until it is dropped. To achieve this goal, the jammer can follow several models. First, we consider a problem where all the actors act simultaneously. In this case the jammer seeks to disrupt the communication by seeking to transmit at times when a communication is present. Second, we consider a Game Model, in which the communication link is the leader and the jammer is the follower. In this case, the jamming system identifies if there is a communication and emits a jamming signal in order to disrupt it. Since the jammer has the ability to detect the transmitted power, the communication transmitter adjusts its emission power accordingly, knowing that the jammer will also increase its transmission power in response. We provide the closed expressions of the equilibrium strategies where the transmitter and the jammer have complete information. Finally, we consider the worst case where the transmitter has incomplete information while the jammer has complete information. We introduce reinforcement through learning method, thus, the transmitter can act autonomously in a dynamic environment without knowing the above game model. It turns out that despite the jamming ability to detect the active channel, the transmitter can improve its efficiency by predicting the jammer's reaction according to its own strategy.

Many study the effect of smart jamming on wireless communication. Some work[6] considered the problem of smart jamming in the uplink of a massive MU-MIMO system. They showed that if a jammer causes pilot contamination during the training phase and optimally allocates its power budget to jam the training and data transmission phases, it can impose dramatic harm to the sum SE of the legitimate system. They showed that the optimal strategy of a smart jammer is highly dependent on the number of BS antennas. In particular, when the BS is equipped with large number of antenna elements, even a low power jammer can achieve a large gain by optimal energy allocation over fixed power jamming. In an other study,[8] presented an in-depth study of the vulnerability of 5G wireless systems to smart jamming attacks. They reviewed different types of jammers, and they showed that 5G NR enhanced the resilience of wireless cellular network to jamming attacks, primarily because of its flexible and dynamic resource allocation, yet 5G NR is still far from being secure against jamming attacks.

But studies also considers on making wireless communication more robust again smart jamming like[8] who reviewed the existing jamming detection techniques and investigated and compared the performance of several machine learning models to detect jamming attacks. They performed feature extraction and feature selection to construct a large dataset constructed to train, validate, and test random forest, support vector machine, and neural network algorithms. These trained machines are able to process a huge number of data within a very short time, which helps increase efficiency and reduce the processing time. Future work includes investigating the efficiency of deep learning in detecting all types of jamming attacks. The authors of[9] have investigated machine learning based jamming detection using RSSI data from both simulation and real networks and proposed an enhanced detection mechanism based on multi-path profile information which are validated with simulation data.

Most of the detection approaches to detect jamming or smart jamming signal to improve the communication are based on ML.

3 Difficulties and Challenges of Electromagnetic Waves Communication Anomaly Detection

In this chapter, the considered attack scenarios correspond to attackers who would use jammers to provoke denial of services. To develop an approach able to detect jamming attacks and to distinguish them, it is needed to higlight difference between a communication and a scenario with jamming.

3.1 Detection on Physical Layers

From the point of view of the physical layer, the only information that is recovered is the power of the signal sent on the communication channel. In an anechoic chamber, the communication signal is found isolated, by design, the only informations measured are: the trace of the communication and the noise of the equipment. In this context, when we add a jamming signal, it is possible to see the effect of this jamming on the recovered spectra.

One of the difficulties in this context is to identify a jamming signal having a low power level which does not disturb the communication signal. In this case, it becomes complex to separate the jamming signal from the noise of the equipment. This becomes problematic when measuring the signal in a context of actual use. Indeed, in such a context of use, many other factors come to disrupt communication. First of all, being outside an anechoic chamber adds ambient noise to the measured signal. The impact of this noise is that it degrades communication and makes it more sensitive to low power jamming signals. As ambient noise is added to the noise of the equipment, it increases the difficulty, already present in an anechoic chamber, of distinguishing the presence of a jamming signal. In addition, the weak jamming signal, having no effect on the communication in the anechoic chamber, disrupts the communication and degrades the latter.

Another difficulty which appears when the communication is carried out outside anechoic room is due to the fact that the communication propagates in all directions and that we will therefore also measure the communication of the surrounding systems which will disturb the monitored communication system.

The challenge is therefore to distinguish a interference signal from ambient noise under such conditions.

3.2 Smart Jamming Detection

The use of smart jamming also poses some difficulties in a context where other communications are present around the monitored communication system. Indeed, smart jamming makes it possible to send a jamming signal in a non-continuous manner. It is therefore complex to be able to measure it. It is therefore very difficult to identify such a jamming system from another communication system. In fact, the jamming signal transmitted can take the form of a communication signal which would be transmitted by another communication system or can be emmitted on some specifics frequencies in order to be better hidden by the surrounding noise. These jamming signals can tackle the protocol flaw in wireless communication systems to prevent them from transmitting. It is therefore the adaptability and the diversity of forms of attack that smart jamming can take that makes it very difficult to detect and that makes this type of jamming a major threat. The use of Machine learning and game theory can counter chanel surfing protocols and increases the performance of the jamming signal and its ability to be undetectable.

3.3   Transmission and Mobility

With the evolution of transport systems, it becomes more and more essential to look at the effect of speed on wireless communication systems. The complexity brought about by mobility can be seen at several levels. The first difficulty is that movement involves a constant change of environment. Indeed, the communication system being in constant movement, the ambient noise and the propagation conditions constantly change. For example, it is easy to imagine that the ambient noise present in the countryside is totally different from the ambient noise in the city center. In addition, the effect of displacement will have an effect on the quality of the transmission. Although this effect can be considered negligible for very short range as it can be the case inside a car, a communication system can be established over longer distances in the case of a train for example. In such a context, the arrangement of the antenna becomes essential. In addition to the difficulty of detecting low intensity jamming as well as smart jamming, the possibility of the system having a certain number of benchmarks is removed. Indeed, in the context of a communication system being located in a fixed environment, it is possible to learn the behavior of the surrounding communication systems in order to have a basis for identifying the interference caused by the other communication systems. Mobility removes this possibility by varying the environment in which the communication is established.

3.4   Transmitter Location

The consequences associated with possible interference are diverse. But in certain areas, jamming can make inoperative many functions sometimes related to security. It is important to protect against this type of attack. Electronic protection includes all devices and procedures to counter electronic attacks and electronic intelligence means. It is either to apply frequency use plans and radio and radar silence procedures, to use electronic identification systems, to use electronic systems with evasion or frequency hopping. Other protection approaches can use systems with short transmissions, codes and encryption, interference filtering or interference cancellation system. The safest way to prevent jamming attacks is to turn off the device sending the jamming signal. However, this requires to identify the location of the source of the jamming signal.

In general, the tracking system uses the RSSI and the mac address of several access points to establish their locations. Jammers do not need to be attached to a network and do not have a mac ID. The only information that can be used to try to locate the jammer is the signal strength. But the power delivered by the jammer can be very variable depending on the model. It is therefore necessary to combine the results obtained on different surveillance antennas in order to be able to locate the jammer more or less precisely. The variability of the power level at the emission of the jamming signal breaks a first problem but the most difficult problem to solve is due to the obstacles that the jamming signal will encounter before being perceived by the surveillance antennas. Indeed, the jamming signal can be emitted in a place different from that where the communication is carried out. The jamming signal perceived by the surveillance system will therefore have already passed through more or less thick walls, windows, etc. In this case, it is easy to imagine that the presence of an object in the path of the signal will make it difficult to precisely locate the source of the signal or even make it impossible. This difficulty will be increased by the fact that the surveillance antennas are positioned at different positions, which implies that the jamming signal will not necessarily encounter the same obstacles or the same number of obstacles.

All of them make the location of the jamming signal transmitters very complex and place location problems as a major challenge to be taken up in the fight against this type of attack.

4 Machine Learning Techniques for Electromagnetic Waves Communication Anomaly Detection

Several types of jamming detection techniques have been proposed, including fuzzy logic, game theory, channel surfing, and time series. Most of these techniques are inefficient in detecting smart jammers. Thus, there is a great need for efficient and fast jamming detection techniques with high accuracy.

4.1 Classification Algorithms Specificities

The purpose of this chapter is to characterize communications subject to interference as well as to detect them. To do this, from the acquired data, we use data mining and classification techniques. As a first step, it is important to identify different possible approaches to perform this task. The compared algorithms are SVM[10], Neural Network[11], Random Forest[12], Decision tree[13], Mixture Model Based Clustering[14], K-means[15] and AHC[16]. To compare these algorithms, we are interested in their application fields. We thus seek to know if the algorithm is supervised, automatic, adaptable and interpretable, as well as its calculation speed and precision. This information is resumed in Table 1.

Depending on the use of the classification, we can choose a different algorithm. For example, SVM, Neural Network, Decision tree and Random Forest are used for discriminate profiles based on a learning approach while Mixture Model based clustering, K-means classification and AHC discriminate data in cluster base on the distribution in the space of these data.

In the literature, most of the learning algorithms used for jamming detection are based on SVM classification or Random Forest algorithm. Stating from these algorithms, most researches try to evolve these algorithms to obtain the best result to solve the problem. For example, fuzzy logic[17] can be one of the most used adaptation in research to improve algorithm quality. In fact, it is less sensible at the presence of distorted, imprecise or noisy input information. The major disadvantage is that we can propose different ways to solve a given problem, which can lead to ambiguity. Moreover, proving the characteristics of fuzzy logic is difficult or impossible in most cases due to not having a mathematical description of the approach. More specifically, we can cite the work of[18] who deployed this logic to detect jamming signal on an RSSI metric and PDR metric. They proposed a fuzzy logic–based jamming detection algorithm for detecting the presence of jamming. This approach includes 3 functional components such as fuzzification, inference, and defuzzification. More recently Vijayakumar et al. deployed an adaptive neuro-fuzzy logic based jamming detection system[19].

Jamming attacks target a wireless network creating an unwanted denial of service. In the following, we will illustrate the use of machine learning algorithms for the detection of jamming signals through different studies.

Table 1: Classification algorithm comparisons.

	Supervised	Automatic	Adaptability	Interpretable	Prediction speed	Accuracy	Number of cluster
Discriminant analysis	×				fast	moderate	fixed a priori
Logistic Regression	×				fast	moderate	fixed a priori
SVM	×				fast	high	fixed a priori
Neural Network	×				fast	high	fixed a priori
Random Forest	×				moderate	high	fixed a priori
XGBoos	×				moderate	high	fixed a priori
Decision tree	×	×			fast	low	fixed a priori
Mixture model		×	×	×	fast	not concerned	fixed a priori
K-means		×	×	×	fast	not concerned	fixed a priori
AHC		×	×	×	fast	not concerned	fixed a posteriori

4.2 ML for Jamming Detection Algorithm for a TETRA Base Station Receiver

Some researchers[20;21] proposed a SVM algorithm for jamming detection at the base station level in cellular networks. The algorithms for jamming detection are independent from the operation and architecture of the wireless communication system used and they are described only to a degree that assists in comprehending the work. The detection process uses only inherent information which is available in common receivers and does not need excessive hardware requirements for external information. It is shown that using SVM algorithm improves the performance of the jamming detection algorithm and decreases the hardware complexity. The application of the proposed jamming detection algorithm is simulated and compared with other conventional methods. The simulation results show a significant improvement in the presence of a wide range of user terminal velocities and for different jammers. They also present a comparison of two proposed jamming detection algorithms based on fuzzy C-means (FCM) and support vector machine (SVM) algorithms. To overcome the training needs for a short period of time and to improve the performance of the FCM-based jamming detection algorithm, a convenient Doppler shift estimation algorithm has been used in order to recognize the information in the channel.

4.3 ML for Jamming Detection in 5G Radio Communication

5G wireless network will be a subject to a variety of cyber-threats from advanced and complex attacks. Given their potential vulnerability to malicious attacks, the security of the networks has attracted significant attention. Among various anomaly-based detection techniques, the most promising one is the machine learning as it learns without human assistance and can provide adjustments accordingly to the actions. Recent research aims to secure the 5G system.

To illustrate this interest, some works[8] compare the efficiency of several machine learning models in detecting jamming signals. They investigated the types of signal features that identify jamming signals, and generated a large dataset using these parameters. Using this dataset, the machine learning algorithms were trained, evaluated, and tested. These algorithms are random forest, support vector machine, and neural network. The performance of these algorithms was evaluated and compared using the probability of detection, probability of false alarm, probability of missed detection, and accuracy. The simulation results show that jamming detection based random forest algorithm can detect jammers with a high accuracy, high detection probability and low probability of false alarm. We can also[22] who focus on deploying a multi-stage machine learning-based intrusion detection (ML-IDS) in 5G C-RAN that can detect and classify four types of jamming attacks: constant jamming, random jamming, deceptive jamming, and reactive jamming. This deployment enhances security by minimizing the false negatives in C-RAN architectures. The evaluation of the solution uses WSN-DS (DataSet), which is a dedicated wireless dataset for intrusion detection. The result shows a classification accuracy of 94.51% with a 7.84% false negative rate. Other works[23] proposes a hierarchical detection scheme based on a reinforcement learning process to secure the main segments of end-to-end 5G network. The distributed attacks detection systems collaborate with a goal to reinforce their learnings, update their optimal defense strategies, and determine the current and futures attacks at different segments. These results demonstrate that, the proposed cyber defense scheme requires a low computation overhead to protect the network from internal and external attacks as compared to the current cyber detection schemes.

Sedjelmaci proposes and develops a new cooperative attack detection based on a hierarchical Reinforcement Learning (RL) process to identify the network attacks. The cooperative detection is performed with a distributed detection systems executed at the different critical 5G network's organs such as access point, base station and servers. According to our experiments results, the proposed RL detection system enhances the detection of new misbehaviors attacks.

4.4 ML for Jamming Detection in IoT Network

The IoT, which will be a ubiquitous fabric for interconnecting huge numbers of machines and human devices, is one of the most critical technologies of the next decade. The IoT generally encompasses a network of interconnected and uniquely identifiable virtual and physical objects, such as sensors, RFID tags, actuators, and cell phones which are able to communicate and exchange data with each other to perform various tasks. Given its large scale and the heterogeneity of its environment, the IoT is more vulnerable to security threats than other networks. Due to these security requirements in the IoT, in the absence of robust security solutions, attacks and malfunctions in the IoT may outweigh any of its benefits. Due to its large attack surface, the security of an IoT system is prone to a variety of attacks such as malicious radio jamming, DoS, SCA, replay attack, node capture, Sybil attack, and wormhole attack. In particular, IoT systems are vulnerable to jamming attacks that could quickly drain the battery of target devices by disrupting data transmission and forcing them to retransmit repeatedly. Moreover, jamming could also lead to DoS which is the most common attack in WSNs and internet.

In this context, many studies develop ML approach to detect jamming signal. Some authors[24] have studied the problem of jamming in an IoT system. In particular, they have proposed a centralized mechanism to address the jamming problem in an IoT system composed of resource constrained devices. In the proposed model, an IoT access point defends against the jammer by allocating its power over the subcarriers in a smart way to defend the system.

Some researches[25;26] focus on the conception of a monitoring system able to detect and classify jamming attacks. To achieve this goal, they proposed to outsource the attack detection function from the network to protect and they used an antenna to monitor the spectrum over the time. The proposed estimation model shows good results in the prediction of attacks. They also studied the very weak jamming signals (perfectly indistinguishable by a visual analysis of the spectrum frequencies) performed in a shared environment in terms of wireless communications. An analysis, using a clustering approach, permitted to characterise the different spectral occupation situations observed in an open environment in which it is needed to control the wireless communication activity. This analysis identified the discriminant clusters with a proportion of spectra, with or without jamming signals, significantly different from the whole data set distribution.

5 A Case Study

The proposed case study focuses on the Wi-Fi system. Nowadays Wi-Fi is not only used to access to internet. There are growing numbers of applications using Wi-Fi, including critical applications in terms of security. For instance, in the railway sector, Wi-Fi is increasingly used to ease the maintenance. Some trains are now equipped with on-board systems that provide maintenance checks and report to a center via Wi-Fi transmissions. Hence, a monitoring system with attack detection functions can help strengthen the Wi-Fi network when is used for critical applications. Wi-Fi communications can use different ethernet standard like 802.11n, 802.11g, 802.11a, 802.11b, 802.11ac and 802.11ax, but in a physical point of view, the communications are perceived as measured power on different frequencies. Based on the similarity, we have the same observed measures even if waveforms could be different (DSSS, OFDM). For this case study, we focus on the 802.11n ethernet standard.

5.1 Preliminary Description of the Measurement Test Site

The experiments analysed in this article were carried out with a Wi-Fi network specifically installed in a room of the Gustave Eiffel University. No specific precautions were taken to avoid ambient ISM emissions intended for the activities of the University's staff. Indeed, this building is equipped with various systems using the ISM frequency band (door remote control system, occupancy sensor, Wi-Fi networks). We only identified in advance the channels the most used by this internal Wi-Fi network to select an unused channel for our test network. We chose the channel located at 2.422 GHz because it was far away enough from the channels used by the university's network and was therefore not likely to disturb them.

By conducting our tests in a space that is not protected from ambient emissions, our conditions can vary considerably from one measurement to an other. For example, the activity on the University network can be more or less important, terminals connected to the University Wi-Fi network can be deployed inside the building and be more or less close to the test area. Smart phones can also be activated in a Wi-Fi gateway mode by guests who do not have access to the internal Wi-Fi network. These Wi-Fi gateways generally scan all the Wi-Fi bands and can use channels that occur to be the same as our test channel. Finally, due to Wi-Fi operating in the ISM band, other devices can also use the Wi-Fi frequency band with a different communication protocol.

In these not controlled variable conditions, we have observed that the Wi-Fi communications of our test networks are more sensitive to jamming signals than in a protected anechoic environment. The presence of other applications in the Wi-Fi band implies that extremely low jamming power signals can be sufficient to interrupt the Wi-Fi communication. Other ambient communications are observed to act as unintentional interferences and have a superimposed impact on the jamming signal, resulting in a communication failure.

Consequently, the objective is to distinguish the presence of a jamming signal and determine for which level power of jamming the detection system unperformed.

5.2 Jamming Signals

The attack by jamming signals consists in intentionally emitting a signal which covers the frequency bands employed by a communication system in order to disturb the reception of a communication device. Generally, the power levels of jamming signals are similar to communication signal power levels. The jamming signals can degrade the performance of the communication networks without damaging the communication devices. Different types of jamming signals can be used[27]. The vast majority of commercial jammers uses a cyclic frequency-sweeping interference signal, which sweeps a frequency band $[f_1, f_2]$ in a time duration T. It can be expressed as:

$$s(t) = A \cos \left(2\pi \left(\frac{f_2 - f_1}{2T} t + f_1 \right) t \right), \quad 0 < t < T, \tag{1}$$

where A is the interference signal amplitude. Here, the Wi-Fi jamming signal that we consider sweeps the $[2.4\ \text{GHz}, 2.5\ \text{GHz}]$ frequency band in $T = 10\ \mu\text{s}$.

The jamming signal waveform defined by (1) is generated with an Arbitrary Waveform Generator(AWG) connected to a variable attenuation control unit in order to reduce the power of the jamming signal and to emulate a jamming source far away from the test site.

According to the wireless communication protocol, the jamming signal power level required to interrupt the communication and to provoke a deny of service on the application, can vary. As a consequence, depending on the wireless application we want to protect, we must be able to detect more or less powerful interference signals. Previous studies analysing the impact of jamming signals on the Wi-Fi communication have shown that a jamming signal with a power 30 dB lower than the power of the considered Wi-Fi signal can be sufficient to interrupt the communication[27].

5.3 Device Setting

For the experiments, a specific Wi-Fi network was set-up in a room of the university Gustave Eiffel by installing a server, an access point and a client computer. The client computer is equipped with the Iperf network testing tool. Iperf allows creating TCP and UDP data streams and measuring the network throughput. The Wi-Fi channel employed is centered on the 2.422 GHz frequency. The jamming signal is emitted with a small omni-directional antenna connected to the arbitrary waveform generator and the attenuation control unit. The variable attenuation control unit allows adjusting the jamming signal power. We measured the bit rate thanks to the Iperf software, and we increased progressively the power of the jamming signal until we observed a very small impact on the bit rate.

To measure the electromagnetic activity, we placed a monitoring antenna nearby the client. The monitoring antenna is a small omni-directional antenna and is connected to a real time spectrum analyzer (see Figure 1).

A 40 MHz frequency band, centred on 2.422 GHz, is monitored by the spectrum analyzer. Each collected spectrum contains 1601 frequencies measured with a 100 kHz resolution bandwidth and a 38.2 μs sweep time. Each spectrum is obtained in applying the "MaxHold" function of the spectrum analyzer over ten successive scans of the 40 MHz frequency band. That means that for each frequency, the maximal measured power behind the ten previous scans is recorded.

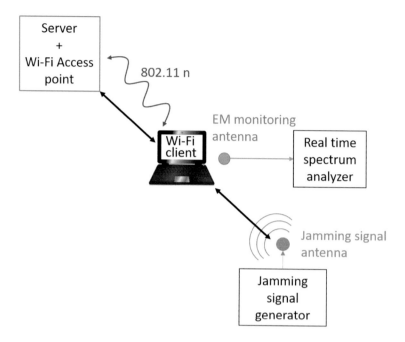

Figure 1: Experimentation with a 802.11 n communication in the presence of jamming attack.

Figure 2 represents the level of power in dBm measure on 1601 frequency points of ten spectra.

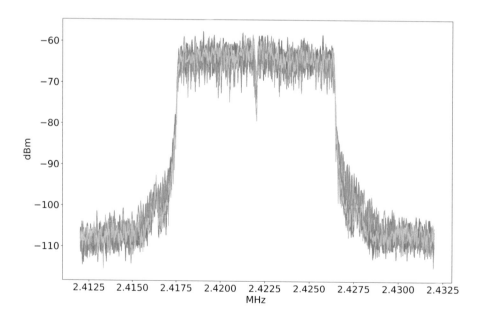

Figure 2: Representation of ten spectra.

Experiments were performed over two test days and alternating measurements with jamming attacks and measurements without jamming. The measurement with jamming attacks are performed at different distances and with or without the presence of a wall between the receiver and the jamming antenna. These changes of distance and the presence of a wall are to emulate different scenarios with different levels of jamming power. So, the antenna emitting the jamming signal is placed from one to twelve meters in line of sight and out of sight (see Figure 3).

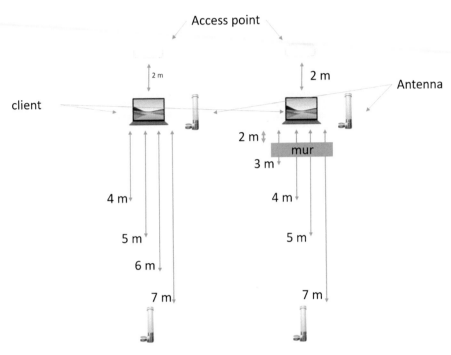

Figure 3: Configuration for the measurement of the jamming signal.

5.4   Spectrum Analysis

The power measured on these frequencies varies between -114 dBm and -49 dBm. As shown in Figure 4, the measured powers are mainly concentrated around 2 power levels, -68 dBm and -109dBm, which correspond to the frequencies present in the central band of 20MHz of the communication channel and the 2 frequency bands of 10MHz located in the vicinity of the communication channel. These values and their observation rate vary slightly depending on the communication configuration and we want to exploit these variations to identify the source of the signal.

Having highlighted the differences between the configurations presented, we will try to distinguish three types of configuration. The first is a communication without intentional disturbance, the second configuration is a communication disturbed by a jamming signal in OS and the last configuration, a communication in the presence of a jamming signal in LoS.

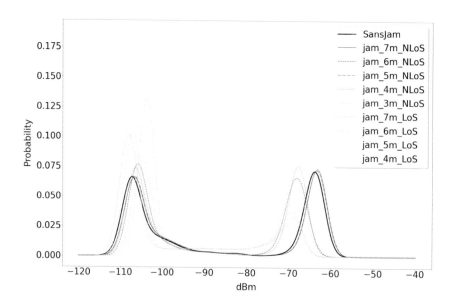

Figure 4: Power distribution density by configuration.

5.5 Learning and Result

In this study, we compare two classification algorithms by learning on their ability to detect the presence of a jamming signal and determine whether the source of the latter is located inside or outside the room where is located the communication. The algorithms compared here are the Wide Margin Separator approaches and the random forest approaches.

Classification is performed on the 40MHz frequency band. We want to identify whether or not the communication network is facing an attack and whether its source is located in the room where the access point and the client are located or outside it. We need to identify the 3 presented configurations. We estimate the attack profile using SVM and RF algorithm. To check the quality of the models, the spectra are divided into 3 data sets, a training set (60 %), a validation set (20%) and a test set (20%) obtained by random drawing without replacement. The learning phase is the phase where the model learns the characteristics of the separation on the learning set and optimizes it on the validation set. The test phase is the phase in which the quality of the model is checked. In this phase, the model prediction error is calculated on the test set. Table 2 represents the distribution of the different configurations in the three classes without interference, OS and LoS that we want to predict. The two learning classification approaches bring different results. Indeed, on the test set the score for the classification error obtained by the SVc algorithm is 16.7% while the RF classification algorithm obtains a score of 22%. On this type of data, it therefore seems more judicious to use an SVc approach to identify the 3 configurations without jamming, with jamming signal transmitted in OS and with jamming signal transmitted in LoS. For these two classification approaches, the most frequent errors correspond to spectra of the interference-free configuration classified in OS, spectra of the OS

Table 2: Confusion matrix.

	Configuration\Cluster	Without jamming	OS	LoS
	without jamming	357	144	0
	under jamming signal at:			
	7m OS	15	486	0
	5m OS	20	476	0
S	4m OS	0	490	0
V	3m OS	0	251	2
c	7m LoS	0	91	151
	6m LoS	0	321	703
	5m LoS	0	55	189
	4m LoS	0	21	223
	without jamming	332	169	0
	under jamming signal at:			
	7m OS	30	470	1
	5m OS	37	457	2
R	4m OS	11	470	9
F	3m OS	2	243	8
	7m LoS	2	107	137
	6m LoS	86	278	660
	5m LoS	1	49	194
	4m LoS	0	38	206

configuration classified without interference and spectra of the LoS configuration classified in OS. We also find that the closer the jamming antenna is to the surveillance antenna, the lower the classification error. It can therefore be deduced that errors are due to a too weak perception of the jamming signal.

Several avenues are envisaged for the continuation of this work. First of all, study the distance for which it is possible to measure the jamming signal with a surveillance antenna in order to improve the results of the classification algorithms by associating them with more adequate cost matrices. In this case, we have studied configurations for which the interference signals come from a single direction, so it will be important to study other configurations to extend the case study. In the next steps, we would like to combine a detection system with a location system. In our work, we studied the spectra using only one antenna but the final goal is to implement a monitoring system using several antennas.

6   Conclusion

In today's society, over-connectivity generates a constant throughput of information. Whether it is through smartphones, connected watches, wireless earphones, car gps or connected homes, the majority of information is transmitted through radio frequencies. This involves many risks. Among these the one we are interested in the problems related to jamming signals which act as a DDoS attack. This attack saturates the communication system and prevents communication transmission. Although the barrage jammers remain the most common, the advent of smart jammers has complexified the detection of such attacks. With the security issues, we have listed different means of detecting these jamming signals. In this context, ML is a powerful tool allowing better protection against jamming attacks and allowing solutions to be provided. Despite these detection systems, all jamming signals are not always detected, which shows the difficulty of protecting our systems against these attacks. And even if the system is able to detect the jamming signal, in order to remedy these attacks it is essential to be able to locate the source of emission to interrupt the jamming signal. But this is not easy and is the work of many research subjects.

References

[1] M. Lichtman, R.P. Jover, M. Labib, R. Rao, V. Marojevic and J.H. Reed. LTE/LTE-A jamming, spoofing, and sniffing: Threat assessment and mitigation. *IEEE Communications Magazine*, 54(4): 54–61, 2016.

[2] R.M. Rao, S. Ha, V. Marojevic and J.H. Reed. LTE PHY layer vulnerability analysis and testing using open-source SDR tools. *Military Communications Conference (MILCOM), MILCOM IEEE.* IEEE, pp. 744–749, 2017.

[3] G. Philippe, F. Montaigne, J.C. Schiel, E. Georgeaux, C. Gruet, P.Y. Roy and P. Mege. LTE resistance to jamming capability: To which extend a standard LTE system is able to resist to intentional jammers. *Military Communications and Information Systems Conference*, 2013.

[4] V. Deniau, N.B. Slimen, S. Baranowski, H. Ouaddi and N. Dubalen. Characterisation of the em disturbances affecting the safety of the railway communication systems. *The European Physical Journal-Applied Physics*, 43(2): 225–230, 2008.

[5] G. Romero, V. Deniau and O. Stienne. LTE Physical layer vulnerability test to different types of jamming signals. In: *2019 International Symposium on Electromagnetic Compatibility-EMC EUROPE.* IEEE, pp. 1138–1143, 2019.

[6] H. Pirzadeh, S.M. Razavizadeh and E. Björnson. Subverting massive MIMO by smart jamming. *IEEE Wireless Communications Letters* 5.1: 20–23, 2015.

[7] Y. Arjoune and S. Faruque. Smart jamming attacks in 5G new radio: A review. In: *2020 10th Annual Computing and Communication Workshop and Conference (CCWC).* IEEE, pp. 1010–1015, 2020.

[8] Y. Arjoune, F. Salahdine, M.S. Islam, E. Ghribi and N. Kaabouch. A novel jamming attacks detection approach based on machine learning for wireless communication. In: *2020 International Conference on Information Networking (ICOIN)*, IEEE, pp. 459–464, 2020.

[9] B. Upadhyaya, S. Sun and B. Sikdar. Machine learning-based jamming detection in wireless IoT networks. In: *2019 IEEE VTS Asia Pacific Wireless Communications Symposium (APWCS).* IEEE, pp. 1–5, 2019.

[10] V. Vapnik. *The Nature of Statistical Learning Theory.* Red Bank: Springer, vol. 2, 2000.

[11] C.M. Bishop. *Neural Networks for Pattern Recognition.* Oxford University Press, 1995.

[12] L. Breiman. Random forests. *Machine Learning*, 45(1): 5–32, 2001.

[13] K. Karimi and H.J. Hamilton. Generation and interpretation of temporal decision rules. *International Journal of Computer Information Systems and Industrial Management Applications*, Volume 3, 2011.

[14] K. Ozonat and R.M. Gray. Gauss mixture model-based classification for sensor networks. *In Data Compression Conference*, IEEE, pp. 322–331, March 2006.

[15] J.B. MacQueen. Some methods for classification and analysis of multivariate observations. *Proceedings of 5th Berkeley Symposium on Mathematical Statistics and Probability, 1, University of California Press*, pp. 281–297, 1967.

[16] T. Hastie, R. Tibshirani and J. Friedman. Hierarchical clustering. *The Elements of Statistical Learning* (2nd ed.), New York: Springer, pp. 520–528, 2009.

[17] L.A. Zadeh, G.J. Klir and B. Yuan. *Fuzzy Sets, Fuzzy Logic, and Fuzzy Systems: Selected Papers*, World Scientific, vol 6, 1996.

[18] K.P. Vijayakumar, P. Ganeshkumar, M. Anandaraj, K. Selvaraj and P. Sivakumar. Fuzzy logic–based jamming detection algorithm for cluster-based wireless sensor network. *International Journal of Communication Systems*, 31(10), 2018.

[19] K.P. Vijayakumar, K.P.M. Kumar, K. Kottilingam, T. Karthick, P. Vijayakumar and P. Ganeshkumar. An adaptive neuro-fuzzy logic based jamming detection system in WSN. *Soft Computing*, 23(8): 2655–2667, 2019.

[20] J.A. Jahanshahi, S.A. Ghorashi and M. Eslami. A support vector machine based algorithm for jamming attacks detection in cellular networks. *Wireless Advanced*, IEEE, 2011.

[21] J.A. Jahanshahi, S.A. Ghorashi and M. Eslami. Utilizing support vector machine and fuzzy C-means algorithms in the base station for jamming detection. *Journal of the Chinese Institute of Engineers*, 36(2): 245–256, 2013.

[22] M. Hachimi, G. Kaddoum, G. Gagon and P. Illy. Multi-stage jamming attacks detection using deep learning combined with kernelized support vector machine in 5g cloud radio access networks. In: *2020 International Symposium on Networks, Computers and Communications (ISNCC)*. IEEE, pp. 1–5, 2020.

[23] H. Sedjelmaci. Cooperative attacks detection based on artificial intelligence system for 5G networks. *Computers & Electrical Engineering*, 91: 107045, 2021.

[24] N. Namvar, W. Saad, N. Bahadori and B. Kelley. Jamming in the internet of things: A game-theoretic perspective. In: *2016 IEEE Global Communications Conference (GLOBECOM)*. IEEE, pp. 1–6, 2016.

[25] J. Villain, V. Deniau, A. Fleury, E.P. Simon, C. Gransart and R. Kousri. EM monitoring and classication of IEMI and protocol-based at-tacks on IEEE 802.11 n communication networks. *IEEE Transactions on Electromagnetic Compatibility*, 61(6): 1771–1781, 2019.

[26] J. Villain, V. Deniau, C. Gransart, A. Fleury and E.P. Simon. Characterization of IEEE 802.11 communications and detection of low-power jamming attacks in non controlled environment based on a clustering study. *IEEE Systems Journal*, 2021.

[27] V. Deniau, C. Gransart, G.L. Romero, E.P. Simon and J. Farah. IEEE 802.11n communications in the presence of frequency-sweeping interference signals. *IEEE Transactions on Electromagnetic Compatibility*, 59(5): 1625–1633, 2017.

Chapter 11

Intellectual Support with Machine Learning for Decision-making in Garment Manufacturing Industry: A Review

Yanni Xu* and Xiaofen Ji

1 Introduction

Machine learning is a subset of artificial intelligence[1]. It is used in a wide variety of applications, where it is difficult or unfeasible to develop conventional algorithms to perform the needed tasks. Garment manufacturing is usually considered a lengthy and complicated process, which transforms two-dimensional fabrics into three-dimensional garments[2]. Industry 4.0[3] aims to manipulate information extracted from large and complex data sets (big data) to support decision-making in manufacturing, intelligently (artificial intelligence), powerfully (cloud computing), and in real-time (industrial internet of things). Based on an overview of decision problems in the garment manufacturing industry, popular machine learning algorithms, and the applications of machine learning in various fields, this study attempts to explore the ability of machine learning to make critical decisions and to find the optimal solution in the new garment manufacturing industry 4.0 era. The content of the study consists of the following four parts based on literature since 2000 to now, as shown in Figure 1.

(1) Expounding the main decision problems in each garment manufacturing-related process including sizing, cutting, sewing, finishing, and packaging.

(2) Analyzing the current applications that attempt to solve these garment manufacturing decision problems by machine learning.

(3) Clarifying the basic and commonly used machine learning methods, identifying their principals, properties, and availabilities.

(4) Seeking out the potential opportunities of using machine learning methods to solve more garment manufacturing decision problems for research in the future.

Zhejiang International Institute of Fashion Technology, Zhejiang Sci-Tech University, Hangzhou 310018, China.
Email: xiaofenji@zstu.edu.cn

* Corresponding author: scorpioni@zstu.edu.cn

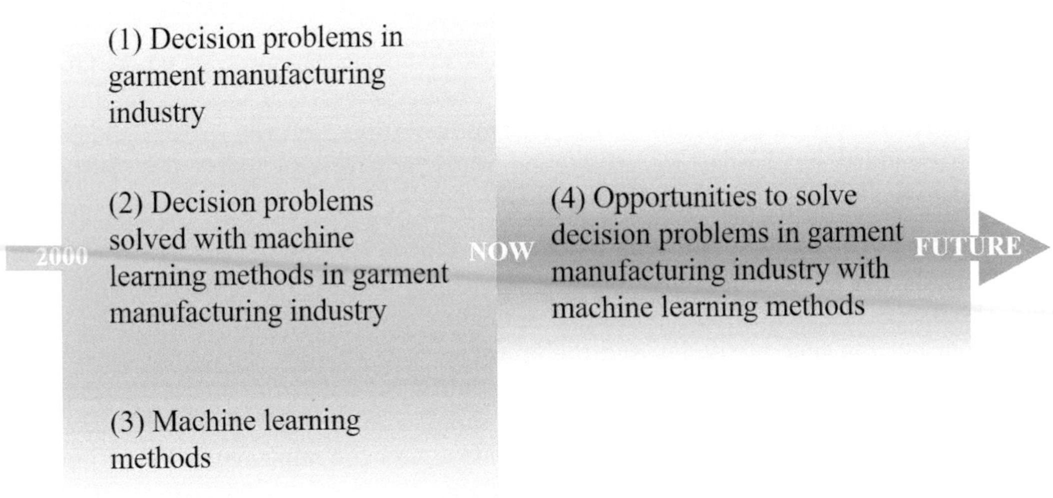

Figure 1: Study content.

2   Problems in Garment Manufacturing

The whole garment manufacturing process contains four main processes, i.e., cutting, sewing, ironing, and packaging, which refers to the entire apparel production process from fabrics to garments, and is mostly described as a lengthy and complicated process[2;4;5]. The sizing process is crucial and should also be considered because patterns used while cutting fabric are produced according to the garment sizing systems which are developed in this process before the cutting process. This section is to give an overview of the garment manufacturing-related processes, i.e., sizing, cutting, sewing, finishing, and packaging, and an analysis of the correspondent prediction and classification problems that can be solved by machine learning.

(1) Sizing and the corresponding problems

The sizing process aims at generating standard garment sizes[6], based on which the patterns can be produced for the subsequent cutting process. Therefore, sizing system development and pattern making are the two critical subprocesses of sizing. Sizing derives a set of sizing systems according to anthropometric data of the population in order to standardize garment sizes and then patterns for each size are made accordingly[7]. Generally, patterns of the medium size being first produced directly, patterns of the rest sizes are generated by grading[8].

Correspondingly, there exists two decision problems, i.e., the body type classification and the pattern grading prediction in the sizing process. The application of machine learning to solve these problems contributes to the improvement of garment fit and the implementation of automatic pattern generation.

(2) Cutting and the corresponding problems

The cutting process is in the first phase of the garment manufacturing process, where fabrics are cut into cut-pieces for being assembled in the next sewing process[9]. The main cutting-related operations, i.e., the spreading operation, the cutting operation, and the sorting and bundling operations are guided by the cutting production planning subprocess with lay planning and marker making included.

There are some prediction and classification problems, such as: the lay number prediction in lay planning, the marker length prediction and the marker cutting length prediction in marker making, the defective fabric detection and the spreading time prediction during the spreading operation, the cutting time prediction and the fabric waste estimation during the cutting operation, the cut pieces classification and the defective cut pieces detection during the sorting and bundling operation. The application of machine learning to solve these problems makes for the cutting time and cost estimation, fabric quality control, and the implementation of automatic fabric cutting.

(3) Sewing and the corresponding problems

The sewing process is the core of the garment manufacturing, assembling cut-pieces into a garment. It is the most critical and intricacy section of the whole garment manufacturing process, dealing with various operations, along with the corresponding materials, operators, and machines[10]. The sewing operation is guided by the sewing production planning, which consists of sewing order planning and sewing assembly line design.

The related prediction and classification problems are the sewing productivity prediction in sewing order planning, the operator skill classification and the operator efficiency prediction in sewing assembly line designing, the defective semi-product detection, the defective semi-product prediction, and the sewing machine fault diagnosis during the sewing operation. The application of machine learning to solve these problems creates sewing quality control and automatic sewing.

(4) Finishing, packaging, and the corresponding problems

Compared with cutting and sewing, these two processes, i.e., finishing and packaging, being simpler, and in most cases, the corresponding operations are arranged in one area. Finishing, is also called ironing, straightens the garments for packaging, while packaging the garments and concerns a series of actions, such as sort, pile, and pack.

The related prediction and classification problems with these two processes are the ironing temperature determination during the finishing operation, the finished product classification, the defective finished product detection, and the defective finished product prediction during the packaging operation. The application of machine learning to solve these problems contributes to the implementation of automatic ironing and packaging.

(5) Prediction and classification problems in the whole process

For the entire garment manufacturing process, the three related prediction problems are found, i.e., the lead time prediction, the productivity prediction, and the carbon emission prediction. The application of machine learning to solve these problems results in the overall control of garment manufacturing.

The related prediction and classification problems that exist in the garment manufacturing process are shown in Figure 2.

Process	Subprocess		Problem
Sizing	sizing system development		body type classification
	pattern making		pattern grading prediction
	production planning	lay planning	lay number prediction
		marker making	marker length prediction
			marker cutting length prediction
Cutting	spreading operation		defective fabric detection
			spreading time prediction
	cutting operation		cutting time prediction
			fabric waste estimation
	sorting and bundling operation		cut pieces classification
			defective cut pieces detection
	production planning	sewing order planning	sewing productivity prediction
		sewing line designing	operator skill classification
			operator efficiency prediction
Sewing			defective semi-product detection
	sewing operation		defective semi-product prediction
			sewing machine fault diagnosis
Finishing	finishing operation		ironing temperature determination
			finished product classification
Packaging	packaging operation		defective finished product detection
			defective finished product prediction
			lead time prediction
Whole			productivity prediction
			carbon emission prediction

Figure 2: Prediction and classification problems in the garment manufacturing process.

It can be summarized that using machine learning to solve these mentioned problems mainly aims to effectively promote the time and cost estimation, the quality control, and the operation automation in the garment manufacturing industry.

3 Garment Manufacturing using Machine Learning

Machine learning has a wide range of applications in the garment industry. It has been seen used in the design and sales processes for fashion image classification[11], garment fit evaluation[12], fashion analysis[13], demand forecasting[14], sales forecasting[15], and so on. While in the manufacturing process, machine learning is gradually being used mainly for population division in the sizing process, and quality control or operation automation in the sewing process. The details are addressed below.

(1) Machine learning used in sizing

To build sizing systems, machine learning is applied to the classification issue dividing the population into homogeneous subgroups based on some key body dimensions. For this application, k-means is the most widely used machine learning algorithm. Some other machine learning algorithms, i.e., decision tree, neural network, and support vector machine are also applied.

In[16], the classification and regression tree technology was used to identify and classify significant patterns in the body shapes of soldiers. In[17], a back propagation neural network algorithm was used to identify young females' body type. In[18], the k-means cluster method was used to segment the subjects into homogenous body size groups, which were validated by a decision tree. In[19;20], Ward's minimum variance method was integrated with the k-means method to group the homogeneous individuals into each figure type. In[21], a k-means algorithm was also used to segment the heterogeneous population to more homogeneous one. In[22], a trimmed version of the partitioning around medoids algorithm based on k-means was used to classify specific population homogeneous subgroups based on some key body dimensions. In[23], different body types are clustered using the Kohonen neural network. In[24], the support vector clustering, an unmonitored support vector machine, was used to military uniform sizes, where a genetic algorithm was used to determine the optimal parameter values. In[25], a k-means clustering was used to derive cluster characteristics.

(2) Machine learning used in sewing

Artificial networks have outstanding performances in quality control and operation automation especially in the sewing process.

Neural networks were proved to be capable in fabric performance prediction or classification for various fabrics, like knitted-fabrics and woven fabrics[26;27;28;29;30;31;32]. Additionally, neural networks were used to predict the amount of sewing thread required to make up a garment[33] and to guide fabrics with curved edges towards sewing[34]. In[35], an approach based on neural network was developed for predicting the position error correction of a 2R robot manipulator. In[32], a neural network was used to estimate the extensibility of two pieces of fabrics.

Other machine learning algorithms, i.e., naïve bayes, decision tree, and k-nearest neighbor were also applied in fabric performance prediction[36;37].

(3) Machine learning used in cutting, finishing, and packaging

Machine learning was used for pattern classification and marker length estimation to solve the marker making problem in the cutting process. In[38], an irregular object packing approach was constructed, where a learning vector quantization neural network was developed as a classification heuristic to divide the objects into three classes. In[39], multiple linear regression and radial basis function neural network were applied to estimate marker lengths as the basis for cutting order planning.

Machine learning was applied to the task of garment inspection in packaging. In[40], the lasso regression was used to measure garments from a single image that speeds up this task. In[41], a novel hybrid model which integrated of genetic algorithm and neural network was proposed to classify garment defects.

The applications of machine learning in garment manufacturing are shown in Figure 3.

It can be summarized that the application of machine learning in the garment manufacturing industry is more concentrated in the two processes, i.e., sizing and sewing. Artificial networks have outstanding performance in quality control and operation automation especially in the sewing process. The mainly used machine learning algorithms in this area are neural networks and k-means. Comparatively, little research has been done on machine learning applications towards cutting, finishing, and packaging.

4   Popular Machine Learning Algorithms

Machine learning is seen as a branch of artificial intelligence, which studies computer algorithms that improve automatically through experience and the use of sample data, or called training data[1]. The term was coined by Arthur Samuel in 1959[42].

Machine learning is performed using various types of models, including regressions, decision trees, random forest, support-vector machines, K-nearest neighbors, K-means, naïve Bayes, artificial neural networks, genetic algorithms, etc[43].

Machine learning models can be validated by accuracy estimation techniques like the holdout method, the K-fold-cross-validation method, bootstrap for overall accuracy, and total operating characteristic for diagnostic ability. It can fail to deliver expected results because of data, model, or evaluation problems.

Machine learning makes computers perform intelligent tasks without explicitly coding them to do so. Based on this feature, machine learning algorithms can turn out to be more effective, and widely used in various applications, where it is difficult or impossible to develop conventional algorithms. The two main tasks of using machine learning are to classify existing data and to predict new data based on developed models.

In the areas of manufacturing, healthcare, finance, media, commerce, and transportation, machine learning has been applied for image recognition, medical diagnosis, fraud detection, email filtering, virtual personal assistant, automatic language translation, stock market trading, prod-

Process	Algorithm	Task
Sizing	decision tree	identify and classify significant patterns in the body shapes of soldiers
	k-means	validate the divided homogenous body size group segment the heterogeneous population to more homogeneous one identify systematic patterns within body dimensions generate useful patterns and rules for standard size charts classify a specific population homogeneous subgroup derive cluster characteristics
	neural network	identify young females' body type cluster different body sizes
	support vector machine	classify military uniform sizes
Cutting	neural network	classify patterns predict maker length
Sewing	linear regression, neural network	predict the amount of sewing thread required to make up a garment
	decision tree, k-nearest neighbors	predict seam appearance
	naïve bayes, decision tree, k-nearest neighbors	predict fabric behavior
	neural network	predict the sewing performance of fabrics predict seam performance predict the sewing performance of fabrics fabric properties estimation predict the quality of the sewed item classify knitted-fabric stitching detect stitching defect guide fabrics with curved edges towards sewing predict the position error correction of a 2R robot manipulator estimate the extensibility of two pieces of fabrics
Packaging	neural network	classify garment defects
	support vector machine	garment size check

Figure 3: Garment manufacturing-related tasks that solved by machine learning algorithms.

uct recommendations, auto-driving, etc[44;45;46]. For better and wider applications of machine learning, there is a growing demand for compound application talents who master machine learning along with domain knowledge.

Here is an overview of the most popular machine learning algorithms and their recent applications.

(1) Linear regression and its current applications

Linear regression is the very basic and widely used machine learning algorithm. The case of one independent variable is called simple linear regression, while for more than one, it is called multiple linear regression, of which a special form is called polynomial or curvilinear regression. Linear regression is used for prediction, e.g., material properties prediction[47], taxi rides demand prediction[48], battery remaining useful life prediction[49], etc.

(2) Logistic regression and its current applications

Logical regression predicts the probability of existence and is mainly used for classification, e.g., sound classification[50], disease diagnosis[51], pipe failures prediction[52], etc.

(3) Decision tree and its current applications

Decision tree establishes a tree-like model to determine the possible results, which can be used for regression or classification, e.g., software fault prediction[53], clothing size classification[54], futures price forecasting[55], etc.

(4) Random forest and its current applications

Random forest is an ensemble learning method, building a large number of decision trees to perform tasks. It is successfully used for large-sized classification[56], e.g., cracked soybean seeds discrimination[57], heart diseases diagnosis[58], avalanche prediction[59], etc.

(5) Support-vector machine and its current applications

Support-vector machine uses the maximum-margin hyperplane for binary classification, e.g., carrot appearance detection[60], machine fault diagnosis[61], agriculture productivity prediction[62], etc.

(6) K-nearest neighbors and its current applications

K-nearest neighbor is a non-parametric classification method first developed by Evelyn Fix and Joseph Hodges in 1951[63], and later expanded by Thomas Cover[64]. The idea is that in the feature space, if most of the k nearest samples near a sample (i.e., the nearest neighbors in the feature space) belong to a certain category, the sample also belongs to this category, so the model is sensitive to the local structure of the data. It is used for classification and regression, e.g., customer demand forecasting[65], scent classification[66], web documents clustering[67].

(7) K-means and its current applications

K-means is a simple and efficient clustering algorithm, classifying and organizing data via an iterative refinement approach, e.g., data leak identification[68], filtering recommendation[69], identification of similarities in satellite images[70].

(8) Naïve Bayes and its current applications

Naïve Bayes and decision tree are both most widely used for building classifiers. Compared with decision tree, naïve Bayes originated from classical mathematical theory, features a solid mathematical foundation, and stable classification efficiency. Abstractly, naïve Bayes is a conditional probability model, applied for mail spam filtering[71], promotion images classification[72], freeway safety prediction[73], etc.

(9) Artificial neural networks and their current applications

Artificial neural networks, or called neural networks, are computing systems vaguely inspired by the biological neural networks, having the ability to reproduce and model nonlinear processes. In many fields such as materials, biology, medicine, finance, agriculture, engineering, etc., they are used for fatigue life prediction[74], passengers' loyalty prediction[75], instantaneous vehicle emission prediction[76], etc.

The above mentioned popular machine learning models are seen to move forward and have broad application prospects. A good ware of the features, types, targets, and typical application cases can help to flexibly apply these algorithms to well solve some prediction or classification problems in the garment manufacturing industry.

The above content is also summarized below in Table 1.

5 Potential Machine Learning Applications in Garment Manufacturing

There are many prediction and classification problems which need to be solved in the garment manufacturing industry. However, the application of machine learning in the garment manufacturing industry is relatively rare. Consequently, there is a lot of room for expansion and exploration for the application of machine learning in this area.

The three topics, i.e., problems found in garment manufacturing, applications of machine learning in garment manufacturing, and popular machine learning technologies and their recent wide applications in various fields are addressed separately in the previous sections, based on which, five potential applications of machine learning in garment manufacturing, i.e., machine learning prediction of marker cutting lengths, machine learning prediction of operator skill levels, machine learning classification of made-up products machine learning classification of cut pieces, machine learning classification of machine breakdown are discussed in this section to provide inspirations for expanding machine learning applications in the garment manufacturing industry so as to better promote the development of fashion industry 4.0.

Table 1: Popular machine learning algorithms and current applications.

Algorithm	Task		Applications
	Prediction	Classification	
Linear regression	YES	NO	material properties prediction
			demand prediction of taxi rides
			battery remaining useful life prediction
Logistic regression	NO	YES	sound classification
			disease diagnosis
			pipe failures prediction
Decision tree	YES	YES	software fault prediction
			clothing size classification
			futures price forecasting
Random forest	YES	YES	cracked soybean seeds discrimination
			heart diseases diagnosis
			avalanche prediction
Support-vector machine	NO	YES	carrot appearance detection
			machine fault diagnosis
			agriculture productivity prediction
K-nearest neighbors	YES	YES	customer demand forecasting
			scent classification
			web documents clustering
K-means	NO	YES	data leak identification
			filtering recommendation
			identification of similarities in satellite images
Naïve Bayes	NO	YES	mail spam filtering
			promotion images classification
			freeway safety prediction
Artificial neural networks	YES	YES	fatigue life prediction
			passengers' loyalty prediction
			instantaneous vehicle emission prediction

(1) Machine learning prediction of marker cutting lengths

In the previous study[40], the marker lengths estimation for various garment size combinations was carried out with the aid of two machine learning technologies, i.e., multiple linear regression and radial basis function neural network. It was proved that both technologies are generally performant in marker length estimation, where the neural network was said to be slightly more powerful. Likewise, the marker cutting length estimation problem also can be regarded as a

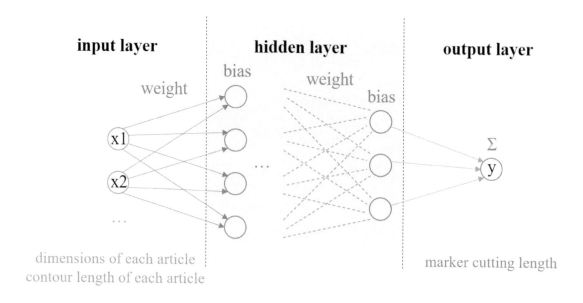

input layer   hidden layer   output layer

Figure 4: A neural network model for predicting marker cutting length.

regression problem of which the underlying regularity is complex to be built. Similarly, the shortest marker cutting length may be predicted by building a neural network model. In this neural network model, the size dimensions (primary and secondary dimensions) and size contour length of contained articles in the marker are taken as input (X) and the marker cutting length is taken as output (Y), as shown in Figure 4. The predicted marker cutting length can be used for the cutting time and cost estimation.

(2) Machine learning prediction of operator skill levels

In the garment manufacturing industry, the traditional labor-intensive industry, the operators' performance largely depends on personal skill levels[77]. It is essential to take into consideration the skill levels of operators to properly assign operations during sewing line designing, in order to make full use of the labor source and improve the production efficiency.

Operator skill level may be predicted by a discrete choice model with logistic regression. It is a multinomial and ordinal logistic regression model, where operator kill levels are modeled as discrete outcomes (excellent skill, good skill, average skill, fair skill and poor skill), and the input variables are years of experience, age, sex, speed, flexibility and so forth.

(3) Machine learning classification of made-up products

In the packaging process, finished products will be packaged and crated. Classifying and grading the made-up products, the machine learning model can help to automize this process.

Decision tree is a good option to build a classification model for classifying finished products into different classes, i.e., qualified products, defective products containing four subclasses (Figure 5). The machine learning-based product classification finally contributes to the automation of the garment packaging process.

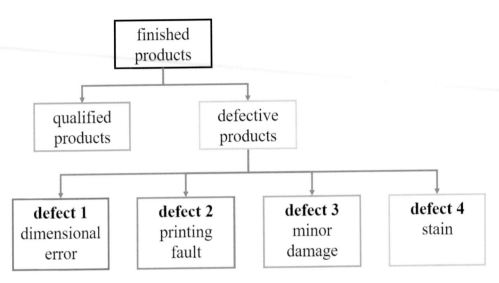

Figure 5: A decision tree model for classifying finished products.

(4) Machine learning classification of cut pieces

In the cutting process, different fabrics are being cut into pieces, the garment components including front, back, sleeve, collar, pocket, etc. Cut components are then sorted and bundled for use in the subsequent sewing process. All components of a garment are sought out and placed together. Size wise sorting and color wise sorting will be required especially in nowadays multi-variety and small-lot manufacturing. Defective cut pieces will be discarded.

A naive Bayes classifier[78], a simple probabilistic classifier (Figure 6), can be constructed for sorting the cut pieces, in which the features including dimensional error, color difference, and material damage are considered.

In the classifier, F_1, refers to dimensional error, F_2 refers to color difference, and F_3 refers to material damage, n=3. There are two class labels including bundle (C_1) and discard (C_2), k=2. Cut pieces can be sorted by the naïve Bayes classifier that the qualified cut pieces will be bundled and sent to the sewing department while the defective cut pieces will be discarded.

(5) Machine learning prediction of machine breakdown

To achieve a production of high efficiency and stable quality, the smooth sewing process is required.

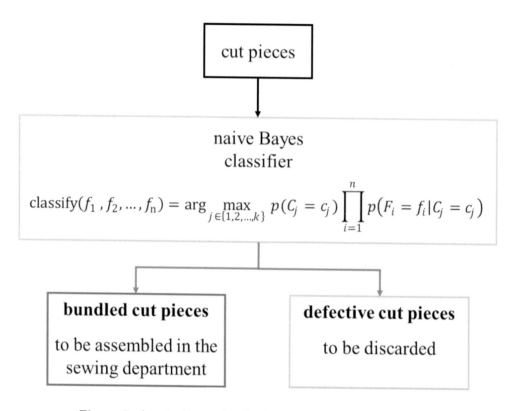

Figure 6: A naïve Bayes classifier for classifying cut pieces.

Markov chains can be applied for a correct machine breakdown prediction, based on which it optimizes the redundant inspection and maintenance tasks for maximum profit. According to the maintenance records of the machine, the machine state is divided into several levels, e.g., normal, minor failure, and major failure. Markov chain is used to analyze and predict the machine breakdown probability with a state trend diagram.

6 Case Study

This is a case study taken from an article on machine learning based marker length estimation[39]. In this case study, a neural network is the used machine learning model to predict the overall marker length. More specifically, the radial basis function neural network (RBF NN) is applied to estimate the overall marker lengths of both mixed markers and group markers (Figure 7) containing one or two garment articles of sizes from a total of 7 mass production sizes from XXS to XXL (Figure 8) of a basic straight skirt.

Figure 8 shows a set of 7 basic straight skirt sizes used in mass production, where the primary dimension is the hip girth and the secondary dimension is the waist girth.

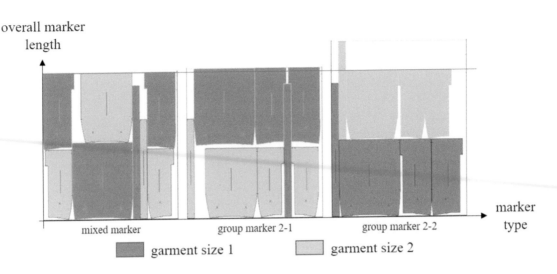

Figure 7: Overall marker lengths of 2-article marker vary with marker types.

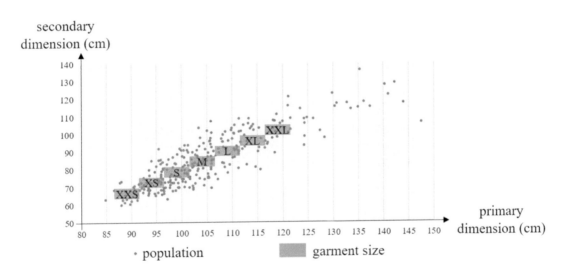

Figure 8: Mass production garment sizes for a certain population.

The experimental marker lengths of the markers generated by Lectra softwares are collected and taken as actual values (Figure 9). Due to the limited data sample, the stratified 10-fold cross-validation used, the data set is divided into training sets and test sets for validation. In the marker length prediction model, the overall marker length is taken as output (Y), the marker lengths of markers only containing itself for each contained garment size is taken as input (X).

The mean square error (MSE) (Figure 10 (a)) and the deviation between predicted value and actual value (Figure 10 (b)) are the selected evaluation criteria to validate the prediction performance. The figure shows that the MSEs are small and the predicted values tally well with

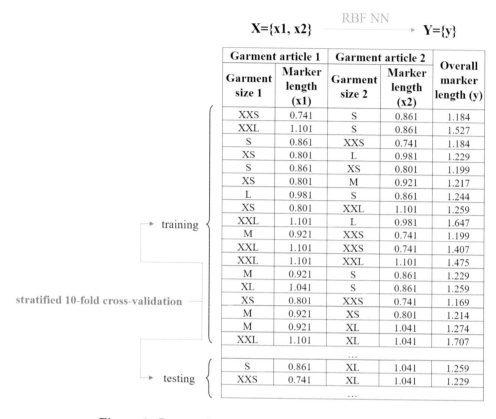

Figure 9: Data used in the RBF NN prediction model.

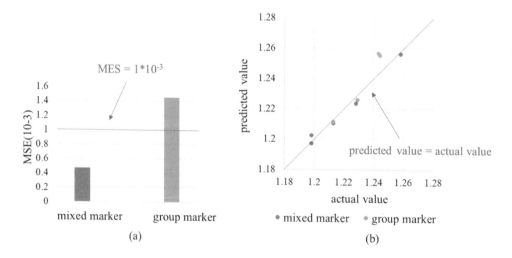

Figure 10: Prediction performance of the RBF NN model.

the actual values. Especially for mixed marker, the MSE is below 10^{-3} and the dots (predicted value, actual value) are located very close to the line where predicted value equals to actual value.

It is proved that the figure that RBF NN performs well in overall marker length prediction for mass production, and the prediction result of mixed markers is better to that of group markers. In summary, machine learning is a potential tool to solve garment manufacturing related problems, so that extension work can be done to explore new applications and to achieve better performances in the further studies.

7 Conclusion

This study focuses on smart manufacturing decisions with the aid of machine learning, mainly contributing to the fourth industrial revolution of garment manufacturing. Literature regarding garment manufacturing-related decision problems and machine learning algorithms were collected. A systematic analysis of the literatures is provided through professional classification schemes based on the main garment production processes, i.e., sizing, cutting, sewing, finishing, and packaging. The characteristics and current application examples of commonly used machine learning algorithms are analyzed. Based on the above review of literature, the potential and feasible extension of machine learning applications in garment manufacturing is specified with five examples for future work in this subject area.

Acknowledgement

This research is jointly supported by Study on fit evaluation of mass customization garment sizes by the General Research Project from the Education Department of Zhejiang Province under the grant number of Y202148250, Intelligent designing of garment size for mass customization funded by the Open Project Program of Anhui Province College Key Laboratory of Textile Fabrics, Anhui Engineering and Technology Research Center of Textile under the grant number of 2021AETKL04 and Optimization of garment industry production processes in the context of mass customization funded by the Scientific Research Start-up Fund Project of Zhejiang Sci-Tech University in 2020 under the grant number of NO. 21192116-Y. The authors thank Professor Kim Phuc Tran for his comments.

References

[1] T.M. Mitchell. *Machine Learning*. New York: McGrawHill, 1997.

[2] R. Nayak and Rajiv Padhye (eds.). *Garment Manufacturing Technology*. Elsevier, 2015.

[3] K. Schwab. The fourth industr←ial revolution. *Currency*, 2017.

[4] T. Karthik, P. Ganesan and D. Gopalakrishnan. *Apparel Manufacturing Technology*. CRC Press, 2016.

[5] R. Nayak and Rajiv Padhye (eds.). *Automation in Garment Manufacturing*. Woodhead Publishing, 2017.

[6] S. Ashdown (ed.). *Sizing in Clothing*. Elsevier, 2007.

[7] K.K. Mullet. *Concepts of Pattern Grading: Techniques for Manual and Computer Grading*. Bloomsbury Publishing USA, 2015.

[8] N. Zakaria and Deepti Gupta (eds.). *Anthropometry, Apparel Sizing and Design*. Woodhead Publishing, 2019.

[9] I. Vilumsone-Nemes. *Industrial Cutting of Textile Materials*. Woodhead Publishing, 2018.

[10] R.E. Glock and Grace I. Kunz. *Apparel Manufacturing: Sewn Product Analysis*. Prentice Hall, 2005.

[11] B. Kolisnik, I. Hogan and F. Zulkernine. Condition-CNN: A hierarchical multi-label fashion image classification model. *Expert Systems with Applications*, 182: 115195, 2021.

[12] K. Liu, X. Zeng, P. Bruniaux, J. Wang, E. Kamalha and X. Tao. Fit evaluation of virtual garment try-on by learning from digital pressure data. *Knowledge-Based Systems*, 133: 174–182, 2017.

[13] X. Gu, F. Gao, M. Tan and P. Peng. Fashion analysis and understanding with artificial intelligence. *Information Processing and Management*, 57(5): 102276, 2020.

[14] İ. Güven and F. Şimşir. Demand forecasting with color parameter in retail apparel industry using artificial neural networks (ANN) and support vector machines (SVM) methods. *Computers and Industrial Engineering*, 147: 106678, 2020.

[15] S. Thomassey. Sales forecasts in clothing industry: The key success factor of the supply chain management. International Journal of Production Economics, 128.2: 470–483, 2010.

[16] C.-H. Hsu and M.-J. J. Wang. Using decision tree-based data mining to establish a sizing system for the manufacture of garments. *The International Journal of Advanced Manufacturing Technology*, 26.5-6: 669–674, 2005.

[17] F.Y. Zou, X.J. Ding, S.J. Zhang, L.J. Wang and Y.H. Zhang. Application of neural network to identification of young females' body type. *2006 IEEE International Conference on Systems, Man and Cybernetics*. Vol. 3. IEEE, 2006.

[18] N. Zakaria, J.S. Mohd, N. Taib, Y.Y. Tan and Y.B. Wah. Using data mining technique to explore anthropometric data towards the development of sizing system. *2008 International Symposium on Information Technology*. Vol. 2. IEEE, 2008.

[19] C.-H. Hsu, H.-F. Lin and M.-J. Wang. Developing female size charts for facilitating garment production by using data mining. *Journal of the Chinese Institute of Industrial Engineers*, 24.3: 245–251, 2007.

[20] C.-H. Hsu. Data mining to improve industrial standards and enhance production and marketing: An empirical study in apparel industry. *Expert Systems with Applications*, 36.3: 4185–4191, 2009.

[21] M.S. Esfandarani and J. Shahrabi. Developing a new suit sizing system using data optimization techniques. *International Journal of Clothing Science and Technology*, 2012.

[22] M.V. Ibáñez, G. Vinué, S. Alemany, A. Simó, I. Epifanio, J. Domingo and G. Ayala. Apparel sizing using trimmed PAM and OWA operators, 2012.

[23] M. Vadood, M.S. Esfandarani and M.S. Johari. Developing a new suit sizing system using neural network. *Journal of Engineered Fibers and Fabrics*, 10.2: 155892501501000212, 2015.

[24] T.C. Hu, J.C., Chen, G.K. Yang and C.W. Chen. Development of a military uniform size system using hybrid support vector clustering with a genetic algorithm. *Symmetry*, 11.5: 665, 2019.

[25] S. Kolose, T. Stewart, P. Hume and G.R. Tomkinson. Cluster size prediction for military clothing using 3D body scan data. *Applied Ergonomics*, 96: 103487, 2021.

[26] T.-H. Lin. Construction of predictive model on fabric and sewing thread optimization. *Journal of Textile Engineering*, 50.1: 6–11, 2004.

[27] C.L. Hui and S.F. Ng. A new approach for prediction of sewing performance of fabrics in apparel manufacturing using artificial neural networks. *Journal of the Textile Institute*, 96.6: 401–405, 2005.

[28] P.C. Hui, K.C. Chan, K.W. Yeung and F.S. Ng. Application of artificial neural networks to the prediction of sewing performance of fabrics. *International Journal of Clothing Science and Technology*, 2007.

[29] C.L. Hui and S.F. Ng. Predicting seam performance of commercial woven fabrics using multiple logarithm regression and artificial neural networks. *Textile Research Journal*, 79.18: 1649–1657, 2009.

[30] C.W.M. Yuen, W.K. Wong, S.Q. Qian, D.D. Fan, L.K. Chan and E.H.K. Fung. Fabric stitching inspection using segmented window technique and BP neural network. *Textile Research Journal*, 79.1: 24–35, 2009.

[31] W.K. Wong, C.W.M. Yuen, D.D. Fan, L.K. Chan and E.H.K. Fung. Stitching defect detection and classification using wavelet transform and BP neural network. *Expert Systems with Applications*, 36.2: 3845–3856, 2009.

[32] P.N. Koustoumpardis and Nikos A. Aspragathos. Intelligent hierarchical robot control for sewing fabrics. *Robotics and Computer-Integrated Manufacturing*, 30.1: 34–46, 2014.

[33] M. Jaouadi, S. Msahli, A. Babay and B. Zitouni. Analysis of the modeling methodologies for predicting the sewing thread consumption. *International Journal of Clothing Science and Technology*, 2006.

[34] P.T. Zacharia. An adaptive neuro-fuzzy inference system for robot handling fabrics with curved edges towards sewing. *Journal of Intelligent and Robotic Systems*, 58.3: 193–209, 2010.

[35] P. Kumar. Artificial neural network based geometric error correction model for enhancing positioning accuracy of a robotic sewing manipulator. *Procedia Computer Science*, 133: 1048–1055, 2018.

[36] D.Z. Pavlinić and J. Geršak. Design of the system for prediction of fabric behaviour in garment manufacturing processes. *International Journal of Clothing Science and Technology*, 2004.

[37] D.Z. Pavlinić, J. Geršak, J. Demšar and I. Bratko. Predicting seam appearance quality. *Textile Research Journal*, 76.3: 235–242, 2006.

[38] W.K. Wong and Z.X. Guo. A hybrid approach for packing irregular patterns using evolutionary strategies and neural network. *International Journal of Production Research*, 48.20: 6061–6084, 2010.

[39] Y. Xu, S. Thomassey and X. Zeng. Machine learning-based marker length estimation for garment mass customization. *The International Journal of Advanced Manufacturing Technology*, 113.11: 3361–3376, 2021.

[40] J. Serrat, F. Lumbreras and I. Ruiz. Learning to measure for preshipment garment sizing. *Measurement*, 130: 327–339, 2018.

[41] C.W.M. Yuen, W.K. Wong, S.Q. Qian, L.K. Chan and E.H.K. Fung. A hybrid model using genetic algorithm and neural network for classifying garment defects. *Expert Systems with Applications*, 36.2: 2037–2047, 2009.

[42] A.L. Samuel. Some studies in machine learning using the game of checkers. *IBM Journal of Research and Development*, 44.1.2: 206–226, 2000.

[43] G. Bonaccorso. *Machine Learning Algorithms*. Packt Publishing Ltd, 2017.

[44] H. Wang, C. Ma and L. Zhou. A brief review of machine learning and its application. *2009 International Conference on Information Engineering and Computer Science*. IEEE, 2009.

[45] M.I. Jordan and T.M. Mitchell. Machine learning: Trends, perspectives, and prospects. *Science*, 349.6245: 255–260, 2015.

[46] S. Chaudhary, S. Yadav, S. Kushwaha and S.R.P. Shahi. A brief review of machine learning and its applications. *SAMRIDDHI: A Journal of Physical Sciences, Engineering and Technology*, 12.SUP 1: 218–223, 2020.

[47] M. Kusano, S. Miyazaki, M. Watanabe, S. Kishimoto, D.S. Bulgarevich, Y. Ono and A. Yumoto. Tensile properties prediction by multiple linear regression analysis for selective laser melted and post heat-treated Ti-6Al-4V with microstructural quantification. *Materials Science and Engineering: A*, 787: 139549, 2020.

[48] T. Kim, S. Sharda, X. Zhou and R.M. Pendyala. A stepwise interpretable machine learning framework using linear regression (LR) and long short-term memory (LSTM): City-wide demand-side prediction of yellow taxi and for-hire vehicle (FHV) service. *Transportation Research Part C: Emerging Technologies*, 120: 102786, 2020.

[49] S.J. Kwon, D. Han, J.H. Choi, J.H. Lim, S.E. Lee and J. Kim. Remaining-useful-life prediction via multiple linear regression and recurrent neural network reflecting degradation information of 20Ah LiNixMnyCo1-x-yO2 pouch cell. *Journal of Electroanalytical Chemistry*, 858: 113729, 2020.

[50] A. Robles-Guerrero, T. Saucedo-Anaya, E. González-Ramírez and J.I. De La Rosa-Vargas. Analysis of a multiclass classification problem by lasso logistic regression and singular value decomposition to identify sound patterns in queenless bee colonies. *Computers and Electronics in Agriculture*, 159: 69–74, 2019.

[51] L. Khairunnahar, M.A. Hasib, R.H.B. Rezanur, M.R. Islam and M.K. Hosain. Classification of malignant and benign tissue with logistic regression. *Informatics in Medicine Unlocked*, 16: 100189, 2019.

[52] C. Jara-Arriagada and I. Stoianov. Pipe breaks and estimating the impact of pressure control in water supply networks. *Reliability Engineering and System Safety*, 210: 107525, 2021.

[53] M.O. Varrà, L. Husáková, J. Patočka, S. Ghidini and E. Zanardi. Classification of transformed anchovy products based on the use of element patterns and decision trees to assess traceability and country of origin labelling. *Food Chemistry*, 360: 129790, 2021.

[54] S. Kolose, T. Stewart, P. Hume and G.R. Tomkinson. Prediction of military combat clothing size using decision trees and 3D body scan data. *Applied Ergonomics*, 95: 103435, 2021.

[55] Q. Gu, Y. Chang, N. Xiong and L. Chen. Forecasting Nickel futures price based on the empirical wavelet transform and gradient boosting decision trees. *Applied Soft Computing*, 109: 107472, 2021.

[56] L. Breiman. Random forests. *Machine Learning*, 45.1: 5–32, 2001.

[57] L. Wang, Z. Huang and R. Wang. Discrimination of cracked soybean seeds by near-infrared spectroscopy and random forest variable selection. *Infrared Physics and Technology*, 115: 103731, 2021.

[58] S. Asadi, S.E. Roshan and M.W. Kattan. Random forest swarm optimization-based for heart diseases diagnosis. *Journal of Biomedical Informatics*, 115: 103690, 2021.

[59] P.D. Sielenou, L. Viallon-Galinier, P. Hagenmuller, P. Naveau, S. Morin, M. Dumont and N. Eckert. Combining random forests and class-balancing to discriminate between three classes of avalanche activity in the French Alps. *Cold Regions Science and Technology*, 187: 103276, 2021.

[60] H. Zhu, L. Yang, J. Fei, L. Zhao and Z. Han. Recognition of carrot appearance quality based on deep feature and support vector machine. *Computers and Electronics in Agriculture*, 186: 106185, 2021.

[61] R.K. Jha and P.D. Swami. Fault diagnosis and severity analysis of rolling bearings using vibration image texture enhancement and multiclass support vector machines. *Applied Acoustics*, 182: 108243, 2021.

[62] G. Prabakaran, D. Vaithiyanathan and M. Ganesan. FPGA based effective agriculture productivity prediction system using fuzzy support vector machine. *Mathematics and Computers in Simulation*, 185: 1–16, 2021.

[63] E. Fix and J.L. Hodges. Nonparametric discrimination: Consistency properties. *Randolph Field, Texas, Project*, 21–49, 1951.

[64] N.S. Altman. An introduction to kernel and nearest-neighbor nonparametric regression. *The American Statistician*, 46.3: 175–185, 1992.

[65] M. Kück and M. Freitag. Forecasting of customer demands for production planning by local k-nearest neighbor models. *International Journal of Production Economics*, 231: 107837, 2021.

[66] P. Müller, K. Salminen, V. Nieminen, A. Kontunen, M. Karjalainen, P. Isokoski and V. Surakka. Scent classification by K nearest neighbors using ion-mobility spectrometry measurements. *Expert Systems with Applications*, 115: 593–606, 2019.

[67] A.S. Abdulameer, S. Tiun, N.S. Sani, M. Ayob and A.Y. Taha. Enhanced clustering models with wiki-based k-nearest neighbors-based representation for web search result clustering. *Journal of King Saud University-Computer and Information Sciences*, 2020.

[68] J. Karthik, V. Tamizhazhagan and S. Narayana. Data leak identification using scattering search K Means in social networks. *Materials Today: Proceedings*, 2021.

[69] Z. Chen, Y. Wang, S. Zhang, H. Zhong and L. Chen. Differentially private user-based collaborative filtering recommendation based on K-means clustering. *Expert Systems with Applications*, 168: 114366, 2021.

[70] P. Ariza-Colpas Paola and A.I. Oviedo-Carrascal. Discovering similarities in Landsat satellite images using the K-means method. *Procedia Computer Science*, 170: 129–136, 2020.

[71] S. Daisy, J. Sickory and A. Rijuvana Begum. Smart material to build mail spam filtering technique using Naive Bayes and MRF methodologies. *Materials Today: Proceedings*, 2021.

[72] P. Phoenix, R. Sudaryono and D. Suhartono. Classifying promotion images using optical character recognition and Naïve Bayes classifier. *Procedia Computer Science*, 179: 498–506, 2021.

[73] J. Yao and Y. Ye. The effect of image recognition traffic prediction method under deep learning and naive Bayes algorithm on freeway traffic safety. *Image and Vision Computing*, 103: 103971, 2020.

[74] H. Kumar and R.P. Swamy. Fatigue life prediction of glass fiber reinforced epoxy composites using artificial neural networks. *Composites Communications*, 100812, 2021.

[75] B. Singh. Predicting airline passengers' loyalty using artificial neural network theory. *Journal of Air Transport Management*, 94: 102080, 2021.

[76] J. Seo, B. Yun, J. Park, J. Park, M. Shin and S. Park. Prediction of instantaneous real-world emissions from diesel light-duty vehicles based on an integrated artificial neural network and vehicle dynamics model. *Science of the Total Environment*, 786: 147359, 2021.

[77] P.K. Mok, C.K. Kwong and W.K. Wong. Optimisation of fault-tolerant fabric-cutting schedules using genetic algorithms and fuzzy set theory. *European Journal of Operational Research*, 177.3: 1876–1893, 2007.

[78] A. McCallum. *Graphical Models, Lecture2: Bayesian Network Represention*. PDF. Retrieved 22, 2019.

Chapter 12

Enabling Smart Supply Chain Management with Artificial Intelligence

Thi Hien Nguyen,[1] Huu Du Nguyen,[2,*] Kim Duc Tran,[2] Dinh Duy Kha Nguyen[3] and Kim Phuc Tran[4]

1 Introduction

Supply Chain Management (SCM) plays a very important role in collaboration among many stakeholders such as producers, suppliers, carriers, distributors, and retailers. The purpose of SCM is to create maximum benefit not as singular realities but also as the result of a sum of interactions between entities sharing common interests. As a consequence, a large number of studies have been devoted to developing effective methods for SCM. In the literature, the number of articles related to the SCM topic has increased dramatically as shown in Figure 1 (extracting from WebofScience). In the period from 2010 to 2020, the number of articles per year has doubled compared to the previous 5 years.

There are different points of view about the definition of SCM. For example, Ellram[1] defined SCM as a network of companies interacting to deliver a product or service to the end customer and involving a set of flows from raw materials to final delivery. The author of[2] referred to SCM as "the management of upstream and downstream relationships with suppliers and customers in order to deliver superior customer value at less cost to the supply chain as a whole". Authors of[3] counted more than 50 definitions of the SCM and classified them into five categories. Regardless of differences in the way to express the definition of SCM, there is a common among all these definitions about the increasing importance of SCM for any organizations or businesses in competing in the global market and networked economy[4].

Due to the growth of Internet businesses and mobile computing, there is a profound change in the way of shopping of customers and the operating of businesses. By allowing customers to contact product distributors directly and encouraging cooperation, these new advances shorten the supply chain. Internet businesses like Amazon have improved their service quality in terms

[1] Laboratoire AGM, UMR CNRS 8088, CY Cergy Paris Université, 95000 Cergy, France.

[2] International Research Institute for Artificial Intelligence and Data Science, Dong A University, Danang, Vietnam.

[3] Université de Technologie de Troyes, 10300 Troyes, France.

[4] Univ. Lille, ENSAIT, ULR 2461 - GEMTEX - Génie et Matériaux Textiles, F-59000 Lille, France.

* Corresponding author: dunh@donga.edu.vn

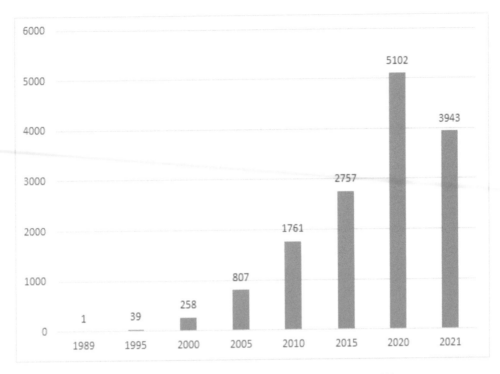

Figure 1: Number of publications on SCM since 1989.

of on-time delivery and convenience. Normalizing features like next-day delivery can increase order fulfillment, but also make it difficult for other parts of the chain. Because orders can be made and received faster, they need to be delivered at a faster rate. As a consequence, several disadvantages can be encountered in the supply chain: it leads to waste when businesses order too many raw materials or they do not supply enough products according to the order in the opposite case. This is only one amongst many challenges a business can meet in its operation and this can only be overcome by developing an efficient SCM method. The application of advanced technologies like the Internet of Things (IoT) and Artificial Intelligence (AI) for SCM is then encouraged.

AI refers to a set of computer algorithms that allows machines to perform complex tasks "as a human" by perceiving the working environment and taking actions to maximize the possibility of success. Shortly, it is regarded as intelligence demonstrated by machines. Recent times witnessed the sharp development and the wide applications of AI in many areas of real life, and SCM is not an exception. In[5] highlighted the recent trends and applications of AI in the retail and manufacturing industry.[6] introduced an SCM solution connecting many components such as suppliers, manufacturers, customers, and other companies to enable efficient inventory management and timely product supply, based on AI and IoT technologies. A systematic review that aims to identify the contributions of AI in SCM has been conducted in[7]. The authors classified the applications of AI in SCM into four main fields, including marketing, logistics, production, and supply chain. Another review on the implementation of machine learning (ML) techniques within SCM in Younis et al.[8] concluded that the ML applications are still at the infant stage and their opportunity for elevating SCM performance is very promising. In this chapter, we provide a survey on the applications and perspectives of AI that enable effective SCM approaches. We focus on the benefits of AI algorithms in the important fields in SCM like demand forecasting, logistics, production, and decision support systems. We also discuss the use of blockchain techniques for SCM. In addition, we suggest a novel method for forecasting retail sales in the fashion industry based on a random forest algorithm.

The chapter is structured as follows: In Section 2, we discuss the applications of AI algorithms for demand forecasting in SCM. The benefits of AI for logistics are presented in Section 3. Section 4 and Section 5 are for the covering of AI technique in the production process and in designing a decision support system, respectively. A case study has been conducted in Section 7 where we present a method for forecasting fashion retail sales using several ML algorithms. Finally, some concluding remarks are given in Section 8.

2   AI for Demand Forecasting

Forecasting refers to the prediction of what is going to happen in the future by analyzing what happened in the past and what is currently going on. Demand forecasting is an essential strategy for improving customer service levels and reducing costs related to supply-demand mismatches. For businesses, is very important to keep the balance between supply and demand. Any oversupply or shortage of goods to meet customer needs leads to negative effects on the businesses, both in terms of economy and operations or even the competitiveness with others. However, the customer demand is an unpredictable quantity and this number can only be estimated using the predictive methods. An accurate forecast of customer demand is able to result in the right decision or an effective policy in managing the supply chain. It facilitates principal business activities such as budgeting, financial planning, sales, marketing planning, material planning, production planning, risk assessment, formulating mitigation plans, and promotional campaigns.

In the literature, a variety of forecasting techniques has been introduced to best suit the specific business environment such as long-term forecasting, short-term forecasting, etc. In general, the core idea in forecasting is that the future needs should follow the past demand patterns, and the forecast is based on the accuracy and validity of historical data no matter the utilized methods. Among many methods applied for demand forecasting, AI algorithms have become increasingly powerful and popular. The authors of[9] proposed a dynamic pattern matching process within an agent-based system framework that combines human expertise and data mining techniques to predict new product demand. The authors in[10] improved the accuracy of the prediction without relying much on historical data by introducing a genetic algorithm-based causal forecasting technique that outperformed traditional regression analysis. These studies are both useful for products that have not yet been introduced to the market because no historical data are required. The authors of[11] presented an overview for the demand forecasting approaches. The authors also made a comparison between the performance of the ML methods and the classical methods for predicting demand, leading to a conclusion that the ML algorithms significantly increase the prediction accuracy. The authors of[12] suggested an AI-based method for the prediction of irregular demands in business aircraft spare parts supply chains. A decomposed deep learning (AL) approach for tourism demand forecasting has been introduced in[13]. Recent studies about the benefits of an accurate prediction for customer's demand and the AI solutions for the problem can be seen in [14;15;16;17;18;19;20;21;22].

3   AI for Logistics

An important objective in SCM is to make sure smooth and efficient operations at the production side of the chain. Once the scale of the production processes increases, several problems in logistics could be faced such as overstocking, stock-out, and delivery delays. Moreover, the logistics operations should be upgraded due to the increasing complexity and variety of customer orders. The inefficient and inaccurate order picking process may lead to negative effects on order fulfillment. That is to say, it is necessary to have good logistics management and AI algorithms are a powerful tool to perform this task: they can lead to a revolution in transportation operations [23]. The assessment of supply chain logistic performance using AI and simulation-based Techniques was presented in [24].

In logistics management, warehousing refers to a storage repository that allows the goods and the cargo to be stored properly. The major operation of the warehouse involves the storage and the protection of goods, risk-bearing, grading/branding, and transportations. A number of the necessity for warehousing was mentioned in [25]. The authors also proposed a method for automated warehouse logistics in which the sensor networks were utilized to gather the information about the number of the items entering and leaving the warehouse and the AI algorithms was applied to handle these data to automatically perform the tasks in the storehouse such as placing the items in the proper rack, picking back the items from the rack as per the order placed. The authors of [26] provided an Internet of things (IoT)-based warehouse management system with an advanced data analytical approach using AI techniques to enable smart logistics that improves the warehouse productivity, picking accuracy, efficiency, and robustness to order variability. The author of [27] discussed many perspectives for the AI adoption in a warehouse along with reviewing a number of studies on warehousing and technology in the literature. Recently, [28] conducted a study to see successful applications of AI in businesses considering an in-depth case study of Alibaba's smart warehouse, a leading e-commerce fulfillment center in China.

Besides the warehouse-related problems, the management of logistics also faces difficulty in transportation. The rapid development of the economy, as well as the expansion of the scale of production, also means increasing the requirements of the efficiency of the transporting system, i.e., the ability to transport goods from the factories to the warehouses, from the warehouses to the supermarkets or stores without breaks in the travel chain regardless of functional ability. The advanced technologies, including AI, serve to reduce difficulty in traveling and tailor solutions to the accessibility of a transportation system. By combining many algorithms like the Back Propagation neural network, the Earliest Deadline First dynamic scheduling algorithm and the Controller Area Network communication network to build an AI-empowered communication system for intelligent transportation Systems, [29] concluded that the application of AI technology can improve significantly the efficiency of vehicle scheduling and the efficiency of the communication system. A large number of studies on the applications of innovative AI algorithms in decision-making, planning, modeling, estimating, and controlling that facilitate the process of transportation planning and operations has been provided in [30]. These studies covered many topics in a transportation system like traffic surveillance, vehicle emission reduction, traffic safety, congestion management, traffic speed forecasting, and ride-sharing strategy. A summary of the potential application of AI in transportation has recently been presented in [31].

4 AI for Production

Thanks to the development of the new advanced technologies in IoT and cloud computing, the use of AI in production is becoming more and more popular. One can mention many applications of AI for production such as detecting abnormality products, planning production, monitoring the production process in real-time, performing predictive maintenance, and optimizing the manufacturing process.

The production scale in modern industrial production is increasingly expanding with large production lines operating continuously. In that process, the problem of detecting defective products plays an important role, both helping to eliminate these defective products to ensure the quality of factory products and, at the same time, allowing for it to detect the cause of defects in the line. The machine learning algorithms like support vector machine, Extra Tree, or the deep learning methods like Recurrent Neural Network (RNN), and the Conventional Neural Network (CNN) are the effective tools in AI to perform the classification mission. In the literature, many studies have been devoted to this problem. The authors of [32] discussed an approach for anomaly detection regarding predictive maintenance in an industrial data-intensive environment. The authors of [33] using a one-class support vector machine algorithm to separate anomalies from multivariate time series data outputted based on the LSTM Autoencoder network. A comprehensive survey on deep learning approaches for anomaly detection was conducted in [34].

The unqualified products maybe because of the degradation of machines in the production lines after a certain time of working. The authors of [35] pointed out that maintenance actions involve high costs, ranging from 15% to 70% of total production costs Therefore, it is necessary to have a good strategy for maintenance. Predictive maintenance refers to a well-known approach that allows determining the right time for maintenance activities. It benefits the production process by minimizing unplanned downtimes, reducing system faults, increasing efficiency in the use of resources, and planning maintenance interventions. Based on the data collected from many sensors appended to the machines, AI algorithms can predict, diagnose, and analyze future maintenance needs. In predictive maintenance, a key idea is to estimate the remaining useful life (RUL) - the remaining time before a machine requires a repair or a replacement when it no longer performs well its function. Several machine learning methods like Linear Regression, Bayesian Linear Regression, Poisson Regression, Neural Network Regression, Boosted Decision Tree Regression and Decision Forest Regression have been applied for RUL prediction in [36]. A hybrid model combining support vector machines for the prediction of the RUL of aircraft engines was presented in [37]. The deep learning algorithms like CNN, RNN, and Long-Short Term Memory (LSTM) network for estimating RUL can be seen in many studies like [38;39;40;41].

Another important application of AI that makes the manufacturing process smart is virtual reality (VR). VR refers to an artificial environment that provides users with three-dimensional images and some effects so that they can feel like being in a real space. In smart manufacturing, VR technology supports engineers in evaluating the performance of an object via virtual prototypes, which saves a lot of expense compared to building physical prototypes. That is, it can allow the implementation of complex engineering theory from industrial real-life practice in a virtual 3D model. Several applications of VR in industrial manufacturing have been discussed in[42], consisting of Design (design and prototyping), Manufacturing Processes (machining, assembly, and inspection), and Operation Management (planning, simulation, and training). The authors of[43] proposed a point cloud-based virtual factory modeling approach for factory layout planning applied in many industries such as aerospace and truck manufacturing. The benefit of the introduction of Additive Manufacturing and Augmented Reality in aeronautical maintenance has been analyzed in[44]. The authors of[45] provided a review of the studies related to virtual manufacturing systems.

All the specific applications discussed above are ultimately for the purpose of optimizing the production process. This is a highly complex task to make the process as good, functional, and effective as possible and it requires the best combination of many controllable parameters. The AI optimization algorithms enable processing data related to products from raw materials, manufacturing, traveling, and storing, to the end of life-cycle and then refining this process which can maximize the yield in a shorter time and at reduced costs. For example,[46] suggested using several machine learning methods for optimizing the production process of methyl and ethyl esters. The authors of[47] solved inventory optimization problems using a reinforcement learning algorithm. A review of machine learning for the optimization of production processes can be seen in[48].

5 AI for Decision Support Systems in SCM

In today's global scale of industrial production, trade, and services, every important decision of managers has a great influence on the benefit and the long-term development of the whole enterprise. The experience-based method is no longer suitable for them to rely on. That is to say, designing an effective Decision Support Systems (DSS) is a must for any business to assist their managers in making the most informed decisions. In fact, the concept of DSS covers not only SCM but also a wide field of applications. Applications of DSS in conjunction with several areas such as database management systems, operations research, AI, involve different levels of DSS complexities in businesses and industry. Table 1 reports the top ten categories that have the most publications on the topic of DSS extracted from WebOfScience. Another report in the same source about the Times Cited and Publications Overtime is reproduced in Figure 2. Namely, the references about the methods to design a DSS and its applications in the literature are abundant. The authors of[49] highlighted the decision-making process, components in a DSS process, and types of DSS in supply chain management. A comprehensive overview of DSS in SCM was made by[50] providing information on the trends, methodologies, and applications on different sectors and platforms used by scientists for building their decision support systems in the supply chain. The author also pointed out that in some research questions about the most effective models used on DSS in the supply chain, the use of DSS covers various problems in the supply chain, the advantages of DSS, etc.[51] developed a practical DSS with the demand management in the health-care supply chain to fight the pandemic Coronavirus disease 2019 (COVID-19) by reducing stress in the community, breaking down the COVID-19 propagation chain, and, generally, mitigating the epidemic outbreaks for health-care supply chain disruption.

Table 1: Top 10 domains that have the most publications on topic DSS and SCM.

Categories	Record Count	% of 1.967 publications
Operations Research Management Science	581	29.537
Engineering Industrial	389	19.776
Management	361	18.353
Engineering Manufacturing	310	15.760
Computer Science Interdisciplinary Applications	255	12.964
Computer Science Artificial Intelligence	220	11.185
Computer Science Information Systems	203	10.320
Environmental Sciences	165	8.388
Green Sustainable Science Technology	144	7.321
Engineering Electrical Electronic	141	7.168

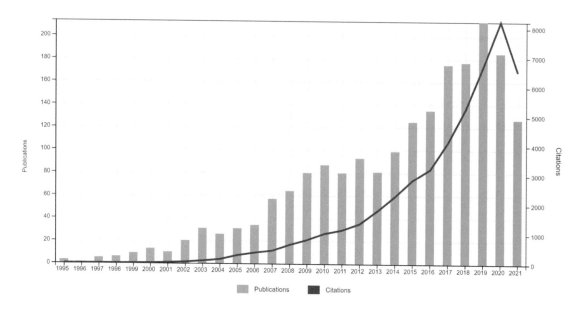

Figure 2: Times Cited and Publications over time.

As discussed in several studies in SCM, there are five main sectors that affect the capacity of a supply chain, including production, inventory, warehouse, location, transportation, and information. An efficient SCM firstly requires an understanding of each sector. The next step is to extend the evaluation of the results achieved by the various combinations of these sectors. Therefore, a supply chain generates a lot of data, its consequence is that there are many systems with inputs and outputs, which are often too complex to model and optimize analytically. Due to its power in analyzing data and the ability to extract important features from data, AI algorithms have been incorporated into the methods to design a DSS in SCM.

The authors of[52] proposed a machine learning algorithm as a potential methodology for system modeling and optimization vis-à-vis traditional design of experiment (DOE) methods. The result shows that these algorithms can obviate the need to perform more complex, expensive, and time-consuming DOE, which usually disrupts system operations. The models resulting from the proposed algorithms had strong explanatory and predictive power, comparable to that of DOE. A new methodology was proposed by[53] to solve a Closed-Loop Supply Chain (CLSC) management problem through a decision-making system based on fuzzy logic built on machine learning decision support tools, more specifically, decision trees. Very recently,[21] developed a predictive decision support system using a Bayesian network analysis featuring the significant factors. It aims to predict an organization's probability of successful blockchain adoption. Other publications about the application of ML technique on DSS can be found in, for example,[54;55;56].

6   Blockchain Technique for SCM

It would be remiss not to mention the contribution of Blockchain to developing effective methods for SCM. Blockchain today is gradually becoming an efficient technology to enhance customer service and enhance company performance. It distributes a database that maintains a continuously growing list of data records that is secure from tampering and modification. So even if the stakeholders are not trusting or unfamiliar, they can share records of data together but still maintain confidentiality. In addition, Blockchain also promotes transaction activities, improves transparency while reducing unnecessary costs. It is showing huge potential for growth in a secure and efficient future economic and social system. The supply chain shows many positives today, but there are also unavoidable challenges such as Lack of traceability, Limited transparency, Outdated means of data sharing. However, with the application of the Blockchain technique, the supply chain will become more efficient, improving efficiency, increasing transparency, and reducing costs. With two keywords "Supply chain management" and "Blockchain", WebofScience shows us a tree-map chart that describes the areas where scientific publications use blockchain technique (BT) in SCM, (see Figure 3). In the sequel, we discuss the main benefits Blockchain to SCM.

Advanced traceability. Blockchain creates a checkable trace of all items that travel through the network. With the help of IoT technology, it can collect a large amount of data of items in real-time along with timestamps and collection location. Thanks to that, Blockchain has created a complete, accurate, and easy to access inspection trail, from the origin of the product to the customer. Moreover, the data in Blockchain is immutable and always requires an electronic signature to confirm ownership of information, so the technique always provides a reliable history of any product and gives provides faster traceability in the event of a compromise. Advanced traceability helps to solve problems faster, reduces product recall costs, and improves product authenticity and quality. For example,[57] found that among the identified enablers, traceability was the most significant reason for blockchain technology implementation in agriculture supply chains (ASC) followed by suitability, immutability, and provenance. Some examples of traceability are mentioned in the following articles[58;59;60;61;62].

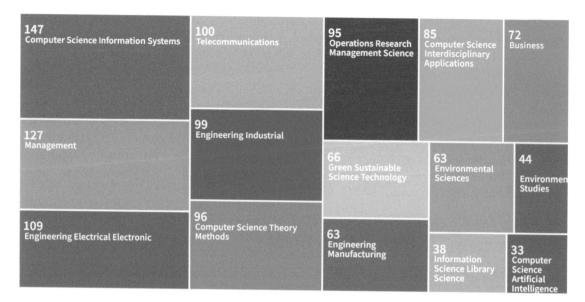

Figure 3: Tree-map chart for number of publications in each the Sciences Categories using Blockchain in SCM.

Improved transparency. Thanks to the transparency and completeness of product information, companies will make better forecasts and decisions against the existence of fake goods. Blockchain technology transparency has become a technological answer to address some sustainability problems, it helps us in improving the processes involved in production. For example,[63] explained how blockchain technology (transparency) helps in the food supply chain management. The work of[64] build an appraisal model of blockchain technology supporting supply chain transparency to mitigate sustainability risks and build global supply chain competitiveness. Like in[65;61;57], the results confirmed that the power of blockchain to enable more transparency in supply chains is real and verifiable.

Greater security. Supply chain security has become a subject of massive interest in both academia and industry. Several recent studies discuss the importance of security in supply chains and the measures required to achieve that, for instance, see[66;67;68]. With the structure of Blockchain (BC), to be able to penetrate a particular loot, all previous blocks in the entire history must be modified. Therefore, hacking to threaten a centralized database in BC is almost impossible. BC technology-powered business and transaction log storage becomes much more secure. With the research in[69], we can understand more about Blockchain technology as a solution to creating and preserving trustworthy digital records, presenting some of the limitations, risks, and opportunities of the approach.

Enhanced trust. From the research of trusted protocol in[70], Blockchain proved better security when it always requires relevant electronic signatures to perform transactions on the supply chain. At the same time, Blockchain also records the time, location, and other data in the Supply chain system and synchronizes all of that data in real-time. This is called a reliable identity management mechanism. As a result, the trust of stakeholders in the Supply chain network has been enhanced. Blockchain technology promises overpowering trust issues and allows a trustless, secure, and authenticated system of logistics (see [71;72;73;74]).

Boosted efficiency. The main purpose of BC when it comes to the Supply chain is to replace outdated processes today. The data will be aggregated, backed up, and updated for relevant parties. Blockchain helps minimize human error and minimizes the need for third parties because transaction information requires instant commitment and authentication from related parties, and Blockchain synchronize also all of this data automatically with local copies.

7 Case Study

In this section, we demonstrate a specific application of a machine learning method in SCM. In particular, we compare the performance of several ML algorithms in forecasting retail sales in the fashion industry.

Fashion has been determined as a factor in the creation of value on a global scale. The business of buying clothes from manufacturers and selling them to customers is known as retail. Retailers make initial purchases for resale three to six months before the customer is able to buy the clothes in-store. For this reason and the "sensibility" of mode, sales forecasting plays a very important task in fashion retailing. A review of several AI approaches for sales forecasting in the fashion retailing service industry can be seen in [75]. In this study, we apply many ML algorithms, including Random Forest (RF), Support Vector Machine (SVM), Linear Regression (LR), and Elastics Net CV to predict the fashion retail sales based on the data set introduced in a part of Kaggle competition (https://www.kaggle.com/c/retail-case-study-batch14/data). This sales data set contains the temporal data like Month, Year, and Product category and Sales, the macroeconomic data like GDP and unemployment rate, the weather data, and the events and holiday data. Based on this information, the goal of applied models is to forecast the retail sales that can help the retailer to plan their budgets or investments in a period (monthly, yearly) among different product categories like "WomenClothing", "MenClothing" and "OtherClothing".

The performance of the proposed methods is evaluated using the measure of Mean Absolute Percentage Error (MAPE)- a measure of prediction accuracy of a forecasting method. Whilst the Mean Absolute Deviation (MAD) calculate the disparity between the predictions and the reality of bookings, the MAPE put a percentage value to that calculation. Namely, it provides the information about how many percentage points a forecasting method are off on average. The formula for MAPE is

$$\text{MAPE} = \frac{1}{n} \sum_{t=1}^{n} \left| \frac{A_t - F_t}{A_t} \right| \times 100\%$$

where A_t is the actual value and F_t is the forecast value, and n is the number of fitted points. The value of MAPE for each method is displayed in Table 2. As can be seen from this table, the RF method is superior to the rest, corresponding to the smallest value of MAPE, which is 13.7328%. The LR model is not effective for the data set as the corresponding value of MAPE is highest: 37.9%. For ElasticNet CV and SVM approaches, the values of MAPE indicate similar

Table 2: The value of Mean Absolute Percentage Error (MAPE) for each method.

Method	The Value of Mean Absolute Percentage Error
Linear Regression	37.9000
ElasticNet CV	20.0387
Support Vector Machine	20.0481
Random Forest	13.7325

accuracy, both are about 20%. That is to say, among all the applied methods, the RF leads to the best performance.

8 Conclusion

In this chapter, we have conducted a survey on the applications of AI algorithms in SCM, aiming to highlight the potential of these advanced techniques to enable a smart SCM. We have focused on several important sectors in SCM, including Demand Forecasting, Logistic, Production, and Decision Support Systems. We have also discussed the benefits of the Blockchain technique for SCM. In addition, a case study where we demonstrated the performance of several ML models to forecast retail sales in the fashion industry has been provided. During the last two years, the Covid-19 pandemic has disrupted the global supply chains due to months of lock-down. However, this is also a motivation for the need to develop applications of advanced technologies such as IoT and AI as the recovery of the global economy requires a more effective SCM to easily adapt to day-to-day changes in current conditions.

References

[1] L.M. Ellram. Supply chain management: The industrial organisation perspective. *International Journal of Physical Distribution & Logistics Management*, 21: 13–22, 1991.

[2] M. Christopher. *Logistics and Supply Chain Management*. Pitman Publishing, London, 1992.

[3] C. Bechtel and J. Jayaram. Supply chain management: A strategic perspective. *International Journal of Logistics Management*, 8(1): 15–34, 1997.

[4] M.C. Cooper, D.M. Lambert and J.D. Pagh. Supply chain management: More than a new name for logistics. *International Journal of Logistics Management*, 8(1): 1–13, 1997.

[5] R. Dash, M. McMurtrey, C. Rebman and U.K. Kar. Application of artificial intelligence in automation of supply chain management. *Journal of Strategic Innovation and Sustainability*, 14(3): 43–53, 2019.

[6] A.-S. Oh. Development of a smart supply-chain management solution based on logistics standards utilizing artificial intelligence and the internet of things. *Journal of Information and Communication Convergence Engineering*, 17(3): 198–204, 2019.

[7] R. Toorajipour, V. Sohrabpour, A. Nazarpour, P. Oghazi and M. Fischl. Artificial intelligence in supply chain management: A systematic literature review. *Journal of Business Research*, 122: 502–517, 2021.

[8] H. Younis, B. Sundarakani and M. Alsharairi. Applications of artificial intelligence and machine learning within supply chains: Systematic review and future research directions. *Journal of Modelling in Management*, 2021.

[9] W. Yu, J.H. Graham and H. Min. Dynamic pattern matching for demand forecasting using temporal data mining. *Proceedings of the 2nd International Conference on Electronic Business*, December. Taipei, Taiwan, pp. 400–402, 2002.

[10] B. Jeong, H. Jung and N. Park. A computerized forecasting system using genetic algorithm in supply chain management. *The Journal of Systems and Software*, 60(3): 223–237, 2002.

[11] L.V. Snyder and Z.J.M. Shen. *Forecasting and Demand Modeling*. Chapter 2, pp. 5–44. John Wiley & Sons, Ltd, 2019. ISBN 9781119584445.

[12] K.N. Amirkolaii, A. Baboli, M.K. Shahzad and R. Tonadre. Demand forecasting for irregular demands in business aircraft spare parts supply chains by using artificial intelligence (ai). *IFAC-PapersOnLine*, 50(1): 15221–15226, 2017.

[13] Y. Zhang, G. Li, B. Muskat and R. Law. Tourism demand forecasting: A decomposed deep learning approach. *Journal of Travel Research*, 60(5): 981–997, 2021.

[14] R. Carbonneau, K. Laframboise and R. Vahidov. Application of machine learning techniques for supply chain demand forecasting. *European Journal of Operational Research*, 184(3): 1140–1154, 2008.

[15] M.Q. Raza and A. Khosravi. A review on artificial intelligence based load demand forecasting techniques for smart grid and buildings. *Renewable & Sustainable energy Reviews*, 50: 1352–1372, 2015.

[16] H. Bousqaoui, S. Achchab and K. Tikito. Machine learning applications in supply chains: Long short-term memory for demand forecasting. In *International Conference of Cloud Computing Technologies and Applications*, pp. 301–317. Springer, 2017.

[17] T. Boone, R. Ganeshan, A. Jain and N.R. Sanders. Forecasting sales in the supply chain: Consumer analytics in the big data era. *International Journal of Forecasting*, 35(1): 170–180, 2019. Special Section: Supply Chain Forecasting.

[18] Y. Zhu, L. Zhou, C. Xie, G.J. Wang and T.V. Nguyen. Forecasting smes' credit risk in supply chain finance with an enhanced hybrid ensemble machine learning approach. *International Journal of Production Economics*, 211: 22–33, 2019.

[19] H.D. Nguyen, K.P. Tran, S. Thomassey and M. Hamad. Forecasting and anomaly detection approaches using lstm and lstm autoencoder techniques with the applications in supply chain management. *International Journal of Information Management*, 57: 102282, 2021.

[20] X.F. Shao, W. Liu, Y. Li, H.R. Chaudhry and X.G. Yue. Multistage implementation framework for smart supply chain management under industry 4.0. *Technological Forecasting and Social Change*, 162: 120354, 2021.

[21] S.S. Kamble, A. Gunasekaran, V. Kumar, Amine Belhadi and Cyril Foropon. A machine learning based approach for predicting blockchain adoption in supply Chain. *Technological Forecasting and Social Change*, 163, 2021.

[22] K. Nikolopoulos, S. Punia, A. Schäfers, C. Tsinopoulos and C. Vasilakis. Forecasting and planning during a pandemic: Covid-19 growth rates, supply chain disruptions, and governmental decisions. *European Journal of Operational Research*, 290(1): 99–115, 2021.

[23] F.-Y. Wang. Toward a revolution in transportation operations: Ai for complex systems. *IEEE Intelligent Systems*, 23(6): 8–13, 2008.

[24] A. Bruzzone and A. Orsoni. Ai and simulation-based techniques for the assessment of supply chain logistic performance. In *36th Annual Simulation Symposium*, pp. 154–164. IEEE, 2003.

[25] A.P. Pandian. Artificial intelligence application in smart warehousing environment for automated logistics. *Journal of Artificial Intelligence*, 1(02): 63–72, 2019.

[26] C.K.M. Lee, Y. Lv, K.K.H. Ng, W. Ho and K.L. Choy. Design and application of internet of things-based warehouse management system for smart logistics. *International Journal of Production Research*, 56(8): 2753–2768, 2018.

[27] K. Mahroof. A human-centric perspective exploring the readiness towards smart warehousing: The case of a large retail distribution warehouse. *International Journal of Information Management*, 45: 176–190, 2019.

[28] D. Zhang, L.G. Pee and L. Cui. Artificial intelligence in e-commerce fulfillment: A case study of resource orchestration at alibaba's smart warehouse. *International Journal of Information Management*, 57: 102304, 2021.

[29] Z. Lv, R. Lou and A.K. Singh. Ai empowered communication systems for intelligent transportation systems. *IEEE Transactions on Intelligent Transportation Systems*, 2020.

[30] K. Sohn. Ai-based transportation planning and operation, 2021.

[31] M. Vasudevan, H. Townsend, T.N. Dang, A. O'Hara, C. Burnier and K. Ozbay. Summary of potential application of ai in transportation. Technical Report, 2020.

[32] A. Graß, C. Beecks and J.A.C. Soto. Unsupervised anomaly detection in production lines. In *Machine Learning for Cyber Physical Systems*, pp. 18–25. Springer, 2019.

[33] H.D. Nguyen, K.P. Tran, S. Thomassey and M. Hamad. Forecasting and anomaly detection approaches using lstm and lstm autoencoder techniques with the applications in supply chain management. *International Journal of Information Management*, 57: 102282, 2021.

[34] R. Chalapathy and S. Chawla. Deep learning for anomaly detection: A survey. *arXiv preprint arXiv:1901.03407*, 2019.

[35] M. Bevilacqua and M. Braglia. The analytic hierarchy process applied to maintenance strategy selection. *Reliability Engineering & System Safety*, 70(1): 71–83, 2000.

[36] O.E. Yurek and D. Birant. Remaining useful life estimation for predictive maintenance using feature engineering. In *2019 Innovations in Intelligent Systems and Applications Conference (ASYU)*, pp. 1–5. IEEE, 2019.

[37] P.J.G. Nieto, E. García-Gonzalo, F.S. Lasheras and F.J. de Cos Juez. Hybrid pso–svmbased method for forecasting of the remaining useful life for aircraft engines and evaluation of its reliability. *Reliability Engineering & System Safety*, 138: 219–231, 2015.

[38] X. Li, Q. Ding and J.Q. Sun. Remaining useful life estimation in prognostics using deep convolution neural networks. *Reliability Engineering & System Safety*, 172: 1–11, 2018.

[39] M. Savargaonkar, A. Chehade, Z. Shi and A.A. Hussein. A cycle-based recurrent neural network for state-of-charge estimation of li-ion battery cells. In *2020 IEEE Transportation Electrification Conference & Expo (ITEC)*, pp. 584–587. IEEE, 2020.

[40] M. Savargaonkar and A. Chehade. An adaptive deep neural network with transfer learning for state-of-charge estimations of battery cells. In *2020 IEEE Transportation Electrification Conference & Expo (ITEC)*, pp. 598–602. IEEE, 2020.

[41] Y. Wu, M. Yuan, S. Dong, L. Lin and Y. Liu. Remaining useful life estimation of engineered systems using vanilla lstm neural networks. *Neurocomputing*, 275: 167–179, 2018.

[42] N.S.S. Hamid, F.A. Aziz and A. Azizi. Virtual reality applications in manufacturing system. In *2014 Science and Information Conference*, pp. 1034–1037. IEEE, 2014.

[43] L. Gong, J. Berglund, A. Fast-Berglund, B. Johansson, Z. Wang and T. Borjesson. Development of virtual reality support to factory layout planning. *International Journal on Interactive Design and Manufacturing (IJIDeM)*, 13(3): 935–945, 2019.

[44] A. Ceruti, P. Marzocca, A. Liverani and C. Bil. Maintenance in aeronautics in an industry 4.0 context: The role of augmented reality and additive manufacturing. *Journal of Computational Design and Engineering*, 6(4): 516–526, 2019.

[45] R. Dobrescu, D. Merezeanu and S. Mocanu. Process simulation platform for virtual manufacturing systems evaluation. *Computers in Industry*, 104: 131–140, 2019.

[46] S.F. Ardabili, B. Najafi, M. Alizamir, A. Mosavi, S. Shamshirband and T. Rabczuk. Using svm-rsm and elm-rsm approaches for optimizing the production process of methyl and ethyl esters. *Energies*, 11(11): 2889, 2018.

[47] A. Oroojlooyjadid, M. Nazari, L.V. Snyder and M. Takáč. A deep q-network for the beer game: Deep reinforcement learning for inventory optimization. *Manufacturing & Service Operations Management*, 2021.

[48] D. Weichert, P. Link, A. Stoll, S. Rüping, S. Ihlenfeldt and S. Wrobel. A review of machine learning for the optimization of production processes. *The International Journal of Advanced Manufacturing Technology*, 104(5): 1889–1902, 2019.

[49] M. Tawfik, M. Younis and T. El Masry. Decision support system in supply chain: A systematic literature review. *European Journal of Logistics, Purchasing and Supply Chain Management*, 5: 40–51, December 2017.

[50] W. Teniwut and C. Hasyim. Decision support system in supply chain: A systematic literature review. *Uncertain Supply Chain Management*, 08, 2019.

[51] K. Govindan, H. Mina and B. Alavi. A decision support system for demand management in healthcare supply chains considering the epidemic outbreaks: A case study of coronavirus disease 2019 (COVID-19). *Transportation Research Part E-logistics and Transportation Review*, 138, 2020.

[52] H.M. Chi, O.K. Ersoy, H. Moskowitz and J. Ward. Modeling and optimizing a vendor managed replenishment system using machine learning and genetic algorithms. *European Journal of Operational Research*, 180(1): 174–193, 2007.

[53] G.G. Rodriguez, J.M. Gonzalez-Cava and J.A.M. Perez. An intelligent decision support system for production planning based on machine learning. *Journal of Intelligent Manufacturing*, 31(5): 1257–1273, JUN 2020.

[54] S. Medina-Gonzalez, A. Shokry, J. Silvente, G. Lupera and A. Espuna. Optimal management of bio-based energy supply chains under parametric uncertainty through a data-driven decision-support framework. *Computer & Industrial Engineering*, 139, 2020.

[55] D. Ni, M.K. Xiao and Z. Lim. A systematic review of the research trends of machine learning in supply chain management. *International Journal of Machine Learning and Cybernetics*, 11(7): 1463–1482, 2020.

[56] B. Alavi, M. Tavana and H. Mina. A dynamic decision support system for sustainable supplier selection in circular economy. *Sustainable Production and Consumption*, 27: 905–920, 2021.

[57] S.S. Kamble, A. Gunasekaran and R. Sharma. Modeling the blockchain enabled traceability in agriculture supply chain. *International Journal of Information Management*, 52: 101967, 2020. ISSN 0268-4012.

[58] M.P. Caro, M.S. Ali, M. Vecchio and R. Giaffreda. Blockchain-based traceability in agrifoodsupply chain management: A practical implementation. In *2018 IoT Vertical and Topical Summit on Agriculture—Tuscany (IOT Tuscany)*, pp. 1–4, 2018.

[59] G.M. Hastig and M.S. Sodhi. Blockchain for supply chain traceability: Business requirements and critical success factors. *Production and Operations Management*, 29(4): 935–954, 2020.

[60] S.F. Wamba and M.M. Queiroz. Blockchain in the operations and supply chain management: Benefits, challenges and future research opportunities. *International Journal of Information Management*, 52: 102064, 2020. ISSN 0268-4012.

[61] J. Sunny, N. Undralla and V.M. Pillai. Supply chain transparency through blockchain based traceability: An overview with demonstration. *Computers & Industrial Engineering*, 150: 106895, 2020. ISSN 0360-8352.

[62] T.K. Agrawal, V. Kumar, R. Pal, L. Wang and Y. Chen. Blockchain-based framework for supply chain traceability: A case example of textile and clothing industry. *Computers & Industrial Engineering*, 154: 107130, 2021. ISSN 0360-8352.

[63] S. Madumidha, P.S. Ranjani, U. Vandhana and B. Venmuhilan. A theoretical implementation: Agriculture-food supply chain management using blockchain technology. In *2019 TEQIP*

III Sponsored International Conference on Microwave Integrated Circuits, Photonics and Wireless Networks (IMICPW), pp. 174–178, 2019.

[64] C. Bai and J. Sarkis. A supply chain transparency and sustainability technology appraisal model for blockchain technology. *International Journal of Production Research*, 58(7): 2142–2162, 2020.

[65] S.F. Wamba, M.M. Queiroz and L.Trinchera. Dynamics between blockchain adoption determinants and supply chain performance: An empirical investigation. *International Journal of Production Economics*, 229: 107791, 2020. ISSN 0925-5273.

[66] T. Salman, R. Jain and L. Gupta. Probabilistic blockchains: A blockchain paradigm for collaborative decision-making. In *2018 9th IEEE Annual Ubiquitous Computing, Electronics Mobile Communication Conference (UEMCON)*, pp. 457–465, 2018.

[67] Y.M. Tukur, D. Thakker and I.U. Awan. Edge-based blockchain enabled anomaly detection for insider attack prevention in internet of things. *Transactions on Emerging Telecommunications Technologies*, 32(6): e4158, 2021.

[68] W. Viriyasitavat, T. Anuphaptrirong and D. Hoonsopon. When blockchain meets internet of things: Characteristics, challenges, and business opportunities. *Journal of Industrial Information Integration*, 15: 21–28, 2019. ISSN 2452-414X.

[69] V.L. Lemieux. Trusting records: Is blockchain technology the answer? *Records Management Journal*, 26(2): 110–139, 2016.

[70] M. Alam. Why the auto industry should embrace blockchain. Available from: http://www.connectedcar-news.com/news/2016/dec/09/why-auto-industry-shouldembraceblockchain/, 2016.

[71] D. Dujak and D. Sajter. Blockchain applications in supply chain, 2019.

[72] B. Oh, T.J. Jun, W. Yoon, Y. Lee, S. Kim and D. Kim. Enhancing trust of supply chain using blockchain platform with robust data model and verification mechanisms. In *2019 IEEE International Conference on Systems, Man and Cybernetics (SMC)*, pp. 3504–3511, 2019.

[73] P. Dutta, T.M. Choi, S. Somani and R. Butala. Blockchain technology in supply chain operations: Applications, challenges and research opportunities. *Transportation Research Part E: Logistics and Transportation Review*, 142: 102067, 2020. ISSN 1366-5545.

[74] M. Alazab, S. Alhyari, A. Awajan and A. Abdallah. Blockchain technology in supply chain management: an empirical study of the factors affecting user adoption/acceptance. *Cluster Computing*, 24, 03 2021.

[75] N. Liu, S. Ren, T.M. Choi, P. Hui and S.F. Ng. Sales forecasting for fashion retailing service industry: A review. *Mathematical Problems in Engineering*, 1-9: 11, 2013.

Index

D

Data analysis 184
Data link layer 254
Data management layer 143, 144
Data perception layer 143
Data pre-processing 144, 166, 167, 209
Data privacy 142
Data sets 166
Data-driven decision-making 1
D-CoDaSVM 198
DDoS-TCP 156
DDoS-UDP 156
Decentralized decision-making 37
Decision boundary 196
Decision making 15, 78, 108, 110, 111–114, 118, 120
Decision problems 287
Decision support systems (DSSs) 1, 8, 19, 26, 34–36, 88, 89, 92, 96, 124, 262, 296, 299, 301, 302, 304
Decision support systems for healthcare 2
Decision tree (DT) 153, 283
Deep learning (DL) 150
Deep neural network (DNN) 14, 150, 152
Demand forecasting 296, 304
Demand prediction 279
Detection rate (DR) 150, 152–154
Diagnosis 75
Digital twin 46
Dimension reduction 146
Dimensionality reduction 145
Directed graphs 10, 11
Dirichlet density 196, 197, 203–207, 209
Dirichlet distribution 205, 208
Dirichlet feature 196
Distribution-free test 216
Domain knowledge 278
DoS 261
DoS-TCP 156
DoS-UDP 156
Double exponential distribution 225, 226, 228, 241–243, 251
Downlink 254
D-part composition 185
Duncan's economic model 222
Dynamic Bayesian Network 75

E

ECG 13, 23
Economic design 217, 223
Economic statistical design 216, 217, 222, 235, 238, 241
Edge 174, 175

Edge computing 126, 128
Edge devices 159
Edge layer 143
Edge-cloud security architecture 142
Edge-machine-learning-based system 45
Efficiency 107
Electromagnetic signal 253
Em interference 254
Encapsulation 79
Energy consumption measurement 170
Enhanced kernel null space (EKNS) 138, 141
Entity characterization 68
Environmental impact 107
Event characterization 68
Evidence lower bound (ELBO) 163, 164
Expected cycle time 222, 223
Experiment set-up 170
Expert 108, 116, 119
Explainable artificial intelligence (XAI) 25, 176
Explained variance 190
Exponentially weighted moving average 221
Extended object oriented bayesian network 80

F

F1-score 154, 168, 169
Failure rate 77
False alarm 219, 222, 223, 227
False negatives 225, 227, 228–230, 234, 236, 239, 242, 247
False positives 225, 228, 230, 234, 236, 239, 242, 247
Fashion industry 4.0 280
Feature evaluator 145
Feature extraction 144, 145, 148
Feature ranker 145
Federated learning 44, 45, 158–160
Federated learning approach 46
Federated learning performance 172–174
Federated learning-based anomaly detection 142
Fitting model 201
Flexibility 80
Forecasting 296, 298, 303, 304
Forward propagation 146
Frequency-sweeping 263
Fuzzy logic 109–111, 113

G

Garment manufacturing 280
Garment manufacturing industry 3
Gaussian kernel 130–132, 136, 140
Gaussian kernel parameter optimization 136